MAKERS OF
WORLD
HISTORY

Volume II

MAKERS OF WORLD HISTORY

Volume II

J. Kelley Sowards, editor

Wichita State University

St. Martin's Press

New York

Editor: Louise Waller
Managing editor: Patricia Mansfield
Project editor: Erica Appel
Production supervisor: Katherine Battiste
Photo researcher: Inge King
Cover design: Nadia Furlan-Lorbek

For information, write:
St. Martin's Press, Inc.
175 Fifth Avenue
New York, NY 10010

ISBN: 0-312-06274-5

Acknowledgments

Akbar: Abu-L-Fazl, *The Akbar Nama,* translated by H. Beveridge, 1972, Vol. 2, pp. 246–
47, 294–96, 316–17, 421; Vol. 3, 2–3, 157–158, 364–366 Atlantic Publishers, 421511
Awsari Road, Darya Ganj, New Delhi, 11002 India.
Abu-l-Qadir, bn-I-Mulak Shah: Al Badaoni, *Muntakhabu-T-Tawrarikh,* translated W. H.
Lowe, *Reed,* 1973, permission granted by Apt. Books, New York.
From Bamber Gascoigne, *The Great Moghuls* (Dorset Press/Rainbird, 1987) Copyright ©
Bamber Gascoigne, 1971, pp. 107–118. Reproduced by permission of Penguin Books, Inc.
Tokugawa Ieyasu Shogun: From *The Makers of Modern Japan: The Life of Tokugawa Ieyasu*
by A. L. Sadler, 1977, pp. 387–389. Reprinted by permission of Unwin Hyman, Ltd., part
of HarperCollins Publishers.
Reprinted from *A History of Japan to 1334* by George Sansone with the permission of the
publishers, Stanford University Press. Copyright © 1958 by the Board of Trustees of the
Leland Stanford, Jr., University
From *Japan: The Story of a Nation* by Edwin O. Reischauer. Copyright © 1970 by Edwin O.
Reischauer. Reprinted by permission of Alfred A. Knopf, Inc.
Shah 'Abbas I: Reproduced by kind permission of Gregg International from the 1972
reprint of *His Relation of his Travels into Persia* by Sir A. Sherley.

Acknowledgments and copyrights are continued at the back of the book on pages
333–334, which constitute an extension of the copyright page.

 The text of this book has been printed on recycled paper.

To Max and Carl, Jan and Jim,
Leona, and Anna Margaret

Preface

Are men and women able to force change upon history by their skill and wits, their nerve and daring? Are they capable of altering history's course by their actions? Or are they hopelessly caught in the grinding process of great, impersonal forces over which they have no real control?

Historians—like theologians, philosophers, and scientists—have long been fascinated by this question. People of every age have recognized great forces at work in their affairs, whether they perceived those forces as supernatural and divine, climatological, ecological, sociological, or economic. Yet obviously at least a few individuals—Alexander, Suleiman—were able to seize the opportunity their times offered and compel the great forces of history to change course. Still others—Confucius, Muhammad, Gandhi—were able, solely by the power of their thoughts or their visions, to shape the history of their periods and of all later times even more profoundly than conquerors or military heroes.

The purpose of this book is to examine the careers and the impact of a number of figures who have significantly influenced world history or embodied much that is significant about the periods in which they lived. At the same time the book introduces the student to the chief varieties of historical interpretation. Few personalities or events stand without comment in the historical record; contemporary accounts and documents, the so-called original sources, no less than later studies, are written by people with a distinct point of view and interpretation of what they see. Problems of interpretation are inseparable from the effort to achieve historical understanding.

The readings in this book have been chosen for their inherent interest and their particular way of treating their subject. Typically, three selections are devoted to each figure. The first selection is usually an autobiographical or contemporary biographical account; in a few instances, differing assessments by contemporaries are included. Next, a more or less orthodox interpretation is presented; it is often a selection from the "standard work" on the figure in question. The final selection offers a more recent view which may reinforce the standard interpretation, revise it in light of new evidence, or dissent from it completely. In some cases, two very different recent views are set side by side.

A book of this size cannot hope to include full-length biographies of all the individuals studied. Instead, each chapter focuses on an important interpretive issue. In some chapters the figure's relative historical importance is at issue; in others the significance of a major point mooted in the sources; in still others the general meaning of the figure's career, as debated in a spread of interpretive positions. In every chapter, it is hoped, the question examined is interesting and basic to an understanding of the figure's place in history.

This book is an alternative edition of an earlier one, *Makers of the Western Tradition*, but adapted for use in World History, as opposed to Western Civilization, courses. The breakpoint between the two volumes lies in the late sixteenth/early seventeenth centuries—a fairly common dividing line between semester-long World History courses. Each volume contains fourteen chapters-figures; thus each fits into the fifteen weeks of a typical college semester. Each volume is also divided equally between Western and non-Western figures. This, I believe, reflects the usual subject emphasis of World History textbooks and courses. An effort was also made to represent a spread of regional civilizations among the non-Western figures—two Chinese, four Indian, two Japanese, three Near Eastern, two African, and one Native American. There is a similar spread among areas of emphasis— seventeen political leaders, seven philosophic-religious leaders, two literary-artistic figures, and three intellectuals.

Even in the selection of the Western figures every effort was made to choose figures or topics that reach out to the larger world. For example, the chapter on Alexander stresses his efforts to incorporate Asians in the management of his empire; the chapter on Cecil Rhodes deals with colonialism; and the chapter on Einstein addresses the worldwide implications of the threat of nuclear war.

For the convenience of both students and instructors, a series of Review and Study Questions has been added to each chapter. In addition, all the chapters conclude with Suggestions for Further Reading, listing in the format of the bibliographic note the best and most up-to-date books on their subjects.

J. K. S.

Contents

AKBAR:
THE GREAT MOGHUL

1542	Born
1556	Succeeded to the throne
1562	Began personal rule
1575	Conquest of Bengal
1579	Infallibility decree
1586	Conquest of Kashmir
1591	Conquest of Sind
1601	Conquest of the Deccan
1605	Died

Jalal-ud-din Muhammad Akbar was only a boy when, in January of the year 1556, his weak and incompetent father Humayun died in an accidental fall. As one chronicler put it, "He stumbled out of life as he had stumbled through it." This was not to be the case with Akbar, whose name means "great": he was destined to be the greatest of all the Moghul emperors.

At his succession Akbar was only thirteen—strong-willed, impulsive, and untrained. He had rejected all efforts to educate him. Earlier, after the court astrologers had laboriously fixed the most propitious day for beginning the boy's education, they found that he "had attired himself for sport and had disappeared." He never returned to school, and he remained illiterate, the only Moghul emperor to do so. Abul Fazl, his dutiful biographer, speaks delicately of this failing and tries to put a good face on it, pointing out "that this lord of lofty wisdom and special pupil of God should not be implicated and commingled with ordinary human learning . . . that the knowledge of this king of knowers was of the nature of a gift, and not of an acquirement."[1]

At his father's death, Akbar could claim to rule only the Punjab, on

---

[1]Abul Fazl, *Akbar-nama*, tr. H. Beveridge (Calcutta: Asiatic Society Bibliotheca Indica, 1907–1939), I, 519.

1

the Indian northwest frontier, and the area around Delhi. His fledgling state was consolidated and extended by the able and faithful regent his father had appointed, Bayram Khan. But by 1562 Akbar had put Bayram Khan aside, and his personal reign began. His chief problem was the jealous independence of the Hindu Rajput princes immediately to the east in the region of Rajasthan. When one of these princes, the Raja of Jaipur, needing a military alliance, offered Akbar his daughter in marriage, Akbar accepted—but only on condition that the *raja* accept his suzerainty. The *raja* agreed. This formula Akbar then proceeded to apply with the other Rajput princes. They were permitted to continue to hold their territories provided they acknowledged Akbar as emperor, paid tribute, supplied troops for him when required, and concluded marriage alliances with him. Further, they and their sons were brought into the emperor's military service, enriched and honored, some becoming generals and provincial governors. But Akbar could be as ruthless as he was accommodating. The state of Mewar refused to acknowledge his supremacy. He personally laid siege to its principal fortress, Chitor, and when it fell in 1568 he massacred all thirty thousand of its defenders. This stern example brought nearly all the remaining Rajput princes into alliance with him.

After conquering the province of Gujarat to the southwest, with its port of Surat, which dominated the trade in Indian goods to the west and the Moslem pilgrim traffic to Mecca, and thus consolidating his power in northwest India, Akbar turned eastward to the rich and ancient region of Bengal. Bengal was held by another Moslem-Afghan ruler. Akbar forced him to recognize his suzerainty in 1575, and when, in the following year, he rebelled and was defeated and killed, Akbar annexed Bengal to the Moghul Empire. In 1586 Kashmir to the north was conquered and in 1591 Sind to the southwest. Between 1596 and 1601 his forces gradually penetrated the great southern plateau of the Deccan. By 1601 Akbar ruled virtually the entire subcontinent.

In Praise of Akbar: Akbar-nama

ABUL FAZL

Akbar had proved himself a mighty conqueror, but in the course of his conquests he had also proved himself a brilliant and innovative ruler by virtue of his religious and administrative reforms. He recognized that his dynasty could not be secure unless it somehow reconciled the vast Hindu majority of the people to Moslem rule, and that his own rule could not be secure unless it recognized the claims and ambitions of the native Hindu princes. We have already noted his policy of conciliation toward the Rajput princes. This in itself was not entirely new. Earlier Moslem rulers had found it necessary to enlist Hindu support. But the Hindus had always been subordinates rather than partners. The ruling force was foreign and alien. It was the genius of Akbar to grant true equality to his Hindu subjects and to confer genuine respect on their institutions. "The essential pillar of this policy was the settlement with the Rajput chiefs and the policy of partnership which sprang from it."[2] They accepted the authority of the Moghul Empire, and in exchange they were left in control of their lands as Moghul agents. To preserve their dignity, they were allowed to beat their drums in the streets of the capital—a sign of royalty—and to enter the Hall of Public Audience fully armed. They were taken into the imperial service as genuine equals. No office or honor was closed to them—some were even among Akbar's most trusted confidential advisers. His policy of intermarriage of his dynasty with Hindu ruling houses was a final recognition of equality.

But Akbar aimed to reconcile himself not only with the Hindu ruling houses but with the Hindu community as a whole. To this end he implemented a series of administrative reforms that marked the entire course of his reign. More important, he granted religious toleration, not only to Hinduism but to other religions, including Judaism and Christianity—nearly unheard of in Moslem lands—and intimately associated himself with these diverse religions.

For an account of these policies we turn to the massive Akbar-nama: The History of Akbar, *written by Abul Fazl. Abu al-Fazl ibn Mubarak (1551–1602) was not only a contemporary of Akbar; he was a close per-*

---

[2]Percival Spear, *India: A Modern History,* new and rev. ed. (Ann Arbor: University of Michigan Press, 1972), p. 132.

sonal friend and, along with his brother the poet Faizi and his father Shaikh Mubarak, a minister of the court. Fazl was Akbar's official court historian, and the emperor not only received Fazl's completed work but had each successive chapter read to him while he corrected and commented on them. This alone would have tended to give a laudatory cast to the work. But the work is more than simply laudatory: its most obvious quality is its outrageously exaggerated flattery. Yet Fazl does not falsify events; he simply presents them in a totally partisan manner. To Fazl's credit, however, he truly believed what he wrote. He was an unabashed advocate of divine right monarchy and an equally unabashed admirer of Akbar, who was, to him, the ideal monarch. He was also, fully as much as Akbar, a freethinker in religion and philosophy and hence an enthusiast for his king's policy of toleration. But with all its faults and limitations, the Akbar-nama *"must be treated as the foundation for a history of Akbar's reign."[3] The work was written in the ornate Persian court language, and some of that quality comes through even in the translation. It is organized, in chronicle fashion, on a year-by-year basis. Our excerpt begins with the year 1562.*

One of the glorious boons of his Majesty the Sh̲āhinsh̲āh[4] which shone forth in this auspicious year was the abolition of enslavement. The victorious troops which came into the wide territories of India used in their tyranny to make prisoners of the wives and children and other relatives of the people of India, and used to enjoy them or sell them. His Majesty the Sh̲āhinsh̲āh, out of his thorough recognition of and worship of God, and from his abundant foresight and right thinking gave orders that no soldier of the victorious armies should in any part of his dominions act in this manner. . . . It was for excellent reasons that His Majesty gave his attention to this subject, although the binding, killing or striking the haughty and the chastising the stiff-necked are part of the struggle for empire—and this is a point about which both sound jurists and innovators are agreed—yet it is outside of the canons of justice to regard the chastisement of women and innocent children as the chastisement of the contumacious. If the husbands have taken the path of insolence, how is it the fault of the wives, and if the fathers have chosen the road of opposition what fault have the children committed? . . .

As the purposes of the Sh̲āhinsh̲āh were entirely right and just, the blissful result ensued that the wild and rebellious inhabitants of portions of India placed the ring of devotion in the ear of obedience, and

---

[3]V. A. Smith, *Akbar the Great Mugal 1542–1605* (Delhi et al.: Chand, 1966), p. 338.

[4]This is a title borrowed from Persian court usage meaning "King of Kings," i.e., Emperor.—Ed.

became the materials of world-empire. Both was religion set in order, for its essence is the distribution of justice, and things temporal were regulated, for their perfection lies in the obedience of mankind. . . .

One of the occurrences [of the year 1563] was that the joyous heart, of H. M.[5] the Sh̲āhin̲s̲h̲āh turned towards hunting, and he went to the neighbourhood of Mathura with a select party. The hunting was successful. One day that tiger-hunter hunted seven tigers. Five were levelled with the dust by arrow and bullet, and one that repository of courage caught alive and so was the subject of a thousand wonderings. The other was caught by the united efforts of a number of bahadurs. In the same hunt he joined worship with pleasure and became distributor of justice. It was brought to his notice that for a long time it was the custom in India for the rulers to take sums from the people who came to sacred spots to worship, proportionate to their rank and wealth. This (worship) was called Karma.[6] The Sh̲āhin̲s̲h̲āh in his wisdom and tolerance remitted all these taxes. . . . He looked upon such grasping of property as blameable and issued orders forbidding the levy thereof throughout his dominions. . . .

One of the great gifts which H. M. the Sh̲āhin̲s̲h̲āh made at the beginning of this year [1564] was the remission of the *Jizya* throughout India.[7] Who can estimate the amount thereof? As the far-seeing glance of the Sh̲āhin̲s̲h̲āh looked to the administration of the world, he paid great attention to the issuing of this edict, which might be regarded as the foundation of the arrangement of mankind. In spite of the disapproval of statesmen, and of the great revenue, and of much chatter on the part of the ignorant, this sublime decree was issued. By this grand gift, thousands of leading-reins and lassoes were made for the stiff-necked ones of the age. . . .

His (Abkar's) keen eye is the astrolabe of the substantive sun—his truth-discerning heart is the celestial observatory of Attributes—he is of noble lineage, of joyous countenance—of right disposition—of open brow—of well-proportioned frame—of magnanimous nature—of lofty genius—of pure purpose—of enduring faith—of perfect wisdom—begirt with varied talents—of wide capacity—of high honour—of splendid courage—of right judgment—of choice counsel—of generosity unfeigned—of boundless forgiveness, abundant in graciousness—at peace with all-compendium of dominion—of plenteous sincerity—multiple of single-minded warriors—abounding

---

[5]This abbreviation, used throughout in the translation, stands for "His Majesty."—ED.

[6]"Fate" or "destiny" in Hindu religious thought.—ED.

[7]This was a yearly tax on all non-Moslem subjects of the Empire—ED.

in wealth—accumulator of the world's rarities—of pure heart—
unspotted by the world—leader of the spiritual realm—of enduring
alertness! How has he been gathered together into one place? Or how
doth a single body upbear him on the shoulders of genius?

At this time[8] when the capital (Fatḥpūr Sikrī) was illuminated by his
glorious advent, H. M. ordered that a house of worship ('Ibādatkhāna)
should be built in order to the adornment of the spiritual kingdom,
and that it should have four verandahs (aiwān). Though the Divine
bounty always has an open door and searches for the fit person, and
the inquirer, yet as the lord of the universe, from his general benevolence, conducts his measures according to the rules of the superficial,
he chose the eve of Friday,[9] which bears on its face the colouring (*ghāza*)
of the announcement of auspiciousness, for the out-pouring (ifāzat). A
general proclamation was issued that, on that night of illumination, all
orders and sects of mankind—those who searched after spiritual and
physical truth, and those of the common public who sought for an
awakening, and the inquirers of every sect—should assemble in the
precincts of the holy edifice, and bring forward their spiritual experiences, and their degrees of knowledge of the truth in various and
contradictory forms in the bridal chamber of manifestation. . . .

At this time, when the centre of the Caliphate (Fatḥpūr Sīkrī) was
glorified by H. M.'s advent, the former institutions were renewed,
and the temple of Divine knowledge was on Thursday nights illuminated by the light of the holy mind. On 20 Mihr, Divine month, 3
October 1578, and in that house of worship, the lamp of the privy
chamber of detachment was kindled in the banqueting-hall of social
life. The coin of the hivers of wisdom in colleges and cells was
brought to the test. The clear wine was separated from the lees, and
good coin from the adulterated. The wide capacity and the toleration
of the Shadow of God were unveiled. Ṣūfī,[10] philosopher, orator,
jurist, Sunnī,[11] Shīa,[12] Brahman,[13] Jatī,[14] Sīūrā,[15] Cārbāk,[16] Nazar-

---

[8]The order for the building of the 'Ibādatkhāna was given in February–March, 1575.

[9]Thursday evening. The Moslem holy day was Friday, but it began with sunset the
previous day.—ED.

[10]Sufi, a modified, mystical form of Islam that attracted millions of former Hindus
and Buddhists to the Moslem faith.—ED.

[11]Sunni, the majority sect of Islam.—ED.

[12]Shia, a minority sect of Islam.—ED.

[13]Brahman, i.e., Hindu.—ED.

[14]Jati, a sect of the Jain religion.—ED.

[15]Siura, another term for the Jains.—ED.

[16]Carbak, an outlawed Hindu sect.—ED.

ene,[17] Jew, Ṣābī (Sabīan),[18] Zoroastrian, and others enjoyed exquisite pleasure by beholding the calmness of the assembly, the sitting of the world-lord in the lofty pulpit (*mimbar*), and the adornment of the pleasant abode of impartiality. The treasures of secrets were opened out without fear of hostile seekers after battle. The just and truth-perceiving ones of each sect emerged from haughtiness and conceit, and began their search anew. They displayed profundity and meditation, and gathered eternal bliss on the divan of greatness. The conceited and quarrelsome from evilness of disposition and shortness of thought descended into the mire of presumption and sought their profit in loss. Being guided by ignorant companions, and from the predominance of a somnolent fortune, they went into disgrace. The conferences were excellently arranged by the acuteness and keen quest of truth of the world's Khedive.[19] . . . The <u>Sh</u>āhin<u>sh</u>āh's court became the home of the inquirers of the seven climes, and the assemblage of the wise of every religion and sect. . . .

In Criticism of Akbar: *Muntakhabu-T-Tawarikh*

AL-BADAONI

Another contemporary historian of Akbar was al-Badaoni (1540–1615), whose great work, Muntakhabu-T-Tawarikh, Abstract of Histories, *is an account, in three large volumes, of the family of Akbar, the reign of Akbar himself, and of the leading intellectuals of the age. It was not an official history but a private work, even a secret one, which might have been lost had it not been discovered among Badaoni's papers after his death. It is as different as possible from Fazl's work. It was motivated by the author's devout, even bigoted commitment to the orthodox, conservative Sunni sect of Islam. He was convinced that Akbar had hopelessly damaged Moslem orthodoxy by his policy of religious toleration. He included in his denunciation his fellow historian Abul Fazl who, in his view, had not only abetted the*

---

[17]Nazarene is the term Fazl usually uses for Christians.—ED.

[18]Sabi, native Indians of a sect converted centuries earlier and sometimes called the Christians of St. John.—ED.

[19]A Turkish term for "ruler."—ED.

*emperor's apostasy but had prevented him (Badaoni) from receiving prefer-
ment at the hands of the emperor. Nevertheless, it is the opinion of the
greatest modern biographer of Akbar that this "hostile criticism of Akbar . . .
is of the highest value as a check on the turgid panegyric composed by the
latitudinarian Abul Fazl. It gives information about the development of
Akbar's opinions on religion which is not to be found in the other Persian
histories."*[20]

*The excerpt begins with Badaoni's account of Akbar's Ibadat-khanah, the
center for the discussion of religions.*

. . . the Emperor came to Fathpūr. There he used to spend much time
in the *'Ibādat-khānah* in the company of learned men and Shaikhs.
And especially on Friday nights, when he would sit up there the
whole night continually occupied in discussing questions of Religion,
whether fundamental or collateral. The learned men used to draw
the sword of the tongue on the battle-field of mutual contradiction
and opposition, and the antagonism of the sects reached such a pitch
that they would call one another fools and heretics. The controversies
used to pass beyond the differences of Sunnī, and Shī'ah, of Hanīfī
and Shāf'i,[21] of lawyer and divine, and they would attack the very
bases of belief.
    . . . Then the Mullās became divided into two parties, and one party
took one side and one the other, and became very Jews and Egyptians
for hatred of each other. And persons of novel and whimsical opinions, in accordance with their pernicious ideas, and vain doubts, coming out of ambush decked the false in the garb of the true, and wrong
in the dress of right, and cast the Emperor, who was possessed of an
excellent disposition, and was an earnest searcher after truth, but
very ignorant and a mere tyro, and used to the company of infidels
and base persons, into perplexity, till doubt was heaped upon doubt,
and he lost all definite aim, and the straight wall of the clear Law, and
of firm Religion was broken down, so that after five or six years not a
trace of Islām was left in him: and every thing was turned topsy
turvy. . . .
    Crowds of learned men from all nations, and sages of various reli-
gions and sects came to the Court, and were honoured with private
conversations. After enquiries and investigations, which were their
only business and occupation day and night, they would talk about

---

[20]V. A. Smith, *Akbar the Great Mogul*, p. 339.
[21]Two of the four schools of Islamic jurisprudence.—ED.

profound points of science, the subtleties of revelation, the curiosities of history, and the wonders of tradition, subjects of which large volumes could give only an abstract and summary: and in accordance with the saying:—"Three things are dangerous, Avarice satisfied: desire indulged: and a man's being pleased with himself." Everything that pleased him, he picked and chose from any one except a Moslem, and anything that was against his disposition, and ran counter to his wishes he thought fit to reject and cast aside. From childhood to manhood, and from manhood to his declining years the Emperor had combined in himself various phases from various religions and opposite sectarian beliefs, and by a peculiar acquisitiveness and a talent for selection, by no means common, had made his own all that can be seen and read in books. Thus a faith of a materialistic character became painted on the mirror of his mind and the storehouse of his imagination, and from the general impression this conviction took form, like an engraving upon a stone, that there are wise men to be found and ready at hand in all religions, and men of asceticism, and recipients of revelation and workers of miracles among all nations and that the Truth is an inhabitant of every place: and that consequently how could it be right to consider it as confined to one religion or creed, and that, one which had only recently made its appearance and had not as yet endured a thousand years! And why assert one thing and deny another, and claim pre-eminence for that which is not essentially pre-eminent?

He became especially firmly convinced of the doctrine of the transmigration of souls, and he much approved of the saying:—*"There is no religion in which the doctrine of Transmigration has not a firm hold."* And insincere flatterers composed treatises in order to establish indisputable arguments in favour of this thesis. And having instituted research into doctrines of the sects of the Hindū unbelievers, of whom there are an endless and innumerable host, and who possess numbers of sacred books, and yet do not belong to the *Ahl-i-Kitāb*,[22] he took so much pleasure in such discussions, that not a day passed but a new fruit of this loathsome tree ripened into existence. . . .

Learned monks also from Europe, who are called *Pādre*, and have an infallible head, called *Pāpā*, who is able to change religious ordinances as he may deem advisable for the moment, and to whose authority kings must submit, brought the Gospel, and advanced proofs for the Trinity. His Majesty firmly believed in the truth of the Christian religion, and wishing to spread the doctrines of Jesus, or-

---

[22]Literally "people of the book," referring to Jews and Christians, who worship the same God as Moslems and whose scriptures contain divine truth.—ED.

dered Prince Murād to take a few lessons in Christianity under good auspices, and charged Abu-l-Fazl to translate the Gospel. . . .

Fire-worshippers also came from Nousārī in Gujrāt, proclaimed the religion of Zardusht[23] as the true one, and declared reverence to fire to be superior to every other kind of worship. They also attracted the Emperor's regard, and taught him the peculiar terms, the ordinances, the rites and ceremonies of the Kaiānians.[24] At last he ordered that the sacred fire should be made over to the charge of Abu-l-Fazl, and that after the manner of the kings of Persia, in whose temples blazed perpetual fires, he should take care it was never extinguished night or day, for that it is one of the signs of God, and one light from His lights. . . .

Every precept which was enjoined by the doctors of other religions he treated as manifest and decisive, in contradistinction to this Religion of ours, all the doctrines of which he set down to be senseless, and of modern origin, and the founders of it as nothing but poor Arabs, a set of scoundrels and highway-robbers, and the people of Islām as accursed. But in the course of time the truth of this verse in its hidden meaning developed itself: "Fain would they put out the light of God with their mouths! but, though the Infidels abhor it, God will perfect his light." By degrees the affair was carried to such a pitch that proofs were no longer considered necessary for abolishing the precepts of Islām. . . .

I have made bold to chronicle these events, a course very far removed from that of prudence and circumspection. But God (He is glorious and honoured!) is my witness, and sufficient is God as a witness, that my inducement to write this has been nothing but sorrow for the faith, and heart-burning for the deceased Religion of Islām, which 'Anqā-like turning its face to the Qāf of exile, and withdrawing the shadow of its wings from the dwellers in the dust of this lower world, thenceforth became a nonentity, and still is so. And to God I look for refuge from reproach, and hatred, and envy, and religious persecution. . . .

And in these days, when reproach began to spread upon the doctrines of Islām, and all questions relating thereto, and ever so many wretches of Hindūs and Hindūizing Musalmāns brought unmitigated reviling against the Prophet, and the villainously irreligious Ulamā[25] in their works pronounced the Emperor to be without sin, and contenting themselves with mentioning the unity of God, they next wrote

---

[23]Persian Zoroastrianism.—ED.

[24]An old Persian dynasty.—ED.

[25]The Islamic learned community.—ED.

down the various titles of the Emperor, and had not the courage to mention the name of the Prophet (God be gracious to him and his family, and give them peace in defiance of the liars!) this matter became the cause of general disgrace, and the seeds of depravity and disturbance began to lift their heads in the empire. Besides this base and low men of the higher and lower classes, having accepted the collar of spiritual obedience upon their necks, professed themselves his disciples. They became disciples through the motives of hope and fear, and the word of truth could not proceed out of their mouths. . . .

At this time a document made its appearance,[26] which bore the signatures and seals of Makhdūm-ul-mulk, of Shaikh 'Abd-un-nabī *çadr-uç-çudūr,* of Qāzī Jalāl-ud-dīn of Multān, *qāzī-l-quzāt,* of Çadr Jahān the *muftī* of the empire, of Shaikh Mubārak the deepest writer of the age, and of Ghāzi Khān of Badakhshān, who stood unrivalled in the transcendental sciences. The subject-matter of the document was the setting of the absolute superiority of the *Imām-i-'ādil* over the *Mujtahid* and the investigation of the grounds of this superiority. . . . I shall copy the document *verbatim:—*

"Petition.

Whereas Hindūstān is now become the centre of security and peace, and the land of justice and beneficence, a large number of people, especially learned men and lawyers, have immigrated and chosen this country for their home. Now we, the principal 'Ulamā, who are not only well-versed in the several departments of the Law and in the principles of jurisprudence, and well acquainted with the edicts which rest on reason or testimony, but are also known for our piety and honest intentions, have duly considered the deep meaning, *first,* of the verse of the Qur'ān: "Obey God, and obey the prophet, and those who have authority among you," and, *secondly,* of the genuine Tradition: "Surely the man who is dearest to God on the day of judgment is the *Imām-i-'ādil;* whosoever obeys the Amīr, obeys Thee; and whosoever rebels against him, rebels against Thee," and, *thirdly,* of several other proofs based on reasoning or testimony; and we have agreed that the rank of *Sultān-i-'ādil,*[27] is higher in the eyes of God than the rank of a *Mujtahid.*[28] Further we declare that the king of Islām, Amīr of the Faithful, shadow of God in the world, *Abu-l-Fatḥ Jalāl-ud-dīn Muḥammad Akbar Padshāh Ghāzī* (whose kingdom God perpetuate!) is a most just, a most wise, and a most God-fearing king.

---

[26]The so-called Infallibility Decree.—ED.

[27] Just ruler.—ED.

[28] Authority on points of law.—ED.

Should therefore in future a religious question come up, regarding which the opinions of the Mujtahids are at variance, and His Majesty in his penetrating understanding and clear wisdom be inclined to adopt, for the benefit of the nation, and as a political expedient, any of the conflicting opinions, which exist on that point, and issue a decree to that effect, we do hereby agree that such a decree shall be binding on us and on the whole nation.

Further, we declare that, should His Majesty think fit to issue a new order, we and the nation shall likewise be bound by it, provided always that such order be not only in accordance with some verse of the Qur'ān, but also of real benefit to the nation; and further, that any opposition on the part of his subjects to such an order passed by His Majesty shall involve damnation in the world to come, and loss of property and religious privileges in this.

This document has been written with honest intentions, for the glory of God, and the propagation of Islām, and is signed by us, the principal 'Ulamā and lawyers, in the month of Rajab of the year nine hundred and eighty-seven (987) [1579–80]."

The draft of this document, when presented to the Emperor, was in the handwriting of Shaikh Mubārak. The others had signed it against their will, but the Shaikh had added at the bottom that he most willingly signed his name; for this was a matter to which for several years he had been anxiously looking forward.

No sooner had His Majesty obtained this legal document, than the road of deciding any religious question was open; the superiority of the intellect of the Imām was established, and opposition was rendered impossible. All orders regarding things which our law allows or disallows were abolished, and the superiority of the intellect of the Imām became law. They called Islām a travesty.

A Modern Assessment of Akbar

BAMBER GASCOIGNE

Every modern writer on the Moghul Empire has had to deal with Akbar's administrative and religious reforms, and most find them the well-spring of his greatness as an emperor. One of the best of the modern commentators is the British journalist and historical popularizer Bamber Gascoigne. His work The Great Moghuls *is one of the most reliable treatments of the complex history of Moghul India, solidly based on the sources—including Fazl and Badaoni—and on the best current specialists' research.*

At the age of twenty-three Abul Fazl arrived at Fatehpur Sikri to enter Akbar's service—in the very same year, 1574, as another equally brilliant young man, Badauni. From early in his childhood Abul Fazl had known Badauni, eleven years his senior, because Badauni had studied at Agra under Abul Fazl's father, Shaikh Mubarak. Each now immediately caught Akbar's eye; each seemed destined for a most promising career; and they were to become, between them, the two most important historians of the period. But their paths rapidly diverged and the vast difference between their two careers and their two books symbolizes neatly the gulf which opened in the second half of Akbar's reign and which made these seem years of calamity to the more orthodox Muslims among Akbar's subjects, many of whom came to believe that the emperor had become a Hindu. Badauni was a strict Sunni, whereas Abul Fazl was a freethinker, as were his elder brother, Faizi, and his father, Shaikh Mubarak. The appointment of the three members of this talented family to positions at court was an ominous reversal for the rigidly orthodox and until now very powerful members of the *ulama,* or religious hierarchy.

Shaikh Mubarak and his two sons rapidly became the most influential group at Akbar's court, largely because their eclecticism chimed so well with his. The shaikh himself took the leading place among the palace divines. His elder son, Faizi, became the poet laureate. And Abul Fazl launched with a will into the many tasks which would bring him ever closer into the emperor's trust. The more affairs at Fatehpur Sikri went the elegant and carefree way of Abul Fazl and Faizi, the more Badauni and his like felt excluded. Badauni claims to have upbraided Abul Fazl one day for his notorious heresies and to have been enraged by the cool reply 'I wish to wander for a few days in the vale of infidelity for sport' though the story does less than justice to the political seriousness underlying Abul Fazl's wish to broaden the regime's religious basis. With poignant irony the two rival intellectuals were each as young men given the rank of twenty horse and were made to share the same task—supervising the branding of horses for muster. Abul Fazl knuckled down to it, and in Badauni's words, 'by his intelligence and time-serving qualities' managed to raise himself from here to the highest positions in the realm, 'while I from my inexperience and simplicity could not manage to continue in the service'. Badauni soon sank to the official level of a mere translator. Akbar, with characteristic lack of concern for Badauni's bigotry, gave him the four-year task of translating into Persian the Hindi classic the *Mahabharata*, which he predictably found nothing but 'puerile absurdities of which the eighteen thousand creations may well be amazed . . . but such is my fate, to be employed on such works'. Badauni hardly appears in Abul Fazl's book, but the latter looms large in Badauni's as the 'man that set the world in flames' and as being 'officious and time-serving, openly faithless, continually studying the emperor's whims, a flatterer beyond all bounds'. The two men's books make together a perfect pair of commentaries on the reign. Badauni's, crotchety, bigoted, ruthlessly honest with himself as well as with others, is much the more readable and in modern terms is far better written. It was compiled in secret and only discovered in 1615 after both Akbar and Badauni were dead. Abul Fazl's, in which a mere list of Akbar's good qualities can run to several pages, was commissioned by the emperor and was read aloud to him as each stage was completed—and no doubt again and again subsequently. Yet it carries one along by the sheer confident profusion of its flowery Persian metaphors and can also be surprisingly vivid, as when a holy man has 'for thirty years in an unnoticed corner been gathering happiness on an old mat'. The difference between the two histories is that between a brilliant diary and the most magnificent of ornamental scrolls.

Akbar's own bent for religious speculation was encouraged not only by Shaikh Mubarak's family but also by wider currents of opinion in India at the time. Within Islam there had long been a tradition of free-thinking mysticism, known as Sufism, which was opposed to the rigid distinctions of orthodoxy, and in the past century this had been joined in India by similar stirrings within Hinduism, in particular the Bhakti movement and the beginnings of the Sikh religion, both of which included a rejection of the caste system and a belief in a personal God. By 1575 Akbar's interest in comparative religion had become so strong that he built a special *ibadat-khana* or 'house of worship' in which to hold religious discussions. The building, which no longer exists, was an extension of a deserted hermit's cell. It was situated behind the mosque at Fatehpur Sikri and Akbar would go there after prayers in the mosque on Thursday evenings—the Muslim day is calculated as beginning at dusk, rather than midnight, so Thursday evening was for Akbar and his mullahs the evening of the holy day, Friday.

His intention, as in his *diwan-i-khas*, was to sit in the middle and digest the arguments from all sides. He was deeply shocked—and sufficiently inexperienced in academic matters to be surprised—when the learned divines whom he invited to participate immediately fell out over who should sit where, but this was finally settled by separating the rival groups to the four sides of the building. The discussions went on long into the night; much perfume was wafted on the air; and Akbar had a pile of money in front of him, as he always did on any comparable occasion, with which he hoped to reward the most persuasive and elegant contributions. But here too he was disappointed. Badauni records that in no time the learned doctors were calling each other 'fools and heretics', and the arguments soon went beyond subtle sectarian differences and threatened to undermine the very foundations of belief, until the participants 'became very Jews and Egyptians for hatred of each other'. The foundations of Akbar's belief, perhaps already shaky, were certainly further disturbed by these performances; such furious differences of opinion within the Muslim community, to whom the discussions were at this stage restricted, seemed to him to cast doubts on Islam itself and his next step was to throw the debate open to learned men from other religions. Eventually he included Hindus, Jains, Zoroastrians, Jews and even a small group who came to play a prominent and most interesting part in the court life at Fatehpur Sikri, three Jesuit fathers from the Portuguese colony at Goa. . . . They were Rudolf Aquaviva, an Italian aristocrat whose uncle became General of the Society of Jesus; Antony Monserrate, a Spaniard who later left a very full account of his experiences in the land of the Moghul; and Francis Henriquez, a Persian convert from Islam who was expected to act as interpreter. . . .

Akbar always treated the 'Nazarene sages', as Abul Fazl called them, with the greatest courtesy; he liked them to sit near him, and would often draw them aside for private conversation; he sent them food from the royal table; when Monserrate was ill he visited him, and he had even gone to the trouble to learn a special Portuguese greeting for the occasion; and he could sometimes be seen walking in public places with his arm around Father Aquaviva. On religious matters he was just as cooperative; he was prepared to kiss their sacred books and holy images; he came to see the crib which they had built for their first Christmas at Fatehpur Sikri, and when he entered their little chapel he took off his turban; he appointed Abul Fazl to teach them Persian and allowed Monserrate to become tutor to his son Murad, then about eleven, even tolerating 'In the name of God and of Jesus Christ, the true Prophet and Son of God' at the head of each of the prince's exercises; he allowed the fathers to preach, to make conversions and to hold a large public funeral for a Portuguese who died at court, processing through the streets with crucifix and candles; he even took in good part the Jesuits' chiding him for his surplus of wives.

It is not surprising that the missionaries felt encouraged, but they were soon to be disappointed. They had mistaken Akbar's fascination with all religions for an inclination to join theirs. It seems that Christianity appealed to him at least as much as any other religion—though he was distressed, among other things, that Christ should have allowed himself the indignity of being crucified and felt that once up there he should have used his special powers to get down—and it has some-times been suggested that Akbar was consciously hoping to find in Christianity a religion with which he could solve his empire's commu-nal hostilities by imposing it from the top on Muslims and Hindus alike, precisely, in fact, as the Jesuits themselves intended. But he was too shrewd a politician to imagine that he could solemnly decree a new religion for India, and it is likely that his interest in Christianity derived almost entirely from his personal love of speculation. It is typical that when he did finally decide on his own religion it should turn out to be so generalized, its main distinguishing feature being a vague nimbus of divinity around his own person, and that he should have made so little effort to spread it beyond his own circle of friends. The announcement in 1582 of this new religion, known as the *din-i-Ilahi* or 'religion of God', finally showed the fathers that their efforts had failed. They returned to Goa but at Akbar's request other missions followed them, and on several more occasions Christian hopes were raised high only to be dashed again. . . .

If the Jesuits were wrong in believing that Akbar was moving towards Christianity, the Muslims were certainly right in their con-viction that he was drifting away from orthodox Islam. That he was doing so was as much as anything a matter of policy. The principle of a medieval Islamic state gave very great powers to the mullahs, since it was believed that the correct way of doing everything could be found in the Koran or in one or two long established commen-taries on it. The ruler must therefore abide by the book and the book was best interpreted by those who had devoted their lives to religion. . . .

Akbar used the undignified squabbles between the Muslim divines in the *ibadat-khana* as an opportunity to limit the power of the priest-hood. In 1579 appeared the famous *mahzar* or so-called decree of infallibility, in which it was stated that if there was disagreement among the learned about the meaning of any part of the Koran, it would in future be Akbar who had the deciding say on which of the contending interpretations should be accepted; and further that if he chose to take any step for the good of the state, it should be accepted by all unless it could be shown to be against the Koran. The decree was sound Islamic theory in so far as it placed the book above all, but it did represent a fairly startling upheaval, at least in concept, in the relationship between the *ulama* or body of learned men and the tem-poral power. . . . The decree of infallibility was signed by several di-vines but only one of them, Abul Fazl's father Shaikh Mubarak, put his name to it with enthusiasm, as a note below his signature testified. Having probably been largely Mubarak's idea, the decree marked a definite advance in the power at court of the shaikh and his two sons, and was a serious blow to the orthodox—particularly when coupled with other indications about this time of the direction which Akbar's thoughts were taking. In 1579 he put an end to the custom of sending vast sums of money each year to Mecca and Medina for distribution to the poor; in 1580 he gave up his annual pilgrimage to Ajmer; in 1584 he rejected the Muslim system of dating events from the Hegira, or flight of the prophet from Mecca to Medina, and replaced it with a new chronology beginning with his own accession (Abul Fazl explains that Akbar found it 'of ominous significance' to date things from the Hegira, presumably because of the mention of flight); finally he had had the effrontery to begin preaching and reciting the *khutba*[29] himself in the mosque, although on the very first occasion he had to stop halfway, when he began trembling in what appears to have been another of his quasi-mystical seizures. Together with the decree of infallibility, this personal performance in the mosque was perhaps the most offensive of all to the orthodox. It implied that Akbar was conferring on himself the status of a learned divine. Their next shock was when he seemed to take the process one stage further and present himself simply as divine.

The *din-i-Ilahi*, Akbar's new religion based on a vague and mystical liberalism, was at the very best unspecific about how far Akbar straddled the dividing line between mortal and divine. The new chronology dating from his accession was known as the Divine Era. And considerable outrage was caused when he decided to stamp on his coins the potentially ambiguous phrase *Allahu akbar;* the ambiguity derives from the fact that *akbar* means great as well as being the emperor's name so that the words could mean either 'God is great' or 'Akbar is God'. This has seemed to various modern historians the most blatant assumption of divinity, but it need not have been so. When a shaikh accused Akbar of having intended the second meaning he replied indignantly that it had not even occurred to him. His claim sounds far-fetched; and the fact that he had taken the unusual step of removing his own name and titles from his coins, in order to substitute this phrase, suggests that he was not unaware that it included his name as well as God's . . . and it seems likely that Akbar was amused by the ambiguity rather than taking it as a serious statement of his own identity.

---

[29]A prescribed sermon read at Friday noon prayers in the mosque, acknowledging the authority of the reigning prince.—Ed.

In all these steps Akbar was energetically supported if not actually led by Shaikh Mubarak and his sons. Abul Fazl's biography of Akbar is liberally sprinkled with epithets suggesting his divinity, and he attributes to the emperor several miracles, including even the making of rain. The emphasis throughout Abul Fazl's writing is on religious toleration—he was a man who practised what he preached, having a Hindu, a Kashmiri and a Persian wife—and within the space of one paragraph he calls the Muslims of Kashmir 'narrow-minded conservatives of blind tradition' but praises the Hindu priests of the same province for not loosening 'the tongue of calumny against those not of their faith'. His stated aim in studying and describing the culture and philosophy of the Hindus was so that 'hostility towards them might abate, and the temporal sword be stayed awhile from the shedding of blood'.

Akbar's progression away from orthodox Islam towards his own vague religion was no doubt part of a conscious effort to seem to represent all his people—the Rajputs, for example, saw their rajas much like Abul Fazl's image of Akbar, both human and divine—and it fitted in with a general policy which included his adoption of Hindu and Parsee festivals and his increasing abstinence from meat in the manner of Hindus. But it also fulfilled a personal need. He was drawn to mysticism, fond of lonely contemplation, eager for any clue to the truth, and if that truth should touch him with divinity there were always precedents within the family; Humayun had indulged in a mystical identification of himself with light, and through light with God; Timur, more conventionally, used to refer to himself as the 'shadow of Allah on earth'. Akbar's religious attitudes seem to have been a happy blend of personal inclination and state policy.

Review and Study Questions

1. How does Abul Fazl manifest his outrageous partisanship in the *Akbar-nama*?

2. How do the two contemporary accounts of Akbar's religious toleration differ from each other?

3. What was the source of al-Badaoni's hostility to Akbar's religious toleration?

4. Why were Abul Fazl and al-Badaoni such bitter enemies? How did this effect their appraisals of Akbar?

5. Given the background of Akbar, could he really be an "infallible" judge of religious and intellectual matters?

Suggestions for Further Reading

The works of Fazl, excerpted for this chapter from Abu-l-Fazl, *The Akbar-nama,* tr. H. Beveridge, 3 vols. (Delhi: Rare Books, 1972) and Badaoni, excerpted for this chapter from Abul-l-Qadir ibn-l-Muluk Shah, Al-Badaoni, *Muntakhabu-T-Tawarikh,* tr. and ed. W. H. Lowe, rev. ed. 3 vols. (Patna, India: Academica Asiatica, 1973), are the only two complete contemporary histories of Akbar's reign, although several partial accounts exist. These can best be sampled in H. M. Elliot and John Dowson, eds., *The History of India, As Told by Its Own Historians,* 2d ed. (Calcutta: Susil Guypta, Ltd., 1955), 8 vols. The interesting account by the Jesuit Father Antony Monserrate is, unfortunately, still in its original Latin, but is summarized with substantial parts translated in Sir. E. D. Maclagan, "The Jesuit Missions to the Emperor Akbar," *Journal of the Asiatic Society of Bengal,* 65, part i (1896), 38–113. Though not a connected history, another large three-volume work by Abul Fazl, *Ain-i Akbari,* tr. H. Blochmann and H. S. Jarrett (Calcutta: Asiatic Society of Bengal, 1873–94), presents a detailed account of Akbar's administrative system.

The best modern biography of Akbar is still Vincent A. Smith, *Akbar the Great Mogul, 1542–1605,* 2nd rev. ed. (Delhi et al.: S. Chand and Co., 1966). A much larger and more detailed work is the learned Ashirbadi Lal Srivastava, *Akbar the Great,* vol. I, *Political History, 1542–1645 A.D.,* vol. II, *Evolution of Administration, 1556–1645 A.D.* (Agra, Delhi, Jaipur: Shiva Lal Agarwala, 1962). There are two old and rather brief biographies of Akbar in English, neither of them critical or based on primary sources: G. B. Malleson, *Akbar and the Rise of the Mughal Empire,* "Rulers of India" (Oxford: Clarendon Press, 1894) and Lawrence Binyon, *Akbar* (Edinburgh: Peter Davies, Ltd., 1932). The chapter on Akbar in Sri Ram Sharma, *The Religious Policy of the Mughal Emperors,* 3rd rev. ed. (New York: Asia Publishing House, 1972) is a very reliable and substantial account.

There are a number of works on the Moghul Empire or on late medieval India, including the Moghul period. The most detailed are two works by A. L. Srivastava, *History of India, 1000–1707* (Jaipur, Agra, Indore: Shiva Lal Agarwala and Co., 1964) and *The Mughal Empire (1526–1803 A.D.),* 7th rev. ed. (Agra: Shiva Lal Agarwala and Co., 1970). Two less satisfactory and older books are Stanley Lane-Poole, *Mediaeval India under Mohammedan Rule (A.D. 712–1764),* 2 vols. (London: Ernest Benn, 1903) with many revised editions; and S. M. Edwardes and H. L. O. Garrett, *Mughal Rule in India* (Delhi et al.: Chand [1900]). The best and most up-to-date history of the Moghuls is Bamber Gascoigne, *The Great Moghuls* (New York et al.: Harper & Row, 1971), excerpted for this chapter.

There are a great many general histories of India that devote chapters or sections to Akbar. Among the most useful are Stanley Wolpert, *A New History of India* (New York: Oxford University Press, 1977); Percival Spear, *India: A Modern History,* new ed. rev. (Ann Arbor: University of Michigan Press, 1972); Francis Watson, *A Concise History of India* (New York: Scribner, 1975); and finally, an old standard work by Vincent A. Smith, in a third edition edited by Percival Spear, with the section containing the Moghuls revised by J. B. Harrison: *The Oxford History of India* (Oxford: Clarendon Press, 1967).

TOKUGAWA IEYASU SHOGUN: "THE OLD BADGER"

1543	Born
1560	Restored to his family lands
1567	Assumed the family name of Tokugawa
1590	Succeeded to Edo (Tokyo)
1600	Won battle of Sekigahara
1603	Appointed shogun
1605	Abdicated in favor of his son Hidetada
1616	Died

The Shogun Tokugawa Ieyasu was a mass of contradictions. Short, squat, and ugly, he was given the enshrinement name, after his death, of "The Light of the East, the Ultimate Made Manifest." A devoted family man, intent upon founding a dynasty, he ordered the suicide of his eldest son and heir on suspicion of sedition, and thus put his dynasty at risk. An unlettered man, he became the great patron of Confucian scholarship in Japan. He relentlessly pursued his last rival, the pretender Hideyori, the son of his old friend and lord, and forced him to commit suicide; yet his self-proclaimed motto was "Requite malice with kindness." A samurai warrior who had devoted his life to battle, he was a devout Buddhist and founded a reign of peace in Japan that would last for more than 250 years.

Ieyasu was born in 1543, the son of a samurai and minor daimyo (feudal landholder) in eastern Japan. Such men had dominated the political life of Japan since the end of the cultivated Heian age in the twelfth century. From time to time a measure of order had been imposed by the appointment of a shogun by the emperor, who was himself strictly a ceremonial and religious figure. The shogun was the military ruler of the nation, the head of the *bakufu*, the military or "tent" government. But there were long periods when no one held the shogunate and when military chaos prevailed. It was in such a period that Ieyasu grew up.

By his warrior skills Ieyasu gained advancement in the service of superior feudal lords, becoming such a lord himself. By the age of forty he had not only been able to secure great military power but had persuaded the emperor to grant him the family name of Tokugawa, thus linking him to the ancient and illustrious warrior family of Mina-moto, the family of past shoguns. In 1582 he offered his services to the leading feudal lord of Japan, Hideyoshi. He quickly became Hideyoshi's most dependable vassal and was rewarded with enor-mous land holdings centered upon the village of Edo—the future Tokyo. He fortified the site and consolidated his position as master of eastern Japan. In the power struggle following the death of Hideyo-shi, Tokugawa defeated all his rivals in a great pitched battle at Sekigahara, northeast of Kyoto, to become the undisputed master of Japan.

By 1603 he was able to demand that the imperial court appoint him shogun. On February 12, a delegation from the Emperor Gayozei called upon Tokugawa with his appointment as shogun and a host of other supporting titles, each contained in a lacquered box. As each box was opened and the appointment letter removed, the box was filled with gold dust and returned. Within a month Tokugawa had taken up residence in a new castle he had ordered built for himself at Kyoto—Nijo Castle. A new shogunal dynasty had begun. Two years later he abdicated in favor of his son Hidetada, thus assuring the succession of the Tokugawa family.

Both as shogun and as retired shogun, Tokugawa retained control of foreign affairs. He was mainly concerned with trade. This came to involve him in a complex set of relations not only with Japan's tradi-tional trading partner, China, but with agents of the European mari-time states, intent upon trade with Japan but intent also upon extend-ing their religious beliefs—whether Catholic or Protestant. Tokugawa welcomed the trade and the new technology that came with it, but he grew increasingly suspicious of western religious motives and the meddling of missionaries in what he regarded as the internal affairs of Japan. By 1614 he had prohibited all western missionary activity—the beginning of the process of closing Japan to the West that would last until the nineteenth century.

By the time of his death in 1616 Tokugawa had fathered sixteen children by an assortment of consorts and concubines—five daugh-ters, who were well and strategically married, and eleven sons, six of them still living when Tokugawa died. The dynasty was secure.

The Legacy

TOKUGAWA IEYASU

Tokugawa was undeniably one of the greatest military figures in his nation's history. But increasingly, especially after becoming shogun, he tried to avoid military engagements and military solutions to political problems. He had concluded that they were not only costly but disruptive; he much preferred conciliation. And he spent the last dozen years of his life creating a system of government that would make peace and order the rule of Japanese life. To a remarkable degree he succeeded. The government he perfected lasted almost totally unchanged for two centuries, the longest period of such peace and order in Japan's history.

In the course of his reign Tokugawa issued many orders, edicts, and codes of conduct to regulate all levels of society, including the imperial court and the court aristocrats, the daimyo, even the religious shrines and temples. One of the most important and interesting of these edicts is the Buke Hyaku Kajo, *the "Legacy of Ieyasu." It was written near the end of Tokugawa's life and is a set of instructions to his successors in the shogunate, embodying his views on how the government should be carried on by them. It exists in a number of editions, including a complete critical edition in the* Transactions of the Japan Society of London, *which takes account of the later revisions of the work. The edition excerpted below is the one edited and translated by A. L. Sadler in his* The Maker of Modern Japan: The Life of Tokugawa Ieyasu, *which is the standard English biography of the great shogun. It consists of those parts of the text that can be incontestably attributed to Tokugawa.*

The instructions take the form, typical of the age of Tokugawa, of a series of maxims in the Chinese manner, presented in a random, seemingly casual order. Despite the apparent lack of order, the document contains recurring themes. There are continual references to the standard Chinese works on governance, especially the Confucian works; the document itself was written in Chinese. It places strong emphasis on benevolence and compassion as principles of governance as well as of personal conduct. There are reminders of the structure of vassalage Tokugawa had created—with House Retainers, Family Vassals, and Outside Lords—and of how he manipulated that structure. There are cautions against the overt use of military power, and the sort of exhortations to craft and patience that caused Tokugawa to be known as "the Old Badger" to his contemporaries. It is filled with spe-

cific advice to future shoguns based on Tokugawa's own experience, and often contains personal reminiscences.

The duty of the lord of a province is to give peace and security to the people, and does not consist in shedding lustre on his ancestors, and working for the prosperity of his descendants. The supreme excellence of T'ang of the Yin dynasty and Wu of the Chou dynasty lay in making this their first principle.[1] There must be no slighting of the Imperial Dignity or confusing the order of Heaven and Earth, Lord and Subject.

The civil and military principles both proceed from Benevolence. However many books and plans there may be the principle is the same. Know therefore that herein lies the way of ruling and administering the Empire. . . .

If the lord is not filled with compassion for his people and the people are not mindful of the care of their lord, even though the government is not a bad one, yet rebellions will naturally follow. But if the lords love Benevolence, then there will be no enemies in the Empire.

If Benevolence abides in the Empire there is no distinction between domestic and foreign or noble and commoner, for the sun and moon shine on the clean and unclean alike. The Sage established the law on this principle, and according to it there are fixed and immutable rules applying to the degree of intimacy, rank, the three allegiances, and the eight rules. If one man is supreme in the Empire then all warriors are his retainers, but he does not make retainers of the whole people. There is the distinction of Outside Families and our own Family, Outside Lords (Tozama) and House Retainers (Hatamoto). Outside houses are those that are temporarily powerful. Family vassals or Fudai are those bound to us by lineage and history, whose ancestors did loyal service to our house as is clear to all by their records. Since their fidelity and affection exceeds that of the Outside houses, these others must not be displeased at this preference, resting as it does on such a basis.

In employing men and recognizing ability, if the Fudai are overlooked and the Tozama elevated there will be inward rage and outward regret, and loyal retainers will naturally be lost. One thing is quite certain, men are not all saints and sages. This fact it is well to bear very much in mind.

All feudatories, whether Fudai or Tozama, are to have their fiefs

---

[1]T'ang of Yin and Wu of Chou were the founders of these two Chinese dynasties.—ED.

changed after a certain number of years, for if they stay long in one place and get used to their positions these lords will lose their fidelity and become covetous and self-willed, and eventually oppress their subjects. This changing of fiefs shall be according to the conduct of these lords.

If there be no direct heir to the Shogunate, then the question of succession must be settled by a conference of the veteran houses of Ii, Honda, Sakai, Sakakibara, and others, after careful consideration.

Should anyone break the laws I have laid down, even if he be a son or heir, he shall not succeed. The Chief Senator (Tairo) and Senators (Roshin) shall then hold a consultation and shall choose a suitable person from among the branch families of our house (Kamon) and make him head of the family.

The right use of a sword is that it should subdue the barbarians whily lying gleaming in its scabbard. If it leaves its sheath it cannot be said to be used rightly. Similarly the right use of military power is that it should conquer the enemy while concealed in the breast. To take the field with an army is to be found wanting in the real knowledge of it. Those who hold the office of Shogun are to be particularly clear on this point. . . .

If your defences are according to my instructions traitors will not be able to spy them out. But even so, if another family plans to over-throw this Empire the attempt will only be made when those who uphold it are given up to drink and dissipation. It is inevitable that those who are incapacitated by these things should be deprived of office and commit suicide.

In ordinary matters, if one does not disobey these instructions of mine, even if he is far from being a sage, he will commit no great fault.

From my youth I have not valued silver or gold or treasures. Virtue only I have treasured. And now I have thus attained this office. If we always consider without ceasing the golden words that declare that it is by learning that emolument comes, we can always attain our purpose. . . .

When the Empire is at peace do not forget the possibility of war, and take counsel with the Fudai vassals that the military arts be not allowed to deteriorate. And be temperate in your habits.

The sword is the soul of the warrior. If any forget or lose it he will not be excused. . . .

The descendants of those retainers who were loyal to our ancestors, except they become traitors to our house, must never have their fiefs confiscated, even if their conduct is not good.

Authority to subdue the whole Empire was granted by Imperial Edict to the Shogun, and he was appointed Lord High Constable

(Sotsui-Hoshi). The orders that the Shogun issues to the country are its law. Nevertheless every province and district has its particular customs, and it is difficult, for example, to enforce the customs of the Eastern Provinces in the Western, or those of the North in the South, so that these customs must be left as of old and not interfered with. . . .

In accordance with ancient precedent, a Court of Judgment is to be established, and there, in the light of these articles I have drawn up and without regarding the high or repressing the low, justice is to be done openly to all.

Now the officials who administer justice in this court are the pillars of the government of the country. Their character shall be carefully considered, and they shall be chosen and appointed after consultation with the veteran councillors. This will be no easy task. . . .

Nagasaki in Hizen is the port at which foreign shipping arrives. It shall be administered by one of the most trusted retainers chosen from the fudai vassals. The great lords of the neighbouring territories shall also be instructed to furnish guards, that our military might may be demonstrated to all countries. It is strictly forbidden that any of these ships shall enter any other port but Nagasaki.

The entertainment tendered to foreigners who come to pay their respects shall be as heretofore. It shall not be rough or scanty. It shall brilliantly reveal the Imperial Benevolence and Divine Might. . . .

Confucianism and Shinto and Buddhism are different systems, but are no more than direction in the way of virtue and punishment of evil. According to this view, their sects may be adopted and their principles followed. They must not be hindered, but disputes among them must be strictly prohibited. It is evident from past history that such have been a misfortune to the Empire. . . .

Since one person differs from another in disposition, when men are appointed to offices this should be tested, and their tendencies observed and their ability estimated, so that the office may be well filled. A saw cannot do the work of a gimlet, and a hammer cannot take the place of a knife, and men are just like this. There is a use for both sharp and blunt at the right time, and if this is not well apprehended the relation of lord and vassal will become disturbed. This article is to be considered carefully.

Lords of provinces both great and small and lords of fiefs and officials both in and outside Edo shall hold official stipend, and rank only if they conduct themselves properly. If he offend, the greatest feudatory or official, even if he be a relation of our house (Kamon), shall be punished. So in their persons shall they the better guard the Shogun's office. . . .

I was born of the family of Matsudaira of the province of Mikawa, of the lineage of Seiwa Genji, but on account of the enmity of a neighbouring province I had for long to suffer hardships among the common people. But now, I am happy to say, encompassed by the grace of Providence I have restored the ancestral lines of Serata, Nitta, and Tokugawa, and from henceforth the successive generations of my family are to use these four names. This is in accordance with the saying (of Confucius): Pay all respect to your parents, and follow the customs of your ancestors. . . .

The distinction between wife and concubine is on the principle of lord and vassal. The Emperor has twelve consorts, the great lords may have eight, high officials five, and ordinary samurai two. Below these are the common people. Thus have the ancient sages specified in the *Li Chi*,[2] and it has always been the rule. But fools ignorant of this treat their wife with less respect than a favourite concubine, and so confuse the great principle. This has always been the cause of the fall of castles and the ruin of countries. Is it not well to be warned? And know too that those who give way to these inclinations are no loyal samurai.

The business of a husband is to protect the family outside, while that of the wife is to look after it at home. That is the order of the world. Should the wife, on the contrary, be the one to guard the house the husband loses his function, and it is a sure sign that the house will be destroyed. It is the disorder of the crowing hen. All samurai should beware of it. Its existence will assist you to judge people.

When I was young I desired nothing but to subdue hostile provinces and take vengeance on the enemies of my father's house. But since I discovered the teaching of Yuyo[3] that helping the people and thus tranquillizing the country is the Law of Nature, I have undeviatingly followed it until now. Let my descendants continue my policy. If they reject it they are no posterity of mine. For be very certain that the people are the foundation of the country.

The Supreme Sovereign of the Empire looks on the people as children under his protecting care, and my family to which the administration of his realm is committed should exhibit this attitude even more. This is what is called Benevolence. Benevolence includes the Five Relationships, and the distinction of superior and inferior. In accordance with it I make a difference in intimacy between the Fudai and the Tozama Daimyos. That is government according to the natural way of the world. It is not favouritism or prejudice or self-interest.

---

[2] The *Li Chi* was the Book of Ceremonies.—ED.

[3] Yuyo: this reference is obscure.—ED.

It must not be polluted either by tongue or pen. And as to the degree of this intimacy with retainers, whether deep or the reverse, you must know how to maintain a deep reserve.

Since I have held this office of Shogun I have drawn up these many statutes, both amplifying and curtailing the ancient regulations of the Minamoto house. But with a view to transmitting and not to creating, for they are no new laws decreed at my will. Thus I have drawn them up in this form as an exemplar. They may not always hit the mark exactly, but they will not be far out. In all things administration is not so much a matter of detail as of understanding past history. I have no time to add more.

Tokugawa's Practical Revolution

GEORGE SANSOM

The earlier Western histories of Japan tended to take the view that the closing of the country to Western influences that took place early in the Tokugawa period resulted in a deadening stagnation from which Japan was rescued only by forceful European intervention in the mid-nineteenth century. Contemporary interpretation has, however, largely revised this Eurocentric judgment. The age of Tokugawa is now seen as one of significant growth in Japan's institutional structures. The dynamic of this period was provided by the conversion of the daimyo into regional rulers and by the creation of a new national hegemony under the Tokugawa shogunate.

One of the leading figures in this contemporary view of the Tokugawa period is the British scholar George Sansom, who has produced "by far the outstanding writing on pre-twentieth-century Japan."[4] His earlier works dealt essentially with cultural history; but then he turned to the long-delayed task of providing an up-to-date political history of Japan. The second volume of this work is A History of Japan, 1334–1615, *which is excerpted below.*

Sansom stresses the practical, revolutionary nature of the reforms instituted by Tokugawa that were essentially responsible for the ensuing long period of peace and order.

---

[4]John Whitney Hall, *Japanese History: New Dimensions of Approach and Understanding* (Washington, D.C.: Service Center for Teachers of History, The American Historical Association, 1961), pp. 10–11.

Ieyasu died on the first of June, 1616, in his seventy-fifth year. Although he had devoted much of his time since the death of Hideyoshi to urgent military problems and had fought two vital campaigns to ensure his supremacy, he had by no means neglected questions of civil government during the last fifteen years of his life. Indeed, in 1605, only two years after his appointment as Shōgun, he resigned the office in favour of his son Hidetada in order to be free to pay full attention to the political structure which was to sustain the power of the house of Tokugawa. His resignation and the succession of Hidetada were also intended to give public notice that the office was to be hereditary in the Tokugawa family. Himself a triumphant warrior, Ieyasu was determined that his family should hold what he had won, and that there should be an end to civil war. It was his purpose to devise a system which would hold in check the ambitions of the most powerful barons, who, though they had submitted to him after Sekigahara, were of uncertain loyalty. . . .

The basis of Ieyasu's civil policy was to distribute fiefs in such a way that his most trusted vassals occupied domains from which they could keep watch and ward upon barons whose allegiance was doubtful. The dependable vassals were known as Fudai, or hereditary lieges of the house of Tokugawa, in contrast to the Tozama, the "Outside Lords," with whom Ieyasu had no hereditary tie. Most of the Fudai daimyos held fiefs of about 50,000 koku[5] or less, with the exception of Matsudaira Tadayoshi (Ieyasu's fifth son) at Kiyosu, who had 500,000 koku, and Ii Naomasa at Hikone with 100,000. They were all placed at strategic points from Kyoto eastward along the Tōkaidō and the Nakasendō to Yedo.

In the Tozama, powerful lords who had been neutral or had adhered to Ieyasu after Sekigahara, he had little trust. He treated them with formal respect, but they were carefully watched and given little opportunity to plan combinations against the Bakufu. They were frequently called upon to perform tasks that put them to great expense, as for example when they were given the unwelcome privilege of building or repairing citadels, supposedly in the interest of the nation. . . .

Ieyasu took all possible steps to thwart alliances and agreements among the Tozama, imposing limits on the size of their castles and on the capacity of the transport craft used by the barons in coastal provinces. Where possible he reduced their freedom of movement by appointing Fudai vassals to neighbouring fiefs. . . .

Although Ieyasu paid unremitting attention to civil affairs, he

---

[5]The *koku* was a measure of rice, about five bushels.—Ed.

made no attempt to organize a coherent system of government. He dealt with problems as they arose, and his methods had a military flavour. He was determined to secure obedience, and it was his method to give direct orders rather than to govern by legislation. He did, it is true, issue a code to guide the behaviour of the military class, but not until the end of his career. It was a collection of rules known as Buke Sho-Hatto, or Ordinances for the Military Houses. . . .

The issuing of this document was little more than a formality or a matter of record, since Ieyasu had already achieved his purpose of subjecting the Tozama by the methods just described, and by increasingly harsh treatment as his earlier forms of pressure succeeded. But even more effective than direct coercion was the great addition to his own strength that resulted from his economic enterprises. He was immensely wealthy, as the Christian missionaries frequently reported in their letters home. After Sekigahara he had vastly enlarged the scope of Tokugawa property rights by taking into his direct jurisdiction the cities of Yedo, Kyoto, Ōsaka, Nagasaki, Yamada, and Nara. . . .

After the establishment of a mint at Fushimi in 1601 he profited by the minting of gold and silver coinage for circulation throughout the country. But perhaps his greatest interest was in foreign trade, which he desired to promote not only as a source of revenue for himself but also on grounds of national policy. The foreign trade of Japan had for too long been in the hands of the Portuguese.

After the invasion of Korea official relations between Japan and China had come to an end, but imports from China were still essential to the Japanese economy or, to put it more correctly, to the economy of the ruling class, who could not dispense with the silks and other luxuries to which they had become accustomed during the period of licensed trade. Fortunately for them the Portuguese, who were allowed to trade with China, could meet Japanese needs by the regular supply of Chinese goods carried in their trading vessels from Macao to Japan. . . .

This favourable treatment of foreigners lasted through the year 1611, when suddenly the Tokugawa government reversed its policy and began to prohibit the preaching and practice of the Christian faith. The reasons for this change are still the subject of controversy, but they were clearly political rather than religious. Ieyasu was determined to get rid of all missionaries, and on January 27, 1614, he issued an edict suppressing Christianity in Japan. The churches in Kyoto were destroyed and the missionaries taken into custody. Some Japanese Christians of high rank were arrested and sent into exile, among them being the "Christian daimyo" Takayama Ukon, who died in Manila a year later. A few poor Japanese believers were punished for refusing to abjure their faith, and some were imprisoned;

but the edict was really directed not against the common people but against members of the military class, because their Christian beliefs were thought to be inconsistent with loyalty to their overlords. During Ieyasu's lifetime no foreign missionary was put to death, though many flouted his decree. . . .

The business of national government was conducted by Ieyasu on the same general lines as the regulation of a fief by a powerful daimyo. He gave orders to his subordinates, who carried them out to the best of their ability. It was characteristic of the early stage of the Tokugawa Bakufu that there was no clear division of functions, for although Ieyasu depended upon his trusted vassals, the Fudai, to carry out his plans, he also depended upon various people of lower standing who happened to come to his notice. He made use of monks and Confucian scholars to draft the Buke Sho-Hatto, and he was in close touch with prominent merchants and other men who had special knowledge or experience. They were usually gifted persons, and they took the place of regular functionaries. . . . From 1615 for two hundred and fifty years Japan was at peace under the rule of the Tokugawa Shōguns.

A More Cautious View

EDWIN O. REISCHAUER

A scholar of Japanese history of equal standing with Sansom is Edwin O. Reischauer. Born in Japan of American missionary parents, Reischauer studied both in the West and in Japan and is a long-time Harvard professor. In the course of World War II he served as a Senior Research Analyst for the War Department and in the Department of State, and from 1961 to 1966 he was ambassador to Japan. For more than forty years he has been the leading interpreter of Japan for American readers, and his many books represent "the most up-to-date interpretations of the causative forces in Japanese history, and provide the best balanced view of the interaction of political, social, and economic factors."[6]

Reischauer's narrative and analysis of the founding of the Tokugawa shogunate does not differ radically from Sansom's. But in interpretive terms he does return to a cautiously modified form of the earlier "stagnation"

---

[6]Hall, *Japanese History,* p. 11.

interpretation. He views the extremely conservative nature of the Tokugawa shogunate as responsible for holding back normal social and economic progress and keeping Japan frozen in an antiquated political and social order.

The political vacuum created by the death of Hideyoshi was soon filled by his foremost vassal, Tokugawa Ieyasu, who had been Hideyoshi's deputy in eastern Japan, where he had built himself a castle headquarters at the small village of Edo, the future Tokyo. In 1600, Ieyasu decisively defeated a coalition of rivals, and fifteen years later he destroyed the remnants of Hideyoshi's family when he captured the great Osaka castle, as much by trickery as by the huge forces he had mustered for the siege. Ieyasu, warned by the fate of the heirs of Nobunaga and Hideyoshi, was obsessed with the idea of building a political system strong enough to survive his death. Political stability became his primary goal, and it was equally sought by his successors. In this they were eminently successful. During the first half of the seventeenth century they created a political system which was to endure almost unchanged for two and a half centuries. In fact, they established a state of absolute peace, internal and external, that has never been matched over a comparable period of time by any other nation. Unfortunately, they secured peace and stability by a series of rigid controls over society, by ruthless suppression of many of the most creative tendencies in the Japan of that day, by isolating Japan from the rest of the world, and by preserving in unchanging form many feudal institutions and attitudes of the late sixteenth century, which became increasingly anachronistic during the next two centuries. In short, the Tokugawa system was extremely conservative even by the standards of early seventeenth-century Japanese society and became increasingly more so as time passed. . . .

The Tokugawa, in their search for stability, froze the political system as it had evolved by the late sixteenth century. They left the bulk of the country divided among a large number of autonomous daimyo, and sought merely to control these daimyo through preponderant military power and a system of careful supervision. . . . The shoguns reserved for themselves a personal domain of about 7 million *koku* (out of a total estimated national yield of 26 million), and also controlled directly all major cities, ports, and mines.

The country was in a sense divided into two halves: the Tokugawa group and the outsiders. On the one side was the shogun, the "related" (*shimpan*) daimyo, who were branches of the Tokugawa family, and the "hereditary" (*fudai*) daimyo, who had been vassals of Ieyasu even before his victory in 1600. These together provided both the military defense and the administration of the Tokugawa shogunate.

On the other side were the "outer" (*tozama*) daimyo. These were the survivors of the allies, neutrals, and enemies of Ieyasu in the great battle of 1600 who had recognized him as their overlord only after his victory. . . .

The holdings of the shogun and daimyo were not scattered haphazardly about Japan. Almost all the central part of the country, including the Kanto Plain in the east and the old capital district in the west, was held by the Tokugawa group. This central area was not only the strategic heart of the country, but contained most of the larger plains, the bulk of the urban population, and was the economically most advanced region. . . .

The outer daimyo, some of whom nursed old hostilities toward the Tokugawa, were relegated largely to the northern and western peripheries of the nation, in north and west Honshu and the islands of Shikoku and Kyushu, where they were sometimes interlarded with related or hereditary daimyo assigned to keep watch over them.

While the daimyo were all in theory autonomous, the Tokugawa actually worked out a careful system of checks and controls to prevent any of them or any combination of them from becoming a military challenge to the shogunate. The bulk of Japan's fighting men remained divided among the daimyo, but the size of their respective forces and the extent of their fortifications were strictly controlled by Edo. Intermarriage and other contracts between the daimyo families were carefully supervised. Though the daimyo domains paid no taxes to the central government, the Tokugawa called on them freely for construction work at Edo or other national services, and so kept them from amassing excessive wealth. The Edo government also developed a category of officials known as *metsuke,* who acted on the one hand as censors in ferreting out cases of maladministration by Tokugawa officials, and on the other hand as secret police spying on all men or groups who could be a menace to Tokugawa rule. The Edo shogunate thus has the dubious distinction of being one of the first governments in the world to develop an extensive and efficient secret police system and to make of it a major organ of state.

The most important measure taken by Edo to ensure its control over the daimyo was the development of a system of hostages and service at the shogunal court. Under the name of *sankin kotai* ("alternating in attendance"), most daimyo spent every other year in Edo, but kept their wives and children permanently there as hostages. A close watch was kept at important barriers on the highways leading into Edo for women leaving and firearms entering the city, since the departure of hostages or the smuggling in of weapons might have foreshadowed a revolt. Naturally, each daimyo had to maintain a large establishment in Edo, and sometimes several in the case of the bigger domains. These were serious economic drains on daimyo resources and an enrichment of the shogun's capital city. The annual comings and goings of the daimyo to Edo, accompanied by long trains of retainers, also constituted a great expense, but at the same time these daimyo processions, particularly on the Tokaido road from Kyoto to Edo, provided one of the more spectacular aspects of life during the Tokugawa period.

To perpetuate their rule, the Tokugawa needed not only to control the daimyo but to guarantee their own solidarity and ensure that the stupidity or ineptness of some future shogun would not destroy the regime. While they left the age-old fiction of imperial rule undisturbed, contenting themselves with the status of shogun, that is, the "generalissimo" of the emperor's military forces, they in fact established close surveillance and strict control over the imperial court, while giving it fairly generous economic treatment as the ultimate source of their own legitimacy. Aware that the deaths of Nobunaga and Hideyoshi had led almost at once to the downfall of their families, Ieyasu passed on the title of shogun to one of his less gifted but more stable sons in 1605, with the result that his own death in 1616 produced no political repercussions. He and his early successors also developed a complicated but strong central administration, quite capable of ruling the land with or without the shoguns, most of whom proved to be little more than figureheads. . . .

Two things should be noted about this governmental system. It was highly bureaucratic, despite its feudal social background. Eligibility for positions was determined primarily by hereditary status, but within this limitation, actual appointments, particularly to the higher posts, depended largely on talent. When Japan had in theory adopted the Chinese bureaucratic form of government in the seventh and eighth centuries, no true bureaucracy had developed. Now, even though the outward forms of government remained feudal, a true bureaucracy started to emerge, and with the passing of the years developed the typical strengths and weaknesses of that form of government. The other point worth mentioning is the strong tendency toward collective responsibility rather than personalized leadership. The figureheads remained individuals, but actual leadership was assumed by councils or officials working in pairs. Japan's genius for anonymous, bureaucratic, group leadership had already become well established. . . .

As early as 1608 Ieyasu appointed a prominent Confucian philosopher to be "attendant scholar" at his court. From this small beginning grew a strong school of Confucianism at Edo that taught the orthodox interpretation as it had been formulated in China in the twelfth century by Chu Hsi (Shushi in Japanese). Soon groups of thinkers, representing various other schools of Confucianism, grew up in opposition to the orthodox school. One of the results of this scholarly interest in Confucianism in Tokugawa Japan was the development within the samurai class of a body of trained scholars and thinkers who, as statesmen, contributed to the efficient administration of the government and, as philosophers and teachers, helped keep Japan intellectually alive despite the oppressive limitations of the political and social system.

The long period of interest in Confucianism also served to imbue the people as a whole with many of the high ethical and moral standards of the Chinese, particularly their ideal of selfless and just public service and their passion for education. Buddhism remained the dominant religion of the masses and enjoyed official patronage, but Confucianism became the strongest intellectual and ethical force in Japan. . . .

Perhaps the most drastic measures taken by the Edo government to ensure political stability were in the field of foreign relations, which, with the coming of Europeans to East Asian waters, assumed a new significance for the Japanese. The first Europeans to reach Japan were Portuguese mariners who landed on an island off the southern tip of Kyushu around 1543. Trade relations sprang up between the Portuguese and the feudal lords of western Kyushu. The Japanese showed immediate interest in the firearms of the Europeans and their use spread rapidly throughout Japan, greatly changing the nature of warfare.

Contacts with the Portuguese took on a new aspect when St. Francis Xavier, the famous Jesuit missionary, introduced Christianity to Japan during a two-year stay from 1549 to 1551. He and the Jesuits who followed him met with considerable success in their proselytizing. . . .

Hideyoshi and the Tokugawa who followed him had no particular objections to Christianity on religious grounds, but they looked upon it with deep suspicion as a political menace to their rule. The Christians, as a sizable group of Japanese owing some sort of allegiance to a remote European "ruler," the pope, were in their eyes a group which could not be trusted and might prove a threat to the reestablished unity of Japan. . . . In 1609 the Dutch established a trading post at Hirado, an island off the northwest coast of Kyushu, and the English, too, set up a trading post there in 1613. At about the same time Ieyasu reverted to Hideyoshi's policy of persecution, and his successor in 1617 reinstated the extreme measure of executing missionaries and native believers. In the next few years all the missionaries were either killed or forced to leave Japan, and thousands of Japanese Christians either apostatized or suffered the death of martyrs. A common practice of the time was to order people suspected of being Christians to tread upon a cross or some other sacred symbol, and to kill those who refused to comply. . . .

Despite this policy of extreme national isolation, the Tokugawa were wise enough not to cut off all contact with other nations. They preserved Nagasaki as a window looking out on the rest of the world. Chinese merchants were allowed to visit and trade there under careful supervision, and the Dutch trading post at Hirado was moved to a small island in Nagasaki harbor, where the Dutch merchants were kept in virtual year-round imprisonment. The measures the early Tokugawa took to ensure the continuance of their regime were indeed drastic. They stifled the normal social and economic development of the country and so isolated Japan from the rest of the world that she began to drop far behind Europe in scientific and industrial achievements. Even Japan's population stopped growing after about 1700 and remained relatively static at about 30 million people during the remaining century and a half of Tokugawa rule.

It must be admitted, however, that the Tokugawa were supremely successful in establishing the political stability they sought. Between the middle of the seventeenth century and the middle of the nineteenth, no revolution, disturbance, or incident in any way threatened their rule. . . .

The long peace of the Tokugawa era was, of course, in many ways a blessing. At the same time, the Tokugawa held back the wheels of normal social and economic progress and fixed on the nation an antiquated political and social order. They preserved in Japan a feudal structure and mentality far longer than these could have lasted in a freer society or one more open to pressures from abroad. What had been essentially a conservative political and social system when founded in the early seventeenth century was preserved almost intact until the middle of the nineteenth century. Then a Japan still intellectually and socially bound by this antiquated system was suddenly confronted again by the Europeans, who during the intervening two centuries had made tremendous strides forward in almost all fields of human endeavor.

Review and Study Questions

1. What are the leading principles of government you can derive from the "Legacy of Ieyasu"?
2. What is your assessment of Tokugawa as a ruler?
3. What were the relations of Tokugawa's Japan with the European nations? How did these relations affect Japan?
4. How does Reischauer's interpretation of Tokugawa differ from Sansom's?

Suggestions for Further Reading

An extremely useful annotated bibliographic guide is John Whitney Hall, *Japanese History: New Dimensions of Approach and Understanding* (Washington, D.C.: Service Center for Teachers of History, The American Historical Association, 1961). The sources for the Tokugawa period—as for all the earlier periods of Japanese history—are a problem. The period is very well documented but the documents are all in Japan and untranslated. A few exist in selections, like *Sources of the Japanese Tradition,* ed. Ryusaka Tsunoda, Wm. T. de Bary, and Donald Keene (New York: Columbia University Press, 1958), or *Sources of Japanese History,* ed. David John Lu, vol. I (New York et al.: McGraw-Hill Book Co., 1974); fewer still exist as insertions or appendices in narrative works, like "The Legacy of Tokugawa Ieyasu," in A. L. Sadler, *The Maker of Modern Japan: The Life of Tokugawa Ieyasu* (London: Allen and Unwin, 1977 [1937]), excerpted for this chapter.

The standard biography of Tokugawa is A. L. Sadler, *The Maker of Modern Japan,* just cited. But there is a recent, excellent biography by Conrad Totman, *Tokugawa Ieyasu: Shogun* (San Francisco: Heian International, Inc., 1983). Totman is one of a very few current western authorities on the Tokugawa period, and students are also referred to his excellent survey, *Japan before Perry: A Short History* (Berkeley: University of California Press, 1987), which stresses the Tokugawa period. A similar work is George Sansom, *A History of Japan, 1334–1615* (Stanford: Stanford University Press, 1961), excerpted for this chapter. An older standard work is still useful—the massive James Murdoch and Isoh Yamagata, *A History of Japan,* vol. II, *During the Century of Early Foreign Intercourse (1542–1651)* (London: Kegan Paul, Trench, Trubner and Co., 1925); as is the topically organized Jonathan Norton Leonard, *Early Japan* in the "Great Ages of Man" series (New York: Time–Life, 1968).

There are a number of very good books on specialized topics in the Tokugawa period: Conrad D. Totman, *Politics in the Tokugawa Bakufu 1600–1843* (Cambridge: Harvard University Press, 1967); Harold Bolitho, *Treasures among Men: The Fudai Daimyo in Tokugawa Japan* (New Haven and London: Yale University Press, 1974); Herschel Webb, *The Japanese Imperial Institution in the Tokugawa Period* (New York and London: Columbia University Press, 1968); *Studies in the Institutional History of Early Modern Japan,* ed. John W. Hall and Marius B. Jansen (Princeton: Princeton University Press, 1968); and Herman Ooms, *Tokugawa Ideology: Early Constructs, 1570–1680* (Princeton: Princeton University Press, 1985).

Among the best general works in which Tokugawa and the Tokugawa period are treated is Edwin O. Reischauer, *Japan: The Story of a*

Nation, 2nd ed. (New York: Knopf, 1974), excerpted for this chapter. There is a third edition (1981) of this book in which the treatment of this period is somewhat abbreviated. Also recommended is another of Reischauer's books, co-authored with Albert M. Craig, *Japan: Tradition and Transformation* (Boston: Houghton Mifflin, 1978) and G. B. Sansom, *Japan: A Short Cultural History,* rev. ed. (New York: Appleton-Century-Crofts, 1962); John Whitney Hall, *Japan from Prehistory to Modern Times* (New York: Delacorte Press, 1970); and Mikiso Hane, *Modern Japan: A Historical Survey* (Boulder and London: Westview Press, 1986).

SHAH 'ABBAS I: "THE GREAT KING OF KINGS"

1571	Born
1587	Ascended the throne
1590	Peace of Istanbul with the Ottomans
1598	Defeat of the Uzbeks
1599	Moved capital to Isfahan
1629	Died

Between the early sixteenth century and the mid-eighteenth century, Safavid Persia was one of the great states of the Middle East. Its greatest king was Shah 'Abbas I (1571–1629): indeed, Shah 'Abbas may be counted one of the great kings of his age. In the judgment of one of his early English biographers, "there have been few sovereigns in the universe who have done more substantial good to their country than Abbas the Great."[1]

'Abbas was the fifth in the line of Safavid kings. The Safavids had been one of several Turkoman peoples who invaded and settled in northern Iran in the later Middle Ages. Their ruling sultans adopted the Shi'a Islamic cult, traditional in Iran, and claimed descent from the founding Imans of the Shi'a movement. This dubious attachment to religion and their own fierce military capabilities enabled the Safavids to conquer most of Iran and allowed Esma'il to assume the crown in 1501, the first of the Safavid kings.

At 'Abbas's succession in 1587, however, both his state and his dynasty were in great peril. His weakling father had been the pawn of court and tribal factions and the rest of his family had been assassi-

---

[1] Sir John Malcolm, *The History of Persia from the Most Early Period to the Present Time*, 2 vols. (London: John Murray, 1815), vol. I, p. 566.

nated. He himself escaped only because he was useful to first one tribal leader, then another.

'Abbas's most pressing problem was to regain control of his own state from the murderous factions who had fought over it for more than a decade. But in addition, huge chunks of Iranian territory had been taken by the Indian Moghuls to the south, the tribal Uzbeks to the east, and the Ottoman Empire to the west; and the Uzbeks and the Ottomans were preparing for new attacks. 'Abbas's internal and external problems were closely related. Any serious military campaign would put him deeper into the debt of the tribal faction leaders—called the Qizilbash emirs from the red turbans they traditionally wore. These men dominated the Safavid military, as the troops were mustered from their family lands, were paid by them, and were substantially loyal to them. The young shah fully realized that he would have to have a new kind of army if he intended to break Qizilbash power. But in the meantime he had no reliable army to fight the Turks and the Uzbeks. He bought peace with the Turks by the humiliating Treaty of Istanbul of 1590, surrendering every inch of Iranian land claimed by the Ottomans. The Uzbeks were forestalled by diplomacy and their own tribal divisions, and finally by direct military action. 'Abbas turned to the Georgians, Armenians, and Circassians—people who were the descendents of those taken prisoner in earlier Safavid wars, hence called *ghulam* or "slave" troops. They were recruited and organized into a standing army that was at last loyal to the crown, and they were paid by the shah. Over a ten-year period he made inroads on the political and fiscal independence of the Qizilbash feudality, converting their lands and others into crown land. And he had started to centralize his state and modernize his nation.

'Abbas also made progress against his military foes. He defeated the Uzbeks and undertook a series of long and bitter wars against the Turks. By 1625 he had recovered most of the territory lost by the Treaty of Istanbul.

In the meantime, 'Abbas had made significant economic advances, not the least of which involved initiatives to the great powers of Europe who might be interested in negotiating military alliances against the common threat of the Ottomans.

'Abbas the Statesman

SIR ANTHONY SHERLEY

In 1598 a mission headed by a bold English adventurer, Sir Anthony Sherley, arrived in Persia, sent by the equally bold and adventurous favorite of Queen Elizabeth I, the Earl of Essex, Robert Devereux. The purpose of the mission was grand enough: to try to persuade the shah to unite with the powers of Europe against the Turks and to open better trade relations with England. For this Essex had not a shred of official authorization: it was a classic example of the overweening ambition that would shortly bring about his downfall. But Shah 'Abbas knew none of this. Indeed, Sherley gave it out that he was the cousin of King James of Scotland and that the other kings of Christendom had empowered him as their ambassador to treat with the shah.² Whether 'Abbas believed this incredible claim or not, he received Sherley well, liked and favored him and shortly sent him back to Europe as his own envoy to negotiate alliances against the Turks as well as trade alliances. Sir Anthony left his younger brother Robert at the Persian court, as a genteel hostage, along with the other members of his party.

He made his way to the Russian court and later to Prague and Rome, where he was well received. But at none of these courts did he succeed in his mission. Further, he was barred from returning to England by the influence of the East India Company, which had ambitions of its own for the Persian trade. Sir Anthony spent his last years in Madrid, where he died in the most abject poverty in 1635. Part of his failure as an ambassador was simply due to the hazards of seventeenth-century diplomacy. But part of it was surely owing to his own tempestuous nature. Shortly before his death, the English ambassador to Spain, Sir Francis Cottington, reported him "as full of vanity as ever he was, making himself believe that he shall one day be a great prince, when for the present he wants shoes to wear."³

Nevertheless, in 1613 he had published, in London, a memoir of his adventures in Persia. Much of the book is "pompous argumentation and tedious ethical reflections,"⁴ but it contains "also a true relation of the great

---

²Sir E. Denison Ross, *Sir Anthony Sherley and His Persian Adventure* (London: George Routledge and Sons, 1933), p. 16.

³*Dictionary of National Biography*, "Shirley."

⁴This is the judgment of an anonymous contemporary, reported in Ross, *Sir Anthony Sherley and his Persian Adventure*, p. xx.

magnificence, valor, prudence, justice, temperance, and other manifold vir-
tues of Abas, now King of Persia." This account is extremely valuable be-
cause, of the several Europeans who wrote of Shah 'Abbas's Persia, Sherley
was the closest to the shah himself. It is true that the account is adulatory;
but it is equally true that this was the honest opinion and the honest ac-
count of Sir Anthony. From it emerges a portrait of Shah 'Abbas as truly
"the King of Kings."

And now that I am in Persia and speak of the king's absence, since
he is both one of the mightiest princes that are and one of the
excellentest, for the true virtues of a prince, that is or has been; and
having come to this greatness, though by right, yet through the
circumstances of the time and the occasions, which then were, solely
his own worthiness and virtue made way to his right. Besides, the
fashion of his government, differing so much from that which we
call barbarousness, that it may justly serve for as great an Idea for a
principality as Plato's commonwealth did for a government of that
sort. I hold it not amiss to speak amply first of his person, the nature
of his people, the distributions of his government, the administration of his justice, the condition of the bordering princes, and the
causes of those wars in which he was then occupied; that by the true
expression of those, this discourse may pass with a more lively and
more sensible feeling.

His person, then, is such as a well-understanding nature would fit
for the end proposed for his being, excellently well shaped, of a most
well proportioned stature, strong, and active; his color somewhat
inclined to a man-like blackness is also more black by the sun's burning: his furniture of mind infinitely royal, wise, valiant, liberal, temperate, merciful, and an exceeding lover of justice, embracing royally
other virtues, as far from pride and vanity, as from all unprincely
signs or acts; knowing his power justly what it is; and the like acknowledgement will also have from others, without any gentilitious adoration; but with those respects which are fit for the majesty of a prince;
which foundeth itself upon the power of his state, general love, and
awful terror. His fortunes determining to make proof of his virtue,
drove him (in his first years) into many dangerous extremities, which
he overcoming by his virtue hath made great use of both in the
excellent increase of his particular understanding and general tran-
quility, strength of his country, and propagation of his empire. For
the laws and customs, or both, of that kingdom being such that,
though the king have a large increase of issue, the first-born only
rules; and to avoid all kind of cause of civil dissention, the rest are not
inhumanly murdered, according to the use of the Turkish govern-

ment, but made blind with burning basons:[5] and have otherwise all
sort of contentment and regard fit for princes' children. . . .

*Sherley goes on to discuss contemporary political events and the shah's
proposed military campaigns.*

Yet before the king would enter into this action, remembering, that
before he had better settled himself in his own state, that he thrust
himself upon a cast of fortune to seek after the winning of others; yet
since he was forced into it, by a certain great necessity, he resolved to
take the best ways for the securing all dangers which might rise
against himself at home; and setting his country in a reposed state
from so many tempests which had contrarily moved it, as well as to
make due and confident provisions for his intended wars. First then
he called unto him to *Casbin*[6] all governors, and all administrators of
justice whosoever had occupied those functions during the usurped
rule of the *Cans*[7] through all his provinces, with the kinsmen, friends,
and children of the said *Cans*: besides, that all men of power, as
Mirzaes, Cans, Sultans, and *Beagues,* which are principal titles of Dukes,
Princes, and Lords, should repair thither without excuse of age, sickness, or any other pretense whatsoever: which being done, he appointed new Governors and Officers of all sorts; he cleared all his
provinces for three years from paying any tribute-custom, or any
other ordinary or extraordinary exaction whatsoever. . . .

Thus having wisely and providently placed through all his estates
those who must be most assured to him, their fortunes depending
only upon him, having no more strength nor authority in themselves
than they received from him: and having all the great ones in his
army with him or such of them as could not be able to follow him,
either by their few or many years, or sickness, so securely left at
Casbin, that they could not by themselves or any other move any
innovation. And moreover, having dispatched all those and keeping
their persons with him which had any obligation to the former *Cans,*
secured by that means (as much as the counsel of any man could
secure him) from peril at home: having called *Oliver di Can*[8] from
Hamadan, and appointed him a successor for that government with
ten thousand new men, he set himself forward to his enterprise with
his old troops and a great part of his rebeled army.

---

[5]A *bason* was a heated iron plate used in hat making.—ED.

[6]Qazvim was the old Safavid capital city northwest of Tehran.—ED.

[7]Khans.—ED.

[8]*Oliver di Can* is Allah Vardi Khan, a trusted subordinate of the shah.—ED.

This was to be his great campaign against the Uzbeks, culminating in a victory over them.

The country being first spoiled and ransomed at a great rate, which they might well bear by reason of their great riches which they had gathered together through a long peace; and the king's army excellently well satisfied; he dispatched instantly ambassadors to the *Turk,* the *Georgians,* and his old friend, the king of *Corassan,* to give them an account of this new victory: not doubting but as it would be exceeding pleasant to some, so it would be as bitter to others: and leaving *Ferrat Can* to govern the country and *Oliver Dibeague*[9] as his assistant but to be commanded by him, he returned himself, full of glory and great victory into Persia, disposing himself to reduce his state to that excellent form of government which now it hath. . . .

It was at this juncture that Sherley first actually met the shah.

The most part of this time I was at *Casbin,* courteously used by *Marganobeague* the Master of the King's House, and not amiss by any. When the king was come within six miles of *Casbin* he stayed there some three days, to the intent to make his entry with such an estimation of his victory as was fit for so great and happy a success of fortune; and, in truth, I think that he did it most to declare the greatness of it to us that were strangers, by such a strange demonstration. The night before he entered there were 30,000 men sent out of the town on foot with horsemen's staves upon which they fastened vizards of so many heads.[10] All those in the morning when we were commanded to meet him (the governor having provided us horses) we found marching in battle array toward the town, and before the two heads of the king and his son, four officers of arms, such as they use, bearing in their hands great axes of shining steel with long helves. After those battalions followed the *Xa-Hammadagae's*[11] horsemen. After those a number of gentlemen of the king's court. After those a hundred spare horses with as many of the king's pages. After those the prisoners accompanied with *Bastan-Aga.*[12] Then a great

---

[9]*Ferrat Can* is Farhad Khan, another trusted administrator. The identification of *Oliver Dibeague* is uncertain, but he may be Ali Quli Beg, who later accompanied Sherley's mission to the West.—ED.

[10]These seem to have been masks.—ED.

[11]*Xa-Hammadagae* is Shah Ahmed Agha, one of the shah's trusted military commanders.—ED.

[12]*Bastan-Aga* is Bastan-Agah, another trusted subordinate.—ED.

rank of his chief princes among whom were all the ambassadors which used to be resident in his court. Then followed the young prince of *Corazan,* accompanied with *Xa-Tamas-Coolibeague,* the king's principal favorite. And then the king himself alone. And after him some five hundred courtiers of his guard. *Marganobeague* was with us and making us large passage through all those troops.

When we came to the king we alighted and kissed his stirrup. My speech was short unto him, the time being fit for no other: that the fame of his royal virtues had brought me from a far country to be a present spectator of them, as I had been a wonderer at the report of them from afar. If there were anything of worth in me, I presented it with myself, to his majesty's service. Of what I was I submitted the consideration to his majesty's judgment which he should make upon the length, the danger, and the expense of my voyage, only to see him of whom I had received such magnificent and glorious relations.

The king's answer unto me was infinitely affable: that his country, while I should stay there, should be freely commanded by me, as a gentleman that had done him infinite honor to make such a journey for his sake; only bid me beware that I were not deceived by rumors which had, peradventure, made him other than I should find him: It was true that God had given him both power and mind to answer to the largest reports which might be made good of him, which, if he erred in the use of, he would ask counsel of me who must need have much virtue in myself that could move me to undergo so much, and so many perils to know that of another. And that he spoke smiling, willing me to get on horseback; which, when I had done, he called *Haldenbeague,* his *Viseire,* and *Oliver Di-Can* his general, and commanded them to take my brother and me between them: and my company was disposed by *Marganobeague,* among the rest of the king's gentlemen of his court. And in that order the king entered *Casbin,* and passing to the great place, he alighted with the chiefest of his princes and officers whom he caused to bring us with them, and went into a kind of banqueting house in which there were stairs to ascend by into a terrace where the king sat down and the greatest of those princes and we among them. . . . While we sat there the king called me again unto him and when I had confirmed in more words the very same I had before said unto him, then, said he, you must have the proof of time to show you either the errors or the truth of these rumors, since you can make no judgment of what you have yet seen, which is but the person of a man, and this eminence which God hath given me, for anything you know, may be more through my fortune than my virtue. But since your pains and travel have had no other aspect but to know me, we must have a more intrinsic acquaintance to perfect that knowledge. And how you will endure the fash-

ions of my country you can judge best yourself, which are master of
your own humor. This I will assure you of, you shall want no respect
from my people, nor honor from myself. And therewith he bade me
farewell, for the present, committing me and my company to *Bastan-
Aga* to be conducted to my lodging.

'Abbas the Tyrant

SIR THOMAS HERBERT

*Sir Anthony Sherley had, as we have seen, extolled the "manifold virtues"
and kingly accomplishments and bearing of Shah 'Abbas. But another contemporary English traveler saw and reported quite a different image of the
shah. He was Sir Thomas Herbert.*

*Herbert was associated with the Sherleys. Sir Anthony Sherley's brother
Robert, who had stayed on in Persia, made himself useful to the shah as a
soldier and military adviser in reorganizing his army. In 1608 Sir Robert,
like his brother, was sent as Persian ambassador to Europe by Shah 'Abbas,
again to negotiate alliances against the Turks and to improve Persian
trade. He was no more successful than his brother had been, and returned
to Isfahan. Immediately the shah sent him on a second embassy to Europe,
with another set of instructions but the same mission. Although he was still
unable to establish favorable relations with the continental powers, he did
gain some entry to the English court which decided to send its own embassy
to Persia. The ambassador was Sir Dodmore Cotton. In his suite traveled
Sir Robert Sherley and a young man of good family, Sir Thomas Herbert,
whose connections at court won him a place on the embassy staff.*

*The party reached Persia early in 1628 and was received by the shah.
Shortly thereafter, both Cotton and Sherley died. Under guarantee of safe
conduct from the shah, Herbert and the rest of the English party traveled
extensively through Persia and returned to England the following year. In
1634 Herbert published* A Description of the Persian Monarchy.

*In the account of Shah 'Abbas that this work contains, there is none of
the admiration that Sir Anthony Sherley had expressed. Instead, Herbert
draws the picture of a sadistic and murderous despot. Some of what Herbert
reports he clearly witnessed himself; some he reports from the accounts of
others. But the overall impression is the same, of the shah "rather beseeming
a bloody tyrant than so famous a king."*

After our ambassador had reposed himself four days in *Asharaffe,*[13] the king sent a *Coozel-bash*[14] to him, with commendations, and that next day he would give him audience. Accordingly next day, which was our Sabbath and with them a day of ceremony, being the first day of their great fast and feast (for on that day it is not permitted to eat or drink, but after sunset they do both excessively) this feast is called *Ramazan, Ramdam,* or *Ramadan,* our ambassador, with Sir *Robert Sherley,* and seven or eight *English* gentlemen, his followers, set forward to the court: and this I remember our ambassador took it ill, none came to usher him or show the way. For that morning having sent to *Mahomet Ally-beg* the great favorite to that end, the infidel returned a footman whom, our ambassador scorning, sent back, and so proceeded with his own company.

At our alighting at the court gate, an officer led us into a little place having a pretty marble pond or tank in center. The rest spread with silk carpets where our ambassador and the rest stayed two hours, and then were feasted with a dish of *Pelo,* which is rice boiled with hens, mutton, butter, almonds, and turmeric: but how mean soever the diet was, the furniture was excellent, pure beaten gold, both dishes, covers, flagons, cups and the rest.

Thence we were led by many *Sultans,* through a large, delicate and odoriferous garden, to a house of pleasure whose chambers both viewed the tops of *Taurus* and the *Caspian* Sea.

Into this lodge we entered. The low room was round and spacious, the ground spread with silk carpets, in the midst a marble tank full of crystaline water (an element of no small account in those torrid habitations) and round about the tank, vessels of pure gold, some filled with wine, others with sweet smelling flowers. Thence into a chamber furnished in manner like the former but with three times more vessels of gold set there for pomp and observation.

At the end sat the *Potshaugh*[15] or great king, cross-legged, and mounted a little higher than the rest, his seat having two or three white silk shags upon the carpets. His attire was very ordinary, his tulipant[16] could not outvalue forty shillings, his coat red calico quilted with cotton, worth very little, his sword hung in a leather belt, its handle or hilt was gold, and in regard the king was so plain attired, most of the court had like apparel on for that day. Yet the plate and

---

[13]The modern city of Ashraf, on the Caspian Sea, founded by Shah ʿAbbas.—ED.

[14]*Coozel-bash* is Qizilbash.—ED.

[15]*Potshaugh* is padshah or chief ruler, one of the titles of the shah.—ED.

[16]Some item of clothing, perhaps a tunic.—ED.

jewels in that house argued against poverty. A merchant then there imagined it worth twenty millions of pounds.

So soon as our lord ambassador came to him, he by his interpreter delivered briefly the cause of his journey which was to congratulate his victorious success against the *Turk,* to renew the traffic of silk and other things to benefit the merchants, and to see Sir Robert Sherley purge himself from those imputations laid on him by *Nogdibeg* the king of Persia his late ambassador.[17]

The king gave him a very gracious reply and whereas he thinks it honor enough to let the great Turk's ambassador kiss the hem of his coat and sometimes his foot, he very nobly gave our ambassador his hand and with it pulled him down and seated him next to him cross-legged, and calling for a cup of wine, drunk to his majesty our famous king, at which he put off his hat, and the king seeing it, put off his turban, and drunk the cup off which our ambassador pledged thankfully. And the people thought it a strange thing to see their king so complemental, for it is a shame with them to be bare headed.

The chamber wherein he was entertained had the sides painted and gilded very beautifully. . . . Round about, with their backs to the wall, were seated fifty or sixty *Beglerbegs, Sultans* and *Chawns,* who sit like so many statues rather than living men. The *Ganymed* boys go up and down with flagons of wine and fill to those that covet it.

The day before this ceremony the king rode to hunt the tiger, accompanied only with two hundred women, his wives and concubines, most of them attired like courageous *Amazons,* with scimitar, bow and arrows, the eunuchs riding abroad to prohibit any to come in view of them, the penalty is no less than loss of life, a dear price for novelties. And though for the most part, when the king is in a progress, he has sometimes ten thousand, other times twenty thousand *Cozel-bashawes,* or soldiers of best reckoning, yet at our being then at court, two thousand was the most then attending him.

I will relate his severe justice acted at our being in *Hyrcania.*[18] A poor man who had traveled from *Cabull* in *India* . . . after so long a journey, got to the court and the weather being very sulphurous, affected rather the grass to sleep on than the town, 'tis so pestered with mosquitos, flies and other vermin. His business was not much, yet had better been none at all. It was his ill fate to be asleep as old

---

[17]There had indeed been continual bickering between Sherley and Nogdibeg in the course of the embassy. Sherley was cleared of wrongdoing by the shah, but was afterwards not particularly well favored. He died within the year.—ED.

[18]Hyrcania is the classical name for the region southeast of the Caspian Sea.—ED.

Abbas was going a-hunting within the path. The king saw him not but his pampered horse startled at him, whereat immediately the king sent a broad arrow into the poor man's heart, and ere all his followers had passed, the man was killed a hundred times over, if so many arrows could have forfeited so many lives, in imitating the king as if the deed were good and commendable.

A soldier's wife, abounding with more lust than love, complains to the king her husband did not satisfy her. Whereat he makes her to be coupled to an *Asinego*, whose villany and lust took away her life.[19]

A *Cozel-bash* here presented him a petition. The writing did not please him. He sends for the clerk, cuts off his hand, and made the petitioner be almost drubbed to death.

Two needy knaves were brought before him and condemned for stealing. The king threatened them more for being ragged and lousy, thereby to disgrace his court, than for the theft. And that they might die neatlier than they lived, he caused new coats to be put upon them and forthwith commanded they should be carried out of town and impaled upon two stakes thrust through their fundaments.

He has other tortures, as poisons, strangling with bow-strings, men-eating dogs (some of which the merchants or seamen bring out of England and sell there) and men from their infancy educated to cannibalism, with many other tortures rather beseeming a bloody tyrant than so famous a king.

A duke who was his viceroy for *Hyrcania* seeing a boy whose father was poor (and under his command) against the boy's will, his parent's knowledge and the law of nature, makes him a sodomite (which crying sin, although licensed by their Alcoran, yet force is not to be used, and therefore have *Ganymeds* in each great city tolerated). The father of this wronged child prostrates himself before the king, and acquaints him with that villany, the king seeing sorrow and truth in the peasant's look, demands of the duke, who then was sitting there, how true it was. His countenance betrays him. The king having at that instant a knife in his hand gives it the poor father and bids him eunuchize him, punishing those parts that had offended. The duke durst not startle or intercede the law of the Persian, never alters the poor man, [who] executes, as was enjoined him. The king, though, continues his jurisdiction to him and has him yet, his obedient slave or servant. His *Seraglio* only lost most by that bargain.

The king by a *Hyrcanian* lady (which countrywoman the *Begoon* his mother also was, wife to *Mahomet*) had two sons, *Ismaell* and another *Mirza*. *Ismaell* died having not attained twenty years and the younger

---

[19]An *asinego* is a small donkey, proverbial for its lust.—Ed.

brother by right and law of birth and nations then became heir apparent to his dignity and expectations.

Shaw Abbas his father by his other paramours had many children,
but this *Mirza* as endued with the prerogatives of years and birthright prevailed more in his father's affection and the establishment of
succession than the other children obtained by his affability (a virtue
of especial luster and value with the *Persian*) courage, bounty, experience in arms and other princely qualities requisite for the place he
lived in, the son of such a father, and the report he aimed at, to beget
love and admiration amongst his friends, and terror with his enemies. . . . All terrene joys are mixed with discontent and periods, and
old *Abbas,* day by day increasing his jealousy and envy to his son,
intends to hinder his further progress into glory or other happiness.
He durst not banish him lest he should convert his rage, to affront his
unnatural father, and when he thought of killing him by treason in
his army (the innocent prince at that time, sweating blood to redeem
the honor of his countrymen against the *Turk*) that frighted him, lest
when his cruelty disclosed itself, upon apprehension of the murderer
his men in revenge and detestation of his tyranny might rebel, or
joining with the enemy, to his irreparable loss of purse and honor. So
that he resolved to execute him at the court when far from friends
and where he could best feign an invented crime, so without more
procrastinations, he sends a shooter or footman to him, and (all ex-
cuses set aside) to post to court where the business should then be told
him.

The prince, to forfeit their amazement and ill opinion of him,
declares the message and assures them of his flying speed thither and
back again, and without more ceremony hastens to receive instead of
thanks destruction. His arrival was quickly known to his father *Abbas,*
who sends him word he was not very well and desired him to repose
where they should carry him and ere long he would come and welcome him.

The credulous prince, without any suspect of treachery (invincible
signs of honesty and a sincere mind) follows the man appointed to
show his lodging whereinto (so soon as that servant was departed)
enters at a trap-door seven great villains, deaf and dumb, armed with
bow-strings and bloody minds, whose habit and weapons without
other interpreters assured the amazed prince that he was betrayed
and sealed to destruction. If oratory or other submissive signs of
entreaty could have begot pity or intermission from these hell-
hounds, but only till he knew the cause of this unnatural project, he
had afforded it, but knowing they were deaf in body and soul, inflamed with rage and sorrow, that he wanted a sword or other weapons to defend himself, he flew upon them all, one after another,

offending them by rare force and agility, a long time preventing the nooses to fasten on him which they threw incessantly toward his neck, presenting pale death in their terrible twangs, and armed with integrity and innocence, ere they could strangle him, he sent three of them to the Devil to receive their recompence, the other four seeing their danger, re-inforced their actions and at last fastened on him who, quite spent with rage and opposals, fell down [seemingly] dead, and as craving a cessation of that horrible fight, and that they would not equalize him in the manner of his death, to abject dogs. But these cannibals continued their cruel cowardice both dead and living and had surely finished their villainy had not the king then entered and prevented them (who, some say, was a secret spectator of this unparalleled barbarism) he forthwith commands his tired arms to be pinioned and ere he had fully recovered his senses makes a hot flaming steel be drawn before his eyes which, though giving no great pain, yet took away his eyesight: forbidding him for ever more sight of what he loved, wife, children, friends, and endeared soldiers. And by this excessive impiety *Asia* lost her chiefest jewel, *Mars* his darling, and *Persia* her incomparable treasure, now undone, blind, imprisoned, and hopeless of any joy or honor ever after.

This could not be so secretely committed but in time all *Persia* knew it and lamented it with tears for him, and imprecations of all mischief upon the authors of it: his army were of long time implacable but when they saw it was past remedy, and the king would in time serve them with like sauce if they continued refractory, they retired and buried in murmur and forced silence what their hearts fully and freely discourse upon.

So soon as the blinded prince perceived himself imprisoned (which he saw with the eyes of grief and understanding) he was more than half-distracted, exclaimed upon his bloody father, cursed his birth day, and vowed the king's destruction and his favorites if it lay in his power to see or touch them: but when he called to mind his impossible desires, he roared hideously, and in a word, expressed all true symptoms of madness and desire of revenge, till his afflicted kinsmen and companions flocked about him and dictated patience: which they bettered by relating their own *quondam* greatness in blood and office, till by the like dislike and mutability of *Shaw Abbas* his humors, they were degraded, trod upon, mutilated, some their eyes put out, some their ear and noses cut off, and others in other members, here captived and almost famished.

A Balanced View of 'Abbas

DAVID MORGAN

Even the greatest admirers of Shah 'Abbas have admitted the cruel side of his nature. Sherley casually referred to the practice of blinding royal princes, which he found preferable to their murder "according to the use of the Turkish government." The contemporary Persian chronicler, Eskander Beg Monshi, though he found Shah 'Abbas's achievements so remarkable that he concluded that "the Shah is guided by divine inspiration and by that alone,"[20] could only explain his cruelty—especially to his own sons— as a "divine mystery."[21] The early nineteenth-century historian of Persia, Sir John Malcolm, excused 'Abbas's "apparent cruelty" as "the dreadful obligation of that absolute power to which he was born."[22]

Modern scholars have tended to a more personal and more balanced view. Obviously these were cruel times in a cruel part of the world. H. R. Roemer, in the Cambridge History of Iran,[23] *while he finds 'Abbas's cruelties to his children "nothing new," still argues that the normalizing of the practices of blinding princes or secluding them in the harem was "the work of Shah 'Abbas himself" and was the "one fateful cause of the later decline of his dynasty and its power." In the passage excerpted below from David Morgan's book,* Medieval Persia 1040–1797, *he shares the conclusion of Roemer that 'Abbas's mistreatment of his sons led to the weakening of the dynasty. But he explains the shah's cruelty by "an incurably distrustful temperament," a relic of his own harrowing youth.*

So, in answer to the implicit question, Was Shah 'Abbas a great statesman or a cruel despot?, the answer must be that he was both.

It might have been doubted whether there was actually a Ṣafawid empire in existence in 995/1587[24] for Shāh 'Abbās to rule. External enemies were in occupation of nearly half of what had been Ṣafawid territory in the time of Shāh Ṭahmāsp. So far as the unoccupied areas

---

[20]Eskander, *History of Shah 'Abbas the Great,* vol. I, p. 517.

[21]*Ibid.,* vol. I, p. 525.

[22]*The History of Persia,* vol. I, pp. 565–66.

[23]Vol. 6, p. 278.

[24]The first date is the Islamic year, the second the Christian.—Ed.

of the country were concerned, factional fighting among the Türk-men *amīrs* had reached the proportions of civil war, and the rump of Persia could very well at this point have dissolved into a conglomera-tion of small Türkmen principalities. Only a quite remarkably strong and determined personality could have put all this to rights. Shāh 'Abbās was such a man, but even with him at the head of affairs the process of recovery and reconstruction took many years.

'Abbās was not strong enough, at the outset of his reign, to make any significant inroads against the Ottomans, in any case he could not hope to fight simultaneously a two-front war against both Ottomans and Özbegs. Indeed, he could hardly expect to achieve much mili-tarily until he had begun the internal reorganization of his empire: but this was a lengthy process which will be considered as a whole later. The Özbegs were, as ever, the less formidable of Persia's two by now traditional enemies: 'Abbās therefore resolved to tackle them first. To free his hands for this, he was obliged to make a humiliating peace with the Ottomans in 998/1590. Vast areas of western and northern Persia, including Tabrīz, the original Ṣafawid capital, were ceded to the Ottoman Empire. Although most of Āzarbāyjān was lost, 'Abbās did manage to retain the town of Ardabīl, headquarters of the Ṣafawid order and site of the shrine of Shaykh Ṣafī al-Dīn. But there were not many sops to Persian sensibilities in the peace treaty. It was simply an acknowledgement of the political realities: a step that was, for the time being, necessary if Shāh 'Abbās and the dynasty were to survive at all.

Success against the Özbegs was by no means immediate. They re-mained for a decade in occupation of most of Khurāsān, as well as of Sīstān further south. In addition, Qandahār was again lost to the Mughals. It was not until the death of the able Özbeg *khān* 'Abd Allāh in 1007/1598 that it was possible to recover substantial parts of these lands for Persia. Harāt was retaken in 1007/1598 and by 1011/1602–3, although things had not all gone the Ṣafawid way, the eastern frontier had been stabilized. 'Abbās was materially helped in this by the prevailing disunity among the various Özbeg *khāns:* he was able to make alliances with a number of those who controlled areas near the frontier, at Marv, Balkh, and Astarābād. This real if limited success was finally followed, though not until 1031/1622, by the recovery of Qandahār from the Mughals.

With the eastern border reasonably secure, it remained to mount a counter-attack on the Ottomans. The war began in 1012/1603 and was a long one, but on the whole the Persians were successful. The Ottoman forces sustained a crushing defeat at Ṣūfiyān, near Tabrīz in 1014/1605, and north-west Persia was reoccupied. By 1015/1607 the Ottoman troops had been driven from most of the territory that had been defined as Persian by the Treaty of Amāsya. But the war dragged on, and the Ottomans did not recognize 'Abbās's right to the reconquered lands until 1027/1618.

Hostilities even then were not at an end: in the 1620s 'Abbās was strong enough to take Diyārbakr and, in 1033/1623, Baghdad, which had long been lost. In the previous year the island of Hurmūz in the Persian Gulf, an important centre of international trade, was taken from the Portuguese, though not without the help of an English fleet. By the end of the reign in 1038/1629 Persia once more had the borders established over a century earlier during the time of Shāh Ismā'īl I. It had recovered all that had been lost since the death of Shāh Ṭahmāsp in 984/1576, and had even expanded its borders significantly.

This was a considerable achievement as far as it went, but such victories did not in themselves solve the long-standing internal problems of the Ṣafawid regime: military success and internal restructuring unavoidably went together. If Shāh 'Abbās had restricted his efforts to the military sphere—to attempting to drive out the Özbegs and the Ottomans—he might have enjoyed an ephemeral success (though he might equally have enjoyed no success at all). But the potential of another descent into Qizilbash factional fighting, opening the way to more loss of territory to the neighbouring powers, would still have been there. As it was, the reforms that 'Abbās inaugurated formed an important part of a major social transformation, one which enabled the Ṣafawid dynasty to survive for a century after his death, despite the on the whole unimpressive quality of his successors on the throne.

The immediate spur to action was the need to bring the turbulent Qizilbash *amīrs* under effective royal control. Right from the start of his reign 'Abbās showed that he intended to achieve this, but the measures he took went far beyond the mere containment of fractious tribal chieftains. Action against rebel and ex-rebel Qizilbash began immediately. 'Abbās's patron, Murshid Qulī Khān, was appointed *wakīl*, and with his assistance the shāh took reprisals especially against those Qizilbash he held responsible for the murder of his brother Ḥamza, during the previous reign. But not long after this 'Abbās evidently decided that Murshid Qulī Khān himself was becoming an over-mighty subject, and the *wakīl* was killed on royal orders.

The fundamental problem of the regime was a direct legacy of the way in which it had come to power in Persia: its military dependence on the Qizilbash tribesmen whose support had been the mainstay first of the Ṣafawid order and then of the dynasty. The religious basis of loyalty to the shāh in his capacity as head of the Ṣafawid order had not disappeared, but by the time of Shāh 'Abbās it was clearly much

weaker than it had been a century earlier. We now hear more of the
Shāh-savanī appeal—let those who love the shāh rally to his assistance.
But still such support could not necessarily be counted on. The
Qizilbash had repeatedly proved fickle, and their undoubted allegiance to the Ṣafawid family did not appear in practice to preclude
supporting a Ṣafawid prince against the reigning shāh. The circumstances of 'Abbās's own accession would have made that fact sufficiently clear to him. What the dynasty needed if it were to achieve
political stability was a counterweight to the Qizilbash, a strong military
force recruited from other sections of the population, on whose loyalty
to himself the shāh could rely even if he were to face a Qizilbash revolt.

'Abbās found his source of recruitment chiefly in the Caucasians.
Here he was following the precedent laid down, at least in embryo, in
the reign of Ṭahmāsp. The Georgians, Armenians and Circassians
who now became so important were in part the descendants of those
who had been taken prisoner at that time. But their numbers were
considerably augmented by further batches of prisoners taken by
'Abbās himself during campaigns in Armenia in 1012/1603–4 and
Georgia in 1023/1614 and 1025/1616.

The forces 'Abbās inherited did not, with the exception of the
comparatively small force of *qūrchīs* (who were Türkmen chosen from
among the Qizilbash tribes), constitute a standing army. According to
the established system, the shāh called on the various Qizilbash chiefs
for levies as and when required. But the new units that were founded
from Caucasian *ghulām* (military slave) manpower were to be a permanent army, answerable to and paid by the shāh himself. . . .

The payment of the new and permanent forces required a radical
change in the way in which the Ṣafawid empire was administered.
The shāh did not pay the Qizilbash troops directly: they were maintained from the revenues of provinces which were granted to the
tribal chiefs as assignments. . . . When, therefore, it was decided to
pay the *ghulām* troops directly from the royal treasury, there was
nothing approaching sufficient revenue available to the shāh for the
purpose. The central government received very little from the
mamālik[25] provinces, what there was being paid into the state treasury
for the general expenses of the empire, rather than into the shāh's
personal treasury. Such provincial tax revenue was administered by
the *Dīwān-i mamālik*. The expenses of the royal household were met
from the crown lands (*khāṣṣa*), which were administered directly by
the shāh. Such lands existed before Shāh 'Abbās's reign, and had at
times been increased. But during the chaotic period before 995/1587

---

[25]Another term for *ghulam* or "slave."—Ed.

they had been considerably eroded. The remedy for the problem of military salaries was evidently to increase the amount of *khāṣṣa* land available. The principal means of achieving this was inevitably a substantial transfer of *mamālik* land to the category of *khāṣṣa*.

This could not be done overnight, but eventually very large areas of Persia became *khāṣṣa* land. Between 996/1588 and 1014/1606 such provinces as Qazwīn, Kāshān, part of Kirmān, Yazd, and Qum ceased to be *mamālik*. The whole of their revenue now went neither to the state treasury nor to the Qizilbash *amīrs* as the yield of their *tiyūls:* it was paid directly to the shāh. 'Abbās had the resources necessary for the maintenance of his new military forces.

The implications of the great *mamālik-khāṣṣa* transfer were not, of course, solely fiscal. Provinces that came under the direct rule of the shāh also ceased to be at the disposal of the Qizilbash *amīrs*. The balance of power between the shāh and the Qizilbash shifted radically. . . .

The administration of the Ṣafawid empire had, in fact, been centralized in the hands of the shāh to an extent previously unparalleled. As long as the shāh himself was a strong ruler, he would now have the power and resources to meet and crush any internal challenge. Even if the shāh himself was ineffective, as many of 'Abbās's successors indeed were, it would no longer be as easy as it had been during the sixteenth century for the Qizilbash or anyone else to usurp the crown's prerogatives. Shāh 'Abbās had laid foundations which would help ensure the survival of the dynasty for a century after his death.

As the new *ghulām* contingents were recruited and organized, and arrangements made for their payment, so the position of their leaders in the state was gradually enhanced. . . .

By the end of the reign, the proportion of provincial governorships held by *ghulāms* was something like half the total, and it has been calculated that they constituted some 20 per cent of all the important *amīrs*. According to information which has been extracted from the most important historian of the reign, Iskandar Beg Munshī, of the 89 principal *amīrs*, 74 were Qizilbash and 15 *ghulām*. It is important to note here both how great had been the inroads on power and influence made by the new military class and the fact that the Qizilbash, however, had by no means been totally superseded. Their stranglehold over the state had been broken by Shāh 'Abbās's vigorous and effective measures, and he had further weakened them by, in some cases, breaking up the tribes and settling them in widely separated parts of the country. . . .

During the years up to 1006/1598 Shāh 'Abbās transferred the capital from Qazwīn to Iṣfahān. . . . Iṣfahān was, of course, already a great and famous city with a long and distinguished history behind it, including a period as capital under the Saljūqs. For all the efforts of

Shāh 'Abbās and his successors, the most impressive and interesting building in the city remains one that was already there when 'Abbās arrived: the Friday Mosque, the Masjid-i-Jāmi', which was built over a very long period but whose most striking features, perhaps, are the two magnificent brick dome chambers of the Saljūq period and the highly elaborate stucco *miḥrāb* commissioned by the Īlkhān Öljeitü.

Nevertheless, Iṣfahān is to this day, to a considerable extent, Shāh 'Abbās's city. It is an impressive example of imperial town planning. A wide, straight thoroughfare, the Chahār Bāgh ("Four Gardens", indicating its leafy character in the Ṣafawid period) leads north from the Zāyanda-rūd across a bridge, named after Allāhvirdī Khān. Off the Chahār Bāgh and to its right is the centre of the Ṣafawid city: the great square, the Maydān. This, which is some distance to the south of the Friday Mosque and the old city centre, is 'Abbās's most spectacular creation. The square was used as a polo ground (the marble goalposts are still *in situ*), and the shāh watched the sport from the balcony of the 'Alī Qāpū, the entrance to a royal palace, on the west side of the square. On the east side is a beautiful little mosque, the Shaykh Luṭf Allāh, named after and built in honour of 'Abbās's father-in-law from Jabal 'Āmil. To the north is the imposing entrance to the bazaar (and the sides of the square, too, were lined with shops). . . .

But Iṣfahān was not merely a centre for the court and for culture. It was also a thriving economic hub. This aspect of its life was vigorously encouraged by Shāh 'Abbās, especially through his policy of population transfers. Of particular importance was the removal of 3,000 industrious Armenian families from the city of Julfā in the north-west to "New Julfā", their own suburb south of the Zāyanda-rūd in Iṣfahān. It remains an Armenian enclave today, its churches exhibiting the unusual sight of Ṣafawid-style domes topped by a cross. . . .

The background to the international commercial history of the sixteenth century was created by the great Portuguese voyages, the most famous landmark being Vasco de Gama's establishment of a feasible sea-route to India in 1498. The sixteenth century was one of Portuguese commercial dominance in the Indian Ocean. . . . In time the creation of the sea-routes damaged the overland trade routes across Asia which passed through Ṣafawid territory, though according to one distinguished economic historian they continued to flourish until the establishment of the great European India Companies in the early seventeenth century. . . . The English East India Company was founded in 1600, and the Dutch equivalent in 1602. The Portuguese trading monopoly was soon broken: in 1024/1615 the English East India Company secured a foothold in the Persian market, and in the following year an agreement was made with Shāh 'Abbās for the exchange of English cloth for Persian silk through the Gulf port of Jāsk. In 1031/1622, as we have seen, the Company assisted the Persians in evicting the Portuguese from Hurmūz. . . . .

Such trading links, and the wish for others, brought European envoys to Iṣfahān, as did proposals for alliances with Persia against the Ottomans; though for such purposes the distances and the difficulties of communication proved too great, and little tangible was achieved on the purely political front. But ambassadors and others who left written accounts of their journeys, especially after 1600, provide the historian with a most important body of source material on Ṣafawid life and politics: on the court, the character and appearance of the shāhs, and on the architecture of the period (much of which no longer survives). . . . .

Most of what has so far been said in this chapter has been very favourable towards Shāh 'Abbās; and indeed the overall verdict on the achievement of this most remarkable monarch must be a positive one. Starting in what must have seemed at the beginning of his reign an almost hopeless situation, he had built up his kingdom to a position in the world which it had rarely reached before and was never to approach again. He had driven out formidable foreign enemies and secured Persia's frontiers. He had dealt decisively with the menace of factionalism which had plagued the Ṣafawid state since its foundation. In so doing he had initiated something of a social transformation in at least some levels of Persian society, and had built up royal absolutism until it was virtually unchallengeable. He had provided the necessary environment and encouragement for a flourishing economy and, perhaps, for at least a tolerable life for most of his subjects. He had made his new capital one of the world's great cities, and in that setting he had made it possible for the arts to flourish. In an age and a place where so much depended on the ability and strength of the ruler, much of this must in justice be ascribed to Shāh 'Abbās as an individual: there is no reason for supposing that similar stability and prosperity would necessarily have come about had some other prince succeeded Muḥammad Khudābanda. All the signs in 995/1587 pointed to a gloomy future for Persia.

But part of his legacy was undeniably malign in its effects. He is remembered, like the great Sasanian Khusraw Anushirvan, as a monarch who dealt out firm but impartial justice to his people. But this benevolence, which always tended towards unpredictability, did not extend to his leading followers, who sometimes faced arbitrary execution, or even to his own family. It would appear that the experiences of 'Abbās's youth, and in particular the circumstances of his own accession to the throne, had left him with an incurably distrustful temperament. In 1024/1615 he had his eldest son, the heir-apparent Ṣafī Mīrzā, murdered on suspicion of plotting rebellion. The prince was almost certainly innocent, as his father realized when it was too late; and remorse for this act clouded the latter years of his reign. Two other sons were blinded for similar reasons, and since blinding was felt to disqualify a prince from the succession and the remaining two sons predeceased their father, there was no prince of the next genera- tion available to succeed 'Abbās in 1038/1629.

Even more destructive to the future of the regime was the general policy towards princes of the royal house which 'Abbās inaugurated. In the early part of his reign, as was normal, they were employed to govern provinces; but signs of revolt, coupled no doubt with a recol- lection of how he had himself been able to displace his father, per- suaded 'Abbās to end this practice. Instead the princes were immured in the harem, and the leading men of the kingdom were kept away from them. So future shāhs (with the exception of 'Abbās II, who came to the throne as a child) grew up ill-educated, with no experi- ence of government, administration, or the world in general, and excessively under the influence of women and eunuchs. Their low quality as rulers, in such circumstances, is hardly a matter for sur- prise; and the fact that the Ṣafawid state nevertheless survived its greatest shāh for a century is no small tribute to the solidity of the work he had done.

Review and Study Questions

1. Do you consider Sherley's account of 'Abbas to be trustworthy? Why?
2. Do you consider Herbert's account to be trustworthy? Why?
3. In your estimation, can a "cruel despot" also be a "great statesman"?
4. Was Shah 'Abbas a "great statesman"? Why?
5. What were the economic policies of the shah?

Suggestions for Further Reading

There are relatively few surviving chronicles for the Safavid period, and the state archives were destroyed when Isfahan fell to the Afghans in 1722. While there are no archival sources, we do have a catalogue of all administrative offices, officers, and functions, in V. Minorsky, ed. and tr., *Tadhkirat al-Muluk, A Manual of Safavid Administration (circa*

1137/1725) (Cambridge and London: Heffer and Sons and Luzac and Co., 1943). For the early Safavids the best surviving chronicle is *A Chronicle of the Early Safawis, Being the Ashanu't-Tawarikh of Hasan-I-Rumlu*, 2 vols., tr. C. N. Seddon (Baroda: Oriental Institute, 1934). The best contemporary Persian chronicle for 'Abbas is Eskander Beg Monshi, *History of Shah 'Abbas the Great*, 2 vols., tr. and ed. Roger M. Savory (Boulder, Colo.: Westview Press, 1978). Eskander was a Safavid bureaucrat and was intimately acquainted with the events of his time; he died in 1632 and his chronicle breaks off at 1628, a year before 'Abbas's death. While the work is very accurate, its emphasis is on a detailed, year by year political narrative with relatively little analysis or interpretation. Thus, the best accounts of 'Abbas are those done by various European travelers such as the accounts of Sherley and Herbert, excerpted for this chapter. The Sherley excerpt is from Sir Anthony Sherley, *His Relation of His Travels into Persia* (London: Gregg Publishing, 1613). There is a very useful guide to Sherley's work—Sir E. Denison Ross, *Sir Anthony Sherley and His Persian Adventure* (London: George Routledge and Sons, 1933). The Herbert narrative is from Thomas Herbert, *A Relation of Some Years Travel . . .* (London: Walter J. Johnson, 1634). One additional European narrative can be recommended, that of Pietro della Valle, available to English-speaking readers in W. Blunt, *Pietro's Pilgrimage* (London: J. Barrie, 1953), though it is not as useful as either Sherley or Herbert.

By far the most valuable, comprehensive, and up-to-date secondary work on the history of Persia is the *Cambridge History of Iran*, a work of multiple authorship, done by leading authorities. See especially vol. 6, ch. 5, "The Safavid Period," by H. R. Roemer, and ch. 6, "The Safavid Administrative System," by R. M. Savory (Cambridge et al.: Cambridge University Press, 1986). A similar work is the *Cambridge History of Islam* (Cambridge et al.: Cambridge University Press, 1970), especially part III, ch. 5, "Safavid Persia" by R. M. Savory.

The older, general Persian histories such as Sir John Malcolm, *The History of Persia from the Most Early Period to the Present Time*, 2 vols. (London: Murray, 1815) or Sir Percy Sykes, *A History of Persia*, 3rd ed., 2 vols (London: Macmillan, 1915) are no longer of much value. More modern critical works such as Alessandro Bausani, *The Persians*, tr. J. B. Donne (London: Elek Books, 1971) are to be preferred, as is David Morgan, *Medieval Persia 1040–1797* (London and New York: Longman, 1988), excerpted for this chapter. There is no modern biography of Shah 'Abbas in English and only one book-length treatment of the Safavid period, the authoritative Roger Savory, *Iran under the Safavids* (Cambridge et al.: Cambridge University Press, 1980).

For the important topic of economic history under Shah 'Abbas see the fine general treatment by R. W. Ferrier, "Trade from the Mid-14th Century to the End of the Safavid Period" in the *Cambridge History of Iran,* vol. 6, or the more specialized work by N. Steengaard, *The Asian Trade Revolution of the Seventeenth Century: The East India Companies and the Decline of the Caravan Trade* (Chicago and London: University of Chicago Press, 1974).

PETER THE GREAT AND THE WESTERNIZATION OF RUSSIA

1672	Born
1682	Joint succession with Ivan V under a regency
1696	Beginning of Peter's sole rule
1697–1698	The Grand Embassy (Peter's tour of the West)
1698	Destruction of the *streltsy* army revolt
1700–1721	The Great Northern War against Sweden
1706	Start of the building of St. Petersburg
1725	Died

Peter the Great was six feet eight inches tall and so strong that he could break a horseshoe with his bare hands. He was practically indifferent to comfort, and he had a manic energy and a capacity for the most savage and destructive rage. Despite an education so scant and faulty that he was virtually illiterate, he became a competent expert in more than a dozen technical crafts and a more than respectable amateur scientist. The enormous mass of laws, regulations, and edicts he framed have not even yet been completely edited. He was apt to invite anyone to eat or drink with him and was fond of stopping in the huts or shops of the humblest artisans to admire their skill or try his own and to chat with them. Yet Peter the Great sacrificed the lives of uncounted thousands of his peasants in the building of his new capital city of St. Petersburg—his "window on Europe"—in the desolate, disease-ridden marshes at the mouth of the Neva River on the Baltic. He could endure a slur to his own son made by a drunken companion, yet he rode rough-shod over the customs and sensibilities of his boyar court nobility, forcing them to set aside their old ways in favor of Western fashions in dress and education. He cut their beards himself and even demonstrated the new Western craft of dentistry on a few unfortunates among them. When a revolt of the *streltsy*, the imperial musketeers, forced him to return to Moscow from his first journey to the West, he disbanded the unit, personally saw to the torture and execution of more than a thousand of them, and displayed their corpses throughout the city as a lesson to other rebels. When, later in his reign, he suspected his weakling son Alexis of taking part in a conspiracy, Peter ordered his arrest and watched the boy be tortured to death.

Peter the Great is, in short, the most contradictory and intriguing figure in Russian history—as well as the most important. For no matter how it is interpreted, the reign of Peter the Great marks the most fundamental turning point in the history of his nation. And the central issue of this significant reign is Peter's policy of Westernization.

The offspring of the second marriage of Czar Alexis and third in the line of succession, Peter was raised by his mother away from the court in the so-called German suburb, where all the foreign residents of Moscow were compelled to live. Here Peter made friends among the Western merchants, artisans, technicians, and adventurers and developed his passion for Western ways. In 1697, after his succession to the throne, Peter made his celebrated first journey to the West, ostensibly to solicit support for a war against the Turks and also to sample for himself the wonders of Western technology. Peter traveled simply as a member of the party, disguised as Bombardier Peter Mikhailov. His true identity was discovered, however, and he was received at the courts of Brandenburg and Hanover, he met William of Orange and the Emperor Leopold, and he made friends with Augustus the Strong of Saxony, the king of Poland. On the whole, Peter's diplomatic initiative failed, but not so his technological mission. He visited iron foundries in Brandenburg. In Amsterdam he actually worked on the docks and in the shipyards as a ship's carpenter. In England he found the shipyards at Deptford and the Woolwich naval arsenal more interesting than London or Parliament.

When the revolt of the *streltsy* forced him to cut short his visit to the West, Peter returned to Russia with the resolve to Westernize his nation. He not only imposed such seemingly trivial reforms as cleanshaven faces and Western clothing; he instituted the most fundamental changes in every aspect of Russian government and society. He reformed the judicial system and created a senate, whose members were appointed by him, to replace the old council of boyars. A series of ministries for public affairs was established; their directors were both Russians and foreigners. Peter recognized the chaotic system of local government, imposing upon it a structure of governorships responsible to him, and he drove the old conservative religious faction of the nobility out of the court. The power of the Patriarch over the Russian church was broken, and in its place an administrative system like the other ministries of the state was instituted. Peter forced Western-style education upon the boyars and created a new structure of nobility and a "Table of Ranks" based entirely on merit and service to the state. He reformed the system of taxation as well. He invited Western advisers and experts to Russia in unprecedented numbers and gave them unheard-of status and authority. At the same time, thousands of young Russians were sent to study and train in the West.

Peter the Great founded a merchant marine and opened up the vast resources of Russia to foreign trade. He created the Russian navy and completely reorganized the military establishment into Russia's first standing army. Never content to stand on the sidelines, Peter himself passed through all the ranks and grades in all the services of both the army and the navy. Even his foreign policy marked a fundamental turn to the West. The war against the Turks, early in his career, was undertaken in the hope of gaining access to the Mediterranean through the Black Sea. And the major conflict of his reign, the Great Northern War (1700–1721), was waged to challenge Swedish supremacy in the Baltic and open Russia to the West. In the course of the war, he faced the greatest military genius of his age in Charles XII of Sweden; and, though defeated by him at Narva in 1700, Peter came back to defeat Charles at Poltava nine years later. In the treaty that ended the war at Nystadt, it was Peter's Russia that gained the lion's share of territory, and Peter gained his long-hoped-for access to the West.

By the end of his reign in 1725, Peter the Great had changed the Russian monarchy into a Western absolutism; he had displaced Sweden as the dominant power in the Baltic; and he had thrust Russia as a new and powerful force into the family of European nations, from which it would never again be excluded.

Panegyric to the Sovereign Emperor Peter the Great

MIKHAIL LOMONOSOV

Peter the Great not only had his detractors and opponents; he also had his champions, some of whom he had raised to high position and others, both contemporaries and near contemporaries, who shared Peter's vision of the future of their nation. One such defender was Mikhail Vasil'evich Lomonosov (1711–1765), as fanatic a champion of Russian cultural modernization as the great Czar himself and the author of "Panegyric to the Sovereign Emperor Peter the Great," from which the following selection is taken. The occasion for the panegyric was the coronation of Peter's daughter Elizabeth in 1741, and its purpose was clearly to remind the new empress of her father's policies. But the panegyric is important not only as a sympathetic retrospective survey of Peter's reign, but also as one of the first important contributions to the myth of Peter the Great, the founder of modern Russia, a man larger than life and altogether heroic. A contemporary of Lomonosov, P. N. Krekshyn, hailed the Czar in these terms, "Our father Peter the Great! Thou broughtest us from nothingness into existence!"[1]—a sentiment thoroughly compatible with Lomonosov's views.

. . . As I embark on this undertaking, with what shall I begin my discourse? With His bodily endowments? With the greatness of His strength? But it is manifest in his mastery of burdensome labors, labors without number, and in the overcoming of terrible obstacles. Shall I begin with His heroic appearance and stature combined with majestic beauty? But apart from the many who vividly call to mind an image of Him engraved in their memory, there is the witness of those in various states and cities who, drawn by His fame, flocked out to admire a figure appropriate to His deeds and befitting a great Monarch. Should I commence with His buoyancy of spirit? But that is proved by the tireless vigilance without which it would have been impossible to carry out deeds so numerous and great. Wherefore I do immediately proceed to present these deeds, know-

---

[1]Quoted in M. S. Anderson, *Peter the Great* (London: The Historical Association, 1969), p. 3.

ing that it is easier to make a beginning than to reach the end and that this Great Man cannot be better praised than by him who shall enumerate His labors in faithful detail, were it but possible to enumerate them.

And so, to the extent that strength and the brevity of limited time will permit, we shall mention only His most important deeds, then the mighty obstacles therein overcome, and finally the virtues which aided Him in such enterprises.

As a part of His grand designs the all-wise Monarch provided as a matter of absolute necessity for the dissemination of all kinds of knowledge in the homeland, and also for an increase in the numbers of persons skilled in the higher branches of learning, together with artists and craftsmen; though I have given His paternal solicitude in this matter the most prominent place, my whole speech would not be long enough to describe it in detail. For, having repeatedly made the rounds of European states like some swift-soaring eagle, He did induce (partly by command and partly by His own weighty example) a great multitude of His subjects to leave their country for a time and to convince themselves by experience how great an advantage a person and an entire state can derive from a journey of inquiry in foreign regions. Then were the wide gates of great Russia opened up; then over the frontiers and through the harbors, like the tides in the spacious ocean, there did flow in constant motion, in the one direction, the sons of Russia, journeying forth to acquire knowledge in the various sciences and arts, and, in the other direction, foreigners arriving with various skills, books, and instruments. Then to the study of Mathematics and Physics, previously thought of as forms of sorcery and witchcraft, but now arrayed in purple, crowned with laurels, and placed on the Monarch's throne, reverential respect was accorded in the sanctified Person of PETER. What benefit was brought to us by all the different sciences and arts, bathed in such a glow of grandeur, is proved by the superabundant richness of our most varied pleasures, of which our forefathers, before the days of Russia's Great Enlightener, were not only deprived but in many cases had not even any conception. How many essential things which previously came to Russia from distant lands with difficulty and at great cost are now produced inside the state, and not only provide for our needs but also with their surplus supply other lands. There was a time when the neighbors on our borders boasted that Russia, a great and powerful state, was unable properly to carry out military operations or trade without their assistance, since its mineral resources included neither precious metals for the stamping of coins nor even iron, so needful for the making of weapons with which to stand against an enemy. This reproach disappeared through the enlightenment brought by

PETER; the bowels of the mountains have been opened up by his mighty and industrious hand. Metals pour out of them, and are not only freely distributed within the homeland but are also given back to foreign peoples as if in repayment of loans. The brave Russian army turns against the enemy weapons produced from Russian mines and Russian hands.

In the establishment of the sizable army needed for the defense of the homeland, the security of His subjects, and the unhindered carrying out of important enterprises within the country, how great was the solicitude of the Great Monarch, how impetuous His zeal, how assiduous His search of ways and means! . . . The impossible was made possible by extraordinary zeal, and above all by an unheard-of example. In former times the Roman Senate, beholding the Emperor Trajan standing before the Consul to receive from him the dignity of Consul, exclaimed: "Through this thou art the greater, the more majestic!" What exclamations, what applause were due to PETER the Great for His unparalleled self-abasement? Our fathers beheld their crowned Sovereign not among the candidates for a Roman consulship but in the ranks of common soldiers, not demanding power over Rome, but obedient to the bidding of His subjects. O you beautiful regions, fortunate regions which beheld a spectacle so wondrous! Oh, how you marveled at the friendly contest of the regiments of a single Sovereign, both commander and subordinate, giving orders and obeying them! Oh, how you admired the siege, defense, and capture of new Russian fortresses, not for immediate mercenary gain but for the sake of future glory, not for putting down enemies but to encourage fellow countrymen. Looking back at those past years, we can now imagine the great love for the Sovereign and the ardent devotion with which the newly instituted army was fired, seeing Him in their company at the same table, eating the same food, seeing His face covered with dust and sweat, seeing that He was no different from them, except that in training and in diligence He was superior to all. By such an extraordinary example the most wise Sovereign, rising in rank alongside His subjects, proved that Monarchs can in no other way increase their majesty, glory, and eminence so well as by such gracious condescension. The Russian army was toughened by such encouragement, and during the twenty years' war with the Swedish Crown, and later in other campaigns, filled the ends of the universe with the thunder of its weapons and with the noise of its triumphs. It is true that the first battle of Narva was not successful; but the superiority of our foes and the retreat of the Russian army have, through envy and pride, been exaggerated to their glorification and our humiliation, out of all proportion to the actual event. For although most of the Russian army had seen only two years' service and faced a veteran army accustomed to battle, although disagreement arose be-

tween our commanders, and a malicious turncoat revealed to the enemy the entire position in our camp, and Charles XII [of Sweden] by a
sudden attack did not give the Russians time to form ranks—yet even
in their retreat they destroyed the enemy's willingness to fight on to
final victory. Thus the only reason the Russian Life Guard, which had
remained intact, together with another sizable part of the army, did not
dare to attack the enemy thereafter was the absence of its main leaders,
who had been summoned by Charles for peace talks and detained as
prisoners. For this reason the Guards and the rest of the army returned
to Russia with their arms and war chest, drums beating and banners
flying. That this failure occurred more through the unhappy circumstances described than through any lack of skill in the Russian troops
and that PETER's new army could, even in its infancy, defeat the seasoned regiments of the enemies, was proved in the next year and
subsequently by many glorious victories won over them. . . .

Having covered Himself and His army with glory throughout the
world by such famous victories, the Great Monarch finally proved
that he had been at pains to establish His army mainly in the interests
of our safety! For He decreed that it should never be dispersed, even
in times of untroubled peace (as had happened under previous Sovereigns, frequently to no little loss of the country's might and glory),
and also that it should always be kept in proper readiness. . . .

Having cast a quick glance over PETER's land forces, which came to
maturity in their infancy and combined their training with victories,
let us extend our gaze across the waters, my Listeners; let us observe
what the Lord has done there, His marvels on the deep, as made
manifest by PETER to the astonishment of the world.

The far-flung Russian state, like a whole world, is surrounded by
great seas on almost every side and sets them as its boundaries. On all
of them we see Russian flags flying. Here the mouths of great rivers
and new harbors scarcely provide space for the multitude of craft;
elsewhere the waves groan beneath the weight of the Russian fleet,
and the sounds of its gunfire echo in the chasms of the deep. Here
gilded ships, blooming like spring, are mirrored on the quiet surface
of the waters and take on double beauty; elsewhere the mariner,
having reached a calm haven, unloads the riches of faraway countries
to give us pleasure. Here new Columbuses hasten to unknown shores
to add to the might and glory of Russia; there a second Tethys dares
to sail between the battling mountains; she struggles with snow, with
frost, with everlasting ice, desirous to unite East and West. How did
the power and glory of Russian fleets come to be spread over so many
seas in a short time? Whence came the materials, whence the skill?
Whence the machines and implements needed in so difficult and
varied an enterprise? Did not the ancient giants tear great oaks from

dense forests and lofty mountains and throw them down for building on the shores? Did not Amphion with sweet music on the lyre move the various parts for the construction of those wondrous fortresses which fly over the waves? To such fancies would PETER's wondrous swiftness in building a fleet truly have been ascribed if an exploit so improbable and seemingly beyond human strength had been performed in far-off ancient times, and if it had not been fixed in the memory of many eyewitnesses and in unexceptionably reliable written records. . . . From that very time when the contriving of a boat (which, though small in dimensions, was great in influence and fame) aroused in PETER's unsleeping spirit the salutary urge to found a fleet and to show forth the might of Russia on the deep, He applied the forces of His great mind to every part of this important enterprise. As He investigated these parts, He became convinced that in a matter so difficult there was no possibility of success unless He Himself acquired adequate knowlege of it. But where was that to be obtained? What should the Great Sovereign undertake? . . .

. . . But greater still was the amazement that He aroused, greater the spectacle that He presented to the eyes of the whole world when, becoming convinced of the untold benefits of navigation—first on the small bodies of water in the Moscow area, then on the great breadth of Lake Rostov and Lake Kubensk, and finally on the expanse of the White Sea—He absented himself for a time from His dominions and, concealing the Majesty of His Person among humble workmen in a foreign land, did not disdain to learn the shipwright's craft. Those who chanced to be His fellow-apprentices at first marveled at the amazing fact that a Russian had not only mastered simple carpentering work so quickly, had not only brought Himself to the point where He could make with His own hands every single part needed in the building and equipping of ships, but had also acquired such skills in marine architecture that Holland could no longer satisfy His deep understanding. Then how great was the amazement that was aroused in all when they learned that this was no simple Russian, but the Ruler of that great state Himself who had taken up heavy labors in hands born and anointed to bear the Scepter and the Orb. But was it merely out of sheer curiosity or, at the most, for purposes of instruction and command, that He did in Holland and Britain attain perfection in the theory and practice of equipping a fleet and in navigational science? Everywhere the Great Sovereign aroused His subjects to labor, not only by command and reward, but also by His own example! I call you to witness, O great Russian rivers; I address myself to you, O happy shores, sanctified by PETER's footsteps and watered by His sweat. How many times you resounded with high-spirited and eager cries as the heavy timbers, ready for launching of the ship, were being slowly moved by the workmen and then, at the touch of His hand, made a sudden spurt toward the swift current, inspiring the multitude, encouraged by His example, to finish off the huge hulks with incredible speed. To what a marvelous and rousing spectacle were the assembled people treated as these great structures moved nearer to launching! When their indefatigable Founder and Builder, now moving topside, now below, now circling round, tested the soundness of each part, the power of the machinery, and the precision of all the preparations and by command, encouragement, ingenuity, and the quick skill of His tireless hands, rectified the defects which He had detected. In his unflagging zeal, this invincible persistence in labor, the legendary prowess of the ancients was shown in PETER's day to have been not fiction but the very truth! . . .

I say nothing of the assistance afforded in this matter by other wise institutions, but will mention the increase of external revenues. Divine Providence aided the good designs and efforts of PETER, through His hand opening new ports of the Varangian [Baltic] Sea at towns conquered by His valor and erected by His own labors. Great rivers were joined for the more convenient passage of Russian merchants, duty regulations were established, and commercial treaties with various peoples were concluded. What benefit proceeded from the growth of this abundance within and without has been clear from the very foundation of these institutions, for while continuing to fight a burdensome war for twenty years Russia was free from debts.

What, then, have all PETER's great deeds already been depicted in my feeble sketch? Oh, how much labor still remains for my thoughts, voice, and tongue! I ask you, my Listeners, out of your knowledge to consider how much assiduous effort was required for the foundation and establishment of a judiciary, and for the institution of the Governing Senate, the Most Holy Synod, the state colleges, the chancelleries, and the other governmental offices with their laws, regulations, and statutes; for the establishment of the table of ranks and the introduction of decorations as outward tokens of merit and favor; and finally, for foreign policy, missions, and alliances with foreign powers. You may contemplate all these things yourselves with minds enlightened by PETER. . . .

Nothing can serve me so well to demonstrate the kindness and gentleness of His heart as His incomparable graciousness toward His subjects. Superbly endowed as He was, elevated in His Majesty, and exalted by most glorious deeds, He did but the more increase and adorn these things by His incomparable graciousness. Often He moved amongst His subjects simply, countenancing neither the pomp that proclaims the monarch's presence nor servility. Often anyone afoot was free to meet Him, to follow Him, to walk along with Him, to start a conversation if so inclined. In former times many Sovereigns were carried on the shoulders and heads of their slaves; graciousness exalted Him above these very Sovereigns. At the very time of festivity and relaxation important business would be brought to Him; but the importance did not decrease gaiety, nor did simplicity lessen the importance. How He awaited, received, and greeted His loyal subjects! What gaiety there was at His table! He asked questions, listened, answered, discussed as with friends; and whatever time was saved at table by the small number of dishes was spent in gracious conversation. Amid so many cares of state He lived at ease as among friends. Into how many tiny huts of craftsmen did He bring His Majesty, and heartened with His presence His most lowly, but skilled and loyal, servants. How often He joined them in the exercise of their crafts and in various labors. For He attracted more by example than He compelled by force. And if there was anything which then seemed to be compulsion, it now stands revealed as a benefaction. . . .

On the Corruption of Morals in Russia

PRINCE M. M. SHCHERBATOV

Lomonosov had proclaimed that the "compulsion" that had brought about Peter's reforms is "now revealed as a benefaction." To many, however, it continued to seem a compulsion. One person who held this view was the conservative aristocrat Prince Mikhail Mikhailovich Shcherbatov (1733– 1790). Shcherbatov belonged to one of the oldest and proudest families of the Russian traditional nobility, and throughout his life he was preoccupied with the status and the condition of the class to which he belonged. He was also a scholar and historian, one of the first to write a systematic, documentary history of his nation. Shcherbatov was commissioned by the Empress Catherine II to edit the private and public papers of Peter the Great. Thus, there was no one of his generation in a better position to assess Peter's accomplishments.

Shcherbatov was an admirer of Peter and even, to an extent, of Peter's Westernizing reforms. But, at the same time, he was alarmed by the consequences of those reforms, which he saw as undermining the position of the old aristocracy and corrupting the moral base that he considered to be fundamental to the greatness of Russia. These views are nowhere better or more succinctly expressed than in Shcherbatov's tract On the Corruption of Morals in Russia, *a work of his old age and a kind of summation of his reflections on the direction of Russian history. In Shcherbatov we have a cautious, even gloomy conservative to set beside Lomonosov, the euphoric enthusiast for Peter's reforms.*

Peter the Great, in imitating foreign nations, not only strove to introduce to his realm a knowledge of sciences, arts and crafts, a proper military system, trade, and the most suitable forms of legislation; he also tried to introduce the kind of sociability, social intercourse and magnificence, which he first learnt from Lefort, and which he later saw for himself. Amid essential legislative measures, the organization of troops and artillery, he paid no less attention to modifying the old customs which seemed crude to him. He ordered beards to be shaved off, he abolished the old Russian garments, and instead of long robes he compelled the men to wear German coats, and the women, instead of the "telogreya" to wear bodices, skirts, gowns and "samaras," and instead of skull-caps, to adorn their heads with fontanges and cornettes. He established various assemblies where the women, hitherto segregated from the company of men, were present with them at entertainments. . . .

The monarch himself kept to the old simplicity of morals in his dress, so that apart from plain coats and uniforms, he never wore anything costly; and it was only for the coronation of the Empress Catherine Alexeevna, his wife, that he had made a coat of blue gros-de-tours with silver-braid; they say he also had another coat, grey with gold braid, but I do not know for what great occasion this was made.

The rest was all so plain that even the poorest person would not wear it today, as can be seen from such of his clothes as have remained, and are kept in the Kunst-Kamera at the Imperial Academy of Sciences.

He disliked cuffs and did not wear them, as his portraits attest. He had no costly carriages, but usually travelled in a gig in towns, and in a chaise on a long journey.

He did not have a large number of retainers and attendants, but had orderlies, and did not even have a bodyguard, apart from a Colonel of the Guard.

However, for all his personal simplicity, he wanted his subjects to have a certain magnificence. I think that this great monarch, who did nothing without farsightedness, had it as his object to stimulate trade, industries and crafts through the magnificence and luxury of his subjects, being certain that in his lifetime excessive magnificence and voluptuousness would not enthrone themselves at the royal court. . . .

As far as his domestic life was concerned, although the monarch himself was content with the plainest food, he now introduced drinks previously unknown in Russia, which he drank in preference to other drinks; namely, instead of domestic brandy, brewed from ordinary wine—Dutch aniseed brandy which was called "state" brandy, and Hermitage and Hungarian wine, previously unknown in Russia.

His example was followed by the grandees and those who were close to the court; and indeed it was proper for them to provide these wines; for the monarch was fond of visiting his subjects, and what should a subject not do for the monarch? . . .

Closely copying him, as they were bound to do by their very rank, other leading officials of the Empire also kept open table, such as Admiral-of-the-Fleet, Count Fyodor Matveevich Apraxin, Field-Marshal-in-Chief, Count Boris Petrovich Sheremetev, the Chancellor, Count Gavrilo Ivanovich Golovkin, and the boyar, Tikhon Nikitich Streshnev, who as first ruler of the Empire during Peter the Great's absence abroad, was given estates in order to provide for such meals.

As these eminent men were copied by their inferiors, so the custom of keeping an open table was now introduced in many homes. The meals were not of the traditional kind, that is, when only household products were used; now they tried to improve the flavor of the meat and fish with foreign seasonings. And of course, in a nation in which hospitality has always been a characteristic virtue, it was not hard for the custom of these open tables to become a habit; uniting as it did the special pleasure of society and the improved flavour of the food as compared with the traditional kind, it established itself as a pleasure in its own right. . . .

With this change in the way of life, first of the leading officials of state, and then, by imitation, of the other nobles, and as expenditure reached such a point that it began to exceed income, people began to attach themselves more and more to the monarch and to the grandees, as sources of riches and rewards.

I fear someone may say that this, at any rate, was a good thing, that people began to attach themselves more and more to the monarch. No, this attachment was no blessing, for it was not so much directed to the person of the monarch as to personal ends; this attachment became not the attachment of true subjects who love their sovereign and his honour and consider everything from the point of view of the national interest, but the attachment of slaves and hirelings, who sacrifice everything for their own profit and deceive their sovereign with obsequious zeal.

Coarseness of morals decreased, but the place left by it was filled by flattery and selfishness. Hence came sycophancy, contempt for truth, beguiling of the monarch, and the other evils which reign at court to this day and which have ensconced themselves in the houses of the grandees. . . .

But despite [his] love of truth and his aversion to flattery, the monarch could not eradicate this encroaching venom. Most of those around him did not dare to contradict him in anything, but rather flattered him, praising everything he did, and never resisting his whims, while some even indulged his passions. . . .

I said that it was voluptuousness and luxury that were able to produce such an effect in men's hearts; but there were also other causes, stemming from actual institutions, which eradicated resoluteness and good behaviour.

The abolition of rights of precedence (a custom admittedly harmful to the service and the state), and the failure to replace it by any granting of rights to the noble families, extinguished thoughts of noble pride in the nobility. For it was no longer birth that was respected, but ranks and promotions and length of service. And so everyone started to strive after ranks; but since not everyone is able to perform straightforward deeds of merit, so for lack of meritorious service men began to try and worm their way up, by flattering and humouring the monarch and the grandees in every way. Then there was the introduction of regular military service under Peter the Great, whereby masters were conscripted into the ranks on the same level as their serfs. The serfs, being the first to reach officer's rank through deeds suited to men of their kind, became commanders over their masters and used to beat them with rods. The noble families were split up in the service, so that a man might never see his own kinsman.

Could virtue, then, and resolution, remain in those who from their youth had gone in fear and trembling of their commanders' rods, who could only acquire respect by acts of servility, and being each without any support from his kinsmen, remained alone, without unity or defence, liable to be subjected to violent treatment?

It is admirable that Peter the Great wished to rid religion of superstition, for indeed, superstition does not signify respect for God and his Law, but rather an affront. For to ascribe to God acts unbecoming to him is blasphemy.

In Russia, the beard was regarded as being in the image of God, and it was considered a sin to shave it off, and through this, men fell into the heresy of the Anthropomorphites.[2] Miracles, needlessly per-

---

[2]Attributing humanlike qualities to God.—ED.

formed, manifestations of ikons, rarely proven, were everywhere acclaimed, attracted superstitious idolatry, and provided incomes for dissolute priests.

Peter the Great strove to do away with all this. He issued decrees, ordering beards to be shaved off, and by the Spiritual Regulation, he placed a check on false miracles and manifestations and also on unseemly gatherings at shrines set up at crossways. Knowing that God's Law exists for the preservation of the human race, and not for its needless destruction, with the blessing of the Synod and the Ecumenical patriarchs, he made it permissible to eat meat on fast-days in cases of need, and especially in the Navy where, by abstaining even from fish, the men were somewhat prone to scurvy; ordering that those who voluntarily sacrificed their lives by such abstinence, should, when they duly fell ill, be thrown into the water. All this is very good, although the latter is somewhat severe.

But when did he do this? At a time when the nation was still unenlightened, and so, by taking superstition away from an unenlightened people, he removed its very faith in God's Law. This action of Peter the Great may be compared to that of an unskilled gardener who, from a weak tree, cuts off the water-shoots which absorb its sap. If it had strong roots, then this pruning would cause it to bring forth fine, fruitful branches; but since it is weak and ailing, the cutting-off of these shoots (which, through the leaves which received the external moisture, nourished the weak tree) means that it fails to produce new fruitful branches; its wounds fail to heal over with sap, and hollows are formed which threaten to destroy the tree. Thus, the cutting-off of superstitions did harm to the most basic articles of the faith; superstition decreased, but so did faith. The servile fear of Hell disappeared, but so did love of God and his Holy Law; and morals, which for lack of other enlightenment used to be improved by faith, having lost this support began to fall into dissolution. . . .

And so, through the labours and solicitude of this monarch, Russia acquired fame in Europe and influence in affairs. Her troops were organized in a proper fashion, and her fleets covered the White Sea and the Baltic; with these forces she overcame her old enemies and former conquerors, the Poles and the Swedes, and acquired important provinces and sea-ports. Sciences, arts and crafts began to flourish there, trade began to enrich her, and the Russians were transformed— from bearded men to clean-shaven men, from long-robed men to short-coated men; they became more sociable, and polite spectacles became known to them.

But at the same time, true attachment to the faith began to disappear, sacraments began to fall into disrepute, resoluteness diminished, yielding place to brazen, aspiring flattery; luxury and voluptuousness laid the foundation of their power, and hence avarice was also aroused, and, to the ruin of the laws and the detriment of the citizens, began to penetrate the law-courts.

Such was the condition with regard to morals, in which Russia was left at the death of this great monarch (despite all the barriers which Peter the Great in his own person and by his example had laid down to discourage vice).

Peter the Great: A Modern View

NICHOLAS V. RIASANOVSKY

Modern historians of Russia, in their efforts to gain an objective view of Peter, have tried to uncover the real person behind the myth of Peter the Great. They have tried to strike a balance between the work of Peter's champions and the work of his detractors in order to put Peter's reign in proper perspective.

Their efforts have been complicated by the myths and prejudices not only of the eighteenth century but of the twentieth century as well. It is precisely on the issue of Peter's Westernization that the greatest difficulty arises. Through the late nineteenth century until the very eve of the revolution of 1917, one of the dominant themes of Russian intellectual life was Pan-Slav nationalism, with its extravagant praise of things Russian and its almost paranoid suspicion of outside, non-Slavic influences. The effect of such a point of view can be seen in the following conclusion of Vasili Klyuchevsky, the greatest Russian historian of the generation just before the revolution. "He was not a blind admirer of the West, on the contrary, he mistrusted it, and was not deluded into thinking that he could establish cordial relations with the West, for he knew that the West mistrusted his country, and was hostile to it. . . . Thus for Peter association with Europe was only a means to an end, and not an end in itself."[3]

Russian hostility toward the West was only increased by the revolution and by the events of Russian history ever since. The kindest treatment Peter the Great has ever received at the hands of Soviet historians is a kind of

---

[3]Vasili Klyuchevsky, *Peter the Great*, tr. Liliana Archibald (London: Macmillan, 1961), pp. 262–63.

faint praise for his advancing of Russia's modernization. But even that faint praise is no longer heard: Peter's Westernization is now simply denounced as "cosmopolitanism,"[4] and work on the editing of the documentary sources for Peter's reign has been halted indefinitely.

Despite such difficulties, a consensus view of Peter the Great is finally beginning to appear among modern, non-Soviet Russian historians. That view is represented in the following selection from A History of Russia *by the American scholar Nicholas V. Riasanovsky, considered by many Russian historians to be the best general treatment of Russia's history.*

After Peter took over the conduct of state affairs and began to reform Muscovy, he found few collaborators. His own family, the court circles, and the boyar duma[5] overwhelmingly opposed change. Because he discovered little support at the top of the state structure, and also because he never attached much importance to origin or rank, the sovereign proceeded to obtain assistants wherever possible. Before long an extremely mixed but on the whole able group emerged. . . .

Among foreigners, the tsar had the valuable aid of some of his old friends, such as Patrick Gordon and the Swiss Francis Lefort, who played a prominent role until his early death in 1699. Later such able newcomers from Germany as the diplomat Andrew Ostermann and the military expert Burkhard Münnich joined the sovereign's entourage. Some of his numerous foreign assistants, for example, the Scot James Bruce who helped with the artillery, mining, the navy and other matters, had been born in Russia and belonged to the second generation of foreign settlers in Muscovy.

Russian assistants to Peter ranged over the entire social gamut. . . .

War against Turkey was the first major action of Peter I after he took the government of Russia into his own hands in 1694, following the death of his mother.[6] In fighting Turkey, the protector of the Crimean Tartars and the power controlling the Black Sea and its southern Russian shore, the new monarch followed in the steps of his predecessors. However, before long it became apparent that he managed his affairs differently. The war began in 1695, and the first Russian campaign against Azov failed: supplied by sea, the fortress remained impregnable to the Muscovite army. Then, in one winter, the tsar built a fleet in Voronezh on the Don River. He worked indefatigably himself, as well as ordering and urging others, and utilized

---

[4]*Rewriting Russian History: Soviet Interpretations of Russia's Past,* ed. Cyril E. Black, 2nd ed. (New York: Random House, 1962), p. 254.

[5]The old council of nobility.—ED.

[6]Who had served as his regent.–ED.

to the best advantage the knowledge of all available foreign specialists along with his own previously acquired knowledge. By displaying his tremendous energy everywhere, Peter the Great brought thirty sea-going vessels and about a thousand transport barges to Azov in May 1696. Some of the Russian fleet, it might be noted, had been built as far away as Moscow and assembled in Voronezh. This time besieged by sea as well as by land, the Turks surrendered Azov in July.

With a view toward a further struggle against Turkey and a continuing augmentation and modernization of the Russian armed forces, the tsar next sent fifty young men to study, above all shipbuilding and navigation, in Holland, Italy, and England. Peter dispatched groups of Russians to study abroad several more times in his reign. After the students returned, the sovereign often examined them personally. In addition to experts, the tsar needed allies to prosecute war against Turkey. The desire to form a mighty coalition against the Ottoman Empire, and an intense interest in the West, prompted Peter to organize a large embassy to visit a number of European countries and—a most unusual act for a Muscovite ruler—to travel with the embassy.

Headed by Lefort, the party of about 250 men set out in March 1697. The sovereign journeyed incognito under the name of Peter Mikhailov. His identity, however, remained no secret to the rulers and officials of the countries he visited or to the crowds which frequently gathered around him. The tsar engaged in a number of important talks on diplomatic and other state matters. But, above all, he tried to learn as much as possible from the West. He seemed most concerned with navigation, but he also tried to absorb other technical skills and crafts, together with the ways and manners and, in fact, the entire life of Europe as he saw it. As the so-called Grand Embassy progressed across the continent and as Peter Mikhailov also took trips of his own, most notably to the British Isles, he obtained some first-hand knowledge of the Baltic provinces of Sweden, Prussia, and certain other German states, and of Holland, England, and the Hapsburg Empire. From Vienna the tsar intended to go to Italy, but instead he rushed back to Moscow at news of a rebellion of the streltsy. Altogether Peter the Great spent eighteen months abroad in 1697–98. At that time over 750 foreigners, especially Dutchmen, were recruited to serve in Russia. Again in 1702 and at other times, the tsar invited Europeans of every nationality—except Jews, whom he considered parasitic—to come to his realm, promising to subsidize passage, provide advantageous employment, and assure religious tolerance and separate law courts.

The streltsy had already caused trouble to Peter and suffered punishment on the eve of the tsar's journey to the West—in fact delaying the journey. Although the new conspiracy—that was aimed at deposing Peter and putting Sophia[7] in power—had been effectively dealt with before the sovereign's return, the tsar acted with exceptional violence and severity. After investigation and torture more than a thousand streltsy were executed, and their mangled bodies were exposed to the public as a salutary lesson. Sophia was forced to become a nun, and the same fate befell Peter's wife, Eudoxia, who had sympathized with the rebels.

If the gruesome death of the streltsy symbolized the destruction of the old order, many signs indicated the coming of the new. After he returned from the West, the tsar began to demand that beards be cut and foreign dress be worn by courtiers, officials, and the military. With the beginning of the new century, the sovereign changed the Russian calendar: henceforth years were to be counted from the birth of Christ, not the creation of the world, and they were to commence on the first of January, not the first of September. More important, Peter the Great rapidly proceeded to reorganize his army according to the Western pattern.

The Grand Embassy failed to further Peter the Great's designs against Turkey. But, although European powers proved unresponsive to the proposal of a major war with the Ottomans, other political opportunities emerged. Before long Peter joined the military alliance against Sweden organized by Augustus II, ruler of Saxony and Poland. . . .

In modern European history the Great Northern War was one of the important wars and Poltava one of the decisive battles. The Russian victory over Sweden and the resulting Treaty of Nystadt meant that Russia became firmly established on the Baltic, acquiring its essential "window into Europe," and that in fact it replaced Sweden as the dominant power in the north of the continent. Moreover, Russia not only humiliated Sweden but also won a preponderant position vis-à-vis its ancient rival Poland, became directly involved in German affairs—a relationship which included marital alliances arranged by the tsar for his and his half-brother Ivan V's daughters—and generally stepped forth as a major European power. . . .

In regard to internal affairs during the reign of Peter the Great, we find that scholars have taken two extreme and opposite approaches. On the one hand, the tsar's reforming of Russia has been presented as a series, or rather a jumble, of disconnected *ad hoc* measures necessitated by the exigencies of the moment, especially by the pressure of the Great Northern War. Contrariwise, the same activity has been depicted as the execution of a comprehensive, radically new, and well-

---

[7]Peter's older half-sister.—ED.

integrated program. In a number of ways, the first view seems closer to the facts. As Kliuchevsky pointed out, only a single year in Peter the Great's whole reign, 1724, passed entirely without war, while no more than another thirteen peaceful months could be added for the entire period. . . .

Yet a balanced judgment has to allow something to the opposite point of view as well. Although Peter the Great was preoccupied during most of his reign with the Great Northern War and although he had to sacrifice much else to its successful prosecution, his reforming of Russia was by no means limited to hectic measures to bolster the war effort. In fact, he wanted to Westernize and modernize all of the Russian government, society, life, and culture, and even if his efforts fell far short of this stupendous goal, failed to dovetail, and left huge gaps, the basic pattern emerges, nevertheless, with sufficient clarity. Countries of the West served as the emperor's model. We shall see, however, when we turn to specific legislation, that Peter did not merely copy from the West, but tried to adapt Western institutions to Russian needs and possibilities. The very number and variety of European states and societies offered the Russian ruler a rich initial choice. It should be added that with time Peter the Great became more interested in general issues and broader patterns. Also, while the reformer was no theoretician, he had the makings of a visionary. With characteristic grandeur and optimism he saw ahead the image of a modern, powerful, prosperous, and educated country, and it was to the realization of that image that he dedicated his life. Both the needs of the moment and longer-range aims must therefore be considered in evaluating Peter the Great's reforms. Other fundamental questions to be asked about them include their relationship to the Russian past, their borrowing from the West—and, concurrently, their modification of Western models—their impact on Russia, and their durability.

Peter the Great hit Muscovy with a tremendous impact. To many of his contemporaries he appeared as either a virtually superhuman hero or the Antichrist. It was the person of the emperor that drove Russia forward in war and reform and inspired the greatest effort and utmost devotion. It was also against Peter the Great that the streltsy, the Bashkirs, the inhabitants of Astrakhan, and the motley followers of Bulavin staged their rebellions, while uncounted others, Old Believers and Orthodox, fled to the borderlands and into the forests to escape his reach.[8] Rumor spread and legends grew that the reformer

---

[8]We have already noted the revolt of the *streltsy*. In Astrakhan an uprising took place in 1705–1707 against Western influence and was headed by a renegade member of the *streltsy* and a fanatic monk. Bulavin led a revolt of the Don Cossacks in 1707 over the same issue and again with religious overtones. The Bashkirs were Turkish subjects

was not a son of Tsar Alexis, but a foreigner who substituted himself for the true tsar during the latter's journey abroad, that he was an imposter, a usurper, indeed the Antichrist. Peter himself contributed much to this polarization of opinion. He too saw things in black and white, hating old Muscovy and believing himself to be the creator of a new Russia. Intolerance, violence, and compulsion became the distinguishing traits of the new regime, and St. Petersburg—built in the extreme northwestern corner of the country, in almost inaccessible swamps at a cost in lives far exceeding that of Poltava—became its fitting symbol. The emperor's very size, strength, energy, and temperament intensified his popular image. . . .

. . . Scholarly investigations of the last hundred years, together with large-scale publication of materials on the reformer's reign, undertaken by a number of men from Golikov to Bogoslovsky, have established beyond question many close connections between Peter the Great and the Muscovite past. Entire major aspects of the reformer's reign, for example, foreign policy and social relations and legislation, testified to a remarkable continuity with the preceding period. Even the reformer's desire to curb and control ecclesiastical landholding had excellent Muscovite precedents. The central issue itself, the process of Westernization, had begun long before the reformer and had gathered momentum rapidly in the seventeenth century. In the words of a modern scholar, Peter the Great simply marked Russia's transition from an unconscious to a conscious following of her historical path.

Although in the perspective of Russian history Peter the Great appears human rather than superhuman, the reformer is still of enormous importance. Quite possibly Russia was destined to be Westernized, but Peter the Great cannot be denied the role of the chief executor of this fate. At the very least the emperor's reign brought a tremendous speeding up of the irreversible process of Westernization, and it established state policy and control, where formerly individual choice and chance prevailed.

Review and Study Questions

1. Why could Peter the Great be regarded as the most important figure in Russian history?

---

of Peter in the lower Volga area who rebelled against heightened Russian interference at about the same time. All these revolts were eventually put down. The Orthodox party and the Old Believers were conservative factions that were opposed to Peter's Westernization and often involved in revolt.—Ed.

2. In what respects is Lomonosov's "Panegyric" an idealistic distortion of the accomplishments of the Czar? In what respects is it a reliable account?

3. What were the reasons for Shcherbatov's somewhat gloomy appraisal of Peter's reign?

4. Do you think that Peter's far-reaching reforms were part of a systematic campaign or impulsive ad hoc measures born of the Czar's own personal enthusiasms?

Suggestions for Further Reading

The historiography of Peter the Great divides along the line separating Russian national scholars from Westerners. As we observed in the headnote to the Riasanovsky selection, this separation is a product not only of the Soviet revolution but of the earlier Pan-Slav movement with its deep suspicions of Western influence. Of this viewpoint of Russian nationalist historians, the best example is Vasily O. Klyuchevsky, whose *A History of Russia*, tr. C. J. Hogarth, 5 vols. (New York: Russell and Russell, 1960), originally published in Russia between 1911 and 1931, is among the monuments of modern Russian historical writing. The section of Klyuchevsky's history dealing with Peter has been separately published: *Peter the Great*, tr. Liliana Archibald (London: Macmillan, 1961). To some extent the views of Klyuchevsky are seconded by M. T. Florinsky, *Russia: A History and an Interpretation*, 2 vols. (New York: Macmillan, 1953), which many admirers consider contains the best general account of Peter the Great. See also his *Russia: A Short History* (New York: Macmillan, 1965). For the Soviet views see the essay by C. E. Black, "The Reforms of Peter the Great" in *Rewriting Russian History: Soviet Interpretations of Russia's Past*, ed. Cyril E. Black, 2nd rev. ed. (New York: Random House, 1962).

In the Western tradition, probably the best full-scale biography of Peter is Ian Grey, *Peter the Great: Emperor of All Russia* (Philadelphia: Lippincott, 1960), while the two best brief accounts are B. H. Sumner, *Peter the Great and the Emergence of Russia*, "Teach Yourself History Library" (London: English Universities Press, 1950), and L. Jay Oliva, *Russia in the Era of Peter the Great* (Englewood Cliffs, N.J.: Prentice-Hall, 1969). Students may prefer the exciting popular biography by Harold Lamb, *The City and the Tsar: Peter the Great and the Move to the West, 1648–1762* (New York: Doubleday, 1948). There are three excellent recent biographies of Peter: Matthew S. Anderson, *Peter the Great* (London: Thames and Hudson, 1978), is a brief, solid, up-to-date survey; Alex DeJonge, *Fire and Water: A Life of Peter the Great* (New York: Coward,

McCann and Geoghegan, 1980), is also a substantial book but more readable; and Robert K. Massie, *Peter the Great: His Life and World* (New York: Knopf, 1980), is a huge, nine-hundred-page work, the most important aspect of which is its detailed description of the setting, the world of Peter the Great. For the interpretive problems of Peter, see *Peter the Great: Reformer or Revolutionary*, ed. Marc Raeff, rev. ed. (Boston: Heath, 1972), as well as Nicholas V. Riasanovsky, *The Image of Peter the Great in Russian History and Thought* (Oxford and New York: Oxford University Press, 1985).

For the role and setting of such figures as Lomonosov and Shcherbatov, see Hans Rogger, *National Consciousness in Eighteenth-Century Russia* (Cambridge, Mass.: Harvard University Press, 1960), and Marc Raeff, *Origins of the Russian Intelligentsia, the Eighteenth-Century Nobility* (New York: Harcourt, Brace and World, 1966).

Of brief general accounts of Russian history for the background to Peter the Great, the best is Nicholas V. Riasanovsky, *A History of Russia,* 2nd ed. (New York: Oxford University Press, 1969), excerpted in this chapter. But students should also see the fine narrative history, George Vernadsky, *A History of Russia,* 6th rev. ed. (New Haven, Conn.: Yale University Press, 1971), and the exciting and readable James H. Billington, *The Icon and the Axe: An Interpretive History of Russian Culture* (New York: Knopf, 1966). For the role of Russia in Europe, see J. B. Wolf, *The Emergence of the Great Powers, 1685–1715* (New York: Harper & Row, 1951).

NAPOLEON: CHILD OR BETRAYER OF THE REVOLUTION?

1769	Born on Corsica
1793	First command, against Toulon
1796–1797	The successful Italian campaign
1799–1804	One of three rulers in the Consulate
1804	Proclaimed emperor
1805–1807	Victories in Europe
1812–1813	The disastrous Russian campaign and defeat at Leipzig
1814	Abdication and exile to Elba
1814–1815	"The Hundred Days," defeated at Waterloo, and second exile, to St. Helena
1821	Died on St. Helena

Was Napoleon the child of the French Revolution? Napoleon himself felt that he was. And in one sense at least, the assertion is undeniably true. The Revolution had broken the caste system of the old military order, just as it had broken the social order of the Old Regime generally. In the struggling revolutionary republic, threatened with invasion and armed reprisal from every side, any man who showed the ability and the willingness to serve could advance in the military—even such an apparently unpromising officer as the young Napoleon Bonaparte, with his heavy Italian accent, his mediocre record as a military cadet and a junior officer, and his consuming interest in the politics of his native Corsica, which seemed to preclude any involvement in the great events that had been shaking France since 1789.

But Napoleon was not indifferent to those events. As early as 1791, he had become a member of the Jacobin Club in his garrison town of Valence, in the south of France, and was an outspoken advocate of Jacobin radicalism. His political views, rather than any proven military ability, secured for him his first important commission as commander of artillery at the siege of Toulon against the royalists and the British. Napoleon was successful, and he caught the eye of the military commissioner Augustin Robespierre, who praised the young officer in a letter to his brother Maximilien, then at the zenith of his political career in Paris. Napoleon was appointed commandant of artillery in the army of Italy. But Robespierre and his faction soon fell from power, and Napoleon, deprived of his command, was arrested. After a brief imprisonment, he departed for Paris to try to rescue his fortunes.

In 1795 the National Convention, its tenure running out, submitted to referendum the so-called Constitution of the Year III,[1] with its accompanying decree that two-thirds of the convention's members must be returned to the new legislative assembly. The royalists, enraged at this attempt to insure continued radical domination of the government, rose in revolt. Someone remembered that the young radical Napoleon was in Paris, and he was given effective command of the defense of the convention. As the rebels marched on 13 Vendémiaire, Year IV (October 5, 1795), Napoleon had already positioned his artillery and coolly ordered it to fire. The famous "whiff of grapeshot" carried the day—though there is no record that Napoleon used the phrase—and friends and enemies alike began to call him "Général Vendémiaire." He was now a force to be reckoned with in the politics of the Revolution.

When the new government was formed, headed by a Directory, Napoleon was its military adviser. Within a year, he was given command of the army of Italy. The Italian campaign was at that time verging on failure, but Napoleon turned it around. He gained the loyalty of his troops—largely by authorizing them to live off the land they conquered in lieu of the pay their republic had failed to provide—and he won battles. Within less than a year, Napoleon was the master of Italy. Far exceeding his authority, he set up a series of Italian republics and forced the Austrians out of Italy entirely. Then Napoleon returned to Paris once more to engineer the Treaty of Campo Formio with the defeated Austrians. Although the Directory was far from pleased, Napoleon was fast becoming a popular hero.

Britain, with its formidable sea power and its wealth and industry, was clearly France's most dangerous enemy, and the Directory had formulated a plan for an invasion of England from across the chan-

---

[1]The early leaders of the Revolution had proclaimed a new calendar dating from the overthrow of the Old Regime. Napoleon would later return France to the common usage.—Ed.

nel. Napoleon was placed in command of the operation. After a cursory inspection, he rejected the plan, arguing instead for a strike at the British lifeline to India—a campaign in Egypt. Napoleon was able to overcome the Directory but not the British sea power and the squadrons of Lord Nelson. The Egyptian campaign was a disaster. But rather than admit defeat, Napoleon returned to France and proclaimed a victory when in fact there was none. The French people believed him.

In 1799 Napoleon, with Abbé Sieyès, an ambitious member of the Directory, engineered a coup d'état. The coup, which took place on 18–19 Brumaire, Year VIII (November 9–10, 1799), was successful, and the Directory was replaced by a Consulate of three men, one of them Napoleon. Within a matter of weeks, a new "Constitution of the Year VIII" was proclaimed, making Napoleon First Consul and the government of France a military dictatorship. It is true that the constitution was overwhelmingly approved by plebiscite, after the fact. It is true that under its authority Napoleon launched far-reaching reforms, moving the nation in the direction of order and stability. But it is also true that the French nation had succumbed to the myth of Napoleon, a myth that was ultimately founded upon his military invincibility and—at least in Napoleon's mind—upon continued military victories.

In 1802 Europe might well have had peace. Even Britain had agreed to the Treaty of Amiens. For achieving this diplomatic coup, Napoleon was granted lifetime tenure as First Consul, but even this did not satisfy his ambition. Napoleon demanded an empire and he got it: on May 18, 1804, he was proclaimed Emperor of the French. In the years that followed, Napoleon compiled an incredible list of military victories: he defeated the Austrians at Ulm and the Austrians and Russians at Austerlitz in the winter of 1805, the Prussians at Jena and Auerstädt in the fall of 1806, and the Russians alone at Eylau and Friedland in the spring and summer of 1807. By this time, Napoleon had redrawn the map of western Europe, and his own relations sat on half a dozen thrones. His plan was to organize the Continent against the stubborn British; to this end, he signed an agreement with the new Russian emperor, Alexander I, dividing Europe between them.

In 1810 Napoleon, standing at the apex of his power, decided to disregard his agreement with Alexander and invade Russia. It was a disastrous miscalculation, and it proved to be the crucial turning point in Napoleon's career. Out of the almost half a million men who had massed on the banks of the Neman in the summer of 1812, fewer than ten thousand remained after the winter's march back from Moscow. The myth of Napoleon was shattered, and the powers of Europe rose up against him. Not only had he defeated and humiliated them, but he had brought them the Revolution. Even if he had subverted the Revolution in France, he had, nevertheless, exported its principles along with his conquests. To the Old Regime of Europe, this was Napoleon's greatest insult, the ultimate betrayal that they could not forgive. But it was also perhaps Napoleon's most enduring claim to having been one of the makers of world history, for, whatever his motives, Napoleon introduced the Age of Revolution that persisted on the Continent, in one guise or another, through most of the nineteenth century and that fundamentally changed the nature of European government and society.

Napoleon was forced to abdicate and was exiled to the Mediterranean island of Elba. But even as the victors were gathering to undo his work and the Bourbons were returning to France, Napoleon escaped from Elba. This was the beginning of his Hundred Days. As Napoleon, with an escort of grenadiers, approached Grenoble, he met the first battalion sent to intercept him. His secretary, the Marquis de Las Cases, described the scene:

> The commanding officer refused even to parley. The Emperor without hesitation, advanced alone, and one hundred of his grenadiers marched at some distance from him, with their arms reversed. The sight of Napoleon, his costume, and in particular his grey military great coat, produced a magical effect on the soldiers, and they stood motionless. Napoleon went straight up to a veteran whose arm was covered with *chevrons,* and very unceremoniously seizing him by the whisker, asked him whether he would have the heart to kill his Emperor. The soldier, his eyes moistened with tears, immediately thrust the ramrod into his musquet, to show that it was not loaded, and exclaimed, "See, I could not have done thee any harm: all the others are the same." Cries of *Vive l'Empereur!* resounded on every side. Napoleon ordered the battalion to make half a turn to the right, and all marched on to Paris.[2]

With every mile resistance melted, and cries of *Vive l'Empereur!* swelled up from the throngs that lined the roads and from garrison troops and militia. Napoleon had returned and France was his. Even after the catastrophe at Waterloo, an officer lying in the mud with a shattered thigh cried out, "He has ruined us—he has destroyed France and himself—yet I love him still."[3]

---

[2]The Count de Las Cases, *Memoirs of the Life, Exile, and Conversations of the Emperor Napoleon,* new ed. (New York: Eckler, 1900), III, 295.

[3]Louis Antoine Fauvelet de Bourrienne, *Memoirs of Napoleon Bonaparte,* ed. R. W. Phipps (New York: Scribners, 1891), IV, 204.

But what of the Revolution? The old veteran on the road to Grenoble and the wounded officer on the field of Waterloo wept for their emperor, not for the lost cause of the Revolution. Thousands unquestionably shared their views. But many thousands more were convinced that, despite the terrible cost of Napoleon's search for glory, he had carried the Revolution to its proper, even to its inevitable conclusion. Napoleon himself wrote:

> I purified a revolution, in spite of hostile factions. I combined all the scattered benefits that could be preserved; but I was obliged to protect them with a nervous arm against the attacks of all parties; and in this situation it may be truly said that the public interest, *the State, was myself.*[4]

The wheel had come full circle. Napoleon "the child of the Revolution" echoed the words often ascribed to Louis XIV, "I am the state."

---

[4]Las Cases, *Memoirs*, III, 255–56.

Napoleon's Memoirs

THE COUNT DE LAS CASES

When, after Waterloo, Napoleon was sent into exile again, this time to the tiny, distant island of St. Helena in the south Atlantic, he was only forty-five years old, apparently in the prime of life. Might he not escape once more, even against all odds? Might he even be called back by one or another of the victorious allies, already beginning to quarrel among themselves? Might not France even summon its emperor again? Napoleon was planning for any eventuality, as carefully and methodically as he might plan a military campaign.

Napoleon had, of course, some limited contact with the Bonapartists in France, but this was restricted by the tight control over the island. He was able to carry on some correspondence, though much of it consisted of complaints to the British government about the conditions of his exile. But mainly Napoleon devoted himself to his memoirs, which he dictated to his secretary, the Marquis de Las Cases. Las Cases carefully transcribed the material, and then Napoleon read and corrected it himself.

Memoirs of the Life, Exile, and Conversations of the Emperor Napoleon *is a vast and complicated work—four volumes in its final published form. In addition to Napoleon's own recollections of events, discourses, and opinions, it contains comments, reflections, and interpolations by Las Cases. It details Napoleon's bitter, petty, continuing controversy with the authorities on the island whose task it was to maintain his captivity. But primarily the book is Napoleon's own apologia, the justification for his policies and his career, directed to his own French people, to the allies, and to the tribunal of history. To Napoleon, the book was his final weapon.*

It is in this work, more than in any other place, that we see the precise terms in which Napoleon considered himself the child, the inheritor, the "purifier" of the Revolution.

"The French Revolution was not produced by the jarring interests of two families disputing the possession of the throne; it was a general rising of the mass of the nation against the privileged classes." . . . The principal object of the Revolution was to destroy all privileges; to abolish signorial jurisdictions, justice being an inseparable attribute of sovereign authority; to suppress feudal rights as being a remnant of the old slavery of the people; to subject alike all citizens and all property to

96

the burdens of the state. In short, the Revolution proclaimed equality of rights. A citizen might attain any public employment, according to his talent and the chances of fortune. The kingdom was composed of provinces which had been united to the Crown at various periods: they had no natural limits, and were differently divided, unequal in extent and in population. They possessed many laws of their own, civil as well as criminal: they were more or less privileged, and very unequally taxed, both with respect to the amount and the nature of the contributions, which rendered it necessary to detach them from each other by lines of custom-houses. France was not a state, but a combination of several states, connected together without amalgamation. The whole had been determined by chance and by the events of past ages. The Revolution, guided by the principle of equality, both with respect to the citizens and the different portions of the territory, destroyed all these small nations: there was no longer a Brittany, a Normandy, a Burgundy, a Champagne, a Provence, or a Lorraine; but the whole formed a France. A division of homogeneous territory, prescribed by local circumstances, confounded the limits of all the provinces. They possessed the same judicial and administrative organization, the same civil and criminal laws, and the same system of taxation. The dreams of the upright men of all ages were realized. The opposition which the Court, the Clergy, and the Nobility, raised against the Revolution and the war with foreign powers, produced the law of emigration and the sequestration of emigrant property, which subsequently it was found necessary to sell, in order to provide for the charges of the war. A great portion of the French nobility enrolled themselves under the banner of the princes of the Bourbon family, and formed an army which marched in conjunction with the Austrian, Prussian, and English forces. Gentlemen who had been brought up in the enjoyment of competency served as private soldiers; numbers were cut off by fatigue and the sword; others perished of want in foreign countries; and the wars of La Vendée and of the Chouans, and the revolutionary tribunals, swept away thousands. Three-fourths of the French nobility were thus destroyed; and all posts, civil, judicial, or military, were filled by citizens who had risen from the common mass of the people. The change produced in persons and property by the events of the Revolution, was not less remarkable than that which was effected by the principles of the Revolution. A new church was created; the dioceses of Vienne, Narbonne, Féjus, Sisteron, Rheims, &c., were superseded by sixty new dioceses, the boundaries of which were circumscribed, in Concordat,[5]

---

[5]The agreement (1801) between Napoleon and Pope Pius VII that restored Catholicism to France, though largely on Napoleon's terms.—ED.

by new Bulls applicable to the present state of the French territory. The suppression of religious orders, the sale of convents and of all ecclesiastical property, were sanctioned, and the clergy were pensioned by the State. Everything that was the result of the events which had occurred since the time of Clovis, ceased to exist. All these changes were so advantageous to the people that they were effected with the utmost facility, and, in 1800, there no longer remained any recollection of the old privileges and sovereigns of the provinces, the old parliaments and bailiwicks, or the old dioceses; and to trace back the origin of all that existed, it was sufficient to refer to the new law by which it had been established. One-half of the land had changed its proprietors; the peasantry and the citizens were enriched. The advancement of agriculture and manufactures exceeded the most sanguine hopes. France presented the imposing spectacle of upwards of thirty millions of inhabitants, circumscribed within their natural limits, and composing only a single class of citizens, governed by one law, one rule, and one order. All these changes were conformable with the welfare and rights of the nation, and with the justice and intelligence of the age.

The five members of the Directory were divided. Enemies to the Republic crept into the councils; and thus men, hostile to the rights of the people, became connected with the government. This state of things kept the country in a ferment; and the great interests which the French people had acquired by the Revolution were incessantly compromised. One unanimous voice, issuing from the plains of France and from her cities and her camps, demanded the preservation of all the principles of the Republic, or the establishment of an hereditary system of government, which would place the principles and interests of the Revolution beyond the reach of factions and the influence of foreigners. By the constitution of the year VIII the First Consul of the Republic became Consul for ten years, and the nation afterwards prolonged his magistracy for life: the people subsequently raised him to the throne, which it rendered hereditary in his family. The principles of the sovereignty of the people, of liberty and equality, of the destruction of the feudal system, of the irrevocability of the sale of national domains, and the freedom of religious worship, were now established. The government of France, under the fourth dynasty, was founded on the same principles as the Republic. It was a moderate and constitutional monarchy. There was as much difference between the government of France under the fourth dynasty and the third, as between the latter and the Republic. The fourth dynasty succeeded the Republic, or, more properly speaking, it was merely a modification of it.

No Prince ever ascended a throne with rights more legitimate than those of Napoleon. The crown was not presented to him by a few

Bishops and Nobles; but he was raised to the Imperial throne by the unanimous consent of the citizens, three times solemnly confirmed.[6] Pope Pius VII, the head of the Catholic religion, the religion of the majority of the French people, crossed the Alps to anoint the Emperor with his own hands, in the presence of the Bishops of France, the Cardinals of the Romish Church, and the Deputies from all the districts of the Empire.[7] The sovereigns of Europe eagerly acknowledged Napoleon: all beheld with pleasure the modification of the Republic, which placed France on a footing of harmony with the rest of Europe, and which at once confirmed the constitution and the happiness of that great nation. Ambassadors from Austria, Russia, Prussia, Spain, Portugal, Turkey, and America, in fine, from all the powers of Europe, came to congratulate the Emperor. England alone sent no ambassador: she had violated the treaty of Amiens, and had consequently again declared war against France. . . .

The English declaration of war (1803) precipitated the imperial phase of Napoleon's career, during which, in victory after victory, he defeated the great powers of Europe. He hoped to complete his plans for Europe and for himself in the attack upon Russia. Here he reflects upon those plans and upon the Russian war.

. . . "That war should have been the most popular of any in modern times. It was a war of good sense and true interests; a war for the repose and security of all; it was purely pacific and preservative; entirely European and continental. Its success would have established a balance of power and would have introduced new combinations, by which the dangers of the present time would have been succeeded by future tranquillity. In this case, ambition had no share in my views. In raising Poland,[8] which was the key-stone of the whole arch, I would have permitted a King of Prussia, an Archduke of Austria, or any other to occupy the throne. I had no wish to obtain any new acquisition; and I reserved for myself only the glory of doing good, and the blessings of posterity. Yet this undertaking failed, and proved my ruin, though I never acted more disinterestedly, and never better

---

[6]A reference to the successive plebiscites that Napoleon used to gain approval of his modifications in the government. The last sanctioned his assumption of the imperial title.—ED.

[7]Though the pope was present, Napoleon placed the crown on his own head, as depicted in the famous painting of the occasion by the court painter Jacques-Louis David.—ED.

[8]His creation of an independent Poland was an indignity Russia would not endure. It was over this matter that the Russian campaign actually began.—ED.

merited success. As if popular opinion had been seized with contagion, in a moment, a general outcry, a general sentiment, arose against me. I was proclaimed the destroyer of kings—I, who had created them! I was denounced as the subverter of the rights of nations—I, who was about to risk all to secure them! And people and kings, those irreconcilable enemies, leagued together and conspired against me! All the acts of my past life were now forgotten. I said, truly, that popular favour would return to me with victory; but victory escaped me, and I was ruined. . . ."

The ruin brought upon him by the Russian war was purely fortuitous, claims Napoleon, and in no way can obscure his true accomplishments.

"I closed the gulf of anarchy and cleared the chaos. I purified the Revolution, dignified Nations and established Kings. I excited every kind of emulation, rewarded every kind of merit, and extended the limits of glory! This is at least something! And on what point can I be assailed on which an historian could not defend me? Can it be for my intentions? But even here I can find absolution. Can it be for my despotism? It may be demonstrated that the Dictatorship was absolutely necessary. Will it be said that I restrained liberty? It can be proved that licentiousness, anarchy, and the greatest irregularities, still haunted the threshold of freedom. Shall I be accused of having been too fond of war? It can be shown that I always received the first attack. Will it be said that I aimed at universal monarchy? It can be proved that this was merely the result of fortuitous circumstances, and that our enemies themselves led me step by step to this determination. Lastly, shall I be blamed for my ambition? This passion I must doubtless be allowed to have possessed, and that in no small degree; but at the same time, my ambition was of the highest and noblest kind that ever, perhaps, existed—that of establishing and of consecrating the empire of reason, and the full exercise and complete enjoyment of all the human faculties! And here the historian will probably feel compelled to regret that such ambition should not have been fulfilled and gratified!" Then after a few moments of silent reflection: "This," said the Emperor, "is my whole history in a few words."

On Politics, Literature, and National Character

MADAME DE STAËL

There were many who, like one hostile critic, regarded Napoleon simply as "the Corsican ogre." But there were other, more thoughtful critics who, though they condemned Napoleon, tried to understand why they did so. One of these was Anne-Louise-Germaine, Madame de Staël (1766–1817). She was the daughter of the Swiss banker Jacques Necker, who, as Minister of Finance to Louis XVI, had tried without much success—and without much imagination—to rescue France from fiscal chaos on the eve of the Revolution. Madame de Staël had grown up in the highest circles of the French aristocracy and the court, marrying the Swedish ambassador to France, Eric Magnus de Staël-Holstein, in 1786. She lived through the Revolution and knew most of its leading figures, as she did Napoleon and the men of the counterrevolution.

But Madame de Staël was more than simply a fashionable aristocrat. She was one of the last great luminaries of the Age of Enlightenment and one of the most important European writers of her time. She was also one of Napoleon's most perceptive and persistent critics. Though Madame de Staël was a passionate champion of liberty and an outspoken French patriot, she was no friend of the Revolution. But then, she observed, neither was Napoleon! He was, in her view, nothing less than its most sinister subverter. Napoleon tried first to moderate her views, then to persuade her of his good intentions, but he failed altogether to understand the basis of her hostility. Finally, he sent her into exile, and from Switzerland, Germany, Russia, and England she continued to observe and to write about the unfolding of the events she had foreseen. We turn now to Madame de Staël: On Politics, Literature, and National Character, *and her account of the rise and fall of Napoleon, so different in every way from his own.*

The Directory was not inclined to peace, not because it wished to extend French rule beyond the Rhine and the Alps but because it believed war useful for the propagation of the republican system. Its plan was to surround France with a belt of republics. . . .

General Bonaparte was certainly less serious and less sincere than the Directory in the love of republican ideas, but he was much more shrewd in estimating a situation. He sensed that peace would become popular in France because passions were subsiding and people were weary of sacrifices; so he signed the Treaty of Campo Formio with Austria.

General Bonaparte distinguished himself as much by his character and mind as by his victories, and the imagination of the French was beginning to attach itself to him strongly. A tone of moderation and nobility prevailed in his style, which contrasted with the revolutionary gruffness of the civil leaders of France. The warrior spoke like a magistrate, while the magistrates expressed themselves with martial violence. . . .

It was with this feeling, at least, that I saw him for the first time in Paris. I could find no words of reply when he came to me to tell me that he had sought my father at Coppet and that he regretted having passed through Switzerland without having seen him. But when I was somewhat recovered from the confusion of admiration, a very strong sense of fear followed. Bonaparte at that time had no power; he was even believed to be somewhat threatened by the jealous suspicions of the Directory. So the fear he inspired was caused only by the extraordinary effect of his person upon nearly all who approached him. I had seen men worthy of respect, and I had seen fierce men: there was nothing in the impression Bonaparte produced upon me that recalled either the former or the latter. I very quickly saw, in the various occasions I had to meet him during his stay in Paris, that his character could not be defined by the words we ordinarily use; he was neither good, nor fierce, nor gentle, nor cruel, like others we know. Such a being, having no equals, could neither feel nor arouse any sympathy: he was more than a human being or less than one. His appearance, his mind, and his speech were foreign in nature—an added advantage for subjugating the French.

Far from being reassured by seeing Bonaparte more often, I was made increasingly apprehensive. I had a vague feeling that no emotions of the heart could influence him. He considers a human being a fact or a thing, not a fellow man. He does not hate nor does he love. For him, there is nothing but himself; all others are ciphers.

Every time I heard him speak I was struck by his superiority: yet it had no resemblance to that of men educated and cultivated by study or by social intercourse, such as may be found in England or France. But his speech showed a feeling for the situation, like the hunter's for his prey. . . .

General Bonaparte, at this same time, the end of 1797, sounded public opinion regarding the Directors; he realized that they were not liked but that republican sentiment made it as yet impossible for a general to take the place of civilian officials. The Directory proposed to him the assault upon England. He went to examine the coasts, and, quickly seeing that this expedition was senseless, returned resolved to attempt the conquest of Egypt.

Bonaparte has always sought to seize the imagination of men and, in this respect, he knows well how one must govern when one is not born to the throne. An invasion of Africa, the war carried to an almost fabulous country like Egypt, must make an impression upon every mind. . . .

But in his climb to power, Napoleon depended not only upon his growing military reputation.

The most potent magic that Bonaparte used to establish his power was the terror the mere name of Jacobinism inspired, though anyone capable of reflection knew perfectly well that this scourge could not reappear in France. People readily pretend to fear defeated parties in order to justify harsh measures. Everyone who wants to promote the establishment of despotism forcefully reminds us of the terrible crimes of demagogy. It is a very simple technique. So Bonaparte paralyzed every form of resistance to his will by the words: *Do you want me to hand you over to the Jacobins?* And France bowed down before him, no man bold enough to reply to him: *We shall be able to fight the Jacobins and you.* In short, even then he was not liked, only preferred. He almost always presented himself in competition with another cause for alarm, in order to make his power acceptable as a lesser evil. . . .

We cannot watch too attentively for the first symptoms of tyranny; when it has grown to a certain point, there is no more time to stop it. One man sweeps along the will of many individuals of whom the majority, taken separately, wish to be free but who nevertheless surrender because people fear each other and do not dare to speak their thoughts freely. . . .

General Bonaparte decreed a constitution in which there were no safeguards. Besides, he took great care to leave in existence the laws announced during the Revolution, in order to select from this detestable arsenal the weapon that suited him. The special commissions, deportations, exiles, the bondage of the press—these steps unfortunately taken in the name of liberty—were very useful to tyranny. To adopt them, he sometimes advanced reasons of state, sometimes the need of the times, sometimes the acts of his opponents, sometimes the need to maintain tranquillity. Such is the artillery of phrases that supports absolute power, for "emergencies" never end, and the more one seeks to repress by illegal measures the more one creates disaffected people who justify new injustices. The establishment of the rule of law is always put off till tomorrow. This is a vicious circle from which one cannot break out, for the public spirit that is awaited in order to permit liberty can come only from liberty itself. . . .

It was particularly advantageous to Bonaparte's power that he had to manage only a mass. All individual existence was annihilated by ten years of disorder, and nothing sways people like military success; it takes great power of reason to combat this tendency instead of profiting from it. No one in France could consider his position secure. Men of all classes, ruined or enriched, banished or rewarded, found themselves one by one equally, so to speak, in the hands of power. Bonaparte, who always moved between two opposed interests, took very good care not to put an end to these anxieties by fixed laws that might let everyone know his rights. To one man he returned his property, while another he stripped of his forever. The First Consul reserved to himself the power of determining, under any pretext, the fate of everything and everyone.

Those Frenchmen who sought to resist the ever-increasing power of the First Consul had to invoke liberty to struggle against him successfully. But at this word the aristocrats and the enemies of the Revolution cried "Jacobinism," thus supporting the tyranny for which they later sought to blame their adversaries. . . .

I sensed more quickly than others—and I pride myself on it—Bonaparte's tyrannical character and intentions. The true friends of liberty are in this respect guided by an instinct that does not deceive them. But my position, at the outset of the Consulate, was made more painful by the fact that respectable society in France thought it saw in Bonaparte the man who had saved them from anarchy or Jacobinism. They therefore vigorously condemned the spirit of opposition I displayed toward him. . . .

Madame de Staël's opposition led to her exile. But even in exile she continued to comment upon Napoleon and upon the rise and finally the decline of his military and political fortunes. In 1813, following the Russian disaster, the allies invaded France, heading for Paris.

From the moment the Allies passed the Rhine and entered France it seemed to me that the prayers of the friends of France must undergo a complete change. I was then in London, and one of the English Cabinet Ministers asked me what I wished for. I ventured to reply that my desire was to see Bonaparte victorious and slain. The English had enough greatness of soul to make it unnecessary for me to conceal this French sentiment from them. Yet I was to learn, in the midst of the transports of joy with which the city of the conquerors reverberated, that Paris was in the power of the Allies. At that moment I felt there was no longer a France: I believed Burke's prediction realized and that where France had existed we should see only an abyss. The Emperor Alexander, the Allies, and the constitutional principles adopted through the wisdom of Louis XVIII banished this gloomy presentiment.

There was, nevertheless, something of grandeur in Napoleon's farewell to his troops and to their eagles, so long victorious. His last campaign had been long and skillful: in short, the fatal magic that bound France's military glory to him was not yet destroyed. Thus the conference at Paris must be blamed for having made his return possible. . . .

Many people like to argue that Bonaparte would still be emperor if he had not attempted the expeditions against Spain or Russia. This opinion pleases the supporters of despotism, who insist that so fine a government could not be overthrown by the very nature of things but only by an accident. I have already said, what observation of France will confirm, that Bonaparte needed war to establish and maintain absolute power. A great nation would not have supported the dull and degrading burden of despotism if military glory had not ceaselessly moved or exalted the public spirit. . . .

I shall never forget the moment when I learned, from one of my friends the morning of March 6, 1815, that Bonaparte had landed on the French coast. I had the misfortune to foresee at once the consequences of that event—as they have since taken place—and I thought the earth was about to open under me. I said, "There will be no liberty if Bonaparte wins and no national independence if he loses." Events, it seems to me, have borne out this sad prediction only too well. . . .

. . . Enlightened men could see in Bonaparte nothing but a despot, but by a rather fatal conjunction of circumstances this despot was presented to the nation as the defender of its rights. All the benefits achieved by the Revolution, which France will never willingly give up, were threatened by the endless rashness of the party that wants to repeat the conquest of Frenchmen, as if they were still Gauls. And that part of the nation that most feared the return of the Old Regime thought they saw in Bonaparte a way to save themselves from it. The most fatal association that could overwhelm the friends of liberty was that a despot should join their ranks—should, so to speak, place himself at their head—and that the enemies of every liberal idea should have a pretext for confusing popular violence with the evils of despotism and thus make tyranny appear to be the result of liberty itself. . . . If it was criminal to recall Bonaparte, it was silly to try to disguise such a man as a constitutional monarch. . . .

Whether Napoleon lives or perishes, whether or not he reappears on the continent of Europe, only one reason moves me to speak of him: the ardent wish that the friends of liberty in France completely separate their cause from his and beware of confusing the principles of the Revolution with those of the Imperial *régime*. I believe I have shown that there is no counter-revolution so fatal to liberty as the one he made.

A Modern Napoleon

GEORGES LEFEBVRE

Napoleon has been the most enduringly fascinating figure in modern history, the subject of literally thousands of books—more than 200,000 by some estimates. Recent opinion has tended to divide along precisely the lines that appeared in Napoleon's own time—as suggested in the first two selections of this chapter—either "for" or "against" him, to borrow from the title of a famous book on the Napoleonic tradition.[9] The following selection is from Napoleon: From 18 Brumaire to Tilsit 1799–1807, *by the distinguished French historian Georges Lefebvre, considered by many competent critics to have been the best modern scholar of the Napoleonic age. But Lefebvre was also a great authority on the French Revolution, and so we turn to him for his view on the relationship of Napoleon to the Revolution and his answer to the question of whether Napoleon was its child or its betrayer. It is the opinion of Lefebvre that the Revolution had betrayed itself long before Napoleon became its conscious heir; that only in the most elementary sense of its giving him the opportunity to rise to power could Napoleon be considered its offspring; that—as Madame de Staël argued— Napoleon was always the same, from the beginning to the end of his career, an autocrat; and that he did not purify the Revolution but rather manipulated it.*

That the French Revolution turned to dictatorship was no accident; it was driven there by inner necessity, and not for the first time either. Nor was it an accident that the Revolution led to the dictatorship of a general. But it so happened that this general was Napoleon Bonaparte, a man whose temperament, even more than his genius, was

[9]Pieter Geyl, *Napoleon: For and Against,* Olive Renier, trans. (New Haven, Conn.: Yale University Press, 1949).

unable to adapt to peace and moderation. Thus it was an unforesee-able contingency which tilted the scale in favour of "la guerre éternelle."

For a long time the republicans had wanted to strengthen the central authority. One need only look at the constitutions they gave to the vassal states: in Holland, the members of the Directory controlled the treasury; in Switzerland, they appointed government officials; in Rome, they appointed judges as well. In the Helvetic and Roman Republics every department already possessed a "prefect." All this is not to mention the Cisalpine Republic, which was Bonaparte's per-sonal fief. . . . The coup d'état of 18 Fructidor had provided the occa-sion sought by Sieyès, Talleyrand, and Bonaparte, but they let the opportunity slip. In Year VII, however, they hoped to bring about a new one. Without realizing it, the republicans were giving way to a tendency which, ever since the start of the civil and foreign wars, was pushing the Revolution in the direction of a permanent and all-powerful executive, that is to say toward dictatorship. It was this social revolution that drove the dispossessed nobility far beyond insurrec-tion. Subsidized by enemy gold, it exploited the wartime hardships—that inexhaustible source of discontent—and particularly the mone-tary and economic crisis, thereby intending to turn the people against the government. The French did not want a return to the Old Regime, but they suffered and they held their leaders responsible for it. At every election the counter-revolution hoped to regain power. It was awareness of this danger that led the Mountain[10] in 1793 to declare the Convention in permanent session until the peace. The Thermidorians had intended to restore elective government, but they immediately returned to Jacobin expediency by passing the Decree of the Two-Thirds. Next, the Directory, overwhelmed by the elections of 1797, re-established the dictatorship on 18 Fructidor. Yet as long as the Constitu-tion of Year III continued to exist, this dictatorship, put to the test each year, required a host of violent measures and could never be brought into working order. So it was still necessary to revive the principle of 1793 and invest it with permanence until such time as peace, settled once and for all, would persuade the counter-revolution to accept the new order. It was in this respect that Napoleon's dictatorship became so much a part of the history of the French Revolution. No matter what he may have said or done, neither he nor his enemies were ever able to break this bond, and this was a fact which the European aristocracy understood perfectly well.

In 1799, as in 1793, the Jacobins wished to establish a democratic

---

[10]The popular name given to the radical faction in the Convention.—ED.

dictatorship by relying on the Sans-culottes[11] to push it through the councils. Taking advantage of the crisis preceding the victory at Zurich, they succeeded in forcing the passage of several revolutionary measures: a compulsory loan, the abolition of exemptions from military service, the law of hostages, a repeal of assignments on public revenues which had been granted to bankers and government contractors, withholdings on the rente and on salaries, and finally, requisitions. These measures constituted a direct attack on bourgeois interests and brought that class to action. Thus it was symbolic that assignments on public revenues were restored the very night of 19 Brumaire. The Idéologues who gathered around Madame de Condorcet at Auteuil or in the salon of Madame de Staël wanted neither a democratic dictatorship nor even a democracy. . . . Madame de Staël expressed their desire: to devise a representative system of government which would assure power to the moneyed and talented "notables." Sieyès, who had become a Director, took his inspiration from the Decree of the Two-Thirds. Together with his friends he wanted to select the membership of the newly constituted bodies which would then expand themselves by co-optation, leaving to the nation only the role of electing candidates. Furthermore, those already in office saw in this plan the chance to keep themselves in power.

The people having been eliminated as an obstacle to the dictatorship of the bourgeoisie, only the army remained. The Directory had already sought its help on 18 Fructidor, Year V, and had managed to keep the upper hand, despite serious incursions. Now, however, the situation was very different in that steadfast republicans, not royalists, were to be driven out. Only a popular general could have carried it through, and Bonaparte's sudden return destined that it should be he. The will of the nation which was invoked to justify 18 Brumaire played no part in the event. The nation rejoiced at the news that Bonaparte was in France because it recognized an able general; but the Republic had conquered without him, and Masséna's victory[12] had bolstered the reputation of the Directory. Consequently, the responsibility for 18 Brumaire lies on that segment of the republican bourgeoisie called the Brumairians, whose leading light was Sieyès. They had no intention of giving in to Bonaparte, and they chose him only as an instrument of their policy. That they propelled him to power without imposing any conditions, without even first delimiting the fundamental character of the new regime, betrays their incredible

---

[11]Another popular name for the urban proletariat, especially of Paris, who tended to support Jacobin radicalism.—ED.

[12]At Zurich over the Russians.—ED.

mediocrity. Bonaparte did not repudiate the notables, for he too was not a democrat, and their collaboration alone enabled him to rule. But on the evening of 19 Brumaire, after they had hurriedly slapped together the structure of the Provisional Consulate, they should not have harboured any more illusions. The army had followed Bonaparte, and him alone. He was complete master. Regardless of what he and his apologists may have said, his rule was from its origins an absolute military dictatorship. It was Bonaparte alone who would decide the questions on which the fate of France and Europe hinged.

What sort of a man was he? His personality evolved in so singular a manner that it defies portrayal. He appeared first as a studious officer full of dreams, garrisoned at Valence and Auxonne. As a youthful general, on the eve of the battle of Castiglione, he could still hold a council of war. But in the final years as Emperor, he was stupefied with his own omnipotence and was infatuated with his own omniscience. And yet distinctive traits appear throughout his entire career: power could do no more than accentuate some and attenuate others.

Short-legged and small in stature, muscular, ruddy, and still gaunt at the age of thirty, he was physically hardy and fit. His sensitivity and steadiness were admirable, his reflexes quick as lightning, and his capacity for work unlimited. He could fall asleep at will. But we also find the reverse: cold humid weather brought on oppression, coughing spells, dysuria; when crossed he unleashed frightful outbursts of temper; overexertion, despite prolonged hot baths, despite extreme sobriety, despite the moderate yet constant use of coffee and tobacco, occasionally produced brief collapses, even tears. His mind was one of the most perfect that has ever been: his unflagging attention tirelessly swept in facts and ideas which his memory registered and classified; his imagination played with them freely, and being in a permanent state of concealed tension, it never wearied of inventing political and strategic motifs which manifested themselves in unexpected flashes of intuition like those experienced by poets and mathematicians. This would happen especially at night during a sudden awakening, and he himself referred to it as "the moral spark" and "the after midnight presence of the spirit." This spiritual fervour shone through his glittering eyes and illuminated the face, still "sulphuric" at his rise, of the "sleek-haired Corsican." This is what made him unsociable, and not, as Hippolyte Taine would have us think, some kind of brutality, the consequence of a slightly tarnished *condottiere* being let loose upon the world in all his savagery. He rendered a fair account of himself when he said, "I consider myself a good man at heart," and indeed he showed generosity, and even kindness to those who were close to him. But between ordinary mortals, who hurried through their tasks in order to abandon themselves to leisure or diversion, and Napoleon

Bonaparte, who was the soul of effort and concentration, there could exist no common ground nor true community. Ambition—that irresistible impulse to act and to dominate—sprang from his physical and mental state of being. . . .

Ever since his military school days at Brienne, when he was still a poor and taunted foreigner, timid yet bursting with passion, Napoleon drew strength from pride in himself and contempt for others. Destined to become an officer, his instinct to command without having to discuss could not have been better served. Although he might on occasion have sought information or opinion, he alone was master and judge. Bonaparte's natural propensity for dictatorship suited the normal practice of his profession. In Italy and in Egypt he introduced dictatorship into the government. In France he wanted to put himself forward as a civilian, but the military stamp was indelibly there. He consulted often, but he could never tolerate free opposition. More precisely, when faced with a group of men accustomed to discussion, he would lose his composure. This explains his intense hatred of the Idéologues. The confused and undisciplined, yet formidable masses inspired in him as much fear as contempt. Regardless of costumes and titles, Bonaparte took power as a general, and as such he exercised it. . . .

. . . Having entered into a life of action, he still remained a thinker. This warrior was never happier than in the silence of his own study, surrounded by papers and documents. In time he became more practical, and he would boast that he had repudiated "ideology." Nevertheless, he was still a typical man of the eighteenth century, a rationalist, a philosophe. Far from relying on intuition, he placed his trust in reason, in knowledge, and in methodical effort. . . .

He seemed to be dedicated to a policy of realism in every way, and he was, in fact, a realist in execution down to the slightest detail. . . . And yet he was a realist in execution only. There lived in him an alter-ego which contained certain features of the hero. It seems to have been born during his days at the military academy out of a need to dominate a world in which he felt himself despised. Above all he longed to equal the semi-legendary heroes of Plutarch and Corneille. His greatest ambition was glory. "I live only for posterity," he exclaimed, "death is nothing, but to live defeated and without glory is to die every day." His eyes were fixed on the world's great leaders: Alexander, who conquered the East and dreamed of conquering the world; Caesar, Augustus, Charlemagne—the creators and the restorer of the Roman Empire whose very names were synonymous with the idea of a universal civilization. From these he did not deduce a precise formulation to be used as a rule, a measure, or a condition of political conduct. They were for him examples, which stimulated his imagination and lent an unutterable charm to action. . . . That is why it is idle to seek for limits to Napoleon's policy, or for a final goal at which he would have stopped: there simply was none. . . .

That a mind so capable of grasping reality in certain respects should escape it in others . . . can only be due to Napoleon's origins as much as to his nature. When he first came to France, he considered himself a foreigner. Until the time when he was expelled from Corsica by his compatriots in 1791, his attitude had been one of hostility to the French people. Assuredly he became sufficiently imbued with their culture and spirit to adopt their nationality; otherwise he could never have become their leader. But he lacked the time to identify himself with the French nation and to adopt its national tradition to the point where he would consider its interests as a limitation upon his own actions. Something of the uprooted person remained in him; something of the *déclassé* as well. He was neither entirely a gentleman nor entirely common. He served both the king and the Revolution without attaching himself to either. This was one of the reasons for his success, since he could so easily place himself above parties and announce himself as the restorer of national unity. Yet neither in the Old Regime nor in the new did he find principles which might have served as a norm or a limit. . . .

What about moral limits? In spiritual life he had nothing in common with other men. Even though he knew their passions well and deftly turned them to his own ends, he cared only for those that would reduce men to dependence. He belittled every feeling that elevated men to acts of sacrifice—religious faith, patriotism, love of freedom—because he saw in them obstacles to his own schemes. Not that he was impervious to these sentiments, at least not in his youth, for they readily led to heroic deeds; but fate led him in a different direction and walled him up within himself. In the splendid and terrible isolation of the will to power, measure carries no meaning.

Review and Study Questions

1. How did Napoleon view himself as the child of the French Revolution?

2. Why did Napoleon, in the end, fail in his imperial military plans?

3. Why was Madame de Staël so bitterly critical of Napoleon?

4. How does Georges Lefebvre interpret Napoleon as regards his relationship to the Revolution?

5. In your view was Napoleon a child or a betrayer of the Revolution?

Suggestions for Further Reading

Napoleon is linked inescapably with both the French Revolution that created him and with the nineteenth-century age of revolution that he created. Thus, the first category of books to be recommended for Napoleon and his age are those which treat this large topic. The best general work is probably Erich J. Hobsbawm, *The Age of Revolution: Europe 1789–1848* (Cleveland: World, 1962); it is a book of ideas rather than a factual survey, and the author is interested in the continuing social and cultural trends of the revolutionary age, in which he includes the topic of England and its industrial revolution. Of the same sort is Norman Hampson, *The First European Revolution, 1776– 1850* (New York: Harcourt, Brace and World, 1969), a brief, attractive survey and analysis which plays down the role of Napoleon in favor of the continuity of the idea of revolution. Donald Sutherland, *France 1789–1815: Revolution and Counterrevolution* (New York and Oxford: Oxford University Press, 1986) is a revisionist social history emphasizing the importance of classes and ideologies across the whole French nation. George Rudé, *Revolutionary Europe, 1783–1815* (New York: Harper & Row, 1966), is a good summary, while somewhat more comprehensive is Franklin L. Ford, *Europe, 1780–1830* (London: Longman, 1970); both are excellent, straightforward accounts.

The outstanding modern work on the French Revolution itself is Georges Lefebvre, *The French Revolution*, 2 vols., Vol. 1, tr. Elizabeth M. Evanson (New York: Columbia University Press, 1962), Vol. 2, tr. John Hall Stewart and James Friguglietti (New York: Columbia University Press, 1964), along with Lefebvre's brilliant analytical work, *The Coming of the French Revolution, 1789*, tr. R. R. Palmer (Princeton, N.J.: Princeton University Press, 1947). R. R. Palmer, *The World of the French Revolution* (New York: Harper & Row, 1969), is a highly interpretive, brief, readable, analytical survey, while M. J. Sydenham, *The French Revolution* (New York: Putnam, 1965), is a brief, largely political history. Alfred Cobban, *The Social Interpretation of the French Revolution* (Cambridge, England: Cambridge University Press, 1964), is a major critical work, revising much of the sociological theorizing about classes that had marked a generation of revolutionary studies. Cobban argues that the land-owning class eventually triumphed in revolutionary France and that in the course of the French Revolution the shift from title to property as the basis for social status was finally made. Norman Hampson, *A Social History of the French Revolution* (Toronto: Toronto University Press, 1963), is a briefer and more balanced treatment of the same themes.

Georges Lefebvre is the most important authority on Napoleon, as he is on the Revolution. See his *Napoleon*, 2 vols., Vol. 1 *Napoleon from*

18 Brumaire to Tilsit, 1799–1807, tr. H. F. Stockhold, Vol. 2 *Napoleon from Tilsit to Waterloo, 1807–1815,* tr. J. E. Anderson (New York: Columbia University Press, 1969) (the first volume is excerpted in this chapter). J. C. Herold, *The Age of Napoleon* (New York: Harper & Row, 1963), is not only a lush and beautiful book but an interpretive study; Herold is not an admirer of Napoleon and considers him at the best an ungrateful child of the Revolution. On the other hand, Robert B. Holtman, *The Napoleonic Revolution* (Philadelphia: Lippincott, 1967), sees Napoleon as a dramatic and important innovator in a score of fields, thus preserving the best gains of the Revolution. Felix M. Markham, *Napoleon and the Awakening of Europe,* "Teach Yourself History Library" (New York: Macmillan, 1954), and his *Napoleon I: Emperor of the French* (New York: New American Library, 1964) are good short biographies. Several special studies are also recommended. For military history see the good, comprehensive, straightforward account in David G. Chandler, *The Campaigns of Napoleon* (New York: Macmillan, 1966) and Owen Connelly, *Blundering to Glory: Napoleon's Military Campaigns* (Wilmington, Del.: Scholarly Resources, 1987), a brilliant study of Napoleon as a strategic improviser. For a specific detailed study of one crucial campaign, see Christopher L. Hibbert, *Waterloo: Napoleon's Last Campaign* (New York: New American Library, 1967). A related work is the dramatic and exciting Edith Saunders, *The Hundred Days* (New York: Norton, 1964). The best book on Napoleon's army is John R. Elting, *Swords around a Throne: Napoleon's Grande Armée* (London: Free Press, 1988).

Two books by R. F. Delderfield deal with the last years of Napoleon's military career, *The Retreat from Moscow* (New York: Atheneum, 1967) and *Imperial Sunset: The Fall of Napoleon, 1813–14* (Philadelphia: Chilton, 1968). An extremely interesting work on a subtopic of Napoleon is J. Christopher Herold, *Bonaparte in Egypt* (New York: Harper & Row, 1962). Pieter Geyl, *Napoleon: For and Against,* tr. Olive Renier (New Haven, Conn.: Yale University Press, 1949), is a famous book of Napoleonic historiography. Finally, highly recommended is the luminous biography by J. Christopher Herold, *Mistress to an Age: A Life of Madame de Staël* (Indianapolis, Ind.: Bobbs-Merrill, 1958).

SHAKA ZULU: "BLACK NAPOLEON"

1787	Born
1810–16	Served under Dingiswayo
1816	Became chief of the Zulus
1817–23	Conquest of Natal
1828	Died

To a remarkable extent the Zulus dominated and defined the history of southern Africa in the nineteenth century. And the man who brought this about was the warrior-chief of the Zulu nation, Shaka the father of his people.

The Zulus belonged to a large ethnic conglomerate, the Bantu. A migratory, cattle-keeping people composed of many subgroups and speaking some two hundred related languages, the Bantu had gradually moved from the north into the eastern portion of southern Africa. A large subgroup of the Bantu, the Nguni, settled in the pleasant coastal strip of rich grazing land between the Drakenberg Mountains and the Indian Ocean, between Cape Colony to the southwest and what would be the Transvaal to the north. One of the Nguni clans was the Zulu, "the people of the Heavens." But they were neither numerous nor powerful, the entire clan probably numbering fewer than two thousand people in the last years of the eighteenth century.

It was into this setting that Shaka was born about 1787. By the end of his reign Zululand had been extended over an area of eighty thousand square miles, containing nearly half a million people. The slaughter of his enemies and the magnification of his own people were the two parallel accomplishments of Shaka, "the great elephant."

From Folklore to History

E. A. RITTER

The central problem of any history of the sub-Saharan African tribal peoples is the absence of written sources. This is the case with the Zulus and their leader, Shaka. These were preliterate people and, like most such people, they preserved their history and their lore, their religion and their magic in an oral tradition scrupulously passed down from generation to generation. Even today that lore has never been systematically written down. But bits and pieces of it have found their way into white people's accounts. One of these is E. A. Ritter's Shaka Zulu: The Rise of the Zulu Empire, *excerpted below. This is a pivotal work in South African history precisely because Ritter has, as the* Manchester Guardian *reviewer wrote, "amalgamated, as perhaps no one else could have done, the printed records and the Zulu oral tradition."[1]*

Ritter was born in 1890 and raised in South Africa, where his father was a magistrate in Natal, in the heart of Zululand. The father's chief court orderly was a Zulu named Njenga-bantu Ema-Bomvini, then almost seventy. His father Mahola had been one of Shaka's fellow-soldiers in Dingiswayo's army, and Mahola had passed down to his son his own recollections of Shaka. Young Ritter's first language was Zulu, which he learned from his nurses. As a boy he was a nearly daily listener to Njenga-bantu's recitals of Shaka's deeds, "taking in every word with the same rapt attention as the other listeners. Thus was laid the foundation of his being able to see Shaka as the Zulus saw him."[2]

Ritter also had access to another aged Zulu, Chief Sigananda Cube, who, as a boy, had been a personal servant of Shaka. At the time of Sigananda's death, about 1906, he had been recognized by Pika Zulu, Shaka's great-nephew and custodian of the Zulu royal family's unwritten history, as the leading exponent of that history.

As Ritter observed, however, "when Zulus give an account of an historical event their method is not dry reportage, it is more akin to drama, and the feelings and words of all protagonists are recounted as in epic poetry."[3] This is clearly evident in Ritter's work, especially in the early part of his account of Shaka, where there are no reliable non-Zulu sources. We start there.

---

[1]*Manchester Guardian*, August 19, 1955.

[2]Ritter, *Shaka Zulu*, p. xi.

[3]*Ibid.*, p. xiv.

Shaka's father, Senzangakona, a young Chieftain of the Zulu clan, is said by the Zulu tradition to have come upon his mother, Nandi, while she was bathing in a woodland pool and, fired by her beauty, to have boldly asked for the privilege of *ama hlay endlela*.[4] To this, after some banter and mutual teasing, she consented, both parties lost their heads, broke the rules governing casual intercourse, with the result that three months later Nandi realised that she was pregnant.

As soon as Nandi's pregnancy was discovered, a messenger was rushed off bearing a formal indictment against the young Zulu chief. But Mudli, Ndaba's grandson and chief elder of the clan, indignantly denied the charge. 'Impossible,' said he, 'go back home and inform them the girl is but harbouring *I-Shaka*.'[5] But in due course Nandi became a mother. 'There now!' they sent word to the Zulu people over the hills; 'there is your beetle' (*I-Shaka*). 'Come and fetch it for it is yours.'

And reluctantly they came, and deposited Nandi, unwedded, in the hut of Senzangakona; and the child was named U-SHAKA—the year 1787.

The unhappy Nandi was now not only illicitly a mother but, what was worse, within the forbidden degrees of kindred—her mother being Mfunda, daughter of Kondlo, the Qwabe chief, with whose clan inter-marriage with the Zulus was taboo. But Senzangakona, being a chief, 'could do no wrong', and without the wedding-feast—there being no ceremonial celebration of the coming of a bride already with child—Nandi, doubly dishonoured, was quietly installed as the chief's third wife. . . . Shaka's first six years were overshadowed by the unhappiness of a mother he adored. At the age of six he went out to care for his father's sheep, with the other herd-boys; in a moment of negligence he allowed a dog to kill a sheep, his father was angry, his mother defended him, and they were dismissed from Senzangakona's kraal.

Shaka now became a herd-boy at his mother's I-Nguga kraal in E-Langeni-land, twenty miles away from his father's kraal. He was im-mediately subjected to much bullying by the elder boys, and what hurt him more deeply still was that his dear mother felt herself to be disgraced through the dismissal by her husband, and tongues were not wanting to rub this in. Thus, his years of childhood in E-Langeni-land were not happy. . . .

Modern psychology has enabled us to understand the importance in after life, of a child's unhappiness. Perhaps we may trace Shaka's subsequent lust for power to the fact that his little crinkled ears and

---

[4]A form of mock, external intercourse called "the pleasures of the road."—ED.

[5]An intestinal beetle thought to cause interruption of menstruation.—ED.

the marked stumpiness of his genital organ were ever the source of persistent ridicule among Shaka's companions, and their taunts in this regard so rankled that he grew up harbouring a deadly hatred against all and everything E-Langeni. . . .

'Never mind, my *Um-Lilwane* (Little Fire), you have got the *isibindi* (liver, meaning courage) of a lion and one day you will be the greatest chief in the land,' Nandi would tell him. 'I can see it in your eyes. When you are angry they shine like the sun, and yet no eyes can be more tender when you speak comforting words to me in my misery.' So the Zulu chroniclers give her words. . . .

In due course Shaka went to Senzangakona's kraal and went through the ceremonial rites of puberty. But when his Royal father presented him with his *umutsha*[6] he rejected it with disdain, and otherwise succeeded in getting himself so generally disliked that his early return to his mother became imperative.

Shaka had a very definite reason for deciding to continue living unclothed. He wished it to be known that he was now physically adequate. In particular he wanted all his associates of the E-Langeni tribe to see and know this, and especially his former tormentors, who would now, if anything, be envious of him. . . .

Nandi now sent the boy to her father's sister, in Mtetwa-land, near the coast. Neither Shaka nor his mother was a person of any consequence at this period; indeed, as destitute vagrants, they were everywhere despised. But the headman, under King Jobe, in charge of the district in which they settled was Ngomane, son of Mqombolo, of the Dletsheni clan, and with him they soon became acquainted. He treated Nandi and her son with a kindness which Shaka never forgot, and there in a 'real home' surrounded by sympathy Shaka at last had come to rest. . . .

The Chief of the Mtetwa tribe, with whom Shaka dwelt, had been Jobe. His sons had conspired against him, one had been put to death and the other, Godongwana, had fled. He changed his name to Dingiswayo (The Wanderer). When Jobe died, Dingiswayo returned and became chief in 1809. He revived the *Izi-cwe* (Bushmen) regiment by calling-up Shaka's age-group, including Shaka. Thus Shaka became a soldier. . . .

Shaka's commander, Buza, and in fact the whole regiment, did not fail to note the prowess of the young warrior; he was allowed to lead the giya or victory dance. Shaka was pleased with his progress, but pondered deeply over the fact that he constantly broke the light throwing assegais with his mighty stabs into the opposing warriors'

---

[6]The ceremonial loincloth or apron worn by adult Zulu men.—ED.

bodies. But the custom of hurling an assegai,[7] mostly without any effect, at a distant foe, was to him as though merely throwing one's weapon away. According to the chronicle, it was then that he conceived the idea of a single, massive-bladed assegai with a stout, short handle. This would mean fighting at close quarters, with deadly physical and psychological effect. . . .

Like other great conquerors, Shaka began his career by reforming not only tactics, but weapons. His own prowess as an infighter had shown him what was needed, but, as we have seen, he had found the throwing spear dangerously fragile when used as a striking or thrusting weapon. He was determined to get his stabbing blade which, however, had to conform with the very definite specifications formulated in his mind. . . .

The Mbonambi clan, south-eastern neighbours of the Mtetwas, were the most renowned blacksmiths and one of their best craftsmen was Ngonyama (Lion), and to him Shaka went with his problem. . . . Shaka now told him exactly what he wanted, and why, and his fervour soon infected the old 'Lion', who agreed that none of the existing blades would quite answer Shaka's purpose. . . .

'What you want, Zulu, you shall have,' responded the 'Lion' at last. 'But it will take time, for we might as well start at the very beginning. A new furnace shall be equipped with new bellows to ensure that the iron is of the best. The blade will be tempered with the strongest fats, and in your hands it will ever be victorious. It will cost me a lot, but for you I will do it for the price of one heifer, and that you may send to me when you are satisfied with my work, and in your own good time.' . . .

With the magic rites completed, Ngonyama once more became a practical and ardent blacksmith, and again the forest resounded to his hammer blows as he put all his craftsmanship into finishing and refining the blade. . . .

Thus was born the blade which was the model of others which were destined to sweep irresistibly over half a continent. As Shaka held it in his hand and gazed at it with admiration his eyes shone, but not yet had he finished with his tests. He tried it for its 'ring' and vibration, and its resiliency, and, as it had not yet been sharpened he gave a part of its forward edge a good rub on a hard sandstone provided for that purpose. It took a lot of rubbing before it became sharp, razor sharp, as Shaka demonstrated by shaving a few of the sparse hairs which grew on his arm. Then at last he was satisfied and expressed his gratitude to the smith. . . .

---

[7]The traditional Zulu spear or lance.—ED.

Very soon the *Izi-cwe* regiment was doctored again for war. . . . In the following campaign Dingiswayo took personal command of the *Izi-cwe* regiment, brigaded with the *Yengondlovu* regiment. The year was 1810 and Shaka twenty-three years old. . . .

In the ensuing battle Dingiswayo's forces are victorious.

After some twenty head of cattle had been killed for the victors and the vanquished, Dingiswayo told Buza, the commander of the Izi-cwe regiment, to present Shaka to him. He had already had a very favourable report on his first battle, and was greatly impressed by what he had seen that day.

At his first glance into the sharp and intelligent eyes of the huge young warrior, he instantly recognized a leader. After putting a number of questions to him, he was agreeably surprised at the prompt and clever replies. He then questioned Shaka on the matter of fighting without sandals, and with a single stabbing assegai, and conceded that Shaka was right as far as war only was concerned, but for the time being he was content to fight in a less sanguinary way, and to achieve his aims by persuasion with the minimum employment of force. However, after conferring with Buza and Ngomane, he there and then promoted Shaka to Captain of 'one hundred', or the equivalent of a leader of two 'guilds', and also presented him with ten head of cattle. . . .

Shaka now joined the other two regimental commanders and the headmen who were in attendance on Dingiswayo, and the heads of the contingents supplied by allied tribes. Presently the campaign was discussed and Shaka remained silent whilst his seniors gave their opinions. In fact he said nothing until he was invited by Dingiswayo to speak.

Shaka then said that in the next battle the army should be drawn up with a central head and chest, with half a regiment on each side thrown out as enveloping horns to ensure the complete annihilation of the enemy force. Only thus would they gain the complete submission of the remnants of the tribe, and do away with the periodical reconquests necessitated by the present easygoing methods which had proved to be so futile and inconclusive. Moreover, in future campaigns the broad-bladed, stout stabbing assegai should replace the light throwing spears, and sandals should be discarded to increase the mobility of the warriors.

Dingiswayo conceded the advantages in an *impi ebomvu* (red war, or war to a finish), but emphasized again that he did not wish to destroy, but merely to teach a lesson, whereupon Shaka sharply rejoined, 'Which will never be learned'. . . .

Nevertheless, Shaka continued to be a successful war leader and to be advanced by Dingiswayo.

Shaka was now promoted to Commander-in-Chief of all Dingiswayo's armed forces, and a member of the inner Council. As such, he insisted on visiting each military kraal in rotation to tighten up the discipline and extend the drill with rapid forced route marches. In fact he constituted himself an Inspector-General of the Forces. . . .

Towards the end of 1815 Senzangakona's health rapidly declined, and early in 1816 he died. Weak and wasted, he had in the end given way to the incessant importuning of his eighth wife, Bibi, to appoint her son Sigujana as his successor. . . . When Shaka and Dingiswayo heard that Sigujana had appropriated the chieftaincy by prevailing upon the dying Senzangakona to nominate him, the former was furious, and the latter much annoyed, as he had not been advised or consulted. . . .

Dingiswayo now summoned Shaka and told him to take over the chieftaincy of the Zulu clan. He put at his disposal the 2nd Izi-cwe regiment (subsequently known as 'Ngomane's Own'), which had recently been formed under Shaka's energetic recruiting policy for the expansion of Dingiswayo's armed forces. He also provided him with an imposing staff, headed by Ngomane and Dingiswayo's own nephew, Siwangu of Mbikwane. At the head of this triumphal and irresistible force Shaka entered his father's Esi-Klebeni kraal—the home of his childhood days.

With his immense size—perfectly proportioned—and in his full gala dress, his regal, dignified bearing, the easy grace of all his movements, his piercing eyes set in a strong, stern face, and the general look of authority, made plain to all that here was a warrior-king indeed. . . .

Ngomane now advanced to address the headmen of the Zulu clan, who, each with their following, had been assembled for the occasion.

'Children of Zulu! To-day I present to you Shaka, son of Senzangakona, son of Jama, descended from Zulu, as your lawful chief. So says the "Great One" (Dingiswayo) whose mouth I am. Is there anyone here who can contest the righteousness of this decision? If so, let him stand forth and speak now, or hereafter be silent.' . . .

'No one speaks,' said Ngomane, 'then salute your chief.' . . .

Finding that he had no army, Shaka at once called up the whole manhood of the Zulus, capable of bearing arms. . . . Shaka was tireless in getting his little army into shape. Nearly every day he visited one of his two other military kraals and woe betide the defaulters. His kingdom was so small—a paltry ten miles by ten—that from his central position he could reach any of its confines within an hour. . . .

Shaka, having effected all his reforms in his own tribe, proposed to extend his reformative and retributive activities. He had dealt with individuals; now he would deal with clans, beginning with the E-Langeni, of which his own mother was a daughter, in which he and she had spent those first hideous years of exile and sorrow, and where they had been so cruelly treated. His army was now a war machine indeed. He marshalled it and made a night march of twenty-five miles over the Mtonjaneni Heights to E-Langeni-land. Before dawn he had silently surrounded the Esiweni kraal, the capital of Makedama, the E-Langeni chief. As soon as it became light the chief was summoned to surrender, and he did so without any waste of time.

Shaka ordered all the inhabitants to be brought before him, and singled out all those who, so many years before, had inflicted untold misery on his mother and himself. Some other kraals which harboured his youthful tormentors had also been surrounded by detachments of the army, and their inhabitants were also brought up for scrutiny and judgment. . . .

Whilst this was being done Shaka called for two bowls of water, and then deliberately disrobed in front of all the gathering. The bound men on the left were ordered to approach and squat on their haunches. Shaka then arose and towered over them.

'You will all die,' he roared. Then after a dreadful pause he resumed in deep, even tones, 'Before I tell you the manner of your going there are some things I have to say to you. You are such a filthy collection of *utuvi* (excrement) that the very sight of you contaminates me, and I must wash before I proceed.' Very deliberately he now poured water over his head, and rinsed his whole body carefully, until the first bowl was empty. Then he reminded them of how they had sneered at his bodily inadequacy and bade them note that they had lied. . . .

'This is the death I have in mind for you. The slayers will sharpen the projecting upright poles in this cattle-kraal—one for each of you. They will then lead you there, and four of them will pick you up singly and impale you on each of the sharpened poles. There you will stay till you die, and your bodies, or what will be left of them by the birds, will stay there as a testimony to all, what punishment awaits those who slander me and my mother.' As the anguished victims were led away Shaka taunted them with 'Hlalani gahle' ('Sit you well!' not the customary 'Salani gahle!' i.e. 'Stay you well'). Then he ordered the second bowl of water, and again washed his whole body to 'cleanse it from the last defiling look' of those he had sent to their doom. . . .

After a time Shaka sent orders to the slayers to end the death agonies of the victims by placing bundles of grass under them and firing them. As the flames licked about them, those who were still conscious shrieked out in their death agonies, which were now short-lived.

The White Man's History of Shaka

HENRY FRANCIS FYNN

White people first came to Zululand in 1824. Francis George Farewell, a Capetown businessman; James Saunders King, the captain of a coastal brig; and several other investors formed the Farewell Trading Company at Port Natal, a harbor about a hundred miles south of Shaka's home kraal. Shortly the company was joined by a young Englishman, Henry Francis Fynn, who had been educated at Christ's Hospital in London and had worked for a while as a surgeon's assistant, but had decided to come to South Africa looking for adventure. He had already learned some African dialects when he joined the Farewell Trading Company. He discovered from the natives near Port Natal that the land they had settled on—indeed all of Natal—was Shaka's personal domain. Fynn decided to visit the great Zulu chief. On his first venture to the north along the coast he came across one of Shaka's military parties and watched in amazement as some 20,000 warriors tramped past him. Fynn sent word ahead that he wanted to meet with the chief, but Shaka was not ready, and bade him return to Port Natal; he did send him a gift of ivory and forty head of cattle.

Later that summer of 1824 Shaka invited the white men to visit his kraal. Farewell and Fynn and several others mounted their horses, packed an assortment of gifts, and set out in mid-July. Fynn, of course, took his medical kit. After meeting Shaka and exchanging gifts, the party returned to Port Natal, but Fynn stayed on. He quickly became fluent in Zulu and was to be in more or less constant contact with Shaka for the next four years. He would later write his account of his adventures, based on his diary, from which the following excerpt is taken.

On entering the great cattle kraal we found drawn up within it about 80,000 natives in their war attire. Mbikwana[8] requested me to gallop within the circle, and immediately on my starting to do so one general shout broke forth from the whole mass, all pointing at me with their sticks. I was asked to gallop round the circle two or three times in the midst of tremendous shouting. . . .

Mbikwana, standing in our midst, addressed some unseen individ-

---

[8]The leader of their native servants, who served as interpreter.—ED.

ual in a long speech, in the course of which we were frequently called upon by him to answer "*Ye6o*," that is to affirm as being true all he was saying, though perfectly ignorant of what was being said.

While the speech was being made I caught sight of an individual in the background whom I concluded to be Shaka, and, turning to Farewell, pointed out and said: "Farewell, there is Shaka." This was sufficiently audible for him to hear and perceive that I had recognised him. He immediately held up his hand, shaking his finger at me approvingly. Farewell, being near-sighted and using an eye-glass, could not distinguish him.

Elephant tusks were then brought forward. One was laid before Farewell and another before me. Shaka then raised the stick in his hand and after striking with it right and left, the whole mass broke from their position and formed up into regiments. Portions of each of these rushed to the river and the surrounding hills, while the remainder, forming themselves into a circle, commenced dancing with Shaka in their midst.

It was a most exciting scene, surprising to us, who could not have imagined that a nation termed "savages" could be so disciplined and kept in order.

Regiments of girls, headed by officers of their own sex, then entered the centre of the arena to the number of 8,000–10,000, each holding a slight staff in her hand. They joined in the dance, which continued for about two hours. . . .

The people now dispersed, and he directed a chief to lead us to a kraal where we could pitch our tents. He sent us a sheep, a basket of corn, an ox, and a pot of beer, about three gallons. At seven o'clock, we sent up four rockets and fired off eight guns. He sent people to look at these, but from fear did not show himself out of his hut. The following morning we were requested to mount our horses and proceed to the King's quarters. We found him sitting under a tree at the upper end of the kraal decorating himself and surrounded by about 200 people. . . .

While he was dressing himself, his people proceeded, as on the day before, to show droves of cattle, which were still flocking in, repeatedly varying the scene with singing and dancing. In the meantime, we observed Shaka gave orders for a man standing close to us to be killed, for what crime we could not learn, but we soon found this to be a very common occurrence.

Mr. Petersen, unfortunately, at this moment placed a musical box on the ground, and, striking it with a switch, moved the stop. Shaka heard the music. It seemed to produce in him a superstitious feeling. He turned away with evident displeasure and went back immediately to the dance.

Those portions of regiments which had separated prior to the dance now returned from the river and from behind the adjoining hills, driving before them immense herds of cattle. A grand cattle show was now being arranged. Each regiment drove towards us thousands of cattle that had been allotted to their respective barracks, the colour of each regiment's cattle corresponding with that of the shield the men carried, which, in turn, served to distinguish one regiment from another. No cattle of differing colour from those allotted to a given regiment were allowed to intermix. . . .

Two oxen were slaughtered for us. After dinner we prepared to retire, but messengers from Shaka requested us to go to him, with Jacob the interpreter. I was then led into the seraglio, where I found him seated in a carved wooden chair and surrounded by about 400 girls, two or three chiefs and two servants in attendance.

My name Fynn had been converted into Sofili by the people in general; by this, after desiring me to sit in front of him, he several times accosted me in the course of the following dialogue:

"I hear you have come from umGeorge, is it so? Is he as great a king as I am?"

Fynn: "Yes; King George is one of the greatest kings in the world."

Shaka: "I am very angry with you," said while putting on a severe countenance. "I shall send a messenger to umGeorge and request him to kill you. He sent you to me not to give medicine to my dogs." All present immediately applauded what Shaka had said. "Why did you give my dogs medicine?" (in allusion to the woman I was said to have brought back to life after death).[9]

Fynn: "It is a practice of our country to help those who are in need, if able to do so."

Shaka: "Are you then the doctor of dogs? You were sent here to be my doctor."

Fynn: "I am not a doctor and not considered by my countrymen to be one."

Shaka: "Have you medicine by you?"

Fynn: "Yes."

Shaka: "Then cure me, or I will have you sent to umGeorge to have you killed."

Fynn: "What is the matter with you?"

Shaka: "That is your business to find out."

Fynn: "Stand up and let me see your person."

Shaka: "Why should I stand up?"

---

[9]Some time had passed and this was an incident which had occurred several days before.—ED.

Fynn: "That I may see if I can find out what ails you."

Shaka stood up but evidently disliked my approaching him closely. A number of girls held up lighted torches. I looked about his person and, after reflecting on the great activity he had shown during the day, was satisfied he had not much the matter with him. I, however, observed numerous black marks on his loins where native doctors had scarified him, and at once said he had pains in his loins. He held his hand before his mouth in astonishment, upon which my wisdom was applauded by all present. Shaka then strictly charged me not to give medicine to his dogs, and, after a few commonplace questions in which he showed good humour, I was permitted to retire for the night. . . .

The following day had been appointed by Shaka for receiving our present, which, fortunately, had been well chosen by Farewell for presentation to so superior a chief as Shaka. It consisted of every description of beads at that time procurable in Cape Town, and far superior to those Shaka had previously obtained from the Portuguese at Delagoa. There was a great variety of woollen blankets, a large quantity of brass bars, turned and lacquered, and sheets of copper, also pigeons, a pig, cats and dogs. There was, moreover, a full-dress military coat, with epaulettes covered with gold lace. Though Shaka showed no open gratitude, we saw clearly that he was satisfied. He was very interested in the live animals, especially the pig, until it got into his milk stores where it committed great havoc, and set all the women in the seraglio screaming for assistance. All this ended in the pig being killed.

The showing of cattle and dancing continued during the day, whilst other regiments, which had come from a great distance, arrived and took part in the festivities. . . .

In conversation on our object in coming to Natal, this part of South Africa, Shaka showed great desire that we should live at the port. Each evening he sent for me and conversed with me through the Kaffir Jacob, the interpreter, for three or four hours.

On the first day of our visit we had seen no less than ten men carried off to death. On a mere sign by Shaka, viz: the pointing of his finger, the victim would be seized by his nearest neighbours; his neck would be twisted, and his head and body beaten with sticks, the nobs of some of these being as large as a man's fist. On each succeeding day, too, numbers of others were killed; their bodies would then be carried to an adjoining hill and there impaled. We visited this spot on the fourth day. It was truly a Golgotha, swarming with hundreds of vultures. The effects of this together with the scenes of death made Mr. Petersen decide at once to dissolve the partnership and leave for the Cape. . . .

During Fynn's visit an assassination attempt is made on Shaka's life, apparently at the instance of a distant rival chief. Fynn is summoned.

I immediately washed the wound with camomile tea and bound it up with linen. He had been stabbed with an assegai through the left arm, and the blade had passed through the ribs under the left breast. It had made the King spit blood. I could not account for the assegai not entering the lungs; it must have been due to mere accident; I was for some time in doubt. His own doctor, who seemed to have a good knowledge of that nature, also attended him. He gave the King a vomit and afterwards administered purges and continually washed the wound with decoctions of cooling roots. He also probed the wound to ascertain if any poison had been used on the assegai.

Shaka cried nearly the whole night, expecting that only fatal consequences would ensue. The crowd had now increased so much that the noise of their shrieks became unbearable, and this noise continued throughout the night. Morning showed a horrid sight in a clear light. I am satisfied I cannot describe the horrid scene in language powerful enough to enable the reader, who has never been similarly situated, to appreciate it aright. The immense crowds of people that arrived hour after hour from every direction began their shouting on coming in sight of the kraal, running and exerting their utmost powers of voice as they entered it and joined those who had got there before them. They then pulled one another about, men and women throwing themselves down in every direction without taking care how they fell. Great numbers fainted from over exertion and excessive heat. The females of the seraglio, more particularly, were in very great distress, having overtaxed themselves during the night. They suffered from the excessive heat and from want of nourishment, which no one dared to touch, whilst the four brass collars each had, fitting so tightly round the neck as to make it impossible for the wearer to turn her head, nearly suffocated them. Several of them died. Finding their situation so distressing, and there being no one to afford them relief, I poured a quantity of water and threw it over them as they fell; this went on till I was myself so tired as to be obliged to desist. They then made some attempt to help one another.

All this time I had been so busily employed as not to see the most sickening part of this tragical scene. They had now begun to kill one another. Some were put to death because they did not cry, others for putting spittle into their eyes, others for sitting down to cry, although strength and tears, after such continuous mourning and exertion, were quite exhausted. No such limits were taken into account.

We then understood that six men had been wounded by the assassins who wounded Shaka. From the road they took, it was supposed that they had been sent by Zwide, King of the Ndwandwes (Ndwandwe tribe), who was Shaka's only powerful enemy. Two regiments were accordingly sent off at once in search of the aggressors.

In the meantime the medicines which, on his leaving, Mr. Farewell had promised to send were received. They came very opportunely, and Shaka was much gratified. I now washed his wounds frequently, and gave him mild purgatives. I, moreover, dressed his wounds with ointment. The King was in a hopeless condition for four days. During all that time people were continuing to flock in from the outskirts of his country and joining in the general tumult. It was not till the fourth day that cattle were killed for the sustenance of the multitude. Many had died in the interval, and many had been killed for not mourning, or for having gone to their kraals for food.

On the fifth day there were symptoms of improvement in the King's condition; these favourable indications were also noticeable on the day following.

At noon on that day the party sent out in search of the would-be murderers returned, bringing with them the dead bodies of three men whom they had killed in the bush (jungle). These were the supposed assassins. The bodies, having been carried off, were laid on the ground in a roadway about a mile from the kraal. Their right ears were then cut off and the two pursuing regiments sat down on either side of the road, while the whole of the people, men and women, who had assembled at the kraal, probably exceeding 30,000, passed up the road crying and yelling. Each one, on coming up to the bodies, struck them several blows with a stick, which was then left at the spot, so that nothing more of these was to be seen; only an immense pile of sticks remained, but the formal ceremony still went on. The whole body now collecting, and three men walking in advance with sticks on which were the ears of the dead and now shattered bodies, the procession moved to Shaka's kraal. The King now made his appearance. The national mourning song was chanted. After this a fire was made in the centre of the cattle kraal where the ears were burnt to ashes. . . .

Early in 1828 Shaka sent his army south to raid clear to the Cape Colony border. When they returned he sent them far to the north. Such random, irrational behavior apparently gave his two brothers their long-awaited opportunity to assassinate Shaka.

During the life of Shaka his despotic sway was so feared that his name was seldom mentioned but as the form of an oath, and much more dangerous was the attempt to trace in any way the particulars of his family, who were not permitted publicly to be known as his relatives. His brothers, though numerous, were not allowed to call themselves so, except Ngwadi, brother on his mother's side. Dingane and Mhlangana were only partially known, the former much resembling Shaka in person. Their apparent fondness was so great that one was seldom seen without the other. In the same house lived Mɓopha, son of Sithayi, a Zulu chief and principal servant of Shaka. These were the three conspirators who put Shaka to death. . . .

On the 24th September, 1828, Shaka, while taking his usual sleep at midday, dreamt he was killed and Mɓopha's sister, one of the seraglio, knowing the result would be likely to prove her brother's death, told him what had transpired, to give him an opportunity of killing a cow as soon as possible, to invoke his spirit. This information induced Mɓopha to urge his accomplices. Some Bechuanas arriving with crane feathers, which Shaka had long expected, these people were brought to him, he being in a small kraal he had built about 50 yards from Dukuza, calling it Nyakomuɓi or Ugly Year. There he went to receive them. The two brothers, being informed of it by Mɓopha, took a circuitous route to come in at the back of the kraal, having concealed assegais under their karosses, and sat behind the fence. Shaka asked the Bechuanas what had detained them so long, in a harsh tone. Mɓopha immediately threw a stick at them. They ran away instantly, supposing it the signal for their death, which had been given to Mɓopha by Shaka unperceived by them, as was his custom in those cases. Shaka asking why he had struck them, Mhlangana embraced the opportunity and, from behind the fence, stabbed at the back of his left shoulder. Shaka had only time to look round and, seeing the two brothers, exclaim: "What is the matter, children of my father?" when Dingane stabbed him. He then threw the blanket from him and, taking the assegai from his side with which Dingane had stabbed him, fell dead near the kraal gate.

A Modern Shaka

BRIAN ROBERTS

The Zulu Kings, *by Brian Roberts, from which the following excerpt is taken, has been called "the first tempered account we have of Shaka and the rise of the Zulu nation."*[10] *He presents us with a healthy skepticism about*

---

[10]*New York Times Book Review,* July 20, 1975, p. 20.

the reports of Europeans such as Fynn. Like E. A. Ritter, Roberts relied on records derived from Zulu oral tradition. But where Ritter tended to reflect the colonial attitudes of the turn of the century, Roberts reflects careful modern research and a skillful reading of both Zulu and non-Zulu sources. He has created both a "plausible" and a "not unsympathetic picture"[11] of Shaka. His assessment follows.

As far as is known, Shaka was forty-one when he died. If he had come to power in 1817—the year Dingiswayo is said to have died—he had been the effective ruler of Zululand for eleven years. In that time he had forged one of the mightiest empires the African continent has ever known. Under his leadership, his small insignificant clan had risen from obscurity and given their name to an all-powerful nation. During his lifetime the Zulu army had been organised into a fearsome military machine which had transformed the age-old pattern of southern African society. The Nguni system of clanships and petty chieftainships had been replaced by a single, authoritarian state, feared by its neighbours and acknowledged far beyond its borders. Few leaders in history have accomplished so much, so quickly. Shaka not only established Zulu supremacy but ensured the lasting renown of his nation. For generations to come the word Zulu was to be synonymous with might. It was an awe-inspiring achievement.

But, like all such achievements, it was not come by gently. Shaka was a tyrant; he could have been nothing else. He rose amid appalling bloodshed. It has been estimated that no less than two million people died as a result of the upheavals created by Shaka. When the white men first arrived in Natal, they found the country desolate, the landscape littered with skeletons. Shaka reigned supreme because he had obliterated all semblance of opposition. He took no advice, he demanded blind obedience; he was intolerant, ruthless and inflexible. He knew nothing of the softer virtues, had he done so he would not have achieved what he did: his strength was derived from his callousness.

Living as he did, in the first quarter of the nineteenth century, it was inevitable that he should be compared with a contemporary despot: he has been called the Black Napoleon. But the comparison is more romantic than real. The system instigated by Shaka was unique. To compare it, even superficially, with that of a European power is misleading. The aims, methods and values of the white men were unknown to Shaka. The society he ruled and the opponents he fought were so far removed from the regimes of nineteenth-century Europe that to set his achievements against those of a sophisticated

---

[11]*Atlantic*, June 1975 (235), p. 95.

conqueror like Napoleon is meaningless. Shaka had no set objectives and was uninfluenced by political and moral considerations. He was guided by intuition; he learned from his own experience. It is necessary to realise this to appreciate his extraordinary genius.

Shocking as was his apparent cruelty, this also must be judged in isolation. The ethics of the white man meant nothing to him. He relied on his own interpretation of humanity. Treachery, disobedience and cowardice were, for him, the cardinal sins; he did not regard life as sacred—any more than did most of his subjects. When white men, fresh from Regency England, were plunged into a society that recognised none of their values, they were appalled. The fact that that society was rigidly organised only increased their horror: the frightful punishments inflicted by Shaka appeared to them all the more cold blooded. It was difficult to reconcile fine discipline with primitive values. But there was nothing so exceptional about the grim Zulu penal code. Shaka was by no means the only African ruler to order summary executions; he was, however, one of the few whose activities have been reported in vivid detail.

One must accept that European and African values were often irreconcilable. Nowhere was this divergence more apparent than in an early conversation between Fynn and Shaka. The Zulu King was flabbergasted to learn that the white men imprisoned offenders for months, even years. Such punishment seemed to him far more sadistic than the tortures he inflicted. To kill a man, however painfully, was preferable to the living death of confinement. As a warrior he could imagine nothing worse than a long, meaningless captivity. . . .

Reports of Shaka spread by the traders, make him appear an unnatural fiend whose activities went far beyond the dictates of even the most primitive code. He is shown as a mass murderer, a depraved ogre who revelled in the tortures he devised and drooled over his victims. 'History,' said James Saunders King, 'perhaps does not furnish an instance of a more despotic and cruel monster than Chaka.' . . . Anyone wishing to present a lively picture of the monster Shaka can find plenty of material in *Travels and Adventures in Eastern Africa* by Nathaniel Isaacs.[12] It does not do, however, to enquire too deeply into the authenticity of Isaacs's account. Many of his observations on Natal and Zulu customs are undoubtedly accurate and will be of lasting value. But when he comes to deal with the terrible Shaka his comments are, to say the least, suspect. . . .

---

[12]Nathaniel Isaacs came to Port Natal somewhat later than Fynn and only knew Shaka at the very end of his reign. His work, however, is second only to Fynn's in value as a contemporary account.—Ed.

Fynn was more honest, less sensational. His account is far more factual; it contains none of the purple patches Isaacs delighted in. . . . [Nevertheless he] had some covering up to do. What is more, his so-called 'diary' was written many years after the events it describes. He is said to have lost the original notes he was collecting for his book when they were mistakenly buried with his brother Frank and he thus had 'to rewrite the whole of the contents from memory as well as he could'. Unfortunately his memory was not all that reliable. The re-written notes were fragmentary; often he gives more than one version of a single incident; invariably the versions differ. It is possible that, when recalling some events, he was influenced by Isaac's *Travels and Adventures in Eastern Africa*.

Fynn does not dwell on Shaka's sadism to the same extent as does Isaacs. Nevertheless he gives many examples of torture and executions. The executions mostly result from some offence to Shaka, often a trivial offence. Fynn says, for instance: 'On one occasion I witnessed 60 boys under 12 years of age despatched before he had breakfasted.' Precisely why these boys were killed he does not say. The implication would seem to be that Shaka did not require a reason for butchery. . . .

What is difficult to understand is the reaction of the traders. If they really believed that Shaka was a capricious, indiscriminate killer, then why did they remain in Natal? They were given repeated opportunities to leave but they refused them all. One would have thought that, with a monster like Shaka breathing down their necks, there would have been a mad scramble to board the first ship that called at Port Natal. Yet Farewell, Fynn, Cane and Ogle stayed for four years under Shaka; King, Isaacs, Hutton and the seamen were there three years. Young boys like Thomas Halstead and John Ross wandered about the country, apparently without fear. King even brought Farewell's wife to Natal.

Did they really think they would be protected by their white skins and magic medicines? Or were they so self-seeking that they were willing to risk their necks for a haul of ivory? Given their picture of Shaka, neither explanation is particularly convincing. A man who murdered his own family and wilfully massacred his own people could hardly be relied upon to respect a difference in skin colour indefinitely. Their medicines were limited and by no means infallible. Shaka is said to have commanded an army of 30,000; if, in one of his unpredictable moods, he had turned against the traders, their fire-arms would have counted for nothing. The chance of a fortune might have inspired them to take a reasonable risk, but it does not explain why they—down to the last seaman—willingly remained at the uncertain mercy of a savage extremist. . . .

But the undeniable fact is that the traders did not recoil 'at the serpent's hiss or the lion's growl'. They stayed on for years with this terrifying fiend who, according to Isaacs, was continually threatening their lives. James Saunders King tried desperately to force the British to occupy Port Natal and thus provide the traders with protection, but his failure to achieve this did not prevent him, or the others, from returning to the Zulu territory. Just how afraid of Shaka were the traders?

There can be little doubt that the tortures and executions described by Isaacs and Fynn did take place. This was part of the Zulu system and was to be observed, independently, by others who later visited those Zulu rulers trained at Shaka's court. Painful death was the inevitable punishment for those who offended the King: and the King was easily offended. An ill-suppressed cough, sneeze or fart in the royal presence could result in a menacing finger being raised and the executioners moving in. The sixty boys whom Fynn says were put to death before breakfast might have done no more than titter at a serious gathering. Immediate death was the only punishment allowed for such offence. Was this, as Isaacs suggests, simply the means by which Shaka indulged a sadistic whim? If it was, then the traders had good reasons for their professed fears.

But it seems more likely that Shaka's behaviour was not as erratic as they pretended. The Zulu system was based on a harsh, rigid, but recognisable discipline. By means of this discipline Shaka had made his army invincible; in the same way he had ensured his supremacy. From Fynn's description of the mass hysteria which was so easily generated among Shaka's subjects, it is obvious that the Zulu nation could never have reached the heights it did under a ruler less severe and determined than Shaka. To say this is not to excuse a cruel despotism, but to understand the motivations of an intelligent but barbarous ruler. Only by resorting to the abnormal could Shaka—like many another tyrant—retain his hold over his people.

The traders must have recognised this. They, as well as Shaka's subjects, must have been aware of the disciplinary code laid down by the King. They must have realised that, as long as they observed that code, they were safe. Safer in fact than a more ignorant and emotional Zulu. . . .

The only first-hand, detailed reports of Shaka are those given by his white visitors. Knowledge of the first Zulu King depends entirely on the biased observations of Isaacs and Fynn. Stripped of their subjective judgements, the few facts to emerge from these accounts are not entirely to Shaka's detriment. Confronted by a group of strange white men, with seemingly mysterious powers, the King offered them friendship when he might have destroyed them from fear. He not only welcomed them but gave every indication of wishing to meet their fellows. He granted them land, he supplied them with ivory, he fell in with their schemes. He stood between them and the wrath of his people. While Shaka lived no white man in Natal was harmed.

It is unfortunate that no contemporary Zulu account of Shaka exists. Did his people loath him as his enemies—both white and black—later maintained? There seems little evidence to support such a claim. Not even Fynn and Isaacs suggest the possibility of a popular rising against Shaka. The only recorded assassination attempt on the King, apart from that which killed him, was, as far as one can tell, that of an enemy agent. This might be explained, in part, by Shaka's iron-handed rule. Nevertheless, the Zulu were a warrior race, by no means servile, and when Shaka's brothers decided to strike they did so with relative ease. If discontent under Shaka was widespread, it was certainly not apparent.

But there is further evidence in Shaka's favour. Zulu sources are not entirely silent on the founder of their nation. Far from it. For generations oral tradition has hailed Shaka as the greatest of Zulu heroes. His name is frequently invoked in Zulu councils, his example is cited as a supreme authority. Any criticism of Shaka can, and often does, earn a sharp rebuke from Zulu elders and statesmen. He is the subject of eulogistic praise chants and poems; the hero of more than one African novel. The Zulu people have erected a monument in his honour at the site of his Dukuza kraal. When, in 1972, the Zulu Territorial Authority nominated a national day for the newly created kwaZulu, they chose the anniversary of their founder's assassination: Shaka's Day.

Review and Study Questions

1. Can the unwritten, oral tradition of such a preliterate people as the Zulus serve as an authentic source for their history?
2. What reforms did Shaka undertake to turn his army into a superb fighting force?
3. Why, do you imagine, did Shaka receive the white men so favorably?
4. How do you assess the nature of Shaka's accomplishments? Were they important in the history of southern Africa?
5. Could Shaka be described as "the Black Napoleon"?

Suggestions for Further Reading

No written Zulu account of the oral tradition about Shaka exists. We have already noted the skillful and sympathetic use of portions of that tradition by E. A. Ritter, *Shaka Zulu: The Rise of the Zulu Empire* (London: Longmans, Green and Co., 1965), excerpted for this chapter. Probably the closest thing we have to an authentic ethno-history of the Zulus is in two works by A. T. Bryant, *The Zulu People as They Were Before the White Man Came* (New York: Negro Universities Press, 1970 [1948]) and *Olden Times in Zululand and Natal* (London and New York: Longmans, Green and Co., 1929), both compendia of Zulu customs and behavior written by a missionary and the most credible Zulu scholar and linguist of the early part of this century.

Of the two important European contemporary accounts of Shaka, the best is *The Diary of Henry Francis Fynn*, ed. James Stuart and D. McK. Malcolm (Pietermaritzburg: Shuter and Shooter, 1950), excerpted for this chapter. But Nathaniel Isaacs, *Travels and Adventures in Eastern Africa . . .* ed. Louis Herman and Percival R. Kirby (Cape Town: C. Struik, 1970) is worthwhile too.

Ritter's book, *Shaka Zulu*, is the only biography of Shaka. But there are several good works on Zulu history that treat him very fully. One of the best is Brian Roberts, *The Zulu Kings* (New York: Charles Scribner's Sons, 1974), excerpted for this chapter. Two excellent ones are also Donald R. Morris, *The Washing of the Spears: A History of the Rise of the Zulu Nation under Shaka and Its Fall in the Zulu War of 1879* (New York: Simon & Schuster, 1965) and T. V. Bulpin, *Natal and the Zulu Country* (Cape Town: Books of Africa, Ltd., 1969).

Some of the more general works on African history are useful in providing a context within which to understand particular leaders and peoples, like Shaka and the Zulus. One of the best and most comprehensive is *The Cambridge History of Africa*, vol. 5, from c. 1790 to c. 1870, ed. John E. Flint (Cambridge et al.: Cambridge University Press, 1976). Though smaller in scope, two other good general African histories are Robert W. July, *A History of the African People*, 3rd ed. (New York: Scribner, 1980) and Robin Hallett, *Africa to 1875: A Modern History* (Ann Arbor: University of Michigan Press, 1970). An elegant and handsome book, though not as useful as the two preceeding ones, is *The Horizon History of Africa* (New York: American Heritage Publishing Co., 1971). Finally, there is an interesting work by the French anthropologist Jacques Maquet, *Civilizations of Black Africa*, tr. and rev. Joan Rayfield (New York: Oxford University Press, 1972) which presents a series of typologies, e.g., "The Civilization of the Bow," "The Civilization of the Granaries," and, including the Zulus, "The Civilization of the Spear."

CECIL RHODES AND THE DREAM OF EMPIRE

1853	Born
1870	First came to South Africa
1888	Formation of De Beers Mining Company
1890	Prime Minister of Cape Colony
1894	Establishment of Rhodesia
1895	Jameson's Raid
1899–1902	Boer War
1902	Died

If the history of Europe in the second half of the nineteenth century was dominated by Bismarck's German Empire, that of the rest of the world was dominated by the imperial England of Queen Victoria. For in that half century the British Empire reached its greatest extent, and England became the model colonial power of the modern world.

The process had begun centuries before, with the expansion of Europe at the end of the Middle Ages, with the age of exploration and the creation of the first great colonial empires of Portugal and Spain. They were followed by the Dutch, the French, and the British. Colonial rivalries became issues between the major European powers in the seventeenth and eighteenth centuries. But with the coming of the Industrial Revolution, the nature of colonialism was dramatically altered, along with nearly everything else in the modern world.

Interest in underdeveloped areas had formerly been largely commercial and mercantile; it now became exploitative. The Western industrial nations needed raw materials for their factories—rubber, petroleum, copra, hemp, jute, cotton, lumber, copper. European populations demanded vast quantities of meat and grain and such products as coffee, tea, and tobacco. At the same time, the underdeveloped countries of the world represented a new market for industrial goods—for many of which the need itself had to be fabricated as well as the goods.

The industrialized nations turned not only to the colonies they already had but to the entire area now popularly called the Third World. They invested enormous amounts of capital, which was to be protected by their military forces. Colonial policy became an extension of national economic policy. When necessary, both political and economic interests manipulated native political naïveté and exploited native labor, usually with the greedy collusion of native political leaders. Colonialism and all its practices were justified as bringing the blessings of civilization to the less fortunate peoples of the world. By most civilized people this was regarded not only as an opportunity but an obligation, to "take up the white man's burden." Part of that burden was, of course, the responsibility of bringing God's word to the remote places and heathen populations now beginning to become known. Throngs of missionaries went out to establish schools, hospitals, and churches. They were often spectacularly successful. But they were sometimes killed, and when this happened, their martyrdom became the provocation for further extension of colonial control. Even the ideas of Darwin were converted into a social gospel and used to justify the supremacy of the Western industrial nations over the poor, uneducated, "less favored," and usually nonwhite peoples of the world.

As Great Britain was the leading industrial power of modern Europe, it was also the leading colonial power. But even imperial Britain was not without rivals in the competition for colonies and spheres of colonial influence—in China, the East Indies, and Southeast Asia; in the Middle East, in Persia, in the lands of the rotting Ottoman Empire, and along the borders of British India. But it was in Africa that the most savage scramble for colonies took place. Even Bismarck's Germany belatedly entered the race.

This was the scene upon which Cecil John Rhodes came in 1870. He was only seventeen years old, the son of a poor Hertfordshire parson. He had been diagnosed as suffering from incipient tuberculosis and, for his health, had decided to join his older brother in South Africa. Shortly after Rhodes's arrival there, the great Kimberley diamond strike was made. Rhodes made his first fortune in this enterprise, and multiplied it many times over by his business acumen. He consolidated existing claims, refinanced bankrupt operations, bought others, and opened new ones. By 1887 his holdings were second only to those of the main Kimberley mine, held by a rough-and-ready diamond merchant and financial genius named Barnett "Barney" Barnato. With backing from the Rothschild Bank, Rhodes bought out his larger rival the following year for more than five million pounds. Thus, he secured absolute control of South African diamond production for his De Beers Consolidated Mines Ltd., the name retained from a former company he had taken over. At the same time, he was deeply involved in gold and had formed the powerful Gold Fields of South Africa Company.

At intervals between making fortunes and suffering bouts of recurring illness, Rhodes had managed to return to England for several periods of residency at Oxford University, from which he was graduated in 1881. In that same year, he stood successfully for the Cape Parliament, and his political career began. Politics to Rhodes was simply business by other means, and he was equally successful at it. He quickly became a dominant figure in South African public life. But Rhodes was a British imperialist to the bone. As he looked to the north, he envisioned British dominion from Cape Colony not only across the Zambezi River to the great lakes of central Africa but to the Sudan and eventually Cairo—to "paint the map of Africa red," as he put it.

Immediately to the north of Cape Colony lay a vast land controlled by native chieftains. The most important of them was Lobengula, King of the Matabele. Rhodes negotiated with him, at the same time hoping to persuade either the Cape government or the British to support his negotiation. Neither was prepared. So Rhodes formed another company, the British South Africa Company, secured a charter for it, and carried through his own negotiations. As a result, he gained virtually sovereign control over the area that would become modern Rhodesia.

Rhodes's further plans were blocked by the opposition of the Boers. The word "boer" means farmer, and the Boer language is an old dialect of Dutch. For the Boers had been Dutch colonists, largely farmers and religious refugees, who had settled in South Africa in the seventeenth century. When the British took control of the Cape following the Napoleonic wars, the Boers had made their "great trek," an epic journey almost a thousand miles to the north. There, they settled in two small republics, the Transvaal and the Orange Free State. They continued to farm, to practice their religion, and to live by a stern, archaic moral code. Their chief representative was Paul Kruger, Prime Minister of the Transvaal, who became Rhodes's most implacable enemy. He disliked Rhodes's plans for British imperial expansion—after all, it was precisely because of such a threat that the Boers had fled from the Cape. He distrusted Rhodes's proposal for federation with the other South African states, suspecting that it was no more than a ploy— which it was not. And more generally, like most Boers, Kruger did not care for foreigners—"uitlanders"—financiers and mining speculators. Indeed, the Transvaal government did everything to discourage such people, including imposing high duties on goods crossing its frontiers and ruinous rail tariffs. The situation reached crisis proportions in 1895 after the discovery of further gold and diamond deposits in the Transvaal "on the Rand." Kruger still refused to consider joining a South African federation, stepped up economic resistance, and even sought support from the German imperial government.

Since 1890, Rhodes had been prime minister of Cape Colony. He now entered into a conspiracy to overthrow the Kruger government in the Transvaal. He organized a raiding party under the command of a friend, Dr. J. S. Jameson. The Jameson Raid was a military fiasco, and Rhodes's complicity in it was revealed. Such behavior by a head of state was intolerable both for the Cape Colony government and the British. Rhodes was stripped of his office and his seat in Parliament and censured by the British House of Commons, whose inquiry into the matter stopped just short of implicating high officials in the British Colonial Office. Rhodes would never totally recover his influence in South Africa, and the Jameson Raid would become a key incident leading to the Boer War. Rhodes himself died in 1902, not yet fifty years old.

Cecil Rhodes was the most obvious embodiment of nineteenth-century British colonialism. He exemplified all its economic rapacity and political ambition, its chauvinism and paternalism, its racism and bigotry. He also exemplified the untrammeled gospel of wealth. In a time of robber barons on a worldwide scale—Cornelius Vanderbilt, J. P. Morgan, Andrew Carnegie, John D. Rockefeller, Baron Krupp, and Lord Rothschild—Rhodes was the greatest both in resources and in vision. There was nothing, he thought, that could not be bought, no one who could not be bribed. He used his wealth to gain political ends and political power to further his fortune. And he dreamed dreams of empire-building that others might applaud or condemn but, for their scope and daring, few could match.

project. He urged me to see Rhodes, and arranged a meeting. At the appointed time I presented myself at the Burlington Hotel. My credentials were duly passed by some members of the little court of secretaries and retainers, whom Rhodes always had about him. He was simple enough in his personal habits, but there was something regal in his dependence upon his suite. He required his trusted favourites and henchmen to be constantly at hand, and he could scarcely write a letter without the assistance of one or other member of his private Cabinet. Eventually I found myself at the end of a large room, in front of a large man, standing before a large fire. Size was the first external impression you received of Cecil Rhodes. In whatever company you met him he seemed the biggest man present. Yet, though tall and broadly built, his stature was not really phenomenal; but there was something in the leonine head, and the massive, loose pose, which raised him to heroic proportions. He received me with a cordial smile and an invitation to sit down in one of the two comfortable arm-chairs, which flanked the fireplace. After a question or two to break the ice, he began to talk, and he went on for an hour almost without intermission. Sometimes I put in a word or two to open the points, and switch him from one track to another; but in the main it was a monologue by Rhodes, or perhaps I should say a lecture on the future of South Africa. As he sat up in his crumpled tweed suit, with his left foot twisted round his right ankle, I lay back in my arm-chair and listened, amazed and fascinated, while the rapid sentences poured out of the broad chest in curiously high notes, that occasionally rose almost to a falsetto. Rhodes's voice was peculiar. It was uneven and apparently under no control. Sometimes it would descend abruptly, but as a rule when he was moved it reached the upper part of the register in odd, jerky transitions. But if it had been full of music and resonance it could have had no more effect upon the listener. I never heard Rhodes make a speech in public, and I am told he was no orator. But a talker he was, of more compelling potency than almost anyone it had been my lot to hear. Readiness, quickness, an amazing argumentative plausibility, were his: illustrations and suggestions were touched off with a rough happy humour of phrase and metaphor: he countered difficulties with a Johnsonian ingenuity: and if you sometimes thought you had planted a solid shot into his defences, he turned and overwhelmed you with a sweeping Maxim-fire of generalisation. Yet in all the intellectual accomplishments of conversation and debate he was inferior to many men one has known. Wittier talkers, more brilliant, far better read, infinitely closer and more logical in argument, it would be easy to name. But these men produced no such impression as Rhodes. It was the personality behind the voice that drove home the words—the restless vivid soul, that set the big body fidgeting in nervous movements, the imaginative mysticism, the absorbing egotism of the man with great ideas, and the unconscious dramatic instinct, that appealed to the sympathies of the hearer. One must add a smile of singular and most persuasive charm. It would break over the stern brickdust-coloured face like the sun on a granite hill, and gave to the large features and the great grey eyes a feminine sweetness that was irresistible. . . .

I came away from my first interview with Rhodes rather fascinated than convinced. It was the character more than the mind one admired. Then, and subsequently, it seemed to me that Rhodes's weakness was on the intellectual side. He was not a clear reckoner or a close thinker, but rather—so he himself admitted—a dreamer of dreams, vague, mighty, somewhat impalpable. Nor did it seem to me that he was an originator of ideas, but one who took up the conceptions of others, expanded them, dwelt upon them, advertised them to the world in his grandiloquent fashion, made them his own. Of late years he has been taken as the typical Imperialist. But in 1892 he seemed to me not an Imperialist at all, in the sense in which we then understood the term. He had risen to power at the Cape, it must be remembered, as the opponent of direct Imperial rule, and of all that was known as "Downing Street." His alliance with the Afrikander Bond was based on joint antipathy against the Colonial Office. When he talked of eliminating the Imperial factor he may have used a casual phrase, with no very precise meaning; but in fact that was what he wanted, though of course he did not mean to eliminate the British flag as well. His ideal was South Africa for the Afrikanders *utriusque juris.* Colonists of both races were to be worked together and federated to form an Afrikander nation, just as the Australians have formed an Australian, and the people of the Dominion a Canadian, nation. To some of us in 1892 the notion of bringing about this result by means of the Dutch, whose hostility to England and the English was well known, seemed dangerous. I asked Mr. Rhodes if the end would not be a secession and the conversion of the Federation to an independent Republic. "Are you going to be the Bismarck or the Washington of South Africa?" I said. Rhodes had his full share of vanity, and was delighted at being linked with these great names; but he hesitated, in order to ponder the question, and then replied with much seriousness, "Oh, Bismarck for choice of course." I suggested that his alliance with the Dutch Nationalists might really involve a danger of separation. He denied it emphatically. He said that he had joined Mr. Hofmeyr, in order to bring the Dutch into Cape constitutional politics and to prepare the way for a United South Africa, able to manage its own affairs, which it had a perfect right to do. "You people at home," he said, "don't understand us." But he laughed at the notion of secession, and he declared that neither Hofmeyr nor any other Dutchman would really want to get rid of English supremacy. "We must have the British Navy behind us," he said, "to keep away foreigners. We all know that." . . .

. . . Rhodes sometimes spoke of England and the English with that kind of irritation which many energetic colonists and Americans feel for this comfortable old country, with its innate conservatism, its arrogant belief in itself, its indifference to new ideas, and its absorption in controversies which, to the pushing new man from beyond the seas, seem time-worn and threadbare. Mr. Kipling's line "What do they know of England who only England know?" had not been written at the date of my first meeting with Rhodes; but the sentiment it conveyed was shared by him to the full. He thought of the British Isles as a few crowded specks of European territory, whose swarming millions should be given room for expansion in the vacant lands of the ampler continents. He was possessed—I had almost said obsessed—by the fear that if we neglected our chances, they would be taken from us by others, and the English people would be throttled for lack of breathing-space. This work seemed to him of such paramount importance that everything else in politics sank into insignificance beside it. He believed sincerely that the service he had rendered the nation by securing Rhodesia as a field for British colonisation could hardly be over-estimated, and he was astonished that the public took the gigantic benefaction so calmly. . . .

. . . The domestic affairs of some forty millions of people seemed to him hardly worth considering when any question of territorial or colonial expansion was in the balance. Lord Salisbury once recommended the use of "large maps" as a corrective to groundless political alarms. Rhodes was fond of large maps too, but they had a different effect upon him. He would gaze upon the great polygon between the Transvaal and the Zambesi which he had coloured red, and expatiate upon the vastness of the country; then he would run his finger northward, and explain how Africa was to be linked up and thrown open by his Cape-to-Cairo telegraph and railway. It was in my first conversation with him that I heard Rhodes mention this project, which was a novel one to me. I hinted some doubts—whether anyone would want to use the through route, whether the native chiefs and slave traders would not interfere with the poles and wires. Rhodes took up the latter point with one of his touches of cynical humour: "The slavers! Why, before my telegraph had been running six months they would be using it to send through their consignment of slaves." Something was said about the Khalifa,[1] and the obvious difficulty of constructing

---

[1]The Caliph, spiritual head of Islam, who was also the Ottoman Sultan, was deeply involved in the colonial scramble in Africa in the late nineteenth century.—Ed.

a railway through the Equatorial Provinces, then in the hands of fanatical barbarians. "You ask me," said Rhodes, in words which, I believe, he afterwards repeated in public, "how I am going to get the railway through the Soudan; well, I don't know. But I tell you, when the time comes we shall deal with the Mahdi[2] in one way or another. If you mean to tell me that one man can permanently check an enterprise like this, I say to you it is not possible." This was very characteristic of Rhodes in two ways. He had a profound belief in destiny and in the power of world-movements to fulfil their ends. And he had also a conviction that almost any man could be "dealt with," if you knew the right way to go to work with him. It was based, I suppose, on his own experience, for he had been singularly successful in manipulating and moulding men to his own purposes. From the keen-eyed speculators in Kimberley to the suspicious savages in the Matoppo caves, there were few with whom he had failed to come to terms when he desired to make them his instruments or allies. Partly I am sure that this was due to the mere personal influence, the "magnetism," to which I have already referred. But Rhodes was always a believer in the arts of bargain and management. He held that most people have their price, though the currency is not always notes or cheques or shares. By appealing to a person's vanity, his patriotism, his ideals, or his cupidity, you can generally contrive to get him to do what you want. It was part of the piquancy of Rhodes's character that he mingled the practical shrewdness of the diamond mart and the gambling table with his prophetic visions and imaginative enthusiasms. . . .

Whatever inconsistency there may have been in his actions, his opinions, so far as I could perceive, did not vary. In fact, he repeated himself a good deal, having a kind of apostolic fervour in expatiating on the broad simple tenets of the Rhodesian religion. His cardinal doctrines I should say were these: First, that insular England was quite insufficient to maintain, or even to protect, itself without the assistance of the Anglo-Saxon peoples beyond the seas of Europe. Secondly, that the first and greatest aim of British statesmanship should be to find new areas of settlement, and new markets for the products that would, in due course, be penalised in the territories and dependencies of all our rivals by discriminating tariffs. Thirdly, that the largest tracts of unoccupied or undeveloped lands remaining on the globe were in Africa, and therefore that the most strenuous efforts should be made to keep open a great part of that continent to

---

[2]A fanatic Moslem religious and political leader in the Sudan. His followers besieged Khartoum in 1885 and took the city with great bloodshed. Among the casualties was the British General Charles George "Chinese" Gordon. See also p. 151.—Ed.

British commerce and colonisation. Fourthly, that as the key to the African position lay in the various Anglo-Dutch States and provinces, it was imperative to convert the whole region into a united, self-governing, federation, exempt from meddlesome interference by the home authorities, but loyal to the Empire, and welcoming British enterprise and progress. Fifthly, that the world was made for the service of man, and more particularly of civilised, white, European men, who were most capable of utilising the crude resources of nature for the promotion of wealth and prosperity. And, finally, that the British Constitution was an absurd anachronism, and that it should be remodelled on the lines of the American Union, with federal self-governing Colonies as the constituent States. . . .

. . . He had a reverence such as is more common now among Americans than Englishmen, for enterprise on an extensive scale. Man in his view was clearly an active animal. He was made to do "big" things, and to do them in a modern, scientific, progressive manner. With the obstructionist, who clogged the wheels of the machine, whether from indolence, ignorance, or an exaggerated regard for the past, he had no patience. Some months before the opening of the South African War I was dining with him and a number of his friends, who were mostly interested in one way or other in Rhodesian or Transvaal affairs. The conversation turned on the condition of Johannesburg, the grievances of the Uitlanders, and the possible attitude of Great Britain. "If I were in the position of the British Government," said Rhodes, "I should say to old Kruger, 'Mr. Kruger, you are interfering with business, and you will have to get out of the way.' " The little speech was characteristic; so, by the way, was the pronunciation of the ex-President's name. Rhodes, as I have said, had no mastery of detail. In his thirty years in South Africa he had not learned how Dutch words should be spoken. He called his ancient enemy "old Krooger," like the man in the street.

My most interesting talk with Rhodes occurred in the early days of February 1896, after the shattering collapse of Jameson's failure, when the deeply compromised Cape Premier hastened to England to "face the music." I was anxious to see him. Knowing that he was an early riser, I thought I should have the best chance of catching him disengaged if I went before most other callers were out of bed. So on the second morning after his arrival, at about eight o'clock, I sent in my name at the Burlington Hotel. My access to Rhodes on this occasion, when few but intimate friends were allowed to approach him, was facilitated by the fact that he had been reading some articles of mine on the events of the preceding month. I was no apologist for the Raid, nor have I ever been able to regard Rhodes's participation in the plot against the Transvaal Republic as anything but an unpardonable breach of trust and a monstrous abuse of the exceptional powers and privileges which had been conferred upon him. But if I did not excuse his conduct, I thought it was possible to explain it; and, as it happened, my explanations were very much on the lines of those which he himself would have framed. On this morning—the 6th of February 1896—I was taken up to Rhodes in his bedroom. He had risen, but was not quite dressed, and as he talked he walked feverishly up and down the room, awkwardly completing his toilet. He had been dining out the evening before; the dress clothes he had worn were scattered in disorder about the room; the large, rather bare, hotel apartment seemed strangely cold and friendless in the chilly light of the grim London morning; and the big man, with the thatch of grey-brown hair, who paced up and down in his shirt-sleeves, was a pathetic, almost a desolate figure. He was much changed by these few bitter weeks of suspense and suffering. Through the ruddy bronze of the sea wind and the veldt breezes his cheeks showed grey and livid; he looked old and worn. He asked me to sit down while he finished dressing; and presently he began to talk about the Raid and the conspiracy. I had felt some diffidence in approaching the subject; but he was full of it—too full to keep silence. He was, as I have said, always candid: but on this occasion, considering the circumstances in which he stood and my own comparatively slight acquaintance with him, I was amazed at his freedom. I thought, indeed, that he was saying too much, and more than once I tried to check him and rose to go; but he evidently wanted to talk—I suppose to ease his mind after a sleepless night—and he begged me to remain till he had finished his story. . . .

. . . From his very candid exposition of his own motives and expectations, I derived a strong, and, I think, perfectly correct impression that Rhodes's intervention in the Johannesburg conspiracy was due quite as much to fear of the Uitlanders as to animosity against Mr. Kruger. Rhodes disliked the reactionary Dutch oligarchy at Pretoria; but he also rather despised it, and believed that it was bound to fall before long by its inherent weakness, which he greatly over-estimated. He was, however, possessed by a genuine apprehension that it might be succeeded by a Republican Government which might be anti-Imperialist and perhaps anti-British. He knew that among the leading reformers at Johannesburg there were Americans, many Australians and Cape Afrikanders, some Germans and other foreigners. They objected to the Krugerite *régime*, which dipped into their pockets and shackled their enterprise; but they had no liking for Downing Street and many of them had even a very qualified affection for the Union Jack. Rhodes put it somewhat in this way:

I knew that in five years there would be 250,000 white settlers on the Rand. In ten years there might be half a million or more. Now, that large European population, with its enormous wealth and industry, would inevitably become the political centre of all South Africa. If we left things alone, the Uitlanders were certain, sooner or later, to turn out Kruger and his lot, to get possession of the Transvaal administration, and to make the Republic a modern, financial, progressive State, which would draw all South Africa after it. But they would have done it entirely by their own efforts. They would owe no gratitude to England, and, indeed, they might feel a grudge against the Home Government for having left them in the lurch so long. They would take very good care to retain their independence and their flag, with perhaps a leaning towards some foreign power, and all the Afrikander world would gradually recognise their leadership. So that, in the end, instead of a British Federal Dominion, you would get a United States of South Africa, with its capital on the Rand, and very likely it would be ruled by a party that would be entirely opposed to the English connection. In fact, you would lose South Africa, and lose it by the efforts of the English-speaking minority in the Transvaal, who are at present anti-British as well as anti-Kruger. I saw that if left to itself this section would become predominant when the Dutch oligarchy was expelled. That was why I went into the movement. I joined with the wealthy men who were ready to give their money to overthrow Kruger, so that we might be able to turn the revolution in the right direction at the right time. You may say, 'Rhodes should have left it alone; it was no business of his.' Yes; and if I had done so, there was the certainty that the revolution would have been attempted—perhaps not just now, but in two years, three years, or five years—all the same; that it would have succeeded; and then the money of the capitalists, the influence of the leading men in Johannesburg, would have been used in favour of this new and more powerful Republican Government, which would have drifted away from the Empire and drawn all South Africa—English as well as Dutch—after it.

I had much more talk with Rhodes on the subject, both on this day and subsequently. But the passage I have reproduced, as nearly as possible in his own words, has always seemed to me the gist of Rhodes's whole defence of his action in 1895.

A South African View of Rhodes

STUART CLOETE

The opinions about Rhodes available in South Africa are, of course, as varied as the political extremes of that troubled region. Most white Rhodesians regard him not only as the founder of their country but as the patron of their way of life. Even the descendants of the South African Boers share many of his views, in particular his racial views. Most black South African intellectuals regard him as the fountainhead of their own present discontent. Stuart Cloete was a native-born white South African who, in a string of highly successful novels, took on the hard task of espousing a middle course on the many questions faced by South Africa today. He was a moderate in a land increasingly dominated by extremists. In his assessment of Rhodes he is as moderate as in his other writings, recognizing at once the blight that Rhodes and his sort laid upon South Africa, but still able to see the person behind the symbol. The following selection is from his Against These Three: A Biography of Paul Kruger, Cecil Rhodes, and Lobengula: Last King of the Matabele.

Rhodes was a man who parodied his own virtues, whose whole life was a paradox of Machiavellian simplicity. An expatriate who devoted his life to the aggrandizement of the country he had left, and all but ruined the Africa he loved. Hero to some. Murderer to others. The godless man whom men worshipped almost as a god. The Colossus with lungs of clay. The great cynic, the great idealist. The financier who was always in debt. The imperialist who shares with Simón Bolívar the liberator the honor of having a great country named after him. The man who chose a mountain for a tomb. The only white man who ever received the Zulu royal salute of "Bayete" from the very people he had destroyed; and who, exposing another facet of his character, left uncompleted the greatest deal of his life to go to the deathbed of a friend. The maker of a million settlers' homes who had none, in the real sense, of his own. The uncrowned king of half a continent. The man, to whom hundreds of women offered themselves in concubinage or as wives, who never touched a woman. The student of history who forgot men were not bloodless pawns. . . .

He was not a man who lived by rote or thought in terms of precedent. His idea was to force on a reluctant Africa a federation resembling the American federation of states. But he went beyond this. He wanted to get America back and said—"Even from an American point of view, just picture what they have lost." At another time he wrote to Stead, "Fancy the charm to young America to share in a scheme to take the government of the world."

This was Rhodes's master plan—the orderly government of the world by a superstate. The limited plan he came near to achieving was the African federation.

The race for Africa was now really on. The preliminary canter was over. The Belgians were in the Congo—led by Stanley, the explorer; the French were in the Congo—led by another explorer, de Branza. Germans were everywhere hunting, prospecting as engineers for gold, as missionaries for souls. The silences of the great rivers were broken by the shots of the hunters and the hymns of the ministers. Soon they were to echo under the crack of the kiboko and the cries of natives being thrashed for failing to produce their quota of rubber. Portugal was claiming more rights. Germany had established her colonies. France was creeping down the Niger. England must make her way up from the Limpopo and join the Cape to Egypt. Is it wonderful, therefore, that the Boers were afraid? That they sought protection, that they wanted an outlet of their own to the sea? That they, who to live, needed farms so large that they could live by the increase of their herds alone, felt themselves hemmed in? Above all they hated and feared England, and England guided by Rhodes was on the march. "I look upon this territory of Bechuanaland as the Suez Canal of the trade of this country," Rhodes said, ". . . the key of its road to the interior. Some honorable members," he went on, "may say this is immorality. The lands they may say belong to the chief, Mankoroane. . . . Now I have not these scruples. I believe the natives are bound gradually to come under the control of Europeans. . . ." Here Rhodes paraphrased Darwin. He knew what he had to do. He felt conquest his duty—not merely to England, but to the world. . . .

Rhodes always looked older than he was, thirty when he was twenty; forty when he was thirty. He is described as thick and heavy—square, with big hands, a double chin, a sensual mouth, and a high falsetto voice. Bismarck, the maker of Germany and competitor for Africa, another big man, had a similar voice.

Rhodes, the so-called solitary—this is part of the fiction that has been built up about him—hated even to have a meal by himself. He loved to surround himself by friends and if friends were not available enemies would do. He had to talk, he had to have an audience. And often, when he had done talking, his enemies became his friends. He hated loafers and, like many childless men, had definite ideas about education. A good education he felt was essential. "Then kick all the props away. If they are worth anything the struggle will make them better men; if they are not, the sooner they go under the better for the world." Here we get the theory of the survival of the fittest introduced into family life. . . . He investigated God factually and gave God his chance—a fifty per cent chance. He decided that Charles Darwin was the best interpreter of God's work, which in terms of fact appeared to be that "dog eats dog": the bigger dog destroying the lesser. It remained merely for man to follow this lead and God's will was done.

God's finest product, according to Rhodes, was the Englishman. Here was the one race which had true ideals of justice, peace, and liberty without any suggestion of equality. . . .

Rhodes's attitude to the natives varied with the political wind. At one time he said—this was when he wanted the natives on his side— "I do not believe they are different from ourselves." But he also said on other occasions, "The natives are children." On the native question at least Rhodes and the Boers had no quarrel. It was their one and lowest common denominator. Rhodes said, "I am no negrophilist"—a superfluous assertion, since he threw so much emphasis on pigmentation. All that was Nordic blond was good to him— in which conclusion he agreed perfectly with the thoughts of Nietzsche, whom he had never seen.

He has been described as overbearing and ruthless. And he was. But he was also reasonable and conciliatory, colloquial; and explanatory when it was worth his while. He was for a time—and not a short time either—successful in being all things to all men. Whether he fooled them or fooled himself, or whether he thought circumstance itself would come to his aid, it seems impossible to determine. He did not believe with Kruger that "alles sal regt kom"—that all would come right; but appears to have thought that he could make things come right if he had control.

Rhodes's charm was undeniable. Barnato said, "You can't resist him." Hofmeyr said, "We had a talk and were friends ever afterwards." The Matabele whom he destroyed said, "You have come again and now all things are clear, we are your children." General Gordon said, "Stay and work with me." Then he asked him to come and help "smash the Mahdi." Rhodes's reply was typical. He would not fight the Mahdi, "but deal with him." To "deal" or to "square" were pleasant euphemisms for bribing: a simpler and a cheaper method of settling difficulties than war. Rhodes is even supposed to have said to Parnell, when he said owing to his divorce, the priests were against him, "Can't you square the Pope?" Nothing daunted

Rhodes. After getting Barney Barnato into the Kimberley Club, "to make a gentleman of him" and bring him onto his side of the diamond fence, Barney said, "But your crowd will never leave me in. They will turn me out in a year or two."

"Then we'll make you a life governor," was Rhodes's answer.

This final act of amalgamation took place in Doctor Jameson's cottage. Rhodes and Biet were on one side. On the other were Woolf Joel and Barnato. The stakes were for millions and none of the men concerned was yet thirty-six years old. The argument went on till dawn, Rhodes talking, Rhodes exhorting, cajoling, threatening. Rhodes's high voice stringing out long estimates of costs and profits. Rhodes getting up and sitting down. The room was filled with smoke. The men were drinking as they talked. Someone would lean forward to adjust the light of the lamp, turning the wick up or down. "If you have an idea and it's a good idea, if you will only stick to it, you will come out all right," was Rhodes's argument, and the amalgamation of the diamond fields and consolidation of diamond interests was a good idea. And then, as the sky began to pale, Rhodes threw in his final argument: he promised Barney Barnato a seat in Parliament. That finished it. Barney gave in. Life governor of the Kimberley Club and the right to put the magic letters M.P. after his name.

Ambition. Rhodes's was endless. He even wanted the stars, he said. "These stars that you see overhead at night, these vast worlds which we can never reach. I would annex the planets if I could. I often think of that. It makes me sad to see them so clear and so far away." This takes us back to the story of the old Boer who said there were no minerals in the moon because if there were the British would have taken possession of it long ago.

But what chance had men like Lobengula, and the others who were against him, with Rhodes? The man who wanted the stars, whose thoughts were so big that men were less than ants. Perhaps he saw them as ants toiling to make the world red for England. . . . Rhodes's sense was of the future, always the future; the present meant little to him. Today was no more to Rhodes than the rung which he must climb to attain tomorrow.

An example of Rhodes's sense of timing is given by Fitzpatrick when he describes his negotiations for the sale of a parcel of diamonds worth half a million sterling. What he wanted was a cash offer for the whole lot made on behalf of all the buyers present. They could agree among themselves afterwards as to the proportions they would take, and how the payment should be made, but he alone, acting for the de Beers shareholders, would decide whether the offer they made was adequate or not. The diamonds were laid out on sheets of paper exactly fitting a teak trough twelve inches wide. The sheets overlapped each other like the tiles of a roof and the diamonds on each sheet were carefully sorted and graded by the de Beers experts—the work, perhaps, in a parcel of this size, of several months. The diamonds in each little heap were identical.

The first offer made was not enough and Rhodes said so. He said, "I know the value as well as you do," and, turning to Brink, said, "That's not good enough."

A few minutes later, the buyers agreed to a much higher price which Rhodes accepted.

At this time the diamond market "was in a very nervous condition and it was realized that the sale, releasing of a mass of stones, would have a very serious effect upon prices." Everyone knew this, but the buyers each thought that he would be first in the field and resell quickly. All knew the enormous advantage of buying well-classified stones. Rhodes, when he signed the contract, had said, "I can make no contract with you binding you to hold these stones off the market. . . ." "The buyers were all rivals and none believed that everybody would exercise this restraint or comply with Rhodes's wishes . . . After all, business is business," Harris says. However, all agreed with Rhodes and there was a little chaff about his idealistic touch. Everything was now signed. The lawyers were finished and Rhodes said, casually: "All right, you will get the stones tomorrow when payment is made. They will be here in the de Beers office. Brink will take care of them for you. . . . Come along, Brink, put them away . . . and you understand, delivery tomorrow morning against payment."

"For a moment everyone was happy. Then Rhodes strolled across the room to speak to Brink from the head of the long trough where the diamonds lay grouped on their white paper. A wooden bucket was at the other end of the trough, and as Rhodes told Brink to put them away, he raised the head of the teak trough and shot the whole in a cataract into the bucket. He did it with the most natural movement, just as indifferently as one would toss an old newspaper onto the table. He did not say a word to those round him; was seemingly quite unconscious of what he had done and strolled out of the room without showing any sign of what had happened.

"Believe me, the faces of our people were a treat . . . the whole work of sorting was wiped out in one second and for six or eight months the entire output was kept off the market as surely as if it had been locked in the de Beers' safe. Someone said, 'My God, we have not a word in the contract about the grading or classifying. We just bought the output. . . .' Then someone else said, 'How the Christian beat the Jews!' and there was a roar of laughter such as you would only get from a gathering of Jews, who can, after all, enjoy a story at their own expense. And mind you, Rhodes was perfectly right. Our stones were locked up, but when we could sell them we realized a much better price than we could possibly have done at the time. His judgment was completely justified."

The Enigma of Rhodes

ROBERT I. ROTBERG

Cecil Rhodes has continued to fascinate not only those whose lives are some-how still touched by his imperial dream, but academic scholars as well. Most such scholars have succumbed to one or another part of the "myth of Cecil Rhodes" that was, in part, Rhodes's own creation. We now have, in Robert I. Rotberg's The Founder: Cecil Rhodes and the Pursuit of Power, *a definitive biography that succeeds in getting beyond the myth to the man. Rotberg, a distinguished African historian, in this book has col-laborated with psychiatrist Miles F. Shore to produce a work of mature and responsible psychohistory. Although Rhodes is still an "enigma" to Rotberg, he is an enigma whose many and contradictory parts can be explained by a comprehensive appraisal of this larger-than-life man.*

Rhodes died both genius and rogue. Even before an aneurysm led to the collapse of his bloated body in middle life, the very magnificence of Rhodes' successes had begun to subordinate the facts of his kaleido-scopic years to the idealistic apotheosizing of his acolytes and himself. His death occasioned an outpouring of part-remembered, part-fanciful, part-true, part-wishful retrospection. Those of his contempo-raries who wrote soon afterward were concerned to improve a glorified memory. So were most of their successors. Others, equally determined, offered appraisals that were as venomous as those of his admirers were adulatory. Those who saw hardly anything but the good were invested in myth. But so, too, were those who could still see the very twitch of the devil's tail.

A century after the decade of his greatest glories, it is important to push aside the veil of myth to reveal the real Rhodes, the man who served both god and mammon, who was as human, fallible, gentle, charismatic, and constructive as he was shameless, vain, driven, ruth-less, and destructive. He deserves to be seen in both the bright and the somber hues of the rainbow. As Colvin, biographer of Jameson, wrote, Rhodes was "such a great example to Englishmen and has been so abominably analyzed that the truth cannot be too often told."

In Rhodes' case, what is that truth? Certain of the cobwebs of misconception can be removed without arousing ire among the faithful—those generations of Rhodes scholars, South Africans, Rhodesians, and even Britons who were taught to enshrine Rhodes as a heroic, nearly perfect, far-seeing, fundamentally idealistic colossus. . . .

It is a measure of Rhodes' magnetism that the men on the frontier to whom he revealed [his] secret dreams in the late 1870s and thereafter believed in him and in those dreams. So did a range of supposedly skeptical Britons. No matter how wildly grandiose his dreams may appear today, Rhodes' own sense of conviction—his utter self-confidence—commanded a growing legion of followers. Rhodes, articulating his plans in a high voice that broke occasionally into falsetto, inducted men both older and more experienced than himself into a growing fraternity of believers. Even men otherwise cynical seemed to accept the compelling magic of Rhodes' charisma. When he angled for the amalgamation of the diamond mines, sought hegemony over the north, or attempted to oust the Portuguese from Mozambique, Rhodes enrolled supporters from all backgrounds. Not least, the Founder crucially gained the support of men more powerful, wealthier, and better-connected than himself. . . .

A ceaseless energy was essential. So was attention to detail. More important may have been his ability to empathize—to appreciate the strengths and weaknesses of others. Rhodes called this talent "squaring"—he sensed what others wanted, what their dreams were, and thereupon made converts. Charm, which he had in abundance, bright blue eyes, a broad smile, and an impressively large head could not have been sufficient, but they assisted. Rhodes, said Low, "could conquer hearts as effectually as any beauty that ever set herself to subjugate mankind." An especial appeal to persons whose sexual preferences were similar to his own doubtless helped among a subset of men on the frontier, in parliament, and in positions of power in Britain. Many of Rhodes' strongest allies were homosexuals. But not all were. . . .

Rhodes "was not a clear reckoner or a close thinker." He hardly originated ideas, but "took up the conceptions of others, expanded them, dwelt upon them, advertised them to the world in his grandiloquent fashion, made them his own." Rhodes had "compelling potency." Low describes his art: "It was the personality behind the voice that drove home the words—the restless vivid soul, that set the big body fidgeting in nervous movements, the imaginative mysticism, the absorbing egotism of the man with great ideas, and the unconscious dramatic instinct, that appealed to the sympathies of the hearer." . . .

It was Rhodes' skills with people and his visionary capacity, not his intellect or a midas touch, which won the mines for the De Beers combine. Rhodes saw and believed in the larger, dramatic possibilities and gave others confidence in himself and therefore in his dreams. He promoted himself and his prospects well, and, without reducing the well-conceived unfairly to the flash of charisma, he made his fortune and the fortunes of others largely because his head for business could encompass vast sums and broad results and because he could sell those goals to men of consequence and ability. In all his endeavors, once he obtained support for defined objectives, he could persuade more scrupulous or more conventional men to take short-cuts, water stock, misrepresent prospects, set up secret reserves of diamonds, and disguise the underlying concessions on which floated companies were based. . . .

The imperial Rhodes is hardly attractive. Lobengula of the Ndebele was tricked into providing a concession, his authority ignored by the Pioneer Column, and fine promises given to him—all with Rhodes' knowledge and approval—until the moment came when whites could overthrow him entirely. That moment, the war of 1893, was unprovoked by the Ndebele, and destroyed their independence. With Her Majesty's Government turning a blind eye, Rhodes personally approved the decision to attack; his troops had Maxim machine guns and the more numerous Ndebele had not. Rhodes also badly wanted copper-rich Katanga and the lands leading down to the Indian Ocean shores of Mozambique, but Lord Salisbury had to balance the needs of peace in Europe against an enhanced dominion under the British flag and in Rhodes' grip.

Without Rhodes, the Rhodesias, Nyasaland, and Bechuanaland— an area the size of western Europe including Great Britain, Italy, and Austria—might have become British anyway, if with fewer incentives for white settlers. But Rhodes decided when and how it did so, provided the organizational and capitalist framework, and personally sustained these young outposts of Europe during their difficult first years. For the Rhodesias, certainly, he justly was the Founder. For present day Zimbabwe and Zambia, he appropriately is the despoiler. . . .

Rhodes was not a good man, but he was great and far-seeing. He believed in himself and in his ability to leave the world richer than it was when he entered it. In the titanic struggle between self-absorption and genuine involvement with others, self-absorption almost invariably won. His love affair with his big ideas ultimately crowded out any lasting or deep concerns for most companions, associates, and friends. Rhodes' few long-term relationships were with those who were prepared to subordinate themselves to his dominating goals. The momentum and scope of his narcissistic dreams devoured the accomplishment of a fulfilling and rounded personal generativity. Yet however hollow he may have been in basic human terms, he left a rich and compelling heritage of achievement and philanthropy for humankind. In that soaring sense, which will hardly satisfy every modern reader, he did not, in fact, fling away the gifts of Providence. He amassed, he acquired, he savaged, he disrupted, and he presided arrogantly over the fate of southern Africa. But he also built lasting economic institutions, furthered transportation and communication, improved agriculture, enhanced education, and fervently believed and preached the doctrine that riches were his primarily to advance the positive interests of a modern southern Africa, and the farther flung English empire, and to uplift the colonies and ex-colonies by sending the very best of their young men to consort with and learn from one another in Britain's oldest cathedral of learning. Rhodes had always tried to find his way back home. The scholarships were meant to unify the original empire, to tie mystical bonds, and to provide a way in which Rhodes, the romantic boy and the irrepressible man, could live on, and do good works.

Review and Study Questions

1. Cecil Rhodes had the ability to influence other people and enlist them in his enterprises. What were some instances of this ability? What elements of his character and temperament enabled him to succeed so brilliantly in persuading others?

2. Rhodes was not only the quintessential imperialist, but also the quintessential capitalist. Compare him with some of the other early leaders of modern capitalism.

3. Why did the Boers resist Rhodes's schemes so persistently? What was the result of their resistance?

4. Colonialism is today usually equated with racism. In what respect were Rhodes's colonial ambitions racist?

5. In the long run, what role do you think Rhodes played in the building of the British Empire in Africa?

Suggestions for Further Reading

The powerful, complex, and enigmatic figure of Cecil Rhodes has persistently eluded his biographers until the recent work of Robert I. Rotberg, *The Founder: Cecil Rhodes and the Pursuit of Power*, with the collaboration of Miles F. Shore (New York and Oxford: Oxford University Press, 1988), the definitive biography, excerpted for this chapter. Nevertheless, there are a number of good and useful biographies. Sarah Gertrude Millin, *Cecil Rhodes* (New York and London: Harper & Bros., 1933), is a standard work on Rhodes, a colorful and exciting account by an experienced novelist and biographer. Both Felix Gross, *Rhodes of Africa* (New York: Praeger, 1956), and John Marlowe, *Cecil Rhodes: The Anatomy of Empire* (London: Elek, 1972), are superficial popular works. Even J. G. Lockhart and C. M. Woodhouse, *Cecil Rhodes: Colossus of Southern Africa* (New York: Macmillan, 1963), though based more fully on documents than any previous study, is timid and indecisive. John Flint, *Cecil Rhodes* (Boston and Toronto: Little, Brown, 1974), although a very small book, is one of the best general treatments of him. There are, however, several special studies that can be recommended: John S. Galbraith, *Crown and Charter: The Early Years of the British South Africa Company* (Berkeley: University of California Press, 1974), tells the dramatic story of the founding of Rhodesia and of Rhodes at the height of his power, with an interesting focus on the internal affairs of the company and its dealings; the massive Arthur Keppel-Jones, *Rhodes and Rhodesia: The White Conquest of Zimbabwe, 1884–1902* (Kingston, Ont.: McGill–Queen's University Press, 1983) is authoritative; Brian Roberts, *Cecil Rhodes and the Princess* (London: Hamilton, 1969), is an intriguing account of a bizarre incident in Rhodes's life, as exciting as an espionage thriller; Jeffrey Butler, *The Liberal Party and the Jameson Raid* (Oxford, England: Clarendon Press, 1968), is a fine study of the political ramifications of a famous incident; and probably the best account of this famous incident is the revised edition of Elizabeth Longford, *Jameson's Raid* (London: Weidenfeld-Nicolson, 1982). An interesting book by a Soviet African specialist is Apollon B. Davidson's *Cecil Rhodes and His Time,* tr. Christopher English (Moscow: Progress Publishers, 1988), which views Rhodes, somewhat predictably, as a "component part" and "agent" of British imperialism.

Rhodes was, of course, the quintessential figure of British economic imperialism, and the enormous literature of that subject almost invariably deals with him. A book dealing specifically with South African economic imperialism is Robert V. Kubicek, *Economic Imperialism in Theory and Practice: The Case of South African Gold Mining Finance, 1886–1914* (Durham, N.C.: Duke University Press, 1979). The definitive work on a key aspect of imperialism is W. L. Langer, *The Diplomacy of Imperialism*, 2nd ed. (New York: Knopf, 1968 [1950]). A smaller book but broader in scope is Heinz Gollwitzer, *Europe in the Age of Imperialism, 1880–1914*, tr. Adam and Stanley Baron (New York: Harcourt, Brace and World, 1969). Raymond F. Betts, *The False Dawn: European Imperialism in the Nineteenth Century* (Minneapolis: University of Minnesota Press, 1975), and *The "New Imperialism": Analysis of Late*

Nineteenth Century Expansion, ed. H. M. Wright, rev. ed. (Boston: Heath, 1975), both deal with the theories and arguments about imperialism. But probably the best and most definitive book on the subject is Winfried Baumgart, *Imperialism: The Idea and Reality of British and French Colonial Expansion, 1880–1914* (London: Oxford University Press, 1982). Also of interest is a specialized work on a long-neglected subject, Daniel R. Headrick, *The Tools of Empire: Technology and European Imperialism in the Nineteenth Century* (London: Oxford University Press, 1981).

With respect to British imperialism, the best survey is Ronald Hyam, *Britain's Imperial Century, 1815–1914: A Study of Empire and Expansion* (New York: Barnes and Noble, 1976). A briefer and more lively book dealing with some of the same matter is Bernard Porter, *The Lion's Share: A Short History of British Imperialism, 1850–1970* (New York: Longman, 1975). *British Imperialism: Gold, God, and Glory,* ed. Robin W. Winks (New York: Holt, Rinehart and Winston, 1963), deals with some of the controversies about the nature and motives of British imperialism, as does Richard Faber, *The Vision and the Need: Late Victorian Imperialist Aims* (New York: Humanities Press, 1966). L. H. Gann and Peter Duignan, *Burden of Empire: An Appraisal of Western Colonialism in Africa South of the Sahara* (New York: Praeger, 1967), also deals with the nature and motives of imperialism in Africa; it is a respected cautionary book, asserting that the benefits of colonialism may have outweighed its more publicized disadvantages for all concerned. A shorter book of readings, *The Scramble for Africa: Causes and Dimensions of Empire,* ed. Raymond F. Betts, rev. 2nd ed. (Boston: Heath, 1972), deals with some of the same issues. The fundamental revisionist monograph on the causes and motives of African imperialism is Ronald Robinson and John Gallagher, *Africa and the Victorians: The Climax of Imperialism in the Dark Continent* (New York: St. Martin's, 1961), but students may prefer *Imperialism: The Robinson and Gallagher Controversy,* ed. William R. Louis (New York: New Viewpoints, 1976). Recommended finally is R. Hallett, *Africa since 1875* (Ann Arbor: University of Michigan Press, 1974), with its focus upon Africa rather than Europe.

V. I. LENIN: ANATOMY OF A REVOLUTIONARY

1870	Born
1897	Exiled to Siberia
1900	Fled to Western Europe
1902	*What Is to Be Done?*, Lenin's first book
1905	Revolution of 1905
1917	Returned to Petrograd
1918	Russian surrender to Germany at Brest-Litovsk
1924	Died

The factual outline of Lenin's biography is well known. He was born Vladimir Ilyich Ulyanov in 1870, the son of a superintendent of public schools for the province of Simbirsk on the Volga and a member of the lesser nobility that provided most of the minor officialdom of Czarist Russia. Vladimir was a bright student. After high school, he went to study law at the regional university of Kazan. His political activities and growing radicalism led to his arrest, and for a year he was under police surveillance. He was soon arrested again, however, and in 1897 was exiled to Siberia. During his exile, he turned away from the tradition of populism, as the native Russian radicalism was called, and became an ardent Marxist. Later, he was to be the principal force in the unlikely task of applying the doctrines of Marx to vast, peasant Russia.

Returning from exile in 1900, Lenin fled Russia for Western Europe. It was at this time that he began writing under the name Lenin. He became active in the underground of radical émigrés and exiles; published a shoestring newspaper, *Iskra (The Spark);* and began to build a group of disciples who would become the inner circle of his revolutionary party. In 1902 he wrote his first major prescription for revolution, a book entitled *What Is to Be Done?* The following year he seized the leadership of the majority of delegates—the Bolsheviks—

161

to the conventions of the tiny, splintered Russian Social-Democratic Workers Party, meeting in London and Brussels. He hurried back to Russia when the Revolution of 1905 broke out. But the Revolution failed, and Lenin returned to his self-imposed exile in the West. When World War I came, he watched anxiously from Geneva as revolution again broke out in Russia under the stress of war.

Lenin was soon approached by the German government. Would he and his radical followers return to Russia under German safe conduct? The Germans, of course, hoped that Lenin would further radicalize the revolution already under way in Russia, paralyze the government, and destroy military resistance. Lenin agreed, and in what is surely one of the most bizarre incidents in modern history, Lenin and his party were put aboard a train, granted extraterritorial rights to pass through Germany and shipped across Germany to the Baltic and to Petrograd. They arrived at the Finland Station in mid-April 1917.

Lenin quickly became involved in the Revolution and soon was its leading figure. By November he had organized his faction and driven the hopeless Provisional Government of Alexander Kerensky out of power. After the fall of Kerensky, Lenin was elected chairman of the new Council of People's Commissars. He was now, in fact, the head of a new state, ready to implement his theoretical ideas by direct political action. "Not a single problem of the class struggle has ever been solved in history except by violence," he told the third All-Russian Congress of Soviets on January 24, 1918.

Lenin had already made the bold and controversial decision to take Russia out of "the imperialist World War," not to please the Germans— though it did—but to preserve his revolution and to save his country from sure defeat. The war had been useful as a "powerful accelerator to overturn the filthy and bloodstained cart of the Romanov monarchy,"[1] but it served no further useful purpose. Lenin accepted the German peace terms at Brest-Litovsk on March 3, 1918. He called it not so much a surrender as a "compromise" with the "bandits of German imperialism," which would enable the imperialists to do whatever they wished while he and his comrades consolidated their revolution.[2]

The treaty of Brest-Litovsk, however, did not signify the end of war for the Russians. Between the collapse of the old Czarist government and a secure new revolutionary government lay years of civil war and invasion by Russia's former allies, outraged at the surrender at Brest-Litovsk and frightened by the apparent success of the Revolution. Lenin later recalled, "Our Red Army did not exist at the beginning of

---

[1] V. I. Lenin, *Selected Works* (New York: International Publishers, 1943), VI, 5.
[2] *Ibid.*, X, 75–76.

the war. . . . Nevertheless, we conquered in the struggle against the world-mighty Entente" and did so with "the alliance between the peasants and the workers, under the leadership of the proletarian state."[3] They indeed did conquer, and by the early 1920s modern Soviet Russia was a reality. Lenin had worked ruthlessly and tirelessly. In 1918 he had been seriously wounded in an assassination attempt from which he never fully recovered. Then in 1922 he suffered a stroke, followed by another that partially paralyzed him. In 1924 he died.

Lenin was the most famous figure in Russia and one of the most famous in the world. As "The Father of the Revolution," his picture looked benignly down from giant posters over Red Square, and countless photographs of him appeared in the Western press. But the man behind the picture was almost unknown—in Russia as well as in the West. Lenin was obsessively secretive about himself. In all his vast collected works, in page after page of mind-boggling theories and bitter polemics, there are no more than a handful of brusque personal anecdotes. When his friends inquired too closely into aspects of his personal life, his tastes, his likes and dislikes, he shoved their questions aside as "trivial" and "unimportant." The cause, the work, the Revolution—these were the things that mattered.

It became almost an obsession with those closest to him to penetrate the "secret corner of his life," that "special room completely to himself," as Lenin called it,[4] in order to understand Lenin the man and to know what made and moved Lenin the leader and revolutionary. His friend the historian M. N. Pokrovsky found the key to Lenin "his tremendous political courage." "Among revolutionaries," Pokrovsky wrote, "there has been no lack of brave people unafraid of the rope and the gallows or of Siberia. But these people were afraid of taking upon themselves the burden of great political decisions." Not so Lenin, "no matter how weighty the decisions."[5] The novelist Maxim Gorky asked a friend, "what, in his opinion, was Lenin's outstanding feature. 'Simplicity! He's as simple as the truth,' he answered without hesitation, as though reiterating a long established fact."[6] Lenin was not simple, of course, and Gorky did not find him so. On the other

[3]*Ibid.*, IX, 246.

[4]Quoted in N. V. Volsky, *Encounters with Lenin* (London: Oxford University Press, 1968), p. 43.

[5]Quoted in Tamara Deutscher, ed., *Not by Politics Alone—The Other Lenin* (London: Allen & Unwin, 1973), p. 71.

[6]Quoted in George Hanna, ed., *About Lenin*, J. Guralsky, trans. (Moscow: Progress Publishers, n.d.), p. 30.

hand, he never did succeed in identifying to his own satisfaction Lenin's "outstanding feature."

At least two others succeeded somewhat better. And they also isolated what they regarded as the causes that moved Lenin to be the person he was.

We now turn to the first of these, Leon Trotsky.

The Young Lenin

LEON TROTSKY

Like Lenin, Trotsky was both a radical revolutionary intellectual and an exile. He opposed Lenin in the split of the Russian Social-Democratic Congress in 1903 and took a middle position between Lenin's Bolsheviks and the Menshevik "minority." Unlike Lenin, Trotsky was one of the heroes of the unsuccessful Revolution of 1905, after which he was imprisoned. In the successful Revolution of 1917, however, he joined forces with Lenin, and his brilliance, audacity, and organizational ability contributed mightily to its success.

In the power struggle following Lenin's death, Trotsky lost out to Stalin and in 1929 was exiled from Russia. Finally, in 1940, he was assassinated in Mexico, allegedly by Stalinist agents. While in exile, as earlier, Trotsky was a prolific writer, and he continued both his struggle against Stalin and his self-justification in his many books and articles. But he often came back to the subject of Lenin and wrote about him extensively, for example, in his My Life *(1930) and his three-volume* History of the Russian Revolution *(1936). In many ways, the most interesting of Trotsky's works on Lenin is* The Young Lenin, *from which the following selection is taken. The book was written in the early 1930s as the first of two volumes on Lenin's life. The second volume was never finished, delayed by other projects and ultimately by Trotsky's death. The work as it stood was translated by the American journalist and publicist Max Eastman, who had translated Trotsky's other works. Then the manuscript was lost, and it did not turn up again until the late 1960s.* The Young Lenin *was at last published in 1972, almost forty years after it was written.*

More interesting than the curious history of the manuscript is the book's insightful treatment of Lenin's early years, very nearly unique among the memoirs and recollections of other Lenin intimates—including the Reminiscences *of Lenin's wife, which reveal almost nothing about him. Especially intriguing is the importance Trotsky attaches to a series of tragic incidents that occurred at the end of Lenin's adolescence. Trotsky finds in these tragedies of Lenin the boy the key to understanding Lenin the man—and the revolutionary.*

"Happy families are all alike," says Tolstoy. "Each unhappy family is unhappy in its own way." The Ulyanov family had lived a happy life for almost twenty-three years, and been like other harmonious and fortunate families. In 1886 the first blow fell, the death of the father. But misfortunes never come singly. Others followed swiftly: the execution of Alexander, the arrest of Anna. And beyond these there were more, and still more, misfortunes to come. Henceforth everybody, both strangers and intimates, began to consider the Ulyanovs an unhappy family. And they had truly become unhappy, though in their own way. . . .

When Ilya Nikolayevich had completed twenty-five years of service, the ministry retained him for but one supplementary year, and not five as was usual with important government officials. . . . In 1884, simultaneously with the new university constitution, new rules were issued for parish schools. Ilya Nikolayevich was opposed to this reform—not out of hostility to the church, of course, for he zealously saw to it that religion was regularly taught in *zemstvo* schools—but out of loyalty to the cause of education. As the winds of reaction grew strong, the Simbirsk superintendent of public schools, by the very fact that he felt concerned for the cause of literacy, willy-nilly found himself opposing the new course. What had formerly been considered his merit had now, it seemed, become a fault. He was compelled to retreat and adapt himself. His whole life's work was under attack. When an occasion presented itself, Ilya Nikolayevich was not averse to pointing out to his older children the disastrous consequences of revolutionary struggle, and how instead of progress it produced reaction. This was the mood of the majority of peaceful educators of the time.

A Simbirsk landowner, Nazaryev, in sending in his regular dispatch to the editor of the liberal journal *Vestnik Yevropy*, wrote to him confidentially about Ulyanov: "He is not in the good graces of the ministry, and is far from doing well." Ilya Nikolayevich took to heart the government's attack upon the elementary schools, although he obeyed the new policy. His former buoyancy had vanished. His last years were poisoned with uncertainty and anxiety. He fell sick suddenly in January 1886, while preparing his annual report. Alexander was in Petersburg, wholly immersed in his zoology term paper. Vladimir, only a year and a half away from high-school graduation, must have been thinking already about the university. Anna was at home for the Christmas holidays. Neither the family nor the physician took Ilya Nikolayevich's illness seriously. He continued to work on his report. His daughter sat reading some papers to him until she noticed that her father was becoming delirious. The next morning, the twelfth, the sick man did not come to the table, but only came to the dining room door, and looked in—"as though he had come to say good-by," remembered Maria Alexandrovna. At five o'clock the mother, in alarm, called Anna and Vladimir. Ilya Nikolayevich lay dying on the sofa which served him for a bed. The children saw their father shudder twice and go still forever. He was not yet fifty-five years old. The physician described the cause of his death—"hypothetically although with overwhelming probability," to quote his own words—as a cerebral hemorrhage. Thus the first heavy blow fell upon the Ulyanov family. . . .

Anna remained in Simbirsk for a time in order to be near her mother. It was at that time that the elder sister and Vladimir grew close to each other. The winter walks together date from that time, and the long conversations in which her brother revealed himself to her as a rebel and nonconformist, the embodiment of protest—so far, however, only in relation to "high-school authorities, high-school studies, and also to religion." During the recent summer vacation, these moods had not yet existed.

The death of the father had suddenly destroyed the lulling flow of life in a family whose well-being had seemed sure to go on indefinitely. How can we avoid assuming that it was this blow that imparted a new critical direction to Vladimir's thoughts? The answers of the church catechism to questions of life and death must have seemed to him wretched and humiliating, confronted with the austere truth of nature. Whether in reality he threw his cross into the garbage, or whether, as is more likely, Krzhizhanovsky's memory converted a metaphorical expression into a physical gesture, one thing is beyond doubt: Vladimir must have broken with religion abruptly, without long hesitation, without attempts at an eclectic reconciliation of truths with lies, with that youthful courage which was here for the first time spreading its wings.

Alexander was staying up nights engrossed in his work when the unexpected news came of his father's death. "For several days he dropped everything," relates a fellow student at the university, "pacing his room from corner to corner as though wounded." But wholly in the spirit of the family, in which strong feelings went hand in hand with discipline, Alexander did not leave the university, and did not hasten to Simbirsk. He pulled himself together and went back to work. After a few weeks his mother received a letter, brief as always: "I have received a gold medal for my zoological study of annelids." Maria Alexandrovna wept with joy for her son and with grief for her husband. . . .

. . . Life was beginning to move again in its new, narrower channel, when a totally unexpected blow, and a double blow at that, descended upon the family: Both son and daughter were involved in a trial for an attempted assassination of the tsar. It was dreadful even to breathe those words!

Anna was arrested on March 1 in her brother's room, which she had entered while a search was in progress. Shrouded in dreadful uncertainty, the girl was locked up in prison in connection with a case in which she had no part. This, then, is what Sasha was busy with! They had grown up side by side, played together in their father's study with sealing wax and magnets, often fallen asleep together to their mother's music, studied together in Petersburg—and yet how little she knew him! The older Sasha grew, the more he withdrew from his sister. Anna remembered bitterly how, when she visited him, Alexander would tear himself from his books with evident regret. He did not share his thoughts with her. Each time he heard of some new vileness of the tsarist authorities his face would darken, and he would withdraw more deeply into himself. "A penetrating observer could have predicted even then his future course. . . ." But Anna was no penetrating observer. During the last year, Alexander had refused to share an apartment with her, explaining to his companions that he did not want to compromise his sister, who showed no desire for public activity. During that winter Anna saw Alexander with some strange objects in his hands. How far she was from the thought of bombs! . . .

A Petersburg relative of the Ulyanovs wrote of the arrest of Alexander and Anna to a former teacher of the children, asking her to prepare the mother cautiously. Narrowing his young brows, Vladimir stood silent a long time over the Petersburg letter. This lightning stroke revealed the figure of Alexander in a new light. "But this is a serious thing," he said. "It may end badly for Sasha." He evidently had no doubt of Anna's innocence. The task of preparing the mother fell to him. But she, sensing tragedy in the first words, demanded the letter, and immediately began to prepare for a journey.

There was still no railroad from Simbirsk; one had to travel by horse and wagon to Syzran. For the sake of economy and for safety on the journey, Vladimir sought a companion for his mother. But the news had already spread through the town. Everyone turned away fearfully. No one would travel with the mother of a terrorist. Vladimir never forgot this lesson. The days that followed were to mean much in the forming of his character and its direction. The youth became austere and silent, and frequently shut himself up in his room when not busy with the younger children left in his charge. So that is what he was, this tireless chemist and dissector of worms, this silent brother so near and yet so unknown! When compelled to speak with Kashka-damova of the catastrophe, he kept repeating: "It means Alexander could not have acted otherwise." The mother came back for a short time to see the children and told them of her efforts and her dream of a life sentence to hard labor for Sasha. "In that case I would go with him," she said. "The older children are big enough and I will take the younger with me." Instead of a chair at a university and scholarly glory, chains and stripes now became the chief object of the mother's hopes. . . . She was admitted to sessions of the court. In his month and a half of confinement, Alexander had grown more manly; even his voice acquired an unfamiliar impressiveness. The youth had become a man. "How well Sasha spoke—so convincingly, so eloquently." But the mother could not sit through the whole speech; that eloquence would break her heart. On the eve of the execution, still hoping, she kept repeating to her son through the double grating: "Have courage!" On May 5, on her way to an interview with her daughter, she learned from a leaflet given out on the street that Sasha was no more. The feelings that the bereaved mother brought to the grating behind which her daughter stood are not recorded. But Maria Alexandrovna did not bend, did not fall, did not betray the secret to her daughter. To Anna's questions about her brother, the mother answered: "Pray for Sasha." Anna did not detect the despair behind her mother's courage. How respectfully the prison authorities, who knew already of the execution of Alexander, admitted this severe woman in black! The daughter did not yet guess that the mourning for her father had become a mourning for her brother.

Simbirsk was fragrant with all the flowers of its orchards when news came from the capital of the hanging of Alexander Ulyanov. The family of a full state counselor, until then respected on every side, became overnight the family of an executed state criminal. Friends and acquaintances, without exception, avoided the house on Moscow Street. Even the aged schoolteacher who had so often dropped in for a game of chess with Ilya Nikolayevich no longer showed his face. Vladimir observed with a keen eye the neighbors around them, their cowardice and disloyalty. It was a precious lesson in political realism.

Anna was set free some days after the execution of her brother. Instead of sending her to Siberia, the authorities agreed to have her restricted, under police surveillance, to the village of Kokushkino, the home of her mother. . . .

What ideas and moods captivated Vladimir in the summer of 1886, on the eve of his last year at high school? In the preceding winter, according to Anna Yelizarova, he had begun "rejecting authority in the period of his first, so to speak, negative formation of personality." But his criticisms, for all their boldness, still had limited scope. They were directed against high-school teachers, and to some extent against religion. "There was nothing definitely political in our conversations." On her return from the capital, Vladimir did not put any questions to his sister about revolutionary organizations, illegal books, or political groupings among the students. Anna adds: "I am convinced that with our relations being what they were at that time, Volodya would not have concealed such interests from me," had he had any. . . . Vladimir remained completely untouched politically and did not show the slightest interest in those economics books that filled Alexander's shelf in their common room. The name of Marx meant nothing to this young man whose interests were almost exclusively in *belles lettres*. Moreover, he gave himself up to literature with passion. For whole days he drank in the novels of Turgenev, page by page, lying on his cot and carried away in his imagination into the realm of "superfluous people" and idealized maidens under the linden trees of aristocratic parks. Having read through to the end, he would begin all over again. His thirst was insatiable. . . .

Some years later, the Social Democrat Lalayants questioned Lenin about the affair of March 1. Lenin answered: "Alexander's participation in a terrorist act was completely unexpected for all of us. Possibly my sister knew something—I knew nothing at all." As a matter of fact, the sister knew nothing either. The testimony of Lalayants fully corroborates Anna's story and coincides with what we know on this subject from Krupskaya's *Recollections*. In explaining this fact, Krupskaya refers to the difference in their ages, which wholly destroys her own account of the closeness of the brothers. But this reference, inadequate to say the least, does not alter the fact itself. Lenin's grief for his brother must have been colored with bitterness at the thought that Alexander had concealed from him what was deepest and most important. And with remorse over his own lack of attentiveness toward his brother and his arrogant assertions of his own independence. His childish worship of Sasha must have returned now with tenfold strength, sharpened by a feeling of guilt and a consciousness of the impossibility of making amends. His former teacher who handed him the fateful letter from Petersburg, says: "Before me sat no longer the carefree cheerful boy but a grown man buried in thought. . . ." Vladimir went through his final high-school experiences with his teeth clenched. There exists a photograph evidently made for the high-school diploma. On the still unformed but strongly concentrated features with the arrogantly pushed-out lower lip, lay the shadow of grief and of a first deep hatred. Two deaths stood at the beginning of the new period of Vladimir's life. The death of his father, convincing in its physiological naturalness, impelled him to a critical attitude toward the church and the religious myth. The execution of his brother awakened bitter hostility toward the hangmen. The future revolutionary had been planted in the personality of the youth and in the social conditions that formed him. But an initial impulse was needed. And this was provided by the unexpected death of his brother. The first political thoughts of Vladimir must inevitably have arisen out of a twofold need: to avenge Sasha and to refute by action Sasha's distrust.

Lenin the Revolutionary

NIKOLAY VALENTINOV

Like Trotsky and so many of Lenin's other early intimates, N. V. Volsky (d. 1964)—who wrote under the name of Nikolay Valentinov—was fascinated by Lenin even though they broke over philosophical disagreements while Lenin was still in exile, long before the Revolution of 1917. But Volsky's recollections of Lenin remained vivid and became the subject of Encounters with Lenin, *the book from which the following excerpt is taken. In a long chapter entitled "My Attempts to Understand Lenin," Volsky described a singular incident when Lenin dropped his "oriental mask" and allowed a handful of friends into "the secret room of his life." What he revealed was not a moving personal tragedy such as Trotsky relates but a passionate intellectual advocacy for a book whose ideas, Volsky was convinced, made Lenin a revolutionary. The book was* What Is to Be Done? *by Nikolai Chernyshevsky (d. 1889). It is not insignificant, as Lenin himself admitted, that he used this title for the first major proclamation of his own revolutionary program, for Chernyshevsky's book was programmatic. The author had been a leading figure in native Russian radicalism and highly regarded by many Russian radicals before the time of Lenin, though hardly known in the West then or later. But what is perhaps more important than the program of Chernyshevsky was Lenin's passion for the book, a clear indication of the debt he owed to its influence. It is also significant that there existed a bridge between the emotional experience that Trotsky saw as Lenin's center and the intellectual experience described by Volsky. Lenin's dead brother Alexander had loved Chernyshevsky's book. Clearly, young Lenin had read at least one of the books on the shelf in their common room.*

During my attempts to understand Lenin, I made some "discoveries" which agreeably surprised me (his love of nature or his attitude to Turgenev, for example), but I also made others which simply nonplussed me. I shall now describe one of these.

At the end of January 1904 I ran into Lenin, Vorovsky, and Gusev in a small café near the square of the Plaine de Plainpalais in Geneva. As I arrived later than the others I did not know how the conversation between Vorovsky and Gusev had started. I only heard Vorovsky mention some literary works which had been very successful in their day but had quickly "dated," and now aroused only boredom and indifference. I remember that he included in this category Goethe's *Werther,* some pieces by George Sand, Karamzin's "Poor Liza," and other Russian works, including Mordovtsev's *A Sign of the Times.* I butted in to say that since he had mentioned Mordovtsev, why not Chernyshevsky's *What Is to Be Done?* too? "One is amazed," I said, "how people could take any interest or pleasure in such a thing. It would be difficult to imagine anything more untalented, crude and, at the same time, pretentious. Most of the pages of this celebrated novel are written in unreadable language. Yet when someone told him that he lacked literary talent, Chernyshevsky answered arrogantly: 'I am no worse than those novelists who are considered great.' "

Up to this moment Lenin had been staring vacantly into space, taking no part in the conversation. But when he heard what I had just said, he sat up with such a start that the chair creaked under him. His face stiffened and he flushed around the cheek-bones—this always happened when he was angry.

"Do you realize what you are saying?" he hurled at me. "How could such a monstrous and absurd idea come into your mind—to describe as crude and untalented a work of Chernyshevsky, the greatest and most talented representative of socialism before Marx! Marx himself called Chernyshevsky a great Russian writer."

"It wasn't *What Is to Be Done?* that made Marx call him a great writer. Marx probably didn't read the book," I said.

"How do you know that Marx didn't read it? I declare that it is impermissible to call *What Is to Be Done?* crude and untalented. Hundreds of people became revolutionaries under its influence. Could this have happened if Chernyshevsky had been untalented and crude? My brother, for example, was captivated by him, and so was I. *He completely transformed my outlook.* When did you read *What Is to Be Done??* It is no good reading it when one is still a greenhorn. Chernyshevsky's novel is too complex and full of ideas to be understood and appreciated at an early age. I myself started to read it when I was 14. I think this was a completely useless and superficial reading of the book. But, after the execution of my brother, I started to read it properly, as I knew that it had been one of his favourite books. I spent not days but several weeks reading it. Only then did I understand its depth. This novel provides inspiration for a lifetime: untalented books don't have such an influence."

"So," Gusev asked, "it was no accident that in 1902 you called your pamphlet *What Is to Be Done?*"

"Is this so difficult to guess?," was Lenin's answer.

Of the three of us I attached the least importance to Lenin's words. On the other hand, Vorovsky became very interested. He began to ask Lenin when he had become acquainted with Chernyshevsky's other works besides *What Is to Be Done?*, and, in general, which writers had had a particularly strong influence on him before he had become familiar with Marxism. Lenin did not usually speak about himself— this in itself distinguished him from most people. However, on this occasion he broke his rule, and answered Vorovsky's question in great detail. The result was a page of autobiography which has never been recorded in print. In 1919 Vorovsky, who was chairman of the Gosizdat (State Publishing House) for a short time, wanted to reconstruct and write down what Lenin said on this occasion. . . .

Vorovsky's reconstruction of Lenin's words throws new light on Lenin's intellectual and political development. I have to admit that it was only very much later that I realized this. It might have been thought that Vorovsky's transcript would be published in the USSR, where even the most worthless scraps of paper connected with Lenin are carefully preserved. However, I have not been able to find it anywhere in the Soviet literature available to me. There is no mention of it whatsoever. What can the explanation be? The point is that Vorovsky records Lenin as saying, in his own words, that he had been "transformed" by Chernyshevsky, and that under his impact he had become a revolutionary before his introduction to Marxism. It is thus impossible, unless one gives credence to a wanton misconception, to believe that Lenin was shaped only by Marx and Marxism. By the time he came to Marxism, Lenin, under Chernyshevsky's influence, was already forearmed with certain revolutionary ideas which provided the distinctive features of his specifically "Leninist" political make-up. All this is extremely important and sharply contradicts both the party canons and Lenin's official biographers. It is very probable that this is the reason why Vorovsky's transcript has not been published. . . .

. . . This is the gist of what Lenin said: "During the year that followed my banishment from Kazan, I used to read greedily from early morning till late at night. I think this was the most intensive period of reading in my whole life, not excluding my time in prison in Petersburg and my exile in Siberia. On the assumption that I might soon be permitted to return to the university, I read my university textbooks. I read a great deal of fiction, I became a great admirer of Nekrasov; what is more, my sister and I used to compete to see who could learn the greater number of Nekrasov's poems by heart. However, I read mainly articles which had once been published in the periodicals *Sovremennik* (Contemporary), *Otechestvennye Zapiski* (Fatherland Notes), and *Vesnik Europy* (Herald of Europe). These periodicals included the best and most interesting social and political writings of the previous decades. Chernyshevsky was my favorite author. I read and reread everything he had published in the *Sovremennik*. Chernyshevsky introduced me to philosophical materialism. It was again Chernyshevsky who first gave me an indication of Hegel's role in the development of philosophical thought, and I got the concept of dialectical method from him; this made it much easier for me to master the dialectic of Marx later on. I read Chernyshevsky's magnificent essays on aesthetics, art, and literature from cover to cover, and Belinsky's revolutionary figure became clear to me. I read all Chernyshevsky's articles on the peasant problem and his notes on the translation of Mill's *Political Economy*. Chernyshevsky's attack on bourgeois economics was a good preparation for my later study of Marx. I read with particular interest and profit Chernyshevsky's surveys of life abroad, which were remarkable for their intellectual depth. I read him pencil in hand, and made long excerpts and abstracts of what I was reading. I kept these notes for a long time. Chernyshevsky's encyclopedic knowledge, the brilliance of his revolutionary views, and his ruthless polemical talent captivated me. I even found out his address and wrote a letter to him; I was very pained when I did not receive any answer, and I was greatly distressed when I heard the news of his death in the following year. Chernyshevsky was hampered by the censorship and could not write freely. Many of his views could only be conjectured at; nevertheless, if one reads his articles carefully for a long time, as I did, one acquires the key to the complete decipherment of his political views, even of those which are expressed allegorically or by means of allusions. It is said that there are musicians with perfect pitch: one could say that there are also people with perfect revolutionary flair. Marx and Chernyshevsky were such men. You can't find another Russian revolutionary who understood and condemned the cowardly, base, and perfidious nature of every kind of liberalism with such thoroughness, acumen, and force as Chernyshevsky did. In the magazines I read there may have been a few things on Marxism too—for example, Mikhaylovsky's and Zhukovsky's articles. I can't say with any certainty whether I read them or not. One thing is certain—they did not attract my attention until I read the first volume of Marx's *Capital* and Plekhanov's book, *Our Differences,* although thanks to Chernyshevsky's articles I had begun to take an interest in economic questions, particularly in Russian rural life. This interest was prompted by essays of Vorontsov, Glep Uspensky, Engelhardt, and Skaldin. Only Chernyshevsky had a real, overpowering influence on me before I got to know the works of Marx, Engels, and Plekhanov, and it started with *What Is to Be Done?* Chernyshevsky not only showed that every right-thinking and really honest man must be a revolutionary, but he also showed—and this is his greatest merit—what a revolutionary must be like, what his principles must be, how he must approach his aim, and what methods he should use to achieve it. This compensates for all his shortcomings which, in fact, were not so much his fault as a consequence of the backwardness of social relations in his day. . . ."

After this conversation with Lenin, on our way back to the hotel, Gusev said laughingly:

"Ilyich could have scratched your eyes out for your disrespectful attitude to Chernyshevsky. Our old man has apparently not forgotten him to this very day. Still, I would never have believed the extent to which Chernyshevsky turned his head when he was a young man."

I found it even more difficult to believe. Lenin's infatuation with Chernyshevsky was quite incomprehensible and bewildering to me. It seemed strange that such a dreary, tedious, and feeble book as *What Is to Be Done?* could "transform his whole outlook" and provide "inspiration for a lifetime." It had never occurred to me that there was a special and hidden, yet strongly revolutionary, ideological, political, and psychological line running from Chernyshevsky's *What Is to Be Done?* to Lenin's *What Is to Be Done?*, and that there was more to it than the identity of titles. I had to admit that I had not understood an apparently very important part of Lenin's way of thinking.

The Lenin of History

ROBERT V. DANIELS

Western scholars of modern Russian history have also been fascinated by Lenin, the person who, more than any other, made the most significant revolution of the modern world. One of the best of these scholars is the American historian Robert V. Daniels, whose book Red October *provides a detailed account of the opening phase of the Revolution of 1917. Daniels's analysis of Lenin is central to his account, and it is an analysis unobscured by either commitment to or disillusionment with one or another revolutionary ideology. Daniels sees the motives of Lenin—the center of the man—in his ruthless drive for personal power and his cynical manipulation of the very dialectic that he mastered and that has been enshrined in Communist methodology since Lenin's time.*

It would be rash to conclude that Daniels's view of Lenin is more "true" than the views of his earlier comrades or of the current crop of Marxian admirers. But it at least has the virtue of a kind of objectivity we cannot expect from those closer either in time or spirit to Lenin.

The Russian Social Democratic Workers Party (of Bolsheviks) had never known any leader but Lenin. It was his personal political creation, starting as a devoted little group of twenty-two Russian *émigrés* (counting Lenin, his wife, and his sister) who met in Geneva in 1904. Their aim was to keep alive his side of the controversy that had split the Russian Marxist movement the year before. . . . Lenin had been adroit enough to seize the label "Bolsheviks"—"Majority men"—for his faction, even though he won only one of the numerous votes that turned around the "hard" political philosophy that he represented. . . .

Lenin had worked out his personal version of Marxist revolutionary philosophy between 1897 and 1900 while serving a sentence of Siberian exile for his revolutionary agitation among the St. Petersburg workers. In 1902, soon after he had left Russia for Western Europe, he published his propositions in the celebrated book, *What Is to Be Done?* Like practically everything Lenin ever said or wrote, the book was couched in the form of a polemic—in this case against the "Economists" because they put the economic progress of the workers ahead of political revolution. "The history of all countries," Lenin insisted, "shows that the working class, exclusively by its own effort, is able to develop only trade union consciousness." What would make them revolutionary, then? "Socialist ideology" and "class political consciousness" that could be "brought to the workers *only from without,* that is, from outside of the economic struggle." By whom? By the Social Democratic Party, and more specifically, "a small compact core of the most reliable, experienced and hardened activists . . . , an organization . . . chiefly of people professionally engaged in revolutionary activity."

Unlike the Mensheviks, who kept to the Marxist doctrine that a bourgeois revolution and capitalism had to precede the proletarian revolution, Lenin took the position that the Russian middle class was too cowardly to revolt, and that the proletariat—led by Lenin—should seize power directly and rule with the peasantry as its "allies." But this revolution would never occur of its own accord. Contrary to Marx, and more in keeping with the tradition of Russian revolutionary conspiracy, Lenin insisted that the proletarian revolution had to be accomplished by the deliberate action of a tightly organized conspiratorial party. He did not trust spontaneous mass movements, and at several crucial moments—in 1905 and in July, 1917—opposed the "adventurism" of Bolsheviks who wanted to exploit a popular outburst. In the fall of 1917, when it seemed as though the proletarian revolution might roll to victory almost as spontaneously as the bourgeois revolution of February, Lenin was beside himself. He was desperate then to demand that his party impose itself by force, to prove its own necessity and keep alive for himself the chance of ruling alone. . . .

Between Lenin and the Mensheviks the basic difference was more temperamental than doctrinal. The Mensheviks, like many earlier critics of Russian injustice, were idealists driven by sympathy for the masses but disinclined to conspire and fight; they admired Western democratic socialism and hoped for a peaceful and legal path to social reform once the Russian autocracy was overthrown. They were appalled by Lenin's elastic political morality and the philosophy they termed "dictatorship over the proletariat."

It is impossible to escape the very strong suspicion that Lenin's deepest motive was the drive for personal power, however he might have rationalized it. Like practically every politician Lenin had a philosophy about the welfare of the people—in his case it was the entire world proletariat—but the philosophy also said or implied that power for him and him alone was the only way this goal could be achieved. Lenin had an inordinate dislike of any sort of political cooperation or compromise, not because it might fail, but because it might succeed, and leave him with less than the whole loaf of power. He never worked honestly under or alongside anyone else, but only as the sole and unquestioned leader of his own forces, even if they had to be whittled down to meet his conditions. He was fascinated by armed force, and did not believe that any revolution worthy of the name could come about without it. "Major questions in the life of nations are settled by force," he wrote when he was a spectator to the Revolution of 1905. "The bayonet has really become the main point on the political agenda . . . , insurrection has proved to be imperative and urgent—constitutional illusions and school exercises in parliamentarism become only a screen for the bourgeois betrayal of the revolution. . . . It is therefore the slogan of the dictatorship of the proletariat that the genuinely revolutionary class must advance."

Many attempts, none very successful, have been made to explain Lenin's psychology. His childhood environment and youthful experiences, hardly exceptional for a family of the nineteenth-century Russian intelligentsia, offer only the sketchiest explanations of the demon that soon came to possess him. He was born in 1870 to a family of the lesser nobility—to be sure, the principal seedbed of the Russian revolutionary movement. His father, Ilya Ulyanov, was the Superintendent of Schools in the Volga city of Simbirsk, also the hometown, interestingly enough, of Alexander Kerensky. Lenin had some traumatic experiences—the untimely death of the father he esteemed; the execution of his older brother Alexander for complicity in an attempt on Tsar Alexander III; and his own expulsion from Kazan University because of a student demonstration. But the most abnormal thing about Lenin was his lack of abnormality among the typically eccentric and extremist Russians. He combined his natural brilliance and energy with an utterly un-Russian rigor and self-discipline which gave him an untold advantage in every political confrontation of his career. "Lenin is sheer intellect—he is absorbed, cold, unattractive, impatient at interruption," wrote John Reed's wife when she met the Bolshevik chief just after the Revolution. In another society Lenin would have risen to Grand Vizier or Corporation Counsel. In fact he did start a legal career in St. Petersburg, in 1893, before the encounter with the circle of Marxist agitators including his future wife Nadezhda Krupskaya finally committed him to the Marxist revolutionary movement.

Most people were either repelled or spellbound by Lenin. He was endowed with an extraordinary force of personality, along with an unbelievably vituperative vocabulary, that made most mortals helpless to oppose him within his own camp—they yielded or left. His extremism attracted many revolutionary romantics of independent mind but none of them were at ease in what Trotsky once called the "barrack regime" of the Bolshevik Party. Lenin hated liberalism and softness and the "circle spirit" of impractical discussion. "Nothing was so repugnant to Lenin," Trotsky recalled, "as the slightest suspicion of sentimentality and psychological weakness." Lenin hated the "spontaneity" of social movements without conscious leadership, and he hated the "opportunism" and "tail-end-ism" of people who went along with such movements. His life was consumed with hatred, and hatred of his rivals for the future of Russia almost more than the old regime. He wrote scarcely anything that was not aimed immediately to abuse an opponent, and usually a democratic and socialist opponent at that.

It is something of a puzzle that young Russian revolutionaries like Lenin embraced the philosophy of Marxism. Literally interpreted, Marx's doctrine of the change of society by deep-seated economic forces held out for an underdeveloped country such as Russia only the prospect of capitalism and middle-class rule for generations—the last thing that the radical intelligentsia wanted. Nor did they plump for Marxism for lack of an alternative philosophy, for the Russian revolutionaries since the 1850's had worked out a substantial body of socialist doctrine—"Populism," it was later termed—based on revolution by the peasants under the direction of the intelligentsia. The conspiratorial methods which so attracted the Russian extremists were an integral part of the Populist philosophy, whereas they were quite foreign to Western Marxism. In short, Marxism did not fit either the way the Russian revolutionaries wanted to work or the goals they wanted to work for, yet they flocked to its banner in ever-increasing numbers. They seem to have been attracted to Marxism because it gave them the secure sense of scientific inevitability and more especially because it stressed the role of the people who were obviously becoming the most vigorous, if small, revolutionary force in Russia, the industrial workers in the big cities. . . .

The stark truth about the Bolshevik Revolution is that it succeeded against incredible odds in defiance of any rational calculation that could have been made in the fall of 1917. The shrewdest politicians of every political coloration knew that while the Bolsheviks were an undeniable force in Petrograd and Moscow, they had against them the overwhelming majority of the peasants, the army in the field, and the trained personnel without which no government could function. Everyone from the right-wing military to the Zinoviev-Kamenev Bolsheviks judged a military dictatorship to be the most likely alternative if peaceful evolution failed. They all thought—whether they hoped or feared—that a Bolshevik attempt to seize power would only hasten or assure the rightist alternative.

Lenin's revolution, as Zinoviev and Kamenev pointed out, was a wild gamble, with little chance that the Bolsheviks' ill-prepared followers could prevail against all the military force that the government seemed to have, and even less chance that they could keep power even if they managed to seize it temporarily. To Lenin, however, it was a gamble that entailed little risk, because he sensed that in no other way and at no other time would he have any chance at all of coming to power. This is why he demanded so vehemently that the Bolshevik Party seize the moment and hurl all the force it could against the Provisional Government. Certainly the Bolshevik Party had a better overall chance for survival and a future political role if it waited and compromised, as Zinoviev and Kamenev wished. But this would not yield the only kind of political power—exclusive power—that Lenin valued. He was bent on baptizing the revolution in blood, to drive off the fainthearted and compel all who subscribed to the overturn to accept and depend on his own unconditional leadership.

To this extent there is some truth in the contentions, both Soviet and non-Soviet, that Lenin's leadership was decisive. By psychological pressure on his Bolshevik lieutenants and his manipulation of the fear of counterrevolution, he set the stage for the one-party seizure of power.

Review and Study Questions

1. Given Lenin's temperament, character, and personality, how do you account for his success in gaining control of revolutionary Russia?

2. What does Trotsky find as the key to understanding Lenin the revolutionary?

3. Valentinov believes that an intellectual advocacy made Lenin a revolutionary. Is his account convincing? Why or why not?

4. How does Daniels explain Lenin's rise to power and his inner motives?

Suggestions for Further Reading

Lenin's own voluminous writings, although they do not illuminate his life, nevertheless reveal his ideas and policies and the scathing declamatory style of virtually everything he wrote. The standard English-language edition is his *Collected Works*, 44 vols. (Moscow: Progress Publishers, 1960–1970), but most students will prefer either his *Collected Works*, rev. and annotated, 3 vols. published in 5 vols. (New York: International Publishers, 1927–   ), or the one-volume *Selected Works* (New York: International Publishers, 1971). There is also a separate edition of *The Letters of Lenin*, tr. and ed. Elizabeth Hill and Doris Mudie (London: Chapman and Hall, 1937), and of his important revolutionary pamphlet, *What Is to Be Done? Burning Questions of Our Movement*, ed. V. J. Jerome, tr. J. Fineberg and G. Hanna (New York: International Publishers, 1969). Nikolai Chernyshevsky, *What Is to Be Done?*, tr. Michael R. Katz, ann. William G. Wagner (Ithaca, N.Y.: Cornell University Press, 1989) is the first full English translation of this important work in Lenin's intellectual background.

Lenin was endlessly fascinating to his own close associates— magnetic, harsh, demanding, domineering, but fascinating all the same. This, added to the fame of Lenin the man and Lenin the symbol, has brought into print a steady stream of memoirs and recollections of uneven quality and usefulness. Two of these are excerpted in this chapter: Trotsky's *The Young Lenin*, tr. Max Eastman (New York: Doubleday, 1972) and Valentinov's *Encounters with Lenin*, tr. Paul Rosta and Brian Pearce (London and New York: Oxford University Press, 1968). Both works are valuable and interesting, as is another work by Trotsky, *Lenin: Notes for a Biography*, tr. Tamara Deutscher (New York: Putnam, 1971), a new translation of a work first published in 1925. Valentinov, *The Early Years of Lenin*, tr. R. H. W. Theen (Ann Arbor: University of Michigan Press, 1969), is part of the same memoir as his *Encounters with Lenin*, but its hostility destroys much of its usefulness. Angelica Balabanoff, *Impressions of Lenin*, tr. Isotta Cesari (Ann Arbor: University of Michigan Press, 1964), is the memoir of another early socialist colleague of Lenin.

N. K. Krupskaia, *Reminiscences of Lenin,* tr. Bernard Isaacs (Moscow: Foreign Language Publishing House, 1959), is the recollections of Lenin's wife, but it is more political polemic than domestic memoir. *About Lenin,* ed. George Hanna, tr. J. Guralsky (Moscow: Progress Publishers, n.d.), is a series of readings from fellow revolutionaries and colleagues, published for "official" purposes and carefully sanitized of all unorthodoxy. Much more interesting and useful is *Not by Politics Alone—The Other Lenin,* ed. Tamara Deutscher (London: Allen and Unwin, 1973), an excellent collection of readings from Lenin himself and many of his contemporaries, about his views on a broad range of topics and revealing Lenin as casual and informal as he ever was.

The same fascination with Lenin that prompted the many recollections of those who knew him has created a flood of biographies. The best and most definitive is Louis F. Fischer, *The Life of Lenin* (New York: Harper & Row, 1964). Two straightforward, unbiased, workmanlike shorter biographies are Harold Shukman, *Lenin and the Russian Revolution* (New York: Putnam, 1967), and Robert Conquest, *V. I. Lenin* (New York: Viking, 1972). Isaac Deutscher, *Lenin's Childhood* (London and New York: Oxford University Press, 1970), is the separately published first chapter of a proposed definitive biography by a great authority; it can be favorably compared with Trotsky's *The Young Lenin.* Another work on Lenin's youth and the influences that formed him is R. H. W. Theen, *Lenin: Genesis and Development of a Revolutionary* (Philadelphia: Lippincott, 1973). A classic piece of exciting history and biography is Bertram D. Wolfe, *Three Who Made a Revolution: A Biographical History,* 5th. rev. ed. (New York: Stein and Day, 1984), the interconnected story of Lenin, Trotsky, and Stalin. A collection of Wolfe's essays on Lenin—most of them not previously published—can also be recommended, *Lenin and the Twentieth Century: A Bertram D. Wolfe Retrospective,* ed. Lennard D. Gerson (Stanford: Hoover Institution Press, 1984). More interesting and informative than Krupskaya's own memoirs is Robert H. McNeal, *Bride of the Revolution: Krupskaya and Lenin* (Ann Arbor: University of Michigan Press, 1972). A work on the history of the Soviet Union, by the French authority Hélène Carrere d'Encausse, tr. Valence Ionescu, is organized, respectively, around the figures of Lenin for the first volume and Stalin for the second: see *Lenin: Revolution and Power* (London and New York: Longman, 1982). Piero Melograni, *Lenin and the Myth of World Revolution: Ideology and Reason of State, 1917–1926,* tr. Julie Lerro (Atlantic Highlands, N.J.: Humanities Press International, 1988), is a major revisionist interpretation of Lenin, holding that he did not advocate world revolution but rather Russian Marxian revolution alone.

Robert V. Daniels, *Red October* (New York: Scribner's, 1967), excerpted in this chapter, is an excellent account of the actual outbreak of the Russian Revolution. Another key event is detailed in J. W. Wheeler-Bennett, *Brest-Litovsk: The Forgotten Peace, March 1918* (London: Macmillan, 1956 [1938]), a brilliant, now classic account. Three important works on the theoretical-intellectual background to Lenin and the revolution must also be recommended: Franco Venturi, *Roots of Revolution: A History of the Populist and Socialist Movements in Nineteenth-Century Russia,* tr. Francis Haskell (New York: Knopf, 1960), is the definitive work on its subject; Edmund Wilson, *To the Finland Station: A Study in the Writing and Acting of History,* rev. ed. (New York: Farrar, Straus, 1972 [1940]), is probably the classic work of the great American social and literary critic, a kind of intellectual history of socialist radicalism ending with Lenin and the outbreak of the Russian Revolution; and Alain Besançon, *The Rise of the Gulag: Intellectual Origins of Leninism,* tr. Sarah Matthews (New York: Continuum, 1980), is a piece of brilliant intellectual history on the ideological framework of the Soviet system and its crucial ties with Lenin's theories. Esther Kingston-Mann, *Lenin and the Problem of Marxist Peasant Revolution* (New York: Oxford University Press, 1983) is a specialized essay dealing with a crucial problem faced by Lenin in adapting classical Marxism to peasant Russia. Finally, Robert V. Daniels, *Russia* (Englewood Cliffs, N.J.: Prentice-Hall, 1964), is an excellent brief book, specifically intended as an introduction to Russia in the twentieth century.

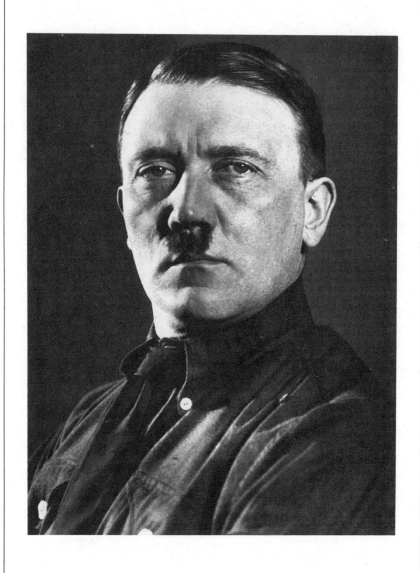

ADOLF HITLER: NIGHTMARE OF OUR CENTURY

1889	Born in Braunau, Austria
1923	Munich beer hall *Putsch*
1933	Became chancellor of Germany
1939	German invasion of Poland: beginning of World War II
1945	Died by suicide

In the early 1920s, the Bavarian city of Munich was a gathering place for the most militant and dissatisfied groups of German war veterans. They despised the weak government of the postwar Weimar Republic; they hated the allies who had defeated Germany in World War I and now seemed bent upon destroying it in peace; and they were desperate in the face of German economic collapse, unemployment, and runaway inflation. In this kind of setting, with a weak and harassed central government far away and the Bavarian state authorities—already distrustful of the national government and disposed to separatism—unwilling or unable to threaten them, a rash of splinter political parties flourished. These parties fought bitterly for support among the veterans and among the equally dissatisfied and hard-pressed working classes from which the bulk of the veterans came. At one extreme were the Communists; at the other a cluster of right-wing extremist groups, which, though they battled each other for supporters, shared a hatred for the Communists and for the Jews, who were a handy—and hated—minority to seize upon. One of these right-wing parties was the National Socialist German Workers' Party—*Nationalsozialistische Deutsche Arbeiterpartei*—Nazi for short. Since 1921 its leader was Adolf Hitler.

In November 1923, Hitler and his party command conceived a plan for a *Putsch,* an armed uprising to capture the leaders of the Bavarian state government and force them to proclaim a revolution against the

Weimar Republic. It was to be the beginning of a new Germany. Hitler had gained the cooperation of General Erich von Ludendorff, one of Germany's war heroes and a right-wing, nationalist fanatic himself, and he was confident that Ludendorff's presence would prevent the military's intervening against the coup. He was also sure that he could count on the Bavarian government's growing hostility toward the government in Berlin. On the evening of November 8, the Bavarian authorities announced a rally and meeting to be held in a Munich beer hall. Hitler and his fellow party leaders—supported by a considerable force of private military police and strong-arm hoodlums already known as stormtroopers—broke into the meeting. They hustled the government officials at gunpoint into a side room and forced them to proclaim a German revolution with Hitler as dictator. As soon as the officials were released, however, they repudiated their action. On the following morning, when the rebels attempted to march on the War Ministry building, they were met by the police. A skirmish ensued and sixteen Nazis were killed. Two days later, Hitler was arrested. The "beer hall *Putsch*" had been a total failure.

The apparently ruined politician who was so ignominiously handled by the Munich police in those autumn days of 1923 had been born in nearby Austria, just across the Bavarian border, in the little town of Braunau, in 1889. The details of his early life are sketchy and contradictory. Hitler's own later accounts of his youth differed as the circumstances demanded, and he generally preferred to remain somewhat mysterious.

His father had been an older man, a retired customs official, stern and domineering. His mother was much younger, usually dominated—if not brutalized—by her husband and idolized by her son. Her death in 1907 was a crushing blow to Hitler. Soon after his mother's death, with his mediocre career in high school completed, Hitler went to Vienna, hoping to be admitted to the state school of art. He failed the entrance examination twice and then drifted into the Viennese underworld of poverty and crime, often near starvation, though he occasionally found work as a sign and postcard painter.

Hitler then went to Munich, and there, with the outbreak of World War I, he joined the German army. Despite a relatively undistinguished military record—he rose only to corporal's rank—the war was the high point in Hitler's life. He belonged at last to a substantial, honored organization engaged in a noble and desperately contested cause. In 1918, as the war was ending, Hitler was hospitalized as the result of a gas attack, and, though not seriously injured, he suffered temporary blindness and loss of speech.

After the war, Hitler joined the obscure political party he was later to lead, and he found a new cause in politics—the obvious end for him being the restoration of the German glory that had come to ruin in 1918. By the time of the failure of the "beer hall *Putsch*," Hitler was a known figure in German radical politics. He should have been finished by the fiasco of the *Putsch*, but he was not. In 1923 his career was only just beginning.

Mein Kampf

ADOLF HITLER

At the insistence of the Bavarian authorities, Hitler and the other leaders of the Putsch *were tried, not in the federal court, but in a provincial Bavarian court and given the minimum sentence of five years—of which Hitler served less than nine months—in nearby Landsberg prison. In prison he was treated more like an exiled head of state than a common criminal, with exemption from work details, extended visiting hours for the streams of political dignitaries that came to see him, and other special privileges. Despite the failure of his uprising, Hitler still commanded several thousand irregular stormtroopers, even though they were scattered throughout Bavaria. And no one knew how many members his party had, nor the exact extent of his influence. It was in Landsberg prison that his secretary, Rudolf Hess, suggested to Hitler the title* der Fuehrer *(the leader). Hitler liked it and adopted it. It was also in prison that he wrote the book "frequently asked of me" by his followers, which he intended to be "useful for the Movement."[1] He called it* Mein Kampf *(My Struggle).*

The title suggests an autobiography, and in part it is an autobiography, though with much falsification of fact. It is also a political polemic against communism and a distorted vision of history, rife with the most savage and hate-filled racism. But most of all, Mein Kampf *is a vision of the future as Hitler intended it to be under the domination of his party—the Movement. In this respect, the book is both a political manifesto and an incredible, step-by-step prescription for what he planned to do. One of the most thoughtful modern scholars of* Mein Kampf, *Werner Maser, has observed that "from 1925 until his suicide in April 1945, Hitler clung faithfully to the ghastly doctrine set out in* Mein Kampf," *and, even more amazingly, despite the notoriety of his doctrine, "he was able to seize power to consolidate it and to carry the German people with him into the abyss."[2]*

The passage excerpted below is from the first chapter of the second volume of Mein Kampf, *written in 1927 after Hitler's release from prison. In it he recalls "the first great public demonstration" of the Movement in Munich in 1920. This was the eve of Hitler's takeover of the Nazi party, which*

---

[1]Adolf Hitler, *Mein Kampf* (New York: Stackpole, 1939), p. 11.

[2]Werner Maser, *Hitler's Mein Kampf: An Analysis,* R. H. Barry, trans. (London: Faber and Faber, 1970), pp. 11–12.

*was already committed to his ideas. These ideas—world conquest, brutal
direct action, glorification of power, Aryan racial supremacy, anti-Semitism,
and anticommunism—show up starkly in the selection that follows.*

On February 24, 1920, the first great public demonstration of our
young movement took place. In the festsaal of the Munich Hofbräu-
haus the twenty-five theses of the new party's program were submitted
to a crowd of almost two thousand and every single point was accepted
amid jubilant approval.

With this the first guiding principles and directives were issued for
a struggle which was to do away with a veritable mass of old traditional conceptions and opinions and with unclear, yes, harmful aims.
Into the rotten and cowardly bourgeois world and into the triumphant march of the Marxist wave of conquest a new power phenomenon was entering, which at the eleventh hour would halt the chariot
of doom.

It was self-evident that the new movement could hope to achieve
the necessary importance and the required strength for this gigantic
struggle only if it succeeded from the very first day in arousing in the
hearts of its supporters the holy conviction that with it political life
was to be given, not to a new *election slogan,* but to a new *philosophy* of
fundamental significance. . . .

Since with all parties of a so-called bourgeois orientation in reality
the whole political struggle actually consists in nothing but a mad rush
for seats in parliament, in which convictions and principles are thrown
overboard like sand ballast whenever it seems expedient, their programs are naturally tuned accordingly and—inversely, to be sure—
their forces also measured by the same standard. They lack that great
magnetic attraction which alone the masses always follow under the
compelling impact of towering great ideas, the persuasive force of
absolute belief in them, coupled with a fanatical courage to fight for
them.

*At a time when one side, armed with all the weapons of a philosophy, a
thousand times criminal though it may be, sets out to storm an existing order,
the other side, now and forever can offer resistance only if it clads itself in the
form of a new faith, in our case a political one, and for a weak-kneed, cowardly
defensive substitutes the battle cry of courageous and brutal attack. . . .*

In the first volume I have dealt with the word "folkish," in so far
as I was forced to establish that this term seems inadequately defined to permit the formation of a solid fighting community. All
sorts of people, with a yawning gulf between everything essential in
their opinions, are running around today under the blanket term
"folkish." Therefore, before I proceed to the tasks and aims of the

National Socialist German Workers' Party, I should like to give a clarification of the concept "folkish," as well as its relation to the party movement.

The concept *"folkish"* seems as vaguely defined, open to as many interpretations and as unlimited in practical application as, for instance, the word "religious. . . ." In it, too, there lie various basic realizations. Though of eminent importance, they are, however, so unclearly defined in form that they rise above the value of a more or less acceptable opinion only if they are fitted into the framework of a political party as basic elements. *For the realization of philosophical ideals and of the demands derived from them no more occurs through men's pure feeling or inner will in themselves than the achievement of freedom through the general longing for it. No, only when the ideal urge for independence gets a fighting organization in the form of military instruments of power can the pressing desire of a people be transformed into glorious reality.*

Every philosophy of life, even if it is a thousand times correct and of highest benefit to humanity, will remain without significance for the practical shaping of a people's life, as long as its principles have not become the banner of a fighting movement which for its part in turn will be a party as long as its activity has not found completion in the victory of its ideas and its party dogmas have not become the new state principles of a people's community. . . .

This transformation of a general, philosophical, ideal conception of the highest truth into a definitely delimited, tightly organized political community of faith and struggle, unified in spirit and will, is the most significant achievement, since on its happy solution alone the possibility of the victory of an idea depends. From the army of often millions of men, who as individuals more or less clearly and definitely sense these truths, and in part perhaps comprehend them, *one* man must step forward who with apodictic force will form granite principles from the wavering idea-world of the broad masses and take up the struggle for their sole correctness, until from the shifting waves of a free thought-world there will arise a brazen cliff of solid unity in faith and will.

The general right for such an activity is based on necessity, the personal right on success.

If from the word "folkish" we try to peel out the innermost kernel of meaning, we arrive at the following:

Our present political world view, current in Germany, is based in general on the idea that creative, culture-creating force must indeed be attributed to the state, but that it has nothing to do with racial considerations, but is rather a product of economic necessities, or, at best, the natural result of a political urge for power. This underlying view, if logically developed, leads not only to a mistaken conception of basic racial forces, but also to an underestimation of the individual.

For a denial of the difference between the various races with regard to their general culture-creating forces must necessarily extend this greatest of all errors to the judgment of the individual. The assumption of the equality of the races then becomes a basis for a similar way of viewing peoples and finally individual men. And hence international Marxism itself is only the transference, by the Jew, Karl Marx, of a philosophical attitude and conception, which had actually long been in existence, into the form of a definite political creed. Without the subsoil of such generally existing poisoning, the amazing success of this doctrine would never have been possible. Actually Karl Marx was only the *one* among millions who, with the sure eye of the prophet, recognized in the morass of a slowly decomposing world the most essential poisons, extracted them, and, like a wizard, prepared them into a concentrated solution for the swifter annihilation of the independent existence of free nations of this earth. And all this in the service of his race.

His Marxist doctrine is a brief spiritual extract of the philosophy of life that is generally current today. And for this reason alone any struggle of our so-called bourgeois world against it is impossible, absurd in fact, since this bourgeois world is also essentially infected by these poisons, and worships a view of life which in general is distinguished from the Marxists only by degrees and personalities. The bourgeois world is Marxist, but believes in the possibility of the rule of certain groups of men (bourgeoisie), while Marxism itself systematically plans to hand the world over to the Jews.

In opposition to this, the folkish philosophy finds the importance of mankind in its basic racial elements. In the state it sees on principle only a means to an end and construes its end as the preservation of the racial existence of man. Thus, it by no means believes in an equality of the races, but along with their difference it recognizes their higher or lesser value and feels itself obligated, through this knowledge, to promote the victory of the better and stronger, and demand the subordination of the inferior and weaker in accordance with the eternal will that dominates this universe. Thus, in principle, it serves the basic aristocratic idea of Nature and believes in the validity of this law down to the last individual. It sees not only the different value of the races, but also the different value of individuals. From the mass it extracts the importance of the individual personality, and thus, in contrast to disorganizing Marxism, it has an organizing effect. It believes in the necessity of an idealization of humanity, in which alone it sees the premise for the existence of humanity. But it cannot grant the right to existence even to an ethical idea if this idea represents a danger for the racial life of the bearers of a higher ethics; for in a bastardized and niggerized world all the concepts of the humanly beautiful and sublime, as well as all ideas of an idealized future of our humanity, would be lost forever.

Human culture and civilization on this continent are inseparably bound up with the presence of the Aryan. If he dies out or declines, the dark veils of an age without culture will again descend on this globe.

The undermining of the existence of human culture by the destruction of its bearer seems in the eyes of a folkish philosophy the most execrable crime. Anyone who dares to lay hands on the highest image of the Lord commits sacrilege against the benevolent creator of this miracle and contributes to the expulsion from paradise.

And so the folkish philosophy of life corresponds to the innermost will of Nature, since it restores that free play of forces which must lead to a continuous mutual higher breeding, until at last the best of humanity, having achieved possession of this earth, will have a free path for activity in domains which will lie partly above it and partly outside it. . . .

. . . Not until the international world view—politically led by organized Marxism—is confronted by a folkish world view, organized and led with equal unity, will success, supposing the fighting energy to be equal on both sides, fall to the side of eternal truth.

A philosophy can only be organizationally comprehended on the basis of a definite formulation of that philosophy, and what dogmas represent for religious faith, party principles are for a political party in the making.

Hence an instrument must be created for the folkish world view which enables it to fight, just as the Marxist party organization creates a free path for internationalism.

This is the goal pursued by the National Socialist German Workers' Party.

That such a party formulation of the folkish concept is the precondition for the victory of the folkish philosophy of life is proved most sharply by a fact which is admitted indirectly at least by the enemies of such a party tie. Those very people who never weary of emphasizing that the folkish philosophy is not the "hereditary estate" of an individual, but that it slumbers or "lives" in the hearts of God knows how many millions, thus demonstrate the fact that the general existence of such ideas was absolutely unable to prevent the victory of the hostile world view, classically represented by a political party. If this were not so, the German people by this time would have been bound to achieve a gigantic victory and not be standing at the edge of an abyss. What gave the international world view success was its representation by a political party organized into storm troops; what caused the defeat of the opposite world view was its lack up to now of a unified body to represent it. Not by unlimited freedom to interpret a general view, but only in the limited and hence integrating form of a political organization can a world view fight and conquer.

Therefore, I saw my own task especially in extracting those nuclear ideas from the extensive and unshaped substance of a general world view and remolding them into more or less dogmatic forms which in their clear delimitation are adapted for holding solidly together those men who swear allegiance to them. In other words: *From the basic ideas of a general folkish world conception the National Socialist German Workers' Party takes over the essential fundamental traits, and from them, with due consideration of practical reality, the times, and the available human material as well as its weaknesses, forms a political creed which, in turn, by the strict organizational integration of large human masses thus made possible, creates the precondition for the victorious struggle of this world view.*

Hitler and His Germany

ERNST NOLTE

Despite the fact, as Maser reminds us, that the German people had Hitler's plan before them in Mein Kampf, *they followed him anyway. Why? The answer may be, to some extent, that they did not take him seriously. There were, after all, other leaders of lunatic rightist movements in Germany in the 1920s, plumping for German nationalism, spouting anti-Semitic and anti-Communist slogans while the Communists shouted back. But to a greater extent, the German people did take Hitler seriously. He preached his doctrine of hatred for the Jews and fear of the Communists, of rabid, militant nationalism more effectively, more tirelessly, more virulently than his competitors—and the German people listened. What Hitler said was crude, but it had a powerful appeal. The Nazi party grew stronger every year, until by the elections of 1932 it was the second most powerful party in Germany. Hitler courted the military establishment, the one great indispensable German national institution, as carefully as he had courted old General Ludendorff in the early 1920s. And he cultivated the economic baronage. Germany's desperate plight was worsened by the world depression of the early 1930s, and the captains of industry, always conservative and disposed to right-wing politics, now frightened by the threat of trade unionism and the Communists, sought a financial-political alliance with Hitler.*

In 1933 the aged President Paul von Hindenburg was compelled by the political situation to name Hitler as chancellor. Hitler persuaded Hindenburg to call for new elections in an effort to achieve a Nazi majority

*in the Reichstag. Then, on February 27, 1933, a spectacular fire gutted
the Reichstag building. It was a case of arson—the arsonist, a Dutch radical, was arrested and confessed—but the fire and the sinister rumors that
the Nazis spread of Communist plots provided the excuse for an emergency
declaration. In this atmosphere of tension, the Nazis polled a working parliamentary majority in the elections. Upon Hindenburg's death the following year, the offices of chancellor and president were merged for Hitler. The
Fuehrer was made. Germany was recovering economically, and part of it
was the result of Hitler's military spending that created a vast public debt
but also jobs and prosperity. Part of it, too, was the beginning of worldwide
recovery. But no matter. Hitler claimed the credit. More Germans supported
him, and those who did not were intimidated by open terrorism. Jews had
already begun to stream out of Germany.*

*Hitler was now ready to implement his foreign policy. In 1935 the Rhineland was reclaimed by plebiscite and the following year remilitarized. In
1938 Austria was united with Germany; Czechoslovakia was surrendered
to Germany; and on September 1, 1939, Poland was invaded. World War
II had begun.*

*That Hitler was a dangerous psychopath is virtually a cliché of modern
European historical studies, and every book that deals seriously with Hitler
or his age must come to terms with it and venture a diagnosis. A more interesting question than what particular aberration Hitler suffered from is why
the German people were willing to follow a madman, in Werner Maser's
phrase, "into the abyss." It is a much more difficult question, a more essential one, and one to which the answers are more diverse. German scholars
of the postwar era have been especially preoccupied with this question.*

In a now famous essay, Three Faces of Fascism: Action Française,
Italian Fascism, National Socialism, *the German historian Ernst Nolte
gave his analysis. Although he subjects Hitler to penetrating study and
finds him "infantile," "monomaniacal," and "mediumistic," Nolte is unwilling to set him down simply as a madman. Rather, he argues that these very
aberrant qualities enabled him to exemplify the experience of his more normal fellow citizens. Hitler told the German people in a passionate and
oversimplified way what they themselves wanted to hear, and for this reason
he came for a brief time "to be lord and master of his troubled era."*

We turn now to Nolte's analysis.

The dominant trait in Hitler's personality was infantilism. It explains
the most prominent as well as the strangest of his characteristics and
actions. The frequently awesome consistency of his thoughts and behavior must be seen in conjunction with the stupendous force of his
rage, which reduced field marshals to trembling nonentities. If at the
age of fifty he built the Danube bridge in Linz down to the last detail
exactly as he had designed it at the age of fifteen before the eyes of his

astonished boyhood friend, this was not a mark of consistency in a mature man, one who has learned and pondered, criticized and been criticized, but the stubbornness of the child who is aware of nothing except himself and his mental image and to whom time means nothing because childishness has not been broken and forced into the sober give-and-take of the adult world. Hitler's rage was the uncontrollable fury of the child who bangs the chair because the chair refuses to do as it is told; his dreaded harshness, which nonchalantly sent millions of people to their death, was much closer to the rambling imaginings of a boy than to the iron grasp of a man, and is therefore intimately and typically related to his profound aversion to the cruelty of hunting, vivisection, and the consumption of meat generally.

And how close to the sinister is the grotesque! The first thing Hitler did after being released from the Landsberg prison was to buy a Mercedes for twenty-six thousand marks—the car he had been dreaming of while serving his sentence. Until 1933 he insisted on passing every car on the road. In Vienna alone he had heard *Tristan and Isolde* between thirty and forty times, and had time as chancellor to see six performances of *The Merry Widow* in as many months. Nor was this all. According to Otto Dietrich he reread all Karl May's boys' adventure books during 1933 and 1934, and this is perfectly credible since in *Hitler's Table Talk* he bestowed high praise on this author and credited him with no less than opening his eyes to the world. It is in the conversations related in *Hitler's Table Talk* that he treated his listeners to such frequent and vindictive schoolboy reminiscences that it seems as if this man never emerged from his boyhood and completely lacked the experience of time and its broadening, reconciling powers.

The monomaniacal element in Hitler's nature is obviously closely related to his infantilism. It is based largely on his elemental urge toward tangibility, intelligibility, simplicity. In *Mein Kampf* he expressed the maxim that the masses should never be shown more than *one* enemy. He was himself the most loyal exponent of this precept, and not from motives of tactical calculation alone. He never allowed himself to face more than one enemy at a time; on this enemy he concentrated all the hatred of which he was so inordinately capable, and it was this that enabled him during this period to show the other enemies a reassuring and "subjectively" sincere face. During the crisis in Czechoslovakia he even forgot the Jews over Beneš.[3] His enemy

---

[3]Eduard Beneš, the heroic president of Czechoslovakia who resisted Hitler's schemes and the machinations of the other great powers. He escaped to the United States in 1938. Later, in Britain, he was the head of the Czech government in exile. At the end of the war, he returned to become president of Czechoslovakia once more until his death in 1948.—ED.

196 Makers of World History

was always concrete and personal, never merely the expression but also the cause of an obscure or complex event. The Weimar system was caused by the "November criminals," the predicament of the Germans in Austria by the Hapsburgs, capitalism and bolshevism equally by the Jews.

A good example of the emergence and function of the clearly defined hate figure, which took the place of the causal connection he really had in mind, is to be found in *Mein Kampf*. Here Hitler draws a vivid picture of the miseries of proletarian existence as he came to know it in Vienna—deserted, frustrated, devoid of hope. This description seems to lead inevitably to an obvious conclusion: that these people, if they were not wholly insensible, were bound to be led with compelling logic to the socialist doctrine, to their "lack of patriotism," their hatred of religion, their merciless indictment of the ruling class. It should, however, have also led to a self-critical insight: that the only reason he remained so aloof from the collective emotions of these masses was because he had enjoyed a different upbringing, middle-class and provincial, because despite his poverty he never really worked, and because he was not married. Nothing of the kind! When he was watching spellbound one day as the long column of demonstrating workers wound its way through the streets, his first query was about the "wirepullers." His voracity for reading, his allegedly thorough study of Marxist theories, did not spur him on to cast his gaze beyond the frontier and realize that such demonstrations were taking place in every city in Europe, or to take note of the "rabble-rousing" articles of a certain Mussolini, which he would doubtless have regarded as "spiritual vitriol" like those in the *Arbeiterzeitung*.[4]

What Hitler discovered was the many Jewish names among the leaders of Austrian Marxism, and now the scales fell from his eyes— at last he saw who it was who, beside Hapsburgs, wanted to wipe out the German element in Austria. Now he began to preach his conclusions to his first audiences; now he was no longer speaking, as until recently he had spoken to Kubizek, to hear the sound of his own voice: he wanted to convince. But he did not have much success. The management of the men's hostel looked on him as an insufferable politicizer, and for most of his fellow inmates he was a "reactionary swine." He got beaten up by workers, and in conversations with Jews and Social Democrats he was evidently often the loser, being no match for their diabolical glibness and dialectic. This made the image of the archenemy appear all the more vivid to him, all the more firmly entrenched. Thirty years later the most experienced statesmen

---

[4]A labor newspaper.—ED.

took him for a confidence-inspiring statesman after meeting him personally; hard-bitten soldiers found he was a man they could talk to; educated supporters saw in him the people's social leader. Hitler himself, however, made the following observations in the presence of the generals and party leaders around his table: though Dietrich Eckart had considered that from many aspects Streicher[5] was a fool, it was impossible to conquer the masses without such people, . . . though Streicher was criticized for his paper, *Der Stürmer;* in actual fact Streicher idealized the Jew. The Jew was far more ignoble, unruly, and diabolical than Streicher had depicted him.

Hitler rose from the gutter to be the master of Europe. There is no doubt that he learned an enormous amount. In the flexible outer layer of his personality he could be all things to all men: a statesman to the statesmen, a commander to the generals, a charmer to women, a father to the people. But in the hard monomaniacal core of his being he did not change one iota from Vienna to Rastenburg.

Yet if his people had found that he intended after the war to prohibit smoking and make the world of the future vegetarian it is probable that even the SS would have rebelled. There are thousands of monomaniacal and infantile types in every large community, but they seldom play a role other than among their own kind. These two traits do not explain how Hitler was able to rise to power.

August Kubizek tells a strange story which there is little reason to doubt and which sheds as much light on the moment when Hitler decided to enter politics as on the basis and prospects of that decision. After a performance of *Rienzi*[6] in Linz, Kubizek relates, Hitler had taken him up to a nearby hill and talked to him with shining eyes and trembling voice of the mandate he would one day receive from his people to lead them out of servitude to the heights of liberty. It seemed as if another self were speaking from Hitler's lips, as if he himself were looking on at what was happening in numb astonishment. Here the infantile basis is once again unmistakable. The identification with the hero of the dramatic opera bore him aloft, erupted from him like a separate being. There were many subsequent occasions testifying to this very process. When Hitler chatted, his manner of talking was often unbearably flat; when he described something, it was dull; when he theorized, it was stilted; when he started up a hymn of hate, repulsive. But time and again his speeches contained pas-

---

[5]Julius Streicher was the publisher of a radical, anti-Semitic newspaper, *Der Stürmer,* and one of Hitler's earliest supporters. He continued to be a functionary of the party, survived the war, and was convicted of war crimes at Nürnberg.—ED.

[6]An opera by Wagner.—ED.

sages of irresistible force and compelling conviction, such as no other speaker of his time was capable of producing. These are always the places where his "faith" finds expression, and it was obviously this faith which induced that emotion among the masses to which even the most hostile observer testified. But at no time do these passages reveal anything new, never do they make the listener reflect or exert his critical faculty: all they ever do is conjure up magically before his eyes that which already existed in him as vague feeling, inarticulate longing. What else did he express but the secret desires of his judges when he declared before the People's Court: "The army we have trained is growing day by day, faster by the hour. It is in these very days that I have the proud hope that he hour will come when these unruly bands become battalions, the battalions regiments, the regiments divisions, when the old cockade is raised from the dust, when the old flags flutter again on high, when at last reconciliation takes place before the eternal Last Judgment, which we are prepared to face."

His behavior at a rally has often been described: how, uncertain at first, he would rely on the trivial, then get the feel of the atmosphere for several minutes, slowly establish contact, score a bull's-eye with the right phrase, gather momentum with the applause, finally burst out with words which seemed positively to erupt through him, and at the end, in the midst of thunderous cheering, shout a vow to heaven or, amid breathless silence, bring forth a solemn Amen. And after the speech he was as wet as if he had taken a steambath and had lost as much weight as if he had been through a week's strict training.

He told every rally what it wanted to hear—yet what he voiced was not the trivial interests and desires of the day but the great universal, obvious hopes: that Germany should once again become what it had been, that the economy should function, that the farmer should get his rights, likewise the townsman, the worker, and the employer, that they should forget their differences and become one in the most important thing of all—their love for Germany. He never embarked on discussion, he permitted no heckling, he never dealt with any of the day-to-day problems of politics. When he knew that a rally was in a critical mood and wanted information instead of *Weltanschauung*,[7] he was capable of calling off his speech at the last moment.

There should be no doubt as to the mediumistic trait in Hitler. He was the medium who communicated to the masses their own, deeply buried spirit. It was because of this, not because of his monomaniacal obsession, that a third of his people loved him long before he became

---

[7]"World view."—Ed.

chancellor, long before he was their victorious supreme commander. But mediumistic popular idols are usually simpletons fit for ecstasy rather than fulfillment. In the turmoil of postwar Germany it would have been *impossible* to love Hitler had not monomaniacal obsession driven the man on and infantile wishful thinking carried him beyond the workaday world with its problems and conflicts. Singly, any one of these three characteristics would have made Hitler a freak and a fool; combined, they raised him for a brief time to be lord and master of this troubled era.

A psychological portrait of Hitler such as this must, however, give rise to doubts in more ways than one. Does the portrait not approach that overpolemical and oversimplified talk of the "madman" or the "criminal"? There is no intention of claiming that this represents a clinical diagnosis. It is not even the purpose of this analysis to define and categorize Hitler as an "infantile mediumistic monomaniac." What has been discussed is merely the existence of infantile, mediumistic, and monomaniacal traits. They are not intended to exhaust the nature of the man Hitler, nor do they of themselves belong to the field of the medically abnormal. Rather do they represent individually an indispensable ingredient of the exceptional. There can be few artists without a streak of infantilism, few ideological politicians without a monomaniacal element in their make-up. It is not so much the potency of each element singly as the combination of all three which gives Hitler his unique face. Whether this combination is pathological in the clinical sense is very doubtful, but there can be no doubt that it excludes historical greatness in the traditional sense.

A second objection is that the psychological description prevents the sociological typification which from the point of view of history is so much more productive. Many attempts have been made to understand Hitler as typical of the angry petit bourgeois. The snag in this interpretation is that it cannot stand without a psychologizing adjective and almost always suggests a goal which is obviously psychological as well as polemical. What this theory tries to express is that Hitler was "actually only a petit bourgeois," in other words, something puny and contemptible. But it is precisely from the psychological standpoint that the petit bourgeois can best be defined as the normal image of the "adult": Hitler was exactly the reverse. What is correct, however, is that, from the sociological standpoint, bourgeois elements may be present in an entirely nonbourgeois psychological form. It remains to be shown how very petit bourgeois was Hitler's immediate reaction to Marxism. However, it was only by means of that "form" which cannot be deduced by sociological methods that his first reaction underwent its momentous transformation.

The third objection is the most serious. The historical phenomenon of National Socialism might be considered overparticularized if it is based solely on the unusual, not to say abnormal, personality of one man. Does not this interpretation in the final analysis even approach that all too transparent apologia which tries to see in Hitler, and only in him, the *"causa efficiens* of the whole sequence of events"? But this is not necessarily logical. It is only from one aspect that the infantile person is more remote from the world than other people; from another aspect he is much closer to it. For he does not dredge up the stuff of his dreams and longings out of nothing; on the contrary, he compresses the world of his more normal fellow man, sometimes by intensifying, sometimes by contrasting. From the complexity of life, monomaniacal natures often wrest an abstruse characteristic, quite frequently a comical aspect, but at times a really essential element. However, the mediumistic trait guarantees that nothing peripheral is compressed, nothing trivial monomaniacally grasped. It is not that a nature of this kind particularizes the historical, but that this nature is itself brought into focus by the historical. Although far from being a true mirror of the times— indeed, it is more of a monstrous distortion—nothing goes into it that is pure invention; and what does go into it arises from certain traits of its own. Hitler sometimes compared himself to a magnet which attracted all that was brave and heroic; it would probably be more accurate to say that certain extreme characteristics of the era attracted this nature like magnets, to become in that personality even more extreme and visible. Hence from now on there will be little mention of Hitler's psyche, but all the more of the conditions, forces, and trends of his environment to which he stood in some relationship. For whether he merely interpreted these conditions or intervened in them, whether he placed himself on the side of these forces or opposed them, whether he let himself be borne along by these trends or fought them: something of this force or this trend never failed to emerge in extreme form. In this sense Hitler's nature may be called a historical substance.

Hitler: A Study in Tyranny

ALAN BULLOCK

Not only German scholars, as we have seen, but other scholars of modern European history have been intrigued with the question of why and how Hitler rose to power. The most widely respected of these is Alan Bullock, whose most important work is Hitler: A Study in Tyranny. *Bullock tends to share Nolte's opinion about Hitler's infantilism—though he does not use the term. Stressing the fact that Hitler was incapable of real growth or change, Bullock finds him at the end of his career the same as at its beginning, unwilling to admit the possibility of his own error and seeing everyone's faults but his own. But even with such serious flaws of character and personality, Bullock, again like Nolte, is unwilling to dismiss Hitler as a madman. He sees him rather as the possessor of gifts amounting to political genius, evil genius admittedly but genius nonetheless. And he sees Hitler as using those gifts to secure a wholly personal tyranny over Germany. On the question of why Germany followed Hitler, Bullock diverges sharply from Nolte and from many other German scholars. He finds the explanation, not in the terrible German experience of defeat in World War I and depression in the postwar era, but more deeply rooted in German history, in German nationalism, militarism, and authoritarianism—of which Hitler's tyranny was the "logical conclusion."*

We pick up Bullock's account of Hitler at its last moment, late in April 1945, in the chancellery bunker in Berlin. While Russian artillery crashes above him, shattering what remains of his capital, he dictates to his secretary, Frau Junge, his will and his political testament. Hitler is on the point of committing suicide.

Facing death and the destruction of the régime he had created, this man who had exacted the sacrifice of millions of lives rather than admit defeat was still recognizably the old Hitler. From first to last there is not a word of regret, nor a suggestion of remorse. The fault is that of others, above all that of the Jews, for even now the old hatred is unappeased. Word for word, Hitler's final address to the German nation could be taken from almost any of his early speeches of the 1920s or from the pages of *Mein Kampf.* Twenty-odd years had changed and taught him nothing. His mind remained as tightly closed as it had been on the day when he wrote: "During these years in Vienna a view of life and a definite outlook on the world took shape in my mind. These became the granite basis of my conduct. Since then I have extended that foundation very little, I have changed nothing in it." . . .

In the course of Sunday, the 29th, arrangements were made to send copies of the Fuehrer's Political Testament out of the bunker, and three men were selected to make their way as best they could to Admiral Doenitz's and Field-Marshal Schoerner's headquarters. One of the men selected was an official of the Propaganda Ministry, and to him Goebbels entrusted his own appendix to Hitler's manifesto. At midnight on 29 April another messenger, Colonel von Below, left carrying with him a postscript which Hitler instructed him to deliver to General Keitel. It was the Supreme Commander's last message to the Armed Forces, and the sting was in the tail:

> The people and the Armed Forces have given their all in this long and hard struggle. The sacrifice has been enormous. But my trust has been misused by many people. Disloyalty and betrayal have undermined resistance throughout the war. It was therefore not granted to me to lead the people to victory. The Army General Staff cannot be compared with the General Staff of the First World War. Its achievements were far behind those of the fighting front.

The war had been begun by the Jews, it had been lost by the generals. In neither case was the responsibility Hitler's and his last word of all was to reaffirm his original purpose:

> The efforts and sacrifice of the German people in this war [he added] have been so great that I cannot believe they have been in vain. The aim must still be to win territory in the east for the German people. . . .

He now began to make systematic preparations for taking his life. He had his Alsatian bitch, Blondi, destroyed, and in the early hours of Monday, 30 April, assembled his staff in the passage in order to say farewell. Walking along the line, he shook each man and woman silently by the hand. Shortly afterwards Bormann sent out a telegram to Doenitz, whose headquarters was at Ploen, between Lübeck and Kiel, instructing him to proceed "at once and mercilessly" against all traitors. . . .

In the course of the early afternoon Erich Kempka, Hitler's chauffeur, was ordered to send two hundred litres of petrol to the Chancellery Garden. It was carried over in jerricans and its delivery supervised by Heinz Linge, Hitler's batman.

Meanwhile, having finished his lunch, Hitler went to fetch his wife from her room, and for the second time they said farewell to Goebbels, Bormann and the others who remained in the bunker. Hitler then returned to the Fuehrer's suite with Eva and closed the door. A few minutes passed while those outside stood waiting in the passage. Then a single shot rang out.

After a brief pause the little group outside opened the door. Hitler was lying on the sofa, which was soaked with blood: he had shot himself through the mouth. On his right-hand side lay Eva Braun, also dead; she had swallowed poison. The time was half past three on the afternoon of Monday, 30 April, 1945, ten days after Hitler's fifty-sixth birthday.

Hitler's instructions for the disposal of their bodies had been explicit, and they were carried out to the letter. Hitler's own body, wrapped in a blanket, was carried out and up to the garden by two S.S. men. The head was concealed, but the black trousers and black shoes which he wore with his uniform jacket hung down beneath the covering. Eva's body was picked up by Bormann, who handed it to Kempka. They made their way up the stairs and out into the open air, accompanied by Goebbels, Guensche and Burgdorf. The doors leading into the garden had been locked and the bodies were laid in a shallow depression of sandy soil close to the porch. Picking up the five cans of petrol, one after another, Guensche, Hitler's S.S. adjutant, poured the contents over the two corpses and set fire to them with a lighted rag.

A sheet of flame leapt up, and the watchers withdrew to the shelter of the porch. A heavy Russian bombardment was in progress and shells continually burst on the Chancellery. Silently they stood to attention, and for the last time gave the Hitler salute; then turned and disappeared into the shelter. . . .

In this age of Unenlightened Despotism Hitler has had more than a few rivals, yet he remains, so far, the most remarkable of those who have used modern techniques to apply the classic formulas of tyranny.

Before the war it was common to hear Hitler described as the pawn of the sinister interests who held real power in Germany, of the Junkers or the Army, of heavy industry or high finance. This view does not survive examination of the evidence. Hitler acknowledged no masters, and by 1938 at least he exercised arbitrary rule over Germany to a degree rarely, if ever, equalled in a modern industrialized State.

At the same time, from the re-militarization of the Rhineland to the invasion of Russia he won a series of successes in diplomacy and war which established an hegemony over the continent of Europe comparable with that of Napoleon at the height of his fame. While these could not have been won without a people and an Army willing to serve him, it was Hitler who provided the indispensable leadership, the flair for grasping opportunities, the boldness in using them. In retrospect his mistakes appear obvious, and it is easy to be complacent about the inevitability of his defeat; but it took the combined efforts of the three most powerful nations in the world to break his hold on Europe.

Luck and the disunity of his opponents will account for much of Hitler's success—as it will of Napoleon's—but not for all. He began with few advantages, a man without a name and without support other than that which he acquired for himself, not even a citizen of the country he aspired to rule. To achieve what he did Hitler needed—and possessed—talents out of the ordinary which in sum amounted to political genius, however evil its fruits.

His abilities have been sufficiently described in the preceding pages: his mastery of the irrational factors in politics, his insight into the weaknesses of his opponents, his gift for simplification, his sense of timing, his willingness to take risks. An opportunist entirely without principle, he showed considerable consistency and an astonishing power of will in pursuing his aims. Cynical and calculating in the exploitation of his histrionic gifts, he retained an unshaken belief in his historic role and in himself as a creature of destiny.

The fact that his career ended in failure, and that his defeat was preeminently due to his own mistakes, does not by itself detract from Hitler's claim to greatness. The flaw lies deeper. For these remarkable powers were combined with an ugly and strident egotism, a moral and intellectual cretinism. The passions which ruled Hitler's mind were ignoble: hatred, resentment, the lust to dominate, and, where he could not dominate, to destroy. His career did not exalt but debased the human condition, and his twelve years' dictatorship was barren of all ideas save one—the further extension of his own power and that of the nation with which he had identified himself. Even power he conceived of in the crudest terms: an endless vista of military roads, S.S. garrisons and concentration camps stretching across Europe and Asia.

The great revolutions of the past, whatever their ultimate fate, have been identified with the release of certain powerful ideas: individual conscience, liberty, equality, national freedom, social justice. National Socialism produced nothing. . . .

The view has often been expressed that Hitler could only have come to power in Germany, and it is true—without falling into the same error of racialism as the Nazis—that there were certain features of German historical development, quite apart from the effects of the Defeat and the Depression, which favored the rise of such a movement.

This is not to accuse the Germans of Original Sin, or to ignore the other sides of German life which were only grossly caricatured by the Nazis. But Naziism was not some terrible accident which fell upon the German people out of a blue sky. It was rooted in their history, and while it is true that a majority of the German people never voted for Hitler, it is also true that thirteen million did. Both facts need to be remembered.

From this point of view Hitler's career may be described as a *reductio ad absurdum* of the most powerful political tradition in Germany since the Unification. This is what nationalism, militarism, authoritarianism, the worship of success and force, the exaltation of the State and *Realpolitik* lead to, if they are projected to their logical conclusion.

There are Germans who will reject such a view. They argue that what was wrong with Hitler was that he lacked the necessary skill, that he was a bungler. If only he had listened to the generals—or Schacht—or the career diplomats—if only he had not attacked Russia, and so on. There is some point, they feel, at which he went wrong. They refuse to see that it was the ends themselves, not simply the means, which were wrong: the pursuit of unlimited power, the scorn for justice or any restraint on power; the exaltation of will over reason and conscience; the assertion of an arrogant supremacy, the contempt for others' rights. As at least one German historian, Professor Meinecke, has recognized, the catastrophe to which Hitler led Germany points to the need to re-examine the aims as well as the methods of German policy as far back as Bismarck.

The Germans, however, were not the only people who preferred in the 1930s not to know what was happening and refused to call evil things by their true names. The British and French at Munich; the Italians, Germany's partners in the Pact of Steel; the Poles, who stabbed the Czechs in the back over Teschen; the Russians, who signed the Nazi-Soviet Pact to partition Poland, all thought they could buy Hitler off, or use him to their own selfish advantage. . . .

Hitler, indeed, was a European, no less than a German phenomenon. . . . The conditions and the state of mind which he exploited, the *malaise* of which he was the symptom, were not confined to one country, although they were more strongly marked in Germany than anywhere else. Hitler's idiom was German, but the thoughts and emotions to which he gave expression have a more universal currency.

Hitler recognized this relationship with Europe perfectly clearly. He was in revolt against "the System" not just in Germany but in Europe, against that liberal bourgeois order, symbolized for him in the Vienna which had once rejected him. To destroy this was his mission, the mission in which he never ceased to believe; and in this, the most deeply felt of his purposes, he did not fail. Europe may rise again, but the old Europe of the years between 1789, the year of the French Revolution, and 1939, the year of Hitler's War, has gone for ever—and the last figure in its history is that of Adolf Hitler, the architect of its ruin. *"Si monumentum requiris, circumspice"*—"If you seek his monument, look around."

Review and Study Questions

1. Given the political climate of Germany in the late 1920s, it was nearly inevitable that some radical political leader and extremist party would come to power. How did it happen that Adolf Hitler and the Nazi party did so?

2. What leading elements of Hitler's later Nazi program appear in *Mein Kampf*?

3. Why do you think the German people were so willing to follow Hilter "into the abyss"?

4. How would you compare the personalities and programs of Hitler and Lenin?

Suggestions for Further Reading

Students are encouraged to read further in Hitler's revealing *Mein Kampf*, tr. Ralph Manheim (Boston: Houghton Mifflin, 1971), beyond the brief passage excerpted in this chapter. The understanding of *Mein Kampf* will be greatly enhanced by reading Werner Maser, *Hitler's Mein Kampf: An Analysis*, tr. R. H. Barry (London: Faber, 1970). Maser, an eminent German authority on Hitler, has also edited *Hitler's Letters and Notes*, tr. Arnold Pomerans (New York: Harper & Row, 1974). Also important for insights into Hitler is *Hitler: Secret Conversations, 1941–1944*, tr. N. Cameron and R. H. Stevens (New York: Octagon, 1972 [1953]), conversations with Hitler's intimates that he himself preserved.

The two best biographies of Hitler are the classic Alan Bullock, *Hitler: A Study in Tyranny*, rev. ed. (New York: Harper & Row, 1962), excerpted in this chapter, and Joachim C. Fest, *Hitler*, tr. Richard and Clara Winston (New York: Harcourt Brace Jovanovich, 1974), which adds some material not available to Bullock. This is the case also with Werner Maser, *Hitler: Legend, Myth and Reality*, tr. Peter and Betty Ross (New York: Harper & Row, 1973). John Toland, *Adolf Hitler* (New York: Doubleday, 1976), is a massive, definitive work on Hitler, based on every shred of material available, but students may still prefer the more interpretive and readable works listed above or the brief, up-to-date, and competent survey by William Carr, *Hitler: A Study in Personality and Politics* (New York: St. Martin's, 1979). There are three interesting psychohistorical works: Walter C. Langer, *The Mind of Adolf Hitler: The Secret Wartime Report* (New York: Basic Books, 1972), the fascinating account of how a team of psychiatrists and psychologists built up a strategic psychological profile of Hitler during World War II; Rudolf Binion, *Hitler among the Germans* (New York: Elsevier, 1976), a psychohistory of Hitler and his Germany; and Robert G. Waite, *The Psychopathic God: Adolf Hitler* (New York: Basic Books, 1977), more decidedly and professionally psychoanalytic than Binion and more up-to-date than Langer. Three special studies are also recommended: Bradley F. Smith, *Adolf Hitler: His Family, Childhood and Youth* (Stanford: Hoover Institute, 1967), and two excellent, detailed accounts of the beer hall

Putsch, Harold J. Gordon, *Hitler and the Beer Hall Putsch* (Princeton, N.J.: Princeton University Press, 1972) and John Dornberg, *Munich 1923, The Story of Hitler's First Grab for Power* (New York: Harper & Row, 1982). An important analytical work is Ian Kershaw, *The "Hitler Myth": Image and Reality in the Third Reich* (New York: Oxford University Press, 1987). See also Kershaw's *The Nazi Dictatorship: Problems and Perspectives of Interpretation* (London and Baltimore: E. Arnold, 1986), an excellent synthesis of the current historiography of the Nazi movement.

In addition to Ernst Nolte's *Three Faces of Fascism,* tr. Leila Vennewitz (New York: Holt, Rinehart and Winston, 1965), excerpted in this chapter, students are urged to read H. R. Kedward, *Fascism in Western Europe, 1900–1945* (London: Blackie, 1969), or F. L. Carsten, *The Rise of Fascism* (Berkeley: University of California Press, 1967). On German fascism, one of the most complete and comprehensive works is K. D. Bracher, *The German Dictatorship: The Origins, Structure, and Effects of National Socialism,* tr. J. Steinberg (New York: Praeger, 1970). Richard F. Hamilton, *Who Voted for Hitler?* (Princeton, N.J.: Princeton University Press, 1982), is a detailed study of the political functioning of German fascism. Probably the best general survey of political, social, and cultural history is Raymond J. Sontag, *A Broken World, 1919–1939,* "Rise of Modern Europe" series (New York: Harper & Row, 1971), but the most readable and exciting popular history is William L. Shirer, *The Rise and Fall of the Third Reich: A History of Nazi Germany* (New York: Simon and Schuster, 1960). A. J. P. Taylor, *From Sarajevo to Potsdam* (New York: Harcourt, Brace and World, 1966), is a vigorous, witty, highly personal interpretive history. Hannah Vogt, *The Burden of Guilt: A Short History of Germany, 1914–1945,* tr. Herbert Strauss (New York: Oxford University Press, 1964), is especially interesting in that it was specifically written for the instruction of post–World War II German young people. Sebastian Haffner, *The Meaning of Hitler,* tr. Ewald Osers (New York: Macmillan, 1979), is a best-selling German book, a reassessment (and condemnation) of Hitler against the tendencies to try to rehabilitate or justify him. Of the several books by those close to Hitler, the best, most important, and most interesting is Albert Speer, *Inside the Third Reich,* tr. Richard and Clara Winston (New York: Macmillan, 1970). Finally, three important books on the German army must be recommended: John W. Wheeler-Bennett, *The Nemesis of Power: The German Army in Politics, 1918–1945* (New York: St. Martin's, 1954); Robert J. O'Neill, *The German Army and the Nazi Party, 1933–1939* (London: Cassell, 1968); and Len Deighton, *Blitzkrieg: From the Rise of Hitler to the Fall of Dunkirk* (New York: Knopf, 1980), an exciting, readable account of the employment of Hitler's army. Ronald Lewin, *Hitler's Mistakes* (New York: Morrow, 1986), is an interesting critical appraisal of Hitler's failures as a military strategist.

ALBERT EINSTEIN AND THE ATOMIC AGE: A QUESTION OF RESPONSIBILITY

1879	Born
1905	First basic papers published
1916	Published fundamental paper on the general theory of relativity
1921	Won Nobel Prize in physics
1933	Fled from Germany to the United States
1939	Manhattan Project to create the atomic bomb begun
1945	Atomic bombs dropped on Hiroshima and Nagasaki
1955	Died

By the early 1930s, Albert Einstein was the most famous scientist in the world. Indeed, he had become a kind of symbol for the abstruseness of modern science itself, an expert in a branch of theoretical physics so remote and lofty that—at least according to the popular press—only a dozen other people could even understand his theories, much less explain them.

Long before this time, Einstein had established the fundamental direction of his work. As early as 1905, at the age of twenty-six, he had published very important papers, among them his theory of relativity, his work on statistical mechanics, and the quantum theory of radiation. When these first papers were published, Einstein was working as a patent clerk in Berne because he could not find an academic position, but by 1914 he held a professorship at the University of Berlin and was director of the Institute of Physics in the Kaiser Wilhelm Society for the Development of Sciences and a member of the Royal Prussian Academy of Sciences. In 1916 he published the fundamental paper on the general theory of relativity that established his worldwide fame, and in 1921 he received the Nobel Prize for Physics.

Although Einstein's main interest through the late 1920s was in the development of what came to be called his general field theory, other developments far removed from the abstractions of science had begun to crowd in upon his world. Hitler was on the rise in Germany, and Einstein was a Jew. In 1933 Einstein resigned his academic appointments, severed the associations of a lifetime, and joined the thousands of Jews, humble and famous, who had already begun to flee Hitler's Germany. An honored position was created for him at the Institute for Advanced Study at Princeton University, and there he remained for the rest of his life.

Einstein maintained contact with other brilliant refugee physicists who had fled the tyrannies of Europe, among them his old friend Max Born in England, the Hungarian Leo Szilard in the United States, and dozens of other scholars. These men, through their ties with what remained of the old international community of physicists, began to hear troubling rumors in the mid-1930s of experimental work being done in Europe in the field of atomic energy. Then in 1939 Niels Bohr brought word that Hahn and Strassman of the Kaiser Wilhelm Society in Berlin had actually produced nuclear fission. An atomic bomb was now a practical possibility. The work that Bohr reported and the work that would subsequently be done in Germany, England, and the United States was based, in the last analysis, upon Einstein's theories.

Twenty years before, Einstein had argued in his special theory of relativity that, as an object approached the speed of light, its acceleration would tend to produce not only increased speed but increased mass. He explained the process in the elegantly simple equation $E = mc^2$, in which the potential energy (E) of an object is equal to its mass (m) multiplied by the square of the speed of light (c^2). The enormous product of energy that would result from even the most infinitesimal transformation of mass—with the speed of light computed at 186,000 miles per second—was quite beyond anything but mathematical comprehension and even theoretically possible in terrestrial physics only at the atomic level. Now, working with unstable, heavy elements and apparently quite by accident, German scientists had produced a nuclear chain reaction, the instantaneous transformation of one element into another with exactly the incredible release of energy that Einstein's equation had described. As Leo Szilard would later write, "The dream of the alchemists came true. . . . But while the first successful alchemist was undoubtedly God, I sometimes wonder if the second successful alchemist may not have been the Devil himself."[1]

If German scientists had discovered the secret of atomic fission, it would probably not be long before the German government would have an atomic bomb. This prospect brought Leo Szilard and Eugene Wigner to Einstein. As a result of their discussion, Einstein immediately agreed to take action and eventually signed the now famous letter to President Roosevelt urging government support of research on nuclear chain reactions. Now, with the alarming news from Germany and the push from Einstein, work on the Manhattan Project seriously began, and with it the chain of events leading to the explosions over Hiroshima and Nagasaki in August 1945.

---

[1]"Creative Intelligence and Society," in *Collected Works of Leo Szilard...*, ed. B. T. Feld and G. W. Szilard (Cambridge, Mass.: M.I.T. Press, 1972), I, 189.

The Complaint of Peace

ALBERT EINSTEIN

Technology is older than science, but through the centuries the two have always been linked together, technology adapting the theoretical findings of science to the practical uses of society. Sad to say, these uses, more often than not, have been military. With "the bomb," society at last had the ultimate weapon, the doomsday machine capable of destroying not only one's enemies but all humanity.

With the bomb there also came the difficult question of the scientists' moral responsibility for the application of their theoretical and experimental work. One of the most troubled by this question was Albert Einstein. In December 1945, within months of the explosions over Japan, Einstein addressed the Nobel Anniversary Dinner in New York, speaking of the parallel between Alfred Nobel and his desire to atone for the invention of "an explosive more powerful than any then known" and the physicists "who participated in producing the most formidable weapon of all time" and who "are harassed by a similar feeling of responsibility, not to say guilt." But, he continued, their choice was as clear as their anguish was real. "We helped create this new weapon in order to prevent the enemies of mankind from achieving it first. . . . The war is won, but the peace is not."[2]

The persistent theme of all Einstein's public statements and the principal concern of the last decade of his life was the creation of a supranational organization to make sure that the bomb would never again be used. Some of Einstein's friends were exasperated with him for his continued refusal to advocate the surrender of the bomb to the United Nations, then in its confident infancy. But Einstein perceived the essential weakness of that organization, later to be so tragically demonstrated: it was not capable of keeping the peace. But his own proposal—the establishment of a world government—was even more unrealistic.

Einstein stated his views in an interview-article with Raymond Swing that originally appeared in the Atlantic Monthly *in November 1945. A slightly revised version of this article, from* Einstein on Peace, *is reprinted below in its entirety. Einstein's statements tended to be brief and simple. But in this piece, it is not his arguments that are striking; rather, it is the*

---

[2]*Einstein on Peace*, ed. Otto Nathan and Heinz Norden (New York: Schocken Books, 1968), p. 355.

tension between his belief that pure science is essentially unmanageable and his profound sense of the scientist's moral responsibility in the realm of human affairs.

The release of atomic energy has not created a new problem. It has merely made more urgent the necessity of solving an existing one. One could say that it has affected us quantitatively, not qualitatively. As long as there are sovereign nations possessing great power, war is inevitable. This does not mean that one can know when war will come but only that one is sure that it will come. This was true even before the atomic bomb was made. What has changed is the destructiveness of war.

I do not believe that the secret of the bomb should be given to the United Nations Organization. I do not believe it should be given to the Soviet Union. Either course would be analogous to a man with capital who, wishing another individual to collaborate with him on an enterprise, starts by giving him half his money. The other man might choose to start a rival enterprise, when what is wanted is his co-operation. The secret of the bomb should be committed to a world government, and the United States should immediately announce its readiness to do so. Such a world government should be established by the United States, the Soviet Union and Great Britain, the only three powers which possess great military strength. The three of them should commit to this world government all of their military resources. The fact that there are only three nations with great military power should make it easier, rather than harder, to establish a world government.

Since the United States and Great Britain have the secret of the atomic bomb and the Soviet Union does not, they should invite the Soviet Union to prepare and present the first draft of a Constitution for the proposed world government. This would help dispel the distrust of the Russians, which they feel because they know the bomb is being kept a secret chiefly to prevent their having it. Obviously, the first draft would not be the final one, but the Russians should be made to feel that the world government will guarantee their security.

It would be wise if this Constitution were to be negotiated by one American, one Briton and one Russian. They would, of course, need advisers, but these advisers should serve only when asked. I believe three men can succeed in preparing a workable Constitution acceptable to all the powers. Were six or seven men, or more, to attempt to do so, they would probably fail. After the three great powers have drafted a Constitution and adopted it, the smaller nations should be invited to join the world government. They should also be free not to join and, though they should feel perfectly secure outside the world government, I am sure they will eventually wish to join. Naturally, they should be entitled to propose changes in the Constitution as drafted by the Big Three. But the Big Three should go ahead and organize the world government, whether or not the smaller nations decide to join.

Such a world government should have jurisdiction over all military matters, and it need have only one other power. That is the power to interfere in countries where a minority is oppressing the majority and, therefore, is creating the kind of instability that leads to war. For example, conditions such as exist today in Argentina and Spain should be dealt with. There must be an end to the concept of non-intervention, for to abandon non-intervention in certain circumstances is part of keeping the peace.

The establishment of a world government should not be delayed until similar conditions of freedom exist in each of the three great powers. While it is true that in the Soviet Union the minority rules, I do not believe that the internal conditions in that country constitute a threat to world peace. One must bear in mind that the people in Russia had not had a long tradition of political education; changes to improve conditions in Russia had to be effected by a minority for the reason that there was no majority capable of doing so. If I had been born a Russian, I believe I could have adjusted myself to this situation.

It should not be necessary, in establishing a world government with a monopoly of authority over military affairs, to change the internal structure of the three great powers. It would be for the three individuals who draft the Constitution to devise ways for collaboration despite the different structures of their countries.

Do I fear the tyranny of a world government? Of course I do. But I fear still more the coming of another war. Any government is certain to be evil to some extent. But a world government is preferable to the far greater evil of wars, particularly when viewed in the context of the intensified destructiveness of war. If such a world government is not established by a process of agreement among nations, I believe it will come anyway, and in a much more dangerous form; for war or wars can only result in one power being supreme and dominating the rest of the world by its overwhelming military supremacy.

Now that we have the atomic secret, we must not lose it, and that is what we would risk doing if we gave it to the United Nations Organization or to the Soviet Union. But, as soon as possible, we must make it clear that we are not keeping the bomb a secret for the sake of maintaining our power but in the hope of establishing peace through world government, and that we will do our utmost to bring this world government into being.

I appreciate that there are persons who approve of world government as the ultimate objective but favor a gradual approach to its establishment. The trouble with taking little steps, one at a time, in the hope of eventually reaching the ultimate goal, is that while such steps are being taken, we continue to keep the bomb without convincing those who do not have the bomb of our ultimate intentions. That of itself creates fear and suspicion, with the consequence that the relations between rival countries deteriorate to a dangerous extent. That is why people who advocate taking a step at a time may think they are approaching world peace, but they actually are contributing by their slow pace to the possibility of war. We have no time to waste in this way. If war is to be averted, it must be done quickly.

Further, we shall not have the secret of the bomb for very long. I know it is being argued that no other country has money enough to spend on the development of the atomic bomb and that, therefore, we are assured of the secret for a long time. But it is a common mistake in this country to measure things by the amount of money they cost. Other countries which have the raw materials and manpower and wish to apply them to the work of developing atomic power can do so; men and materials and the decision to use them, and not money, are all that is needed.

I do not consider myself the father of the release of atomic energy. My part in it was quite indirect. I did not, in fact, foresee that it would be released in my time. I only believed that it was theoretically possible. It became practical through the accidental discovery of chain reaction, and this was not something I could have predicted. It was discovered by Hahn in Berlin, and he himself at first misinterpreted what he discovered. It was Lise Meitner who provided the correct interpretation and escaped from Germany to place the information in the hands of Niels Bohr.[3]

In my opinion, a great era of atomic science cannot be assured by organizing science in the way corporations are organized. One can organize the application of a discovery already made, but one cannot organize the discovery itself. Only a free individual can make a discovery. However, there can be a kind of organization wherein the scientist is assured freedom and proper conditions of work. Professors of science in American universities, for instance, should be relieved of

---

[3]Einstein is in error on a minor point. . . . Lise Meitner did not "escape from Germany to place the information [about atomic fission] in the hands of Niels Bohr." She was already in Sweden at the time.—Ed.

some of their teaching so as to have more time for research. Can you imagine an organization of scientists making the discoveries of Charles Darwin?

I do not believe that the vast private corporations of the United States are suitable to the needs of the times. If a visitor should come to this country from another planet, would he not find it strange that, in this country, private corporations are permitted to wield so much power without having to assume commensurate responsibility? I say this to stress my conviction that the American government must retain control of atomic energy, not because socialism is necessarily desirable but because atomic energy was developed by the government; it would be unthinkable to turn over this property of the people to any individual or group of individuals. As for socialism, unless it is international to the extent of producing a world government which controls all military power, it might lead to wars even more easily than capitalism because it represents an even greater concentration of power.

To give any estimate as to when atomic energy might be applied for peaceful, constructive purposes is impossible. All that we know now is how to use a fairly large quantity of uranium. The use of small quantities, sufficient, say, to operate a car or an airplane, is thus far impossible, and one cannot predict when it will be accomplished. No doubt, it will be achieved, but no one can say when. Nor can one predict when materials more common than uranium can be used to supply atomic energy. Presumably, such materials would be among the heavier elements of high atomic weight and would be relatively scarce due to their lesser stability. Most of these materials may already have disappeared through radioactive disintegration. So, though the release of atomic energy can be, and no doubt will be, a great boon to mankind, this may not come about for some time.

I myself do not have the gift of explanation which would be needed to persuade large numbers of people of the urgency of the problems that now face the human race. Hence, I should like to commend someone who has this gift of explanation: Emery Reves, whose book *The Anatomy of Peace* is intelligent, clear, brief, and, if I may use the absurd term, dynamic on the topic of war and need for world government.

Since I do not foresee that atomic energy will prove to be a boon within the near future, I have to say that, for the present, it is a menace. Perhaps it is well that it should be. It may intimidate the human race into bringing order to its international affairs, which, without the pressure of fear, undoubtedly would not happen.

Einstein and the Bomb

OTTO NATHAN AND HEINZ NORDEN

Einstein clearly did not consider himself to be the father of the bomb. Indeed, as he stated in the preceding article, he felt his role to be quite indirect. How Einstein came to be involved in the American effort to construct the atomic bomb is a fascinating story, especially in light of the fact that as late as 1939 he did not seem to be very optimistic about practical applications of nuclear fission. But international events finally prompted Einstein to advise President Roosevelt and the American government to undertake the work that became the Manhattan Project and ultimately produced the bomb. The circumstances leading to Einstein's action are described by Otto Nathan, one of Einstein's confidants and the executor of his Last Will, and Heinz Norden in Einstein on Peace, *from which the following selection is excerpted.*

It was only . . . in the early summer of 1939 that Einstein, through Szilard, became involved in the efforts to experiment with the construction of atomic bombs. It would appear that, several years before, Einstein had been very doubtful about the possibility of splitting the atom. At the winter session of the American Association for the Advancement of Science in Pittsburgh in January 1935, reporters asked Einstein whether he thought that scientists would ever be able to transmute matter into energy for practical purposes. In the subsequent newspaper account, which should be considered with caution, Einstein is reported to have replied that he felt almost certain it would not be possible, and to have referred to the vast amount of energy required to release energy from a molecule. "It is," he is reported to have added, "something like shooting birds in the dark in a country where there are only a few birds."

It is possible that Einstein may have learned early in 1939 about the Hahn-Strassmann-Meitner-Frisch work as well as about subsequent publications concerning these developments. It does not appear, however, that he was very optimistic regarding the possibility of a practical application of the new scientific discoveries at an early date. In a statement made in reply to a question submitted to him on the occasion of his sixtieth birthday, March 14, 1939, and published in *The New York Times,* Einstein made the following remarks:

The results gained thus far concerning the splitting of the atom do not justify the assumption that the atomic energy released in the process could be economically utilized. Yet, there can hardly be a physicist with so little intellectual curiosity that his interest in this important subject could become impaired because of the unfavorable conclusion to be drawn from past experimentation.

Szilard's first contact with Einstein in the matter of nuclear fission took place several months later. When he first considered consulting with Einstein about the new scientific discoveries and their implications, he did not contemplate any approach to the United States Government. Szilard recalls that he and Wigner had by this time become very perturbed by the thought that Germany might obtain large quantities of uranium from the Belgian Congo, the chief source of the material. Germany might thus be greatly helped in her research on atomic energy and ultimately in the production of atomic bombs. Szilard and Wigner felt that the Belgian Government should be advised of these eventualities in order that uranium exports to Germany might be halted if Belgium so desired. Szilard knew that Einstein had for years been on friendly terms with Queen Elizabeth of Belgium. When he and Wigner decided to visit Einstein at Nassau Point, Peconic, Long Island, where Einstein was spending the summer, it was, as Szilard has reported, their intention to suggest to Einstein that he communicate with Queen Elizabeth. It is one of the dramatic aspects of the whole atomic development that this visit, with a relatively modest and probably inconsequential purpose, led to events of completely different and, eventually, momentous import. The visit took place around July 15, 1939.

Szilard recalls that Einstein, when told about the possibility of producing a chain reaction, exclaimed, "*Daran habe ich gar nicht gedacht!*" (That never occurred to me.) Szilard reports that Einstein immediately recognized the implication of Germany's access to uranium in the Congo and declared he would be prepared to assist in informing the Belgian Government accordingly. Several approaches to the problem were discussed by the three scientists. Wigner apparently emphasized not only the desirability of advising the Belgian Government through the Queen or the Belgian Ambassador in Washington of the dangers involved in uranium exports to Germany but also the need for large imports of uranium into the United States. Whether recommendations were made as to how to secure such imports or who might be approached on the matter is not known. Einstein is reported to have favored a suggestion, apparently also offered by Wigner, to submit to the State Department a draft of a projected letter to the Queen of Belgium. The letter would be mailed to the Queen only if no objection were raised by the State Department. There is no information available as to whether, at this original meeting, Einstein, Szilard and Wigner considered advising the American Government of the implications of the new scientific discoveries with a view to engaging its interest in promoting or subsidizing further research in the atomic field.

Even before his visit to Einstein, Szilard had discussed the entire problem with a New York friend in the financial world; he had felt that the financial resources of the physics department of Columbia University would not suffice for the additional research contemplated by Fermi and himself and that outside funds would therefore be necessary. Upon Szilard's return to New York from his visit to Einstein, the finance expert informed him that he had consulted with Dr. Alexander Sachs, a well-known economist connected with the New York banking house of Lehman Brothers and sometimes one of President Roosevelt's unofficial advisers. When it was suggested to Szilard that he communicate with Dr. Sachs, he did so, apparently without delay. It was undoubtedly Sachs who recognized the magnitude and significance of the problem and realized that, to obtain results, the matter should be brought to the attention of the White House. He, therefore, suggested to Szilard that Einstein's letter be addressed to President Roosevelt rather than to the Belgian Queen or the Belgian Ambassador. Sachs offered to see to it that the letter would reach the President personally. Writing to Einstein on July 19, 1939, Szilard stated that, although he had seen Sachs only once in his life and had not been able to form an opinion of him, he nonetheless recommended accepting the course of action outlined by him. Szilard added that this recommendation was also supportred by Professor Edward Teller, then a guest professor at Columbia University, with whom he had consulted. Szilard further suggested that Einstein's projected letter be entrusted to Sachs since he believed that Sachs was in a position to do as he had promised. Szilard enclosed a draft of the letter. Since Sachs was to play an important role during the ensuing months, and since Einstein's letter to Roosevelt was to release a "chain reaction" which possibly no move by any other individual could have effected at that time, Szilard's casually arranged meeting about an all-important matter with a person completely unknown to him, his subsequent confidence in that person on the basis of a single meeting, and Sachs's perception of Roosevelt's capacity for bold decisions are startling incidents in the drama that was to unfold.

While it is not possible to reconstruct all the developments during the two weeks following Szilard's meeting with Sachs, it is known that, during this period, Szilard once again called on Einstein at his Long Island summer home. Since Wigner was out of town, Szilard was accompanied on his second visit by Edward Teller. At this meeting with Szilard and Teller, if not before by phone or mail, Einstein accepted Sachs's suggestion to bring the matter to the attention of the President and to have a letter to Roosevelt transmitted through Sachs. Einstein dictated to Teller the draft of a letter in German which is preserved in his files. This draft contains some of the main points of the history-making communication to Roosevelt that Einstein was eventually to sign. . . .

Einstein's draft is an indication of how, in possibly less than a week, the initial modest proposition to write a letter to the Belgian Queen had developed into a meaningful and highly suggestive approach to the President of the United States. Whether Einstein's dictated draft was inspired by the draft which Szilard had prepared after his meeting with Sachs and had mailed to Einstein before his second visit cannot be ascertained. On August 2, 1939, Szilard wrote to Einstein that, in his discussions with Sachs about additional recommendations, K. T. Compton, Bernard Baruch and Charles Lindbergh had been suggested for the position of liaison man between the government and the atomic scientists, the position recommended in Einstein's draft and also in his final letter to Roosevelt. Szilard added that Lindberg was the "favorite" at the time of writing.

On the basis of Einstein's German draft, Szilard prepared, after a further meeting with Sachs, two English versions of a letter to the President, which he forwarded to Einstein in his letter of August 2, 1939. Einstein favored the shorter of the two Szilard drafts. The letter actually sent to Roosevelt and dated August 2, 1939, reads as follows:

> *Albert Einstein*
> *Old Grove Road*
> *Nassau Point*
> *Peconic, Long Island*
> *August 2, 1939*

F. D. Roosevelt
President of the United States
White House
Washington, D.C.

Sir:

Some recent work by E. Fermi and L. Szilard, which has been communicated to me in manuscript, leads me to expect that the element uranium may be turned into a new and important source of energy in the immediate future. Certain aspects of the situation seem to call for watchfulness and, if necessary, quick action on the part of the Administration. I believe, therefore, that it is my duty to bring to your attention the following facts and recommendations.

In the course of the last four months it has been made probable—through the work of Joliot in France as well as Fermi and Szilard in America—that it may become possible to set up nuclear chain reactions in a large mass of uranium, by which vast amounts of power and large quantities of new radium-like elements would be generated. Now it appears almost certain that this could be achieved in the immediate future.

This new phenomenon would also lead to the construction of bombs, and it is conceivable—though much less certain—that extremely powerful bombs of a new type may thus be constructed. A single bomb of this type, carried by boat or exploded in a port, might very well destroy the whole port together with some of the surrounding territory. However, such bombs might very well prove to be too heavy for transportation by air.

The United States has only very poor ores of uranium in moderate quantities. There is some good ore in Canada and the former Czechoslovakia, while the most important source of uranium is the Belgian Congo.

In view of this situation you may think it desirable to have some permanent contact maintained between the Administration and the group of physicists working on chain reactions in America. One possible way of achieving this might be for you to entrust with this task a person who has your confidence and who could perhaps serve in an unofficial capacity. His task might comprise the following:

a) To approach Government Departments, keep them informed of the further developments, and put forward recommendations for Government action, giving particular attention to the problem of securing a supply of uranium ore for the United States.

b) To speed up the experimental work which is at present being carried on within the limits of the budgets of University laboratories, by providing funds, if such funds be required, through his contacts with private persons who are willing to make contributions for this cause, and perhaps also by obtaining the cooperation of industrial laboratories which have the necessary equipment.

I understand that Germany has actually stopped the sale of uranium from the Czechoslovakian mines which she has taken over. That she should have taken such early action might perhaps be understood on the ground that the son of the German Under-Secretary of State, von Weizsäcker, is attached to the Kaiser Wilhelm Institute in Berlin, where some of the American work on uranium is now being repeated.

Yours very truly,

A. Einstein

This letter, addressed by the then greatest living scientist to one of the most important political leaders of the world, bearing on dramatically important scientific and military developments and suggesting crucial moves by the American Government, was actually not submitted to President Roosevelt for over two months, during which period the Germans might have made much progress in the search for a nuclear chain reaction. The available documents in Einstein's files and all other sources of information fail to provide an adequate explanation for the delay in transmitting Einstein's communication. In a letter of September 27, 1939, Szilard conveyed to Einstein his impression that the letter "had already been in Washington for some time." But in another letter, dated October 3, 1939, Szilard reported that he and Wigner had called on Sachs, and Sachs admitted still having Einstein's letter in his possession; Sachs explained that he had gained the impression from several telephone conversations with Roosevelt's secretary that it was advisable to see the President at a later time since he was overburdened with work. In his testimony of November 27, 1945, before the Special Committee on Atomic Energy of the United States Senate, Sachs stated that he had not wanted to accept an appointment with the President as long as the President was involved in revising the existing neutrality legislation. However, the neutrality legislation did not become an acute issue until the war broke out in Europe on September 1, 1939, which was more than four weeks after Einstein had signed the letter.

In his letter to Einstein of October 3, 1939, Szilard remarked that he and Wigner had begun to wonder whether it might not become necessary to entrust another person with the mission Dr. Sachs had volunteered to perform. But Sachs did finally see President Roosevelt on October 11, 1939, and submitted to the President Einstein's letter, a more technical memorandum by Szilard, as well as considerable background material. The Szilard memorandum stated that, if fast neutrons could be used, "it would be easy to construct extremely dangerous bombs . . . with a destructive power far beyond all military conceptions." Sachs also submitted to the President a written statement of his own in which he summarized the main problems involved and listed the steps which he thought should be taken by the United States in the matter of further exploring the problem of nuclear fission.

President Roosevelt acted at once. He appointed an "Advisory Committee on Uranium," which was to report to him as soon as possible; a few days later, he addressed the following letter to Einstein:

The White House
Washington

October 19, 1939

My dear Professor,
   I want to thank you for your recent letter and the most interesting and important enclosure.
   I found this data of such import that I have convened a board consisting of the head of the Bureau of Standards and a chosen representative of the Army and Navy to thoroughly investigate the possibilities of your suggestion regarding the element of uranium.
   I am glad to say that Dr. Sachs will co-operate and work with this committee and I feel this is the most practical and effective method of dealing with the subject.

Very sincerely yours,
Franklin D. Roosevelt

. . . The further history of the many stages in the development of the atomic bomb is recorded in other publications and need not be repeated. What is of interest here are the few instances when Einstein again intervened.
   After the first meeting of the Advisory Committee, other scientists were invited to participate in subsequent consultations. Sachs continued to play a very important role as the representative of the President and, as he himself frequently emphasized, as the individual who maintained contact with Einstein: he consulted with Einstein and presented Einstein's opinions and suggestions to the President or the committee orally or in writing, as circumstances would dictate. . . .
   Although the Advisory Committee continued to operate, Szilard and Sachs were perturbed at its relatively slow progress and, in February 1940, they decided once again to secure Einstein's intervention. It took the form of another letter from Einstein, dated March 7, 1940.

In this letter, Einstein reviewed the rapid development of atomic research—Szilard's and Fermi's continuing work, for example, and the likelihood that similar work was going forward in Europe, especially in Germany.

On March 15, 1940, Sachs brought Einstein's second letter to the attention of the President, who, on April 5, 1940, proposed an enlarged meeting of the Advisory Committee on Uranium which would include Einstein and others whom Einstein might suggest. Briggs, the chairman of the committee, invited Einstein to participate in such a meeting. Since Einstein was unable to accept the invitation, he addressed, on April 25, 1940, the following letter to Briggs:

> I thank you for your recent communication concerning a meeting of the Special Advisory Committee appointed by President Roosevelt.
>
> As, to my regret, I shall not be able to attend this meeting, I have discussed with Dr. Wigner and Dr. Sachs particularly the questions arising out of the work of Dr. Fermi and Dr. Szilard. I am convinced as to the wisdom and the urgency of creating the conditions under which that and related work can be carried out with greater speed and on a larger scale than hitherto. I was interested in a suggestion made by Dr. Sachs that the Special Advisory Committee submit names of persons to serve as a board of trustees for a nonprofit organization which, with the approval of the government committee, should secure from governmental or private sources, or both, the necessary funds for carrying out the work. It seems to me that such an organization would provide a framework which could give Dr. Fermi and Dr. Szilard and co-workers the necessary scope. The preparation of the large-scale experiment and the exploration of the various possibilities with regard to practical applications is a task of considerable complexity, and I think that given such a framework and the necessary funds, it could be carried out much faster than through a loose co-operation of university laboratories and government departments.

As far as can be established, Einstein had no further connection either with the work that preceded the atomic bomb project or with the project itself. The Advisory Committee did not continue much longer as such. When, in June 1940, Roosevelt created the National Defense Research Committee, which was to develop into a very significant organization with regard to America's military preparations, he asked that the Advisory Committee be reorganized, again under the chairmanship of Dr. Briggs, as a subcommittee of the newly created National Defense Research Committee. The President specifically assigned to the new committee the responsibility for research on nuclear problems. "This meant," Professor Karl T. Compton, a member of the new committee, remarked, "reviewing and acting upon the recommendations of Dr. Briggs's committee."

Viewed in historical perspective, it would appear that the decision to use Einstein's unique authority in the attempt to obtain the government's direct participation and financial assistance in atomic research may well have been decisive, since his intervention succeeded in securing the attention of President Roosevelt. The Advisory Committee on Uranium was organized by the President as an immediate result of Einstein's intervention and was the germinal body from which the whole huge atomic effort developed. Whether, without Einstein's intervention, similar developments would have taken place around the same period, and whether the atomic bomb would still have been produced around the time it was produced—that is, before the end of the war—are legitimate questions. . . .

. . . We shall never know with any degree of certainty what would have happened if Szilard had not called on Einstein in July 1939, or if Einstein, in turn, had not been immediately willing to lend his authority to supporting a request to the President of the United States that was partly based on scientific assumptions and speculations.

A New Vision Out of the Ashes

BERNARD T. FELD

In this chapter, we have already considered Einstein's own proposal for a world government as the only alternative he saw to nuclear war. And we considered the circumstances leading to Einstein's involvement in the American atom bomb project. Despite Einstein's statement that his role in that project was indirect and passive and his assertion that he did not consider himself "the father of the release of atomic energy," his last years were haunted by the prospect of nuclear war that the "release of atomic energy" had made possible. Those last years were also haunted by a sense of his own culpability—notwithstanding his protests to the contrary. The activities of Einstein in the years following World War II were devoted to his passionate advocacy of peace, a cause he had long advocated but which now became an obsession. These activities are sympathetically described by the MIT physicist and peace activist Bernard T. Feld in the article "Einstein and the Politics of Nuclear Weapons," published as one of the symposium papers in The Centennial Symposium in Jerusalem, one of several such celebrations of the centenary of Einstein's birth in 1979.

If relativity captured the public imagination in the period between the wars, the atomic bomb, which ended World War II, propelled Einstein even more directly into the limelight, but under circumstances that caused him acute moral, as well as personal, embarrassment. To the popular mind, Einstein was, and to a large extent remains, the "father of the atomic bomb." Is there any person so ignorant that he or she does not recognize his famous discovery of the equivalence between mass and energy, $E = mc^2$, which provides the theoretical basis for the release of nuclear energy? Add to this Einstein's audacious intervention with President Franklin D. Roosevelt, to convince him of the military potential of the discovery of nuclear fission, and you have the two ingredients of that aspect of the Einstein legend that he worked most diligently and unsuccessfully, to debunk.

Einstein's role in the successful American effort during World War II to develop a nuclear bomb was indeed peripheral. On this score, he tried hard to put the record straight. Thus, in response to a request from the editor of a Japanese journal demanding to know why Einstein, "as a great scientist who played an important role in producing the atomic bomb, . . . co-operate[d] in [its] production . . . although you were well aware of its tremendous destructive power?" he protested:

> My participation in the production of the atomic bomb consisted of one single act: I signed a letter to President Roosevelt, in which I emphasized the necessity of conducting a large-scale experimentation with regard to the feasibility of producing an atom bomb.
>
> I was well aware of the dreadful danger which would threaten mankind were the experiments to prove successful. Yet I felt impelled to take the step because it seemed probable that the Germans might be working on the same problem with every prospect of success. I saw no alternative but to act as I did, *although I have always been a convinced pacifist.*

Yet the myth persisted that through his earlier discovery of the fundamental mass-energy relationship, Einstein somehow bore responsibility for the final outcome. With great patience, he explained:

> Now you seem to believe that I, poor fellow that I am, by discovering and publishing the relationship between mass and energy, made an important contribution to the lamentable situation in which we find ourselves today. You suggest that I should then, in 1905, have foreseen the possible development of atomic bombs. But this was quite impossible since the accomplishment of a "chain reaction" was dependent on the existence of empirical data that could hardly have been anticipated in 1905. But even if such knowledge had been available, it would have been ridiculous to attempt to conceal the particular conclusion resulting from the Special Theory of Relativity. Once the theory existed, the conclusion also existed and could not have remained concealed for any length of time. As for the theory itself, it owes its existence to the efforts to discover the properties of the "luminiferous ether"! There was never even the slightest indication of any potential technological application.

Even now, some forty years later, the importance of Einstein's role in the American development of nuclear weapons before the end of the war against Japan remains a source of legitimate controversy. Some feel it was seminal, that without his intervention the atomic bomb project would never have received the government attention and support that was indispensable to its success. Others believe that the physics was so compelling that once the early (and very inexpensive) demonstrations of the potentiality had taken place—and they would probably have happened even without government support—not even the most obtuse bureaucracy could have resisted the inevitable pressures of the cream of the American physics community. . . .

In any event, Einstein learned of the success of the Manhattan Project as did the rest of the world—by the public announcement on 8 August 1945 that a single bomb using the fission of an isotope of uranium had destroyed the Japanese city of Hiroshima. Einstein is alleged to have responded to this news with the time-honored lament, "*Oy Weh!*" (woe upon us).

There can be no question as to where Einstein would have stood with respect to the dropping of the bombs on Japan. In a letter of 19 March 1955 to Max von Laue, one of the few German physicists with whom he retained a lifelong friendship, he explained:

My action concerning the atomic bomb and Roosevelt consisted merely in the fact that, because of the danger that Hitler might be the first to have the bomb, I signed a letter to the President which had been drafted by Szilard. Had I known that that fear was not justified, I, no more than Szilard, would have participated in opening this Pandora's box. For my distrust of governments was not limited to Germany.

Unfortunately, I had no share in the warning made against using the bomb against Japan. Credit for this must go to James Franck. If they had only listened to him!

The use of the bomb against Japanese civilians was especially painful to Einstein, because he had formed very strong friendships and a special fondness for the people during his visit to Japan in 1922. Not only was there not a single racist bone in his body, but Einstein never held the Japanese people responsible for the war in the sense that he held the German people responsible. Thus, in an uncharacteristically harsh response to an appeal for a "soft peace" from his old friend and fellow refugee James Franck in December 1945, he wrote:

I remember too well the campaign of tears staged by the Germans after the First World War to be fooled by its repetition. The Germans slaughtered several millions of civilians according to a well-thought-out-plan. If they had murdered you too, some crocodile tears would undoubtedly have been shed. The few decent people who are among them do not change the picture as a whole. I have gauged from several letters received from over there, as well as from the information supplied by some reliable persons, that the Germans do not feel one iota of guilt or sorrow.... Dear Franck, do not involve yourself in this dirty mess! They will first misuse your kindness and then they will ridicule you for being a fool. But if I am unable to persuade you to refrain, I, for one, will certainly not get mixed up in this affair. Should the opportunity present itself, I shall publicly oppose the appeal.

Nevertheless, he certainly would have opposed the bomb's use against Germany had it been ready in time, as attested in a letter to a Japanese correspondent written on 23 June 1953:

I am a *dedicated* [*entschiedener*] but not an *absolute* pacifist; this means that I am opposed to the use of force under any circumstances, except when confronted by an enemy who pursues the destruction of life as an *end in itself*. I have always condemned the use of the atomic bomb against Japan. However, I was completely powerless to prevent the fateful decision for which I am as little responsible as you are for the deeds of the Japanese in Korea and China.

I have never said I would have approved the use of the atomic bomb against the Germans, I did believe that we had to avoid the contingency of Germany under Hitler being in *sole* possession of this weapon. This was the real danger at the time.

I am not only opposed to war against Russia but to all war—with the above reservation....

It is far from surprising, therefore, that with World War II over and the intellectual battle lines forming—between those who would have taken advantage of the American nuclear monopoly to establish the dominance of American military influence over all national and international institutions and those who saw the atomic bomb as an opportunity finally to establish international institutions with the intention *and the power* to provide supranational control over future conflict and war—Einstein again plunged enthusiastically into the arena of public affairs. He firmly supported the fledgling atomic scientists' movement, organized into a Federation of Atomic Scientists, and encouraged its voice, *The Bulletin of the Atomic Scientists*. ...

In support of the various national and international enterprises of the atomic scientists, Einstein agreed in May 1946 to serve as chairman of an Emergency Committee of Atomic Scientists. Its program was based on an agreed set of principles concerning the dangers of atomic weapons:

These facts are accepted by all scientists:

1. Atomic bombs can now be made cheaply and in large numbers. They will become more destructive.
2. There is no military defense against the atomic bomb and none is to be expected.
3. Other nations can rediscover our secret processes by themselves.
4. Preparedness against atomic war is futile, and if attempted will ruin the structure of our social order.
5. If war breaks out, atomic bombs will be used and they will surely destroy our civilization.
6. There is no solution to this problem except international control of atomic energy and, ultimately, the elimination of war.

The program of the committee is to see that these truths become known to the public. The democratic determination of this nation's policy on atomic energy must ultimately rest on the understanding of its citizens.

The immediate objective was to raise a fund of $1,000,000 in support of the various educational activities of the atomic scientists aimed at civilian national and international control of future nuclear energy activities. However, although the committee had a certain amount of success in raising money, as time passed it became increasingly clear to Einstein and his fellow committee members that the world was drifting in the wrong direction. In considering the root causes of their failure, Einstein and his colleagues were convinced that the seriousness of the problem demanded more drastic remedies. Their views moved more and more in the direction of "world government" as the only logical solution. . . .

From then on, Einstein became ever more outspoken in his insistence that nothing short of an effective supranational authority able to exercise unquestioned control over international issues of war and peace was needed to save the world from nuclear disaster. He maintained that such an international authority could and should be established promptly through the United Nations, irrespective of whether all the major world powers were ready immediately to join. . . . Although this view was openly and pointedly attacked by Soviet officials, as well as by some Soviet scientists, as playing into the hands of right-wing, anti-Soviet forces, Einstein stood his ground and steadfastly maintained until the end of his life his adherence to the "world government" approach as the only means of saving humankind from the disastrous consequences of the uninhibited national exploitation of inevitable technological progress. . . .

But eternal optimist that he was, Einstein could never give up hope. Thus, in the spring of 1955 he and Bertrand Russell, with typical youthful enthusiasm, launched a project aimed at starting a world-wide movement among scientists to reverse the Cold War trend toward nuclear war. The credo of this movement was the Russell-Einstein Manifesto signed by Einstein on 11 April 1955, exactly one week before his death. The text of this manifesto serves well as a summing up of Einstein's view of the state of the world and of the responsibilities of scientists as world citizens:

> In the tragic situation which confronts humanity, we feel that scientists should assemble in conference to appraise the perils that have arisen as a result of the development of weapons of mass destruction. . . .
>
> We are speaking on this occasion, not as members of this or that nation, continent or creed, but as human beings, members of the species man, whose continued existence is in doubt. The world is full of conflicts; and, overshadowing all minor conflicts, the titanic struggle between Communism and anti-Communism.
>
> Almost everybody who is politically conscious has strong feelings about one or more of these issues; but we want you, if you can, to set aside such feelings and consider yourselves only as members of a biological species which has had a remarkable history, and whose disappearance none of us can desire.
>
> We shall try to say no single word which should appeal to one group rather than to another. All, equally, are in peril, and, if the peril is understood, there is hope that they may collectively avert it. . . .
>
> The general public, and even many men in positions of authority, have not realized what would be involved in a war with nuclear bombs. The general public still thinks in terms of the obliteration of cities. It is understood that the new bombs are more powerful than the old, and that, while one A-bomb could obliterate Hiroshima, one H-bomb could obliterate the largest cities, such as London, New York and Moscow.
>
> No doubt in an H-bomb war great cities would be obliterated. But this is one of the minor disasters that would have to be faced. If everybody in London, New York and Moscow were exterminated, the world might, in the course of a few centuries, recover from the blow. But we now know, especially since the Bikini test, that nuclear bombs can gradually spread destruction over a very much wider area than had been supposed.
>
> It is stated on very good authority that a bomb can now be manufac-

tured which will be 2,500 times as powerful as that which destroyed Hiroshima.

Such a bomb, if exploded near the ground or under water, sends radioactive particles into the upper air. They sink gradually and reach the surface of the earth in the form of a deadly dust or rain. It was this dust which infected the Japanese fishermen and their catch of fish.

No one knows how widely such lethal radioactive particles might be diffused, but the best authorities are unanimous in saying that a war with H-bombs might quite possibly put an end to the human race. It is feared that if many H-bombs are used there will be universal death—sudden only for a minority, but for the majority a slow torture of disease and disintegration.

Many warnings have been uttered by eminent men of science and by authorities in military strategy. None of them will say that the worst results are certain. What they do say is that these results are possible, and no one can be sure that they will not be realized. We have not yet found that the views of experts depend in any degree upon their politics or prejudices. They depend only, so far as our researchers have revealed, upon the extent of the particular expert's knowledge. We have found that the men who know most are the most gloomy.

Here, then, is the problem which we present to you, stark and dreadful and inescapable: Shall we put an end to the human race; or shall mankind renounce war? People will not face this alternative because it is so difficult to abolish war.

The abolition of war will demand distasteful limitations of national sovereignty. But what perhaps impedes understanding of the situation more than anything else is that the term *mankind* feels vague and abstract. People scarcely realize in imagination that the danger is to themselves and their children and their grandchildren, and not only to a dimly apprehended humanity. They can scarcely bring themselves to grasp that they, individually, and those whom they love are in imminent danger of perishing agonizingly. And so they hope that perhaps war may be allowed to continue provided modern weapons are prohibited.

This hope is illusory. Whatever agreements not to use the H-bombs had been reached in time of peace, they would no longer be considered binding in time of war, and both sides would set to work to manufacture H-bombs as soon as war broke out, for, if one side manufactured the bombs and the other did not, the side that manufactured them would inevitably be victorious.

Although an agreement to renounce nuclear weapons as part of a general reduction of armaments would not afford an ultimate solution, it would serve certain important purposes.

First: Any agreement between East and West is to the good in so far as it tends to diminish tension. Second: The abolition of thermonu-

232 Makers of World History

clear weapons, if each side believed that the other had carried it out sincerely, would lessen the fear of a sudden attack in the style of Pearl Harbor, which at present keeps both sides in a state of nervous apprehension. We should, therefore, welcome such an agreement, though only as a first step.

Most of us are not neutral in feeling, but, as human beings, we have to remember that, if the issues between East and West are to be decided in any manner that can give any possible satisfaction to anybody, whether Communist or anti-Communist, whether Asian or European or American, whether white or black, then these issues must not be decided by war. We should wish this to be understood, both in the East and in the West.

There lies before us, if we choose, continual progress in happiness, knowledge and wisdom. Shall we, instead, choose death, because we cannot forget our quarrels? We appeal, as human beings, to human beings: Remember your humanity and forget the rest. If you can do so, the way lies open to a new paradise; if you cannot, there lies before you the risk of universal death.

Review and Study Questions

1. How was the scientific community—including Einstein—responsible for the creation of the Atomic Age?

2. Was Einstein's preoccupation with world government in his last years an implicit admission of guilt in creating the atomic bomb?

3. In light of events since World War II, was the world government proposed by Einstein a realistic plan?

4. To what extent, in your opinion, was Einstein instrumental in beginning the actual work on the atomic bomb?

Suggestions for Further Reading

Einstein's own statements about the atomic bomb and scientific responsibility were as brief and often cryptic as were his public statements on other subjects. His most substantial one is the interview with Raymond Graham Swing reproduced in this chapter ("Einstein on the Atomic Bomb," *Atlantic Monthly*, 176, No. 5 [Nov. 1945], 43–45), but some parallel statements are to be found in his *Out of My Later Years* (New York: Philosophical Library, 1950), especially the section "Science and Life." These, as well as nearly all his other related statements, are reprinted and edited in *Einstein on Peace*, ed.

Otto Nathan and Heinz Norden (New York: Simon and Schuster, 1960), excerpted for this chapter. Some of his concern comes through in *The Born–Einstein Letters: Correspondence between Albert Einstein and Max and Hedwig Born from 1916–1955*, commentary by Max Born, tr. Irene Born (London: Macmillan, 1971), but this book is much more revealing of Born's anguish. The same sentiment is expressed throughout the world community of nuclear physicists, as Werner Heisenberg, *Physics and Beyond: Encounters and Conversations,* tr. A. J. Pomerans (New York: Harper & Row, 1971), demonstrates, as well as Otto Hahn, *My Life . . .* , tr. E. Kaiser and E. Wilkins (New York: Herder and Herder, 1970). The same sorts of views are expressed in the United States by J. Robert Oppenheimer in *The Flying Trapeze: Three Crises for Physicists* (London: Oxford University Press, 1964), especially the third crisis dealing with the atomic bomb and the moral responsibility of scientists; and in *The Open Mind* (New York: Simon and Schuster, 1955).

Most of the books about Einstein deal with his scientific and technical work: Lincoln Barnett, *The Universe and Dr. Einstein,* 2nd rev. ed. (New York: W. Sloane, 1957), or Jeremy Bernstein, *Einstein* (New York: Viking, 1973), for example. The best of these scientific biographies is Abraham Pais, *'Subtle is the Lord . . .' The Science and the Life of Albert Einstein* (Oxford and New York: Oxford University Press, 1982). *Some Strangeness in the Proportion: A Centennial Symposium to Celebrate the Achievements of Albert Einstein,* ed. Harry Woolf (Reading, Mass.: Addison-Wesley Publishing, 1980) is also entirely devoted to the evaluation of his work as a scientist and scientific theorist.

The best and most comprehensive book on him, Ronald W. Clark, *Einstein: The Life and Times,* 3rd ed., (New York: World, 1984), does focus on the political and social implications of his work rather than strictly on the work itself. To a somewhat lesser extent, this is the case with Banesh Hoffman, *Albert Einstein: Creator and Rebel* (New York: Viking, 1972). Antonia Vallentin, *Einstein: A Biography,* tr. M. Budberg (London: Weidenfeld and Nicolson, 1954), is interesting in that it deals more fully than any other book with the intimacies, family relations, and day-to-day affairs of Einstein. This area of his life is also revealed in *Albert Einstein, the Human Side: New Glimpses from His Archives,* ed. Helen Dukas and Banesh Hoffman (Princeton, N.J.: Princeton University Press, 1979). Jamie Sayen, *Einstein in America: The Scientist's Conscience in the Age of Hitler and Hiroshima* (New York: Crown, 1985) is a somewhat too adulatory treatment of its subject.

Lansing Lamont, *Day of Trinity* (New York: Atheneum, 1965), is a fascinating account of the making and employment of the atomic bomb. The implications of that employment are dealt with in several important books: Herbert Feis, *The Atom Bomb and the End of the War in the Pacific,* rev. ed. (Princeton, N.J.: Princeton University Press, 1966), Martin J. Sherwin, *A World Destroyed: The Atomic Bomb and the Grand Alliance* (New York: Knopf, 1975), Gar Alperovitz, *Atomic Diplomacy: Hiroshima and Potsdam; The Use of the Atomic Bomb and the American Confrontation with Soviet Power* (New York: Simon and Schuster, 1965), and in a brilliant and controversial work by a leading defense analyst, Fred Kaplan, *The Wizards of Armageddon* (New York: Simon and Schuster, 1983). Some of these issues and others are conveniently presented in a book of readings, *The Atomic Bomb: The Critical Issues,* ed. Barton J. Bernstein (Boston: Little, Brown, 1975).

MAHATMA GANDHI: SOLDIER OF NONVIOLENCE

1869	Born
1888–91	Studied law in England
1893–1914	Lived in South Africa
1915–20	Leader of the Indian National Congress
1922–24	Imprisoned for sedition
1928–34	Leader of the cause of Indian independence
1947	Indian independence achieved
1948	Died

Mahatma Gandhi was one of the best-known people in the world in the 1930s and 1940s, instantly recognizable from the pictures of him in newspapers, magazines, and newsreels—a frail little brown man in a loincloth, swathed in a shawl that he had woven himself out of yarn he had spun himself on a hand spinning wheel. He had no wealth and, for most of his life, no official political position. He was not an intellectual nor a political theorist. He was a moral leader, for millions in his native India and for millions more throughout the world. The American general and secretary of state George C. Marshall called him "the spokesman for the conscience of all mankind."[1] But it was not the whole world where he chose to play out the drama of his life. It was India. And his cause was Indian independence from the British Empire. Gandhi became the driving force in its final achievement in 1947, after two centuries of colonial rule. In that process he became a world figure.

Mohandas K. Gandhi was born in 1869, the fourth and youngest child of his father's fourth wife. He was born in the poor little provincial capital of Porbandar on the west coast of India. His father was an

---

[1]Louis Fischer, *The Life of Mahatma Gandhi* (New York: Harper, 1950), p. 10.

official in the state administration of the Indian ruling prince, and by native standards the family was reasonably well off. His mother was a deeply religious woman and Gandhi was raised as a devout Hindu.

After completing grammar school Gandhi, following his father's wishes, traveled to England to study law in 1888. He was enrolled in the Inner Temple and was called to the bar in 1891. He immediately returned to India. He had made an unimpressive record as a law student; he was even less impressive as a struggling young lawyer in Porbandar. In 1893 a business firm in the city offered to send him to South Africa for a year as its representative, and he accepted.

In South Africa Gandhi came face to face with the racial segregation policies of the government. He was a "colored," hence an inferior person. The indignities he suffered there—and more, the indignities suffered by his fellow Indians—galvanized Gandhi and started him on his life's work. He did not return to India after his year's contract was up. Instead he stayed in South Africa, opened a law office in Durban, and quickly became the spokesman for the rights of the many Indians there. He organized the Natal Indian Congress; he wrote dozens of eloquent petitions to the government on behalf of Indian rights; he wrote pamphlets to the same purpose. His activities and his views gained him wide coverage in the press in India and in Britain; at the same time, these activities and views—and their coverage in the foreign press—infuriated South African white extremists. He was threatened, even assaulted. He neither resisted nor brought charges against his attackers.

Then in 1899 the Boer War broke out and Gandhi, to the consternation of many of his fellow Indians, organized and led an Indian Ambulance Corps of over a thousand volunteers. Gandhi argued that if they claimed the right to be treated as subjects of the British Empire, they incurred the obligation of defending the Empire.

The Origin of Nonviolence

M. K. GANDHI

In spite of the most heroic service in the war, at its conclusion the Indians of South Africa found their status not at all improved, either with the Boers or with the British. Indeed, the situation deteriorated. In the late summer of 1906 an ordinance was proposed by the Transvaal government that would require all Indians to register with the authorities and to carry a certificate at all times on penalty of imprisonment or deportation. Gandhi, along with most of the Indian leaders, was convinced that this "Black Act" would mean absolute ruin for the Indians of South Africa. After a preliminary strategy session among the leaders, a public meeting was called. In the course of it Gandhi discovered the tactic that would be the fundamental center of his life's work—nonviolence, or as he called it, Satyagraha.

Here is his own account of the event.

The meeting was duly held on the 11th September 1906. It was attended by delegates from various places in the Transvaal. But I must confess that even I myself had not then understood all the implications of the resolutions I had helped to frame; nor had I gauged all the possible conclusions to which they might lead. The old Empire Theatre was packed from floor to ceiling. I could read in every face the expectation of something strange to be done or to happen. Mr. Abdul Gani, Chairman of the Transvaal British Indian Association, presided. He was one of the oldest Indian residents of the Transvaal, and partner and manager of the Johannesburg branch of the well-known firm of Mamad Kasam Kamrudin. The most important among the resolutions passed by the meeting was the famous Fourth Resolution, by which the Indians solemnly determined not to submit to the Ordinance in the event of its becoming law in the teeth of their opposition and to suffer all the penalties attaching to such non-submission.

I fully explained this resolution to the meeting and received a patient hearing. . . . The resolution was duly proposed, seconded and supported by several speakers one of whom was Sheth Haji Habib. He too was a very old and experienced resident of South Africa and made an impassioned speech. He was deeply moved and went so far as to say that we must pass this resolution with God as witness and must never yield a cowardly submission to such degrading legislation. He then went on solemnly to declare in the name of God that he would never submit to that law, and advised all present to do likewise. Others also delivered powerful and angry speeches in supporting the resolution.

When in the course of his speech Sheth Haji Habib came to the solemn declaration, I was at once startled and put on my guard. Only then did I fully realize my own responsibility and the responsibility of the community. The community had passed many a resolution before and amended such resolutions in the light of further reflection or fresh experience. There were cases in which resolutions passed had not been observed by all concerned. Amendments in resolutions and failure to observe resolutions on the part of persons agreeing thereto are ordinary experiences of public life all the world over. But no one ever imports the name of God into such resolutions. In the abstract there should not be any distinction between a resolution and an oath taken in the name of God. When an intelligent man makes a resolution deliberately he never swerves from it by a hair's breadth. With him his resolution carries as much weight as a declaration made with God as witness does. . . .

Full of these thoughts as I was, possessing as I did much experience of solemn pledges, having profited by them, I was simply taken aback by Sheth Haji Habib's suggestion of an oath. I thought out the possible consequences of it in a single moment. My perplexity gave place to enthusiasm. And although I had no intention of taking an oath or inviting others to do so when I went to the meeting, I warmly approved of the Sheth's suggestion. But at the same time it seemed to me that the people should be apprised of all the consequences and should have explained to them clearly the meaning of a pledge. And if even then they were prepared to pledge themselves, they should be encouraged to do so; otherwise I must understand that they were not still ready to stand the final test. I therefore asked the President for permission to explain to the meeting the implications of Sheth Haji Habib's suggestion. The President readily granted it and I rose to address the meeting. I give below a summary of my remarks just as I can recall them now:

"I wish to explain to this meeting that there is a vast difference between this resolution and every other resolution we have passed up to date and that there is a wide divergence also in the manner of making it. It is a very grave resolution we are making, as our existence in South Africa depends upon our fully observing it. The manner of making the resolution suggested by our friend is as much of a novelty as of a solemnity. I did not come to the meeting with a view to getting the resolution passed in that manner, which redounds to the credit of

Sheth Haji Habib as well as it lays a burden of responsibility upon him. I tender my congratulations to him. I deeply appreciate his suggestion, but if you adopt it you too will share his responsibility. You must understand what is this responsibility, and as an adviser and servant of the community, it is my duty fully to explain it to you.

"We all believe in one and the same God, the differences of nomenclature in Hinduism and Islam notwithstanding. To pledge ourselves or to take an oath in the name of that God or with Him as witness is not something to be trifled with. If having taken such an oath we violate our pledge we are guilty before God and man. Personally I hold that a man, who deliberately and intelligently takes a pledge and then breaks it, forfeits his manhood. . . .

"I know that pledges and vows are, and should be, taken on rare occasions. A man who takes a vow every now and then is sure to stumble. But if I can imagine a crisis in the history of the Indian community of South Africa when it would be in the fitness of things to take pledges that crisis is surely now. There is wisdom in taking serious steps with great caution and hesitation. But caution and hesitation have their limits, which we have now passed. The Government have taken leave of all sense of decency. We would only be betraying our unworthiness and cowardice, if we cannot stake our all in the face of the conflagration which envelopes us and sit watching it with folded hands. There is no doubt, therefore, that the present is a proper occasion for taking pledges. But every one of us must think out for himself if he has the will and the ability to pledge himself. Resolutions of this nature cannot be passed by a majority vote. Only those who take a pledge can be bound by it. This pledge must not be taken with a view to produce an effect on outsiders. No one should trouble to consider what impression it might have upon the Local Government, the Imperial Government, or the Government of India. Every one must only search his own heart, and if the inner voice assures him that he has the requisite strength to carry him through, then only should he pledge himself and then only would his pledge bear fruit.

"A few words now as to the consequences. . . .

"We might have to go to jail, where we might be insulted. We might have to go hungry and suffer extreme heat or cold. Hard labor might be imposed upon us. We might be flogged by rude warders. We might be fined heavily and our property might be attached and held up to auction if there are only a few resisters left. Opulent today we might be reduced to abject poverty tomorrow. We might be deported. Suffering from starvation and similar hardships in jail, some of us might fall ill and even die. In short, therefore, it is not at all impossible that we might have to endure every hardship that we can imagine, and wisdom lies in pledging ourselves on the understanding that we shall have to suffer all that and worse. If some one asks me when and how the struggle may end, I may say that if the entire community manfully stands the test, the end will be near. If many of us fall back under storm and stress, the struggle will be prolonged. But I can boldly declare, and with certainty, that so long as there is even a handful of men true to their pledge, there can only be one end to the struggle, and that is victory.

"A word about my personal responsibility. If I am warning you of the risks attendant upon the pledge, I am at the same time inviting you to pledge yourselves, and I am fully conscious of my responsibility in the matter. It is possible that a majority of those present here might take the pledge in a fit of enthusiasm or indignation but might weaken under the ordeal, and only a handful might be left to face the final test. Even then there is only one course open to the like of me, to die but not to submit to the law. . . . Although we are going to take the pledge in a body, no one should imagine that default on the part of one or many can absolve the rest from their obligation. Everyone should fully realize his responsibility, then only pledge himself independently of others and understand that he himself must be true to his pledge even unto death, no matter what others do."

I spoke to this effect and resumed my seat. The meeting heard me word by word in perfect quiet. Other leaders too spoke. All dwelt upon their own responsibility and the responsibility of the audience. The President rose. He too made the situation clear, and at last all present, standing with unraised hands, took an oath with God as witness not to submit to the Ordinance if it became law. I can never forget the scene, which is present before my mind's eye as I write. The community's enthusiasm knew no bounds.

None of us knew what name to give to our movement. I then used the term "passive resistance" in describing it. I did not quite understand the implications of "passive resistance" as I called it. I only knew that some new principle had come into being. As the struggle advanced, the phrase "passive resistance" gave rise to confusion and it appeared shameful to permit this great struggle to be known only by an English name. Again, that foreign phrase could hardly pass as current coin among the community. A small prize was therefore announced in *Indian Opinion*[2] to be awarded to the reader who invented the best designation for our struggle. We thus received a number of suggestions. The meaning of the struggle had been then fully discussed in *Indian Opinion* and the competitors for the prize had fairly sufficient material to serve as a basis for their exploration. Sr.

---

[2]A journal founded by Gandhi for which he often wrote.—ED.

Maganlal Gandhi[3] was one of the competitors and he suggested the word "Sadagraha," meaning "firmness in a good cause." I liked the word, but it did not fully represent the whole idea I wished it to connote. I therefore corrected it to "Satyagraha." Truth (Satya) implies love and firmness (Agraha) engenders and therefore serves as a synonym for force. I thus began to call the Indian movement "Satyagraha," that is to say, the Force which is born of Truth and Love or non-violence, and gave up the use of the phrase "passive resistance," in connection with it, so much so that even in English writing we often avoided it and used instead the word "Satyagraha" itself or some other equivalent English phrase. This then was the genesis of the movement which came to be known as Satyagraha, and of the word used as a designation for it. . . .

Gandhi and Civil Disobedience in India

JUDITH M. BROWN

For the next decade Gandhi's program of Satyagraha *led thousands of Indians in South Africa to resist the government, to endure hardship and danger and deprivation, even imprisonment. Gandhi himself was jailed for two months in 1908, the first of several such terms of prison for him in South Africa. Thousands of Indians were deported with the loss of all their property, and thousands of Indian indentured servants and miners who remained went on strike. The government remained firm, although many liberal whites, including many clergymen, openly supported Gandhi and the cause of Indian justice in South Africa. Gandhi made two trips to England to appeal to the imperial government, but to no avail. In South Africa the government tightened its restrictions. By 1914, largely under the pressure of world opinion and in the face of even more massive resistance than it could handle, the government of what was by now the Union of South Africa offered Gandhi a compromise. By its terms some of the most outrageous provisions against Indians were repudiated. It was no more than half a victory for Gandhi, but he accepted it as the best he could do. He shortly left South Africa for India.*

---

[3]A second cousin of Gandhi's who had joined him in his work in South Africa.—ED.

When he arrived in Bombay on January 9, 1915, Gandhi already had a worldwide reputation as a nonviolent political activist because of his work in South Africa. He also had a considerable knowledge of Indian affairs, which he had followed closely during the years of his absence. There were programs being advocated by various factions for Indian self-rule, or swaraj. *But Gandhi was reluctant to embrace any of them too quickly. He took the better part of a year to travel all over India—always by third-class rail—to get to know the people. He spoke, quietly but emphatically, whenever he was invited to do so, often on disturbing topics such as the shame of the untouchables or peasant poverty. He set up a headquarters in the form of a communal farm.*

With allied victory in World War I, British repression in India tightened. In 1919 the government proposed a series of antisedition bills that were bitterly opposed by most Indians. It was at this point that Gandhi entered the battle for swaraj. *In the spring of 1919 he announced a* Satyagraha *struggle. It swept the country, with work stoppages, boycotts, and nearly total noncooperation. Gandhi was its inspiration: he had begun to be called* Mahatma *or "great soul," a traditional Hindu title of respect. He had also become the spokesman of the Indian National Congress, which was rapidly becoming the political vehicle for his program of Indian independence. The British authorities reacted to Gandhi's campaign of nonviolent resistance with a proclamation of martial law and mass imprisonment for sedition. Gandhi himself was in prison from 1922 to 1924. In 1928 he formally proposed in the Congress a resolution calling for dominion status for India within a year. It was ignored, and repression continued.*

Early in 1930 Gandhi led a Satyagraha *against the salt tax, which was a longstanding burden on the poor. Again he was spectacularly successful. The British were forced to imprison more than 60,000 people. In the following year Gandhi was imprisoned again. The British had proposed a new constitution for India as an alternative to independence, but Gandhi found both the concept and its provisions unacceptable. While still in prison he took up a fast. The threat to the Mahatma's life quickly brought the cancellation of the most odious provisions of the constitution, but not of the proposal for the constitution itself. While Gandhi was still far from his goal of* purna swaraj *or "total independence," by the early 1930s he had attained a unique position of leadership in his nation.*

The following excerpt is from the most detailed and authoritative history of this period of Gandhi's life and of the Indian struggle for independence, Judith M. Brown, Gandhi and Civil Disobedience: The Mahatma in Indian Politics, 1928–34.

In the 1920s and 1930s, despite and in a sense because of the growing experience of reformed political institutions in Delhi, the provincial capitals and the localities, India did not have a single well-defined political system in which Indians encountered their compatriots and their rulers, but a cluster of intermeshing systems in each of which ideals, strategies and alliances were being created. In this complicated environment of political interaction Gandhi played a crucial role for over a quarter of a century. He was for much of the period the figurehead of the Indian National Congress; and at particular times led agitations which constituted a serious challenge to the raj's moral authority and its power to control its subjects. He evoked popular adulation of a kind and to an extent never before enjoyed by an Indian politician; and he attracted the respect of numerous idealists outside India. Gandhi's role and standing in Indian politics were extraordinary phenomena when seen against the barriers to continental political leadership created by regional and social divisions and the limited development of mass media. . . .

At the level of conscious aspiration Gandhi was compelled into politics by a consuming vision of the nature of man and the type of society and government which permitted men to realize their true nature. He believed that in satyagraha he possessed the perfect mode of political action because he saw it as means and end, by its action producing the sort of people whose personal transformation was the foundation of the Indian society. . . . Here was an explosive political mixture: a man careless of the conventional trappings of power, with the iron will of a fanatic, who entered politics with a messianic zeal for the purification of individuals and their relations with each other, one who was willing to bend on many matters but refused to compromise on what he considered essentials though others considered them mere fads, one who would only participate in organized politics if he was undisputed leader. He claimed to be guided by an 'inner voice'; and his willingness to suffer privation and the prospect of death in the pursuit of what he perceived as Truth suggests that he was utterly convinced of the reality of his inner guidance and was neither charlatan nor humbug, covering the tracks of self-seeking ambition with the cloak of religion.

Gandhi's vision of the span of public work essential to his pursuit of swaraj was a significant aspect of his perception of his public role. His interest in health, diet, hygiene, clothing, social customs and religious practice was as strong as his concern for politics. Such activities contributed to Gandhi's continental and international reputation, generating respect for him among segments of Indian society which it was difficult to touch with a more conventional political appeal. They also gave him a flexibility which few other political leaders possessed. If he felt at a particular juncture that he could not act as a political leader without compromising his ideals, he could devote himself to these matters temporarily without a sense of defeat, secure in the belief that they were as important steps on the road to the final goal as promoting resistance to the raj through civil disobedience. The absence of any internal constraint of aspiration to a political career through office in Congress or the governmental structures gave the Mahatma a flexibility which paradoxically was vital in enabling his continued political importance in a period of rapid change. . . .

The most dramatic manifestations of public response to Gandhi were the crowds who flocked to see him and hailed him as a Mahatma. But theirs was not truly political support. Curiosity and veneration were rarely emotions which impelled men into following his exhortations, whether to wear *khadi*,[4] to abandon the observation of Untouchability or to join the ranks of the satyagrahis. Nonetheless Gandhi's public image across the land among vast multitudes was a factor which impinged on the attitudes towards Gandhi of men who were active in politics. The British acknowledged this in their agonized discussions on the time and place to jail him, and the need to avoid his death in prison. Responsivists became reluctant satyagrahis, and moderates refrained from public criticism, in deference to the Mahatma's unprecedented repute among their compatriots. . . .

It was in the all-India gatherings that Gandhi achieved his greatest prominence and influence because as all-India leader he performed a multiplicity of service roles in the particular context of 1928–31. He proved pre-eminent among Congressmen as an arranger of compromises because of his skill with words, his aloofness from factional strife and his ability to set a goal which could provide a focus of unity and a propaganda weapon. It was to achieve a vital unity that some of them deliberately called him back to Congress in 1928, and because of his success in satisfying this need that he was able to assert a new authority at the Calcutta session with the acquiescence of the majority.

Thereafter, as the civil disobedience 'expert', Gandhi was of extraordinary value to Congressmen in circumstances where a campaign of opposition to parts of the imperial structure seemed the best tactic to exert pressure on the raj and to mask their own divisions. Satyagraha solved many of the dilemmas conflict posed in their relations with their rulers and their compatriots. It was a mode of direct action which permitted them temporarily to leave the paths of cooperation while avoiding the pitfalls of violent resistance, which they were ill equipped to organize, and would not only have threatened many of their vested interests but also alienated many Indians and foreign observers whose sympathy was important if they were to put pressure

---

[4]Homespun cloth.—ED.

on the British. Civil disobedience provided an umbrella for a host of individual and corporate protest movements, as it coincided fortuitously with the onset of the depression. It helped them to cement local followings, to elicit support from businessmen, and to exert pressure on more moderate Hindu politicians who felt themselves isolated and their constitutional endeavours threatened by the evidence of widespread support for the movement. It also attracted considerable foreign sympathy. . . . Added to the advantages of placing Gandhi in a leadership position as civil disobedience 'expert' were his skill in fund-raising and his energy as an organizer, qualities which convinced Vallabhbhai Patel, for example, that the Mahatma was a man who meant business and was worth following.

Gandhi reached the peak of his influence early in 1931. His dominance was however only in the realm of all-India politics, because only in that context were his skills valued. Even in that arena the pressures to which he was subjected by those who looked to him for leadership, and his failures in asserting authority, most markedly among Muslims, showed the weakness inherent in a position which hinged on the ability to perform a lubricant function in the processes of political action rather than the capacity to forward the clear interests of a cohesive group. The nature of his leadership was even clearer in 1933–4, when his position of ascendancy was rapidly eroded. The civil disobedience campaign inaugurated in 1932 elicited far less popular support than the 1930 campaign, and was soon stifled by the government. Consequently it strengthened neither Congressmen's cross-regional alliances nor their links with those who should have been the rank and file. . . . It had far less influence than the 1930 campaign on moderate politicians who continued, though with considerable gloom, to cooperate in British reform plans. Ultimately it even alienated those Bombay businessmen who had financed it in the hope that it would assist them in gaining control over economic policy. The cumulative result was the campaign's failure to put pressure on the British and bring Congress into negotiations on the forthcoming constitution. Now Gandhi's tactic was a force isolating and dividing Congressmen instead of uniting them and integrating their different levels of political activity. Moreover Gandhi's skills and potential as an ally were judged of little use by the British. . . .

In 1934 Gandhi recognized that in the changing circumstances he could no longer act as continental leader in the role of civil disobedience 'expert'. Such were his personal aspirations and priorities that he preferred to solve the dilemma his presence and insistence on satyagraha created for his Congress colleagues by liberating them from a technique which for them was a mere tactic and so preserve it and his own integrity, and 'retire' rather than retain an all-India leadership position by performing the functions they now desired of him. However, these decisions did not mean the end of Gandhi as an all-India political leader. Congressmen would not lightly ignore him; and civil disobedience remained an important tactic for use when confrontation with the raj offered more benefits than cooperation, or when no other programme could secure among them an essential unity. Nor had Gandhi himself lost interest in politics: he had merely redirected his energies to preserve himself and his technique from compromise. Ironically, by 'retiring' Gandhi did for himself what the British had done for him in 1922. He took time to review the changing situation where the politics of elections, conciliar activity and even acceptance of office would probably become Congressmen's primary concerns. In this political context men like Vallabhbhai Patel who could weld the disparate elements in the Congress movement into a coherent and disciplined party would be of supreme importance. It was a leadership function Gandhi was ill fitted to perform either by inclination or by expertise. What his role might be in the new context was unclear late in 1934; but by abandoning a role which had proved redundant for his contemporaries he freed himself to adopt another on which a new position of continental leadership could be based, if a situation developed where his personal inclinations and expertise dovetailed with the needs of contemporaries, and offered him a sphere and mode of political action which could forward both their aims and his vision of swaraj.

Nonetheless, Gandhi's civil disobedience campaigns between 1930 and 1934 were of lasting importance in the development of Indian politics. Although civil disobedience neither led to *purna swaraj* nor very significantly influenced the process of constitutional reform, it proved a powerful bonding agent among Indians within and across regions under the Congress banner. It gave many activists a new sense of unity born of shared illegal activities and sojourns in jail. Participation in it became one qualification for political place and a source of prestige in the years which followed. Moreover the campaigns were recruiting grounds for Congress, involving younger people and numbers of women in Congress organizations and activities for the first time and educating them for future positions in the Congress and state structures. The experience of running a continental campaign and Gandhi's emphasis on efficiency were also significant factors in Congress's success in turning itself into an all-India party geared to attract the votes of an enlarged electorate. The Congress name and organization, sketchy though the latter was, had been an important resource in politics in the 1920s. This importance was magnified as Congress emerged from civil disobedience into constitutional competition for power. Few Hindus would now lightly isolate themselves from it, and the influence of those who controlled its central organs was increased because they offered rewards and wielded sanctions which the Mahatma had never had at his command.

In less material ways civil disobedience also equipped Congress for a new political dispensation. It had been a remarkable publicity operation, demonstrating political ideas and actions throughout the land and generating political awareness even in remote villages. It convinced many Indians, and to a lesser extent their rulers, that Congress was a significant factor in political life which could not be ignored. Although its claims to be the people's intermediary with government had not received formal recognition, once Congress returned to constitutional politics most Hindus with political ambitions regarded it as the natural channel through which to pursue them, while the majority of the community who had no aspirations to political activism were sympathetic to its aims and claims. Gandhi's political activities had provided Congress with a pedigree. . . . This was soon clear, in the 1934 Assembly elections, when the poll was higher than in any previous Assembly election and Congress successes outstanding. No other group came near it in organization, resources and appeal. . . .

Gandhi and Indian Independence

JAWAHARLAL NEHRU

In 1934 Gandhi resigned completely from the Indian National Congress, convinced that the other leaders of the movement had adopted nonviolence only as a political tactic rather than as a fundamental political and philosophic commitment. He was disillusioned with politics. In the next few years he devoted himself to increasingly severe asceticism and to the advocacy of social reforms. He restricted his diet to a mere handful of vegetables a day. His personal possessions were reduced to little besides his spectacles, his food bowl, and his sandals, loincloth, and homespun shawl. He kept a small ivory carving of "The Three Wise Monkeys" given him by a friend in South Africa. Though his wife and family continued to live in the commune, Gandhi himself had long since renounced all sexual contact and stayed alone in a small cell where he slept, took his meals, worked and wrote.

He continued to defend the cause of the untouchables: he called them Harijans *or "children of God." He was equally concerned about the vast number of Indian peasants, almost universally impoverished, ignorant, and hopeless. For them he prepared educational texts, proposed the teaching of a single language, and strongly advocated a return to Indian cottage industry—the making of* khadi *or homespun cloth, for example. This, of course, meant his rejection of industrialization, which the British had brought to India and which many progressive Indian leaders had welcomed.*

With the outbreak of World War II the question of Indian independence became hopelessly mixed with that of India's role in the war. In 1942 the British cabinet minister Sir Stafford Cripps came to India with a proposal. The Cripps proposal called for complete British control of India as part of the allied war effort but held out the promise of full dominion status after the war. Gandhi said to Cripps, "Why did you come if this is what you have to offer? If this is your entire proposal to India, I would advise you to take the next plane home."[5] *To Gandhi the plan was fatally flawed in that it called not for a united but a pluralistic India, with independence for Hindus and Moslems, even for the Indian princely states. The other congress leaders objected to the plan on other grounds.*

Gandhi now reentered the political arena. Within months of the rejection of the Cripps proposal he demanded immediate British withdrawal from India. This became the famous "Quit India Resolution." The British reacted by jailing the entire leadership of the congress, including Gandhi. Britain and India were now totally estranged.

With the end of the war it was clear that Indian independence, at long last, was at hand. There were intense negotiations over its terms. The stumbling block was the Moslem insistence on a separate state, an insistence underscored by widespread violence. Partition was finally accepted in the plan that Lord Louis Mountbatten, the last British viceroy, proposed in the early summer of 1947. This plan became the basis for independence and for the creation not of one India but of the two new nations of India and Pakistan, in August 1947.

Gandhi was brokenhearted at the failure to achieve a united independent India. Nevertheless, he worked unceasingly to heal the divisions between Hindus and Moslems and bring an end to the religious violence. On January 30, 1948, he died, a victim of that religious violence, shot to death by a Hindu fanatic on his way to his evening prayers.

Gandhi had been, unquestionably, the leading force in the independence movement. His role in the last years of the struggle is evaluated by his lifelong friend, fellow congress leader, and the man who would become the first prime minister of India, Jawaharlal Nehru. The selection is taken from Nehru's biographical reflection on Gandhi's life, Mahatma Gandhi, *written a few months after his assassination.*

---

[5]Louis Fischer, *The Life of Mahatma Gandhi*, p. 358.

When Gandhiji[6] raised in 1940 the question of non-violence in relation to the war and the future of free India, the Congress Working Committee had to face the issue squarely. They made it clear to him that they were unable to go as far as he wanted them to go and could not possibly commit India or the Congress to future applications of this principle in the external domain. This led to a definite and public break with him on this issue. Two months later further discussions led to an agreed formula which was later adopted as part of a resolution by the All-India Congress Committee. That formula did not wholly represent Gandhiji's attitude; it represented what he agreed, perhaps rather unwillingly, for Congress to say on this subject. At that time the British Government had already rejected the latest offer made by the Congress for co-operation in the war on the basis of a national government. Some kind of conflict was approaching, and, as was inevitable, both Gandhiji and Congress looked toward each other and were impelled by a desire to find a way out of the deadlock between them. The formula did not refer to the war, as just previously our offer of co-operation had been unceremoniously and utterly rejected. It dealt theoretically with the Congress policy in regard to non-violence, and for the first time stated how, in the opinion of Congress, the free India of the future should apply it in its external relations. That part of the resolution ran thus:

[The A.I.C.C.] firmly believes in the policy and practice of non-violence not only in the struggle for Swaraj, but also, in so far as this may be possible of application, in free India. The Committee is convinced, and recent world events have demonstrated, that complete world disarmament is necessary and the establishment of a new and juster political and economic order, if the world is not to destroy itself and revert to barbarism. A free India will, therefore, throw all her weight in favour of world disarmament and should herself be prepared to give a lead in this to the world. Such lead will inevitably depend on external factors and internal conditions, but the state would do its utmost to give effect to this policy of disarmament. Effective disarmament and the establishment of world peace by the ending of national wars depend ultimately on the removal of the causes of wars and national conflicts. These causes must be rooted out by the ending of the domination of one country over another and the exploitation of one people or group by another. To that end India will peacefully labour, and it is with this objective in view that the people of India desire to attain the status of a free and independent nation. Such freedom will be the prelude to the close association with other coun-

---

[6]The suffix is an indication of respect and affection.—ED.

tries within a comity of free nations for the peace and progress of the world.

This declaration, it will be noticed, while strongly affirming the Congress wish for peaceful action and disarmament, also emphasized a number of qualifications and limitations.

The internal crisis within the Congress was resolved in 1940, and then came a year of prison for large numbers of us. In December 1941, however, the same crisis took shape again when Gandhiji insisted on complete non-violence. Again there was a split and public disagreement, and the president of the Congress, Maulana Abul Kalam Azad, and others were unable to accept Gandhiji's view. It became clear that the Congress as a whole, including some of the faithful followers of Gandhiji, disagreed with him in this matter. The force of circumstances and the rapid succession of dramatic events influenced all of us, including Gandhiji, and he refrained from pressing his view on the Congress, though he did not identify himself with the Congress view.

At no other time was this issue raised by Gandhiji in the Congress. When later Sir Stafford Cripps came with his proposals, there was no question of non-violence. His proposals were considered purely from the political point of view. In later months, leading up to August 1942, Gandhiji's nationalism and intense desire for freedom made him even agree to Congress participation in the war if India could function as a free country. For him this was a remarkable and astonishing change, involving suffering of the mind and pain of the spirit. In the conflict between that principle of non-violence, which had become his very lifeblood and meaning of existence, and India's freedom, which was a dominating and consuming passion for him, the scales inclined toward the latter. That did not mean, of course, that he weakened in his faith in non-violence. But it did mean that he was prepared to agree to the Congress not applying it in this war. The practical statesman took precedence over the uncompromising prophet.

The approach of the war to India disturbed Gandhiji greatly. It was not easy to fit in his policy and programme of non-violence with this new development. Obviously civil disobedience was out of the question in the face of an invading army or between two opposing armies. Passivity or acceptance of invasion were equally out of the question. What then? His own colleagues, and the Congress generally, had rejected non-violence for such an occasion or as an alternative to armed resistance to invasion, and he had at last agreed that they had a right to do so. But he was none the less troubled, and for his own part, as an individual, he could not join any violent course of action. But he was much more than an individual; whether he had any official status or not in the nationalist movement, he occupied an outstanding and dominating position, and his word carried weight with large numbers of people. . . .

While this struggle was going on in India's mind and a feeling of desperation was growing, Gandhiji wrote a number of articles which suddenly gave a new direction to people's thoughts, or, as often happens, gave shape to their vague ideas. Inaction at that critical stage and submission to all that was happening had become intolerable to him. The only way to meet that situation was for Indian freedom to be recognized and for a free India to meet aggression and invasion in co-operation with allied nations. If this recognition was not forthcoming then some action must be taken to challenge the existing system and wake up the people from the lethargy that was paralyzing them and making them easy prey for every kind of aggression. . . .

Some of us were disturbed and upset by this new development, for action was futile unless it was effective action, and any such effective action must necessarily come in the way of war effort at a time when India herself stood in peril of invasion. Gandhiji's general approach also seemed to ignore important international considerations and appeared to be based on a narrow view of nationalism. During the three years of war we had deliberately followed a policy of non-embarrassment, and such action as we had indulged in had been in the nature of symbolic protest. That symbolic protest had assumed huge dimensions when thirty thousand of our leading men and women were sent to prison in 1940–41. And yet even that prison-going was a selected individual affair and avoided any mass upheaval or any direct interference with the governmental apparatus. We could not repeat that, and if we did something else it had to be of a different kind and on a more effective scale. Was this not bound to interfere with the war on India's borders and encourage the enemy?

These were obvious difficulties, and we discussed them at length with Gandhiji without converting each other. The difficulties were there, and risks and perils seemed to follow any course of action or inaction. It became a question of balancing them and choosing the lesser evil. Our mutual discussions led to a clarification of much that had been vague and cloudy, and to Gandhiji's appreciating many international factors to which his attention had been drawn. His subsequent writings underwent a change, and he himself emphasized these international considerations and looked at India's problem in a wider perspective. But his fundamental attitude remained: his objection to a passive submission to British autocratic and repressive policy in India and his intense desire to do something to challenge this. Submission then, according to him, meant that India would be broken in spirit, and whatever shape the war might take, whatever its end might be, her people would act in a servile way and their freedom would not be achieved for a long time. It would mean also submission to an invader and not continuing resistance to him regardless even of temporary military defeat or withdrawal. It would mean the complete demoralization of our people and their losing all the strength that they had built up during a quarter of a century's unceasing struggle for freedom. It would mean that the world would forget India's demand for freedom and the postwar settlement would be governed by the old imperialist urges and ambitions. . . .

Gandhiji was getting on in years, he was in the seventies, and a long life of ceaseless activity, of hard toil, both physical and mental, had enfeebled his body. But he was still vigorous enough and he felt that all his lifework would be in vain if he submitted to circumstances then and took no action to vindicate what he prized most. His love of freedom for India and all other exploited nations and peoples overcame even his strong adherence to non-violence. He had previously given a grudging and rather reluctant consent to the Congress not adhering to this policy in regard to defence and the state's functions in an emergency, but he had kept himself aloof from this. He realized that his halfhearted attitude in this matter might well come in the way of a settlement with Britain and the United Nations. So he went further and himself sponsored a Congress resolution which declared that the primary function of the provisional government of free India would be to throw all her great resources in the struggle for freedom and against aggression and to co-operate fully with the United Nations in the defence of India with all the armed as well as other forces at her command. It was no easy matter for him to commit himself in this way, but he swallowed the bitter pill, so overpowering was his desire that some settlement should be arrived at to enable India to resist the aggressor as a free nation. . . .

While we were doubting and debating, the mood of the country changed and from a sullen passivity it rose to a pitch of excitement and expectation. Events were not waiting for a Congress decision or resolution; they had been pushed forward by Gandhiji's utterances, and now they were moving onward with their own momentum. It was clear that whether Gandhiji was right or wrong, he had crystallized the prevailing mood of the people. . . .

On August 7 and 8, 1942, in Bombay the All-India Congress Committee considered and debated in public the resolution which has since come to be known as the "Quit India Resolution." That resolution was a long and comprehensive one, a reasoned argument for the immediate recognition of Indian freedom and the ending of British rule in India "both for the sake of India and for the success of the cause of the United Nations. The continuation of that rule is degrading and enfeebling India and making her progressively less capable of defending herself and of contributing to the cause of world freedom. . . . The possession of empire, instead of adding to the strength of the ruling power, has become a burden and a curse. India, the classic land of modern imperialism, has become the crux of the question, for by the freedom of India will Britain and the United Nations be judged, and the peoples of Asia and Africa be filled with hope and enthusiasm." The resolution went on to suggest the formation of a provisional government which would be composite and would represent all important sections of the people, and whose "primary function must be to defend India and resist aggression with all the armed as well as the non-violent forces at its command, together with its Allied Powers." This government would evolve a scheme for a constituent assembly which would prepare a constitution for India acceptable to all sections of the people. The constitution would be a federal one, with the largest measure of autonomy for the federating units and with the residuary powers vesting in those units. "Freedom will enable India to resist aggression effectively with the people's united will and strength behind it."

This freedom of India must be the symbol of and prelude to the freedom of all other Asiatic nations. Further, a world federation of free nations was proposed, of which a beginning should be made with the United Nations.

The committee stated that it was "anxious not to embarrass in any way the defence of China and Russia, whose freedom is precious and must be preserved, or to jeopardize the defensive capacity of the United Nations." (At that time the dangers to China and Russia were the greatest.) "But the peril grows both to India and these nations, and inaction and submission to a foreign administration at this stage is not only degrading India and reducing her capacity to defend herself and resist aggression but is no answer to that growing peril and is no service to the peoples of the United Nations."

The Committee again appealed to Britain and the United Nations "in the interest of world freedom." But—and there came the sting of the resolution—"the Committee is no longer justified in holding the nation back from endeavouring to assert its will against an imperialist and authoritarian Government which dominates over it and prevents it from functioning in its own interest and in the interest of humanity. The Committee resolves therefore to sanction, for the vindication of India's inalienable right to freedom and independence, the starting of a mass struggle on non-violent lines" under the inevitable leadership of Gandhiji. That sanction was to take effect only when Gandhiji so decided. Finally, it was stated that the Committee had "no intention of gaining power for the Congress. The power, when it comes, will belong to the whole people of India."

The resolution was finally passed late in the evening of August 8, 1942. A few hours later, in the early morning of August 9, a large number of arrests were made in Bombay and all over the country.

Freedom came to us, our long-sought freedom, and it came with a minimum of violence. But immediately after, we had to wade through oceans of blood and tears. Worse than the blood and tears was the shame and disgrace that accompanied them.

Review and Study Questions

1. How did Gandhi's experiences in South Africa prepare him for his later work on behalf of Indian independence?
2. How important to his lifelong work was Gandhi's commitment to peaceful nonresistance?
3. How important to his lifelong work were Gandhi's spiritual and religious views?
4. How was the strident problem of the religious conflict between Hindus and Moslems dealt with in the struggle for Indian independence?

Suggestions for Further Reading

Gandhi himself was a prolific writer. The official collection of his works fills sixty-four volumes: Mahatma Gandhi, *Collected Works* (Delhi: Publications Division, Ministry of Information and Broadcasting, Government of India, 1958–76). His autobiography, while it appears in the *Collected Works*, was originally written in Gujarati in 1927–29 but translated into English by Mahadev Desai and separately published as *Gandhi's Autobiography: The Story of My Experiments with Truth,* 2 vols. (Washington: Public Affairs Press, 1948). It was written very early in his life and is not very useful as a source of biographical information. There are, of course, many anthologies and collections of his works. Some of these reflect the adoring discipleship of his followers and emphasize his personal qualities and his philosophy: see, for example, *Gandhi's India: Unity in Diversity, Selections Prepared by the National Integration Sub-Committee of the National Committee for Gandhi Centenary* (New Delhi: National Book Trust, 1968) or *The Quintessence of Gandhi in His Own Words,* ed. Shakti Batra (New Delhi: Madhu Muskan, 1984). Others contain more substantial selections dealing with his political career as well as with his life and philosophic concerns. These include *The Gandhi Reader: A Source Book of His Life and Writings,* ed. Homer A. Jack (Bloomington: Indiana University Press, 1956), excerpted for this chapter; *The Essential Gandhi, An Anthology: His Life, Work, and Ideals,* ed. Louis Fischer (New York: Vintage, 1963); *Gandhi in India in His Own Words,* ed. Martin Green (Hanover and London: University Press of New England, 1987). Of rather special interest is a series of selections collected and translated by Professor Nirmal Kumar Bose, *Selections from Gandhi* (Ahmedabad: Navajivan, 1968 [1948]), endorsed in a Foreword by Gandhi himself just a year before his death.

There are a number of biographical reminiscences of Gandhi by people who knew him well. One of the most valuable of these is Jawaharlal Nehru, *Mahatma Gandhi* (Bombay et al.: Asia Publishing House, 1966 [1949]), excerpted for this chapter—not only because of Nehru's lifelong friendship with Gandhi but because of his central position in Indian affairs. An equally useful work devoted to Gandhi's early years was written by his personal secretary and is rich in detail: Pyarelal Nair, *Mahatma Gandhi—The Early Phase,* 2 vols., 2nd ed. (Ahmedabad: Navajivan Publishing House, 1965). Of the same sort is Nirmal Kumar Bose, *My Days with Gandhi* (Bombay: Orient Longman, 1953).

There are several works by western journalists who knew Gandhi and spent time with him. Vincent Sheean, *Lead, Kindly Light* (New York: Random House, 1949) is a luminous appreciation of Gandhi as a philosophical, and especially religious, figure. More gritty and realistic are William L. Shirer, *Gandhi: A Memoir* (New York: Simon & Schuster, 1979), based on Shirer's acquaintance with Gandhi in the early 1930s, and Louis Fischer, *The Life of Mahatma Gandhi* (New York: Harper, 1950), based on Fischer's close association with Gandhi through the crucial 1940s. The latter is also a full-scale biography, the first to appear after Gandhi's assassination.

There are a number of other excellent biographies: the two best are Geoffrey Ashe, *Gandhi* (New York: Stein and Day, 1968), and Robert Payne, *The Life and Death of Mahatma Gandhi* (New York: Dutton, 1969). And there are a number of important scholarly books on specialized topics. One of the best of these is Judith M. Brown, *Gandhi and Civil Disobedience: The Mahatma in Indian Politics, 1928–34* (Cambridge et al.: Cambridge University Press, 1977), excerpted for this chapter. Equally good is her earlier book, *Gandhi's Rise to Power: Indian Politics 1915–1922* (Cambridge: Cambridge University Press, 1972). Two other excellent studies of yet other periods of Gandhi's life are Robert A. Huttenback, *Gandhi in South Africa: British Imperialism and the Indian Question, 1860–1914* (Ithaca and London: Cornell Univer-

MAO TSE-TUNG:
THE PEOPLE'S EMPEROR

1893	Born
1912	Formation of the Republic of China
1921	Joined Communist Party
1934–35	The Long March
1937–45	The Japanese War
1949	Formation of People's Republic of China
1966–69	The Cultural Revolution
1976	Died

Mao Tse-tung, the man who was to become China's great proletarian revolutionary, was born into a well-to-do peasant family in Hunan province, in central China, in 1893. As a boy he received a traditional Confucian education in the local primary school. At sixteen he went to a neighboring town to attend a "radical" new, Western-style school, teaching such things as foreign history and geography. He went on to secondary school in the provincial capital of Chang-sha.

But his education was overwhelmed by the rush of political events. Sun Yat-sen was preaching cultural and political revolution. In 1911 the revolution actually broke out against the Manchu dynasty. Mao joined the army. His military service was brief and unimpressive. In the spring of 1912 the Republic of China was proclaimed and he was mustered out of the army.

After trying several kinds of schools Mao finally graduated from the First Provincial Normal School of Chang-sha in 1918. He then enrolled at Peking University. The six months he spent there were to turn his life around. He was exposed to the radical new doctrines of Marxism-Leninism. In 1921 he was one of the founders of the Chinese Communist Party.

The fledgling Communist Party joined with Sun Yat-sen's Nationalist Party (Kuomintang) against the imperial government in Peking. With the death of Sun Yat-sen in 1925, Chiang Kai-shek became head of the Kuomintang and broke with the Communists. The Chinese civil war had begun. Mao was one of the organizers of the Chinese Red Army and emerged as its leader in the Long March—a harrowing retreat from Chiang Kai-shek's forces. But the war against Japan brought Communists and Nationalists together against their common enemy. In the course of the war Mao Tse-tung became the leader of the spreading Communist movement throughout China.

With the end of the war the old rivalry between the Communists and the Kuomintang resurfaced, but with far different results this time. In the spring of 1949 the People's Liberation Army, as the Red Army was now called, forced Chiang out of the country, eventually to rule Nationalist China on the island of Taiwan. Mao was the master of mainland China. For a while he followed the lead of Stalin's Soviet Union. But he was increasingly disillusioned both with the Soviet leadership of world communism and with the Soviet model of socialist development that had been promoted in China.

In 1955 he vigorously stepped forward with a program of his own for China. He advocated the abandonment of the emphasis on heavy industry and capital production and the classical Soviet preference for central planning in agriculture. He announced instead a nationwide program of cooperative agricultural communes. Further, he encouraged Chinese intellectuals and technical and managerial experts to speak out in criticism of the party's failures and the defects of the system. "Let a hundred flowers bloom," he declared in early 1956. But the intellectuals and specialists not only criticized the failures of the system, they criticized the system itself—and its leadership under Chairman Mao. At this point things changed abruptly. Writers who had been too outspoken found themselves cleaning toilets or scrubbing floors; indiscreet managers of plants and businesses were reassigned as laborers on distant farm communes. From the disappointing intellectuals, administrators, and specialists Mao turned to the unlettered masses, the peasants. If China was to be changed, let them change it. These new policies, begun in the fall of 1957, were to be called the Great Leap Forward. Not only agriculture but all forms of economic activity were organized at the grass roots in small communal units, relying on local initiative. Equally important, there was a decentralizing of political power into the hands of communal party secretaries.

The Great Leap Forward turned out to be a dismal failure: the economy was disrupted and there were severe food shortages. Mao's policies were reversed. He retired as chairman of the Chinese People's Republic and settled into a period of reflection and inactivity. But he retained the chairmanship of the Communist Party and he retained his popularity with the People's Liberation Army.

Differences grew between Mao and his chief rival in the party, Liu Shao-ch'i, who had replaced him as chairman of the People's Republic. In 1966 Mao once more seized control of the party and of the nation in the most radical experiment in the history of Communist China, the Great Proletarian Cultural Revolution.

The Great Proletarian Cultural Revolution

CHAIRMAN MAO

The Great Proletarian Cultural Revolution was, in part, a substantive program that grew naturally out of much that Mao had thought and advocated—in particular his suspicion of intellectuals and his almost mystical bond with the Chinese peasants. But it was also powerfully motivated by Mao's bitterness toward Liu and his faction in the Central Committee of the party, his conviction that the party was moving in the wrong direction, and his consequent intention of regaining undisputed control over it. As early as 1962–63 he and Liu had clashed over party objectives. Then in the late summer of 1966 Mao, through his great personal prestige, convinced the Central Committee to adopt his bold new scheme.

Mao proclaimed a new stage in China's socialist revolution that would reclaim the leadership in education, literature, and the arts from the "bourgeois" corruption of experts and authorities and restore it to the true proletariat, the Chinese masses. It is essential, Mao argued, to trust the masses and not to fear disorder or disruption. They can educate themselves. Schools must be reformed according to the aims of Chairman Mao; in order to serve the needs of the proletariat, education must be combined with productive labor to teach students not only their academic subjects but farming, military affairs, and industrial work. If this program is followed the people will achieve greater, faster, better, and more economical results in all fields of work. In all this the guide is to be Mao Tse-tung's thought.

Mao himself traveled widely through China to assess the progress of the Cultural Revolution, and from the fall of 1967 to the summer of 1969 he issued a series of "directives" that appeared in the major Chinese newspapers. They analyzed the results of the revolution and suggested some courses of action. The following are the most pertinent of those "directives."

April 19, 1968

The great proletarian cultural revolution is in essence a great political revolution made under the conditions of socialism by the proletariat against the bourgeoisie and all other exploiting classes; it is a continuation of the prolonged struggle between the Chinese Communist Party and the masses of revolutionary people under the Party's leadership on the one hand and the Kuomintang reactionaries on the other, a continuation of the class struggle between the proletariat and the bourgeoisie.

August 2, 1968
It is still necessary to have universities; here I refer mainly to colleges of science and engineering. However, it is essential to shorten the length of schooling, revolutionize education, put proletarian politics in command and take the road of the Shanghai Machine Tools Plant in training technicians from among the workers. Students should be selected from among workers and peasants with practical experience, and they should return to production after a few years' study.

August 23, 1968
Our country has 700 million people and the working class is the leading class. Its leading role in the great cultural revolution and in all fields of work should be brought into full play. The working class also should continuously enhance its political consciousness in the course of the struggle.

August 30, 1968
In carrying out the proletarian revolution in education, it is essential to have working-class leadership; it is essential for the masses of workers to take part and, in co-operation with Liberation Army fighters, bring about a revolutionary "three-in-one" combination, together with the activists among the students, teachers and workers in the schools who are determined to carry the proletarian revolution in education through to the end. The workers' propaganda teams should stay permanently in the schools and take part in fulfilling all the tasks of struggle-criticism-transformation in the schools, and they will always lead the schools. In the countryside, the schools should be managed by the poor and lower-middle peasants—the most reliable ally of the working class.

The struggle-criticism-transformation in a factory, on the whole, goes through the following stages: establishing a revolutionary committee based on the "three-in-one" combination, mass criticism and repudiation, purifying the class ranks, rectifying the Party organization, simplifying organizational structure, changing irrational rules and regulations and sending people who work in offices to grass-roots levels.

October 11, 1968
Sending the masses of cadres to do manual work gives them an excellent opportunity to study once again; this should be done by all

cadres except those who are too old, weak, ill or disabled. Cadres at work should also go group by group to do manual work.

December 27, 1968

It is very necessary for educated young people to go to the country-side to be re-educated by the poor and lower-middle peasants. Cadres and other people in the cities should be persuaded to send their sons and daughters who have finished junior or senior middle school, college or university to the countryside. Let us mobilize. Comrades throughout the countryside should welcome them.

July 4, 1969

Every Party branch must reconsolidate itself in the midst of the masses. This must be done with the participation of the masses and not merely a few Party members; it is necessary to have the masses outside the Party attend the meetings and give comments.

In the Great Proletarian Cultural Revolution, some tasks have not yet been fulfilled and they should now be carried on, for instance, the tasks of struggle-criticism-transformation.

A Contemporary Analysis

STUART SCHRAM

The resolution adopted by the Central Committee of the Chinese Communist Party on August 8, 1966, giving authorization for the Cultural Revolution, was implemented immediately. The first agency was the People's Liberation Army. Since 1959 it had been headed by Lin Piao, a dedicated supporter of Chairman Mao. Under his leadership the army had become "a great school of Mao Tse-tung's thought." The official army newspaper carried the thoughts of the chairman on page one of every issue, and the Quotations from Chairman Mao, *the famous "Little Red Book," was first published by the army in 1964. Each edition contained a foreword by Lin that began "Comrade Mao Tse-tung is the greatest Marxist-Leninist of our era." Clearly a part of the intent of the Cultural Revolution was to put forward a position favored by both Mao and the army, that China must be separated from Russia and Russian-style communism, and the parallel position that China was the natural leader of the Third World.*

With the army benignly in the background, Mao pushed forward as the leading element in his Cultural Revolution a quasi-military group known as the Red Guards or, as he called them, the "little devils." They were young people, totally dedicated to Chairman Mao, guided by his thoughts in the "Little Red Book" and utterly contemptuous of both their cultural betters and the Communist Party leaders. They smashed temples and burned books and called party leaders to task before people's courts. Thousands of people were deprived of their livelihoods; thousands more were killed in the streets amid mindless riots.

In the confusion of the Cultural Revolution, and with the resulting paralysis of the Chinese Communist Party, Mao had little trouble dismissing Liu Shao-ch'i, his hated rival, from office and reasserting his own firm control of the party and the nation.

The excerpt presented below deals with the onset and early course of the Cultural Revolution. It is from a biography of Mao written by Stuart Schram. Schram is not only a distinguished international authority on Communist China; he was in China at the beginning of the Cultural Revolution and his knowledge of it is first hand. Because the Cultural Revolution was still going on at the time the book was written, his conclusions about it are very cautious. But his analysis of the forces that set it moving and, in particular, his analysis of Mao's motives are extremely interesting and germane to our understanding of Mao Tse-tung.

If Mao no doubt sincerely identifies himself with the anti-imperialist struggles of other peoples, his primary concern remains, as it has always been, the fate of China. At the same time, it must be added that in his eyes China's internal evolution has now taken on decisive international importance. For to the extent that he sees China as the only genuinely socialist great power—the Soviet Union having definitively taken the road of revisionism and the restoration of capitalism—the ideological purity and firmness of will of the Chinese revolutionaries is henceforth the principal guarantee of ultimate victory on a world scale.

It is therefore of the utmost importance that China, in Mao's phrase, should not "change color"—i.e., alter her political character. In order to guard against this danger, the hard lessons of past struggles must be brought home to the young people who have grown to maturity since the victory of 1949.

This preoccupation with training succeeding generations of revolutionaries, in order that China may continue to play her role as the vanguard of the world revolution, lies at the heart of the "Great Proletarian Cultural Revolution" that has swept across China during the past year. . . .

The problem of "revolutionizing" young people, in order to make of them revolutionaries forever, both at home and abroad, was the central theme of the Ninth Chinese Communist Youth League Congress in June 1964. It figures extensively in the last and most remarkable of the nine Chinese replies to the Soviet blast of July 14, 1963, entitled "On Khrushchev's Phony Communism and Its Historical Lessons for the World," issued on the first anniversary of the Soviet article. In this text Mao is credited with the view that a very long period of time is necessary to decide the issue of the struggle between capitalism and socialism. "Several decades won't do it; success requires anywhere from one to several centuries." During this period, the proletarian dictatorship must be maintained and strengthened. . . .

The most important factor in these developments was the growing rôle of the army. Early in 1964, a campaign was launched to "learn from the People's Liberation Army." The army was held up as a model of political loyalty and political consciousness, and "political departments" similar to those in the army were set up in the organizations responsible for administering economic enterprises. . . . Mao regards the army as the natural repository of the ethos of struggle and sacrifice which is for him the hallmark of every true revolutionary movement. The army also tends naturally toward the combination of discipline and initiative which is Mao Tse-tung's constant preoccupation. It is thus not surprising that the heroes recommended as models to Chinese youth in the last few years have been soldiers.

The campaign launched in 1964 did not appear to involve the modification of the Chinese political system by the transfer of political authority to the army. It was, however, a portent of such developments in the future. How much so has only recently been revealed, as the Red Guards' bible, *Quotations from Chairman Mao . . .* , has become available outside China. For the first edition of this book, we now learn, was published in May, 1964, on the eve of the Chinese Communist Youth League Congress, and thereafter it was distributed widely as a reward for the meritorious study of Chairman Mao's works. And this volume, which was thus to play a key role in the ideological training of cadres of the party and other organizations, was published by the Political Department of the Army.

It is clear today that the Army was also involved in two other trends which emerged during 1964, and which are central to the current "Great Proletarian Cultural Revolution": the attack on tradition, and the increasingly extravagant cult of Mao Tse-tung and his thought. . . . Developments since 1964, and especially in the course of 1966, have none the less lifted the Mao cult to a completely new level as regards its intensity and all-pervasiveness, and have also brought striking changes in the nature of that cult. To understand the significance and function of these tendencies, it is necessary to put them in the context of the current political situation as a whole.

Before reviewing the extraordinary events in China since the spring of 1966, it will be well to pause and ask ourselves who launched this movement, and why. There is no doubt that it corresponds to Mao's temperament and political style, and that he fully supports it and gives his approval to all major decisions. . . .

If the current Great Proletarian Cultural Revolution is to a considerable extent stage-managed for Mao by someone else, a large part of the responsibility obviously rests on Lin Piao. . . .

Although it is clear that the army is not entirely united behind Lin Piao, he does speak, of course, for the group now in control of the military establishment. Thus, it is surely no accident that Lin's ascension into public view should have begun immediately after the issuance of the current edition of *Quotations from Chairman Mao*, the preface of which is dated August 1, 1965—August 1st, the anniversary of the Nanchang Uprising, being Army Day in China.

Another key figure in the events of 1966, who also emerged from semiretirement to play a leading role in the Great Proletarian Cultural Revolution, is none other than Mao's wife, today known not under her stage name of Lan-p'ing, but as Comrade Chiang Ch'ing. Since her marriage to Mao in Yenan she had played no open political role whatever, though according to some reports she persistently endeavored to intervene in cultural affairs. . . .

Chiang Ch'ing's rise to eminence found its culmination in her appointment as adviser on cultural work to the People's Liberation Army, which was announced on November 28, 1966, at a meeting celebrating the mass induction into the army of the Peking opera troupe and several other musical and theatrical organizations. In her speech on that occasion—which was greeted by a "thunderous ovation"—Chiang Ch'ing revealed that her "fairly systematic contact with certain sections of literature and art" had begun "a few years" previously. We may assume that one of the first episodes in her intervention in this field was precisely the reform of the Peking opera beginning in 1964. As regards the substance of cultural policy, she affirmed flatly that the "critical assimilation" of the Chinese heritage was "impossible," thus completely reversing the position of her husband, who in the past had come out repeatedly in favor of the selective assimilation of all that was precious in China's past. She also displayed her discriminating knowledge of Western culture by lumping together "rock-and-roll, jazz, strip-tease, impressionism, symbolism, abstractionism, fauvism, modernism" as things "intended to poison and paralyze the minds of the people."

Assuming that leadership in the Great Proletarian Cultural Revolution belongs largely to the trio Mao Tse-tung–Lin Piao–Chiang Ch'ing, why did they decide to launch this movement? Fairly obviously, it was in order to deal with opposition within the Chinese Communist Party toward the radical policies they favor.

If I am correct in assuming that for the past five years Mao has been waiting until the time was ripe to impose a new leap forward, economic policy must have been a major issue. This time Mao was resolved to eliminate opposition *before* launching a new leap, and his suspicion undoubtedly fell on all those who had shown a lack of enthusiasm for his policies in 1958–59, of whom Liu Shao-ch'i was evidently one. These skeptics perhaps also ventured to think that "Mao Tse-tung's thought" placed too heavy an accent on the omnipotence of the human will, as compared to the rational elements in Marxism, and was better adapted to inspiring guerrilla fighters than to building a modern economy.

Undoubtedly the war in Vietnam and the possibility of an American attack against China herself were also subjects of discussion. Some observers of the Chinese scene have made of this the central point and have suggested that the Great Proletarian Cultural Revolution as a whole should be viewed primarily as an attempt to prepare for a war with the United States, which Mao regards as henceforth inevitable. I cannot subscribe to this view. The events of the past year appear to me to be above all an attempt to reshape China and the Chinese people. But it is very likely that the anxiety inspired in Peking by events in Southeast Asia helped Mao and Lin Piao to impose their radical and uncompromising line on the Central Committee.

Whatever the issues in the debate, it is clear from the events since the spring of 1966 that Mao's position by no means won universal acceptance throughout the party apparatus. For if it had, Mao would hardly have embarked on the extraordinary and perilous adventure of creating an entirely new organization, the "Red Guards," which is beyond the control of the party officials except Mao and his henchmen. This enterprise is, of course, entirely without precedent in the forty-nine-year history of Communist regimes, which have always taken as their most fundamental axiom the predominance of the party over all other forms of political and social organization. It is also in contradiction to Mao's own principle, laid down in 1938: "The party commands the gun; the gun must never be allowed to command the party." For the Red Guards, although they harness the enthusiasm of adolescents delighted to occupy the center of the stage, were created and guided by the army, and continue to take the army as their model and inspiration. . . .

At first glance it appears exceedingly singular that Mao should encourage young people to revolt in a country which has been under communist rule for seventeen years, especially as this revolt is directed against "persons within the party who have been in authority, and have taken the capitalist road." To be sure, these persons are said to be only a handful, but in fact the resistance of the party apparatus is obviously much greater than these optimistic official statements would imply, and Mao's aim is not merely to eliminate a few individuals. He is bent on nothing less than smashing the entire party organization as it now exists, and building it up again from the bottom—no doubt incorporating into it in the process a great many revolutionary cadres and militants drawn from the Red Guards and others who have come to the fore in the course of the Great Proletarian Cultural Revolution. In order to attain this end, he has not shrunk back from the possible consequences of a period of disorganization. As the Red Guards of the Middle School attached to Tsinghua University wrote in their first poster, the aim is to "turn the old world upside down, smash it to pieces, pulverize it, and create chaos—the greater the confusion the better!"

What does Mao want to bring out of this chaos? His ambition is apparently to create a party organization of a new type, with built-in safeguards against "bureaucracy." In particular, the "Cultural Revolution Groups" which emerged during the spring and summer of 1966 are to be made permanent. . . . A careful reading of the innumerable "philosophical" articles by workers and peasants published in the Chinese press revealed that what their authors had learned from the study of Mao's thought was to be resourceful, to look at all sides of a problem, to test their ideas by experiment, and to work hard for the sake of the common good.

This rational kernel in the Great Proletarian Cultural Revolution, while it has not entirely disappeared from view, has been largely swallowed up in a mass movement which has attained levels—or at least forms—of irrationality previously unknown even in Stalin's Russia. In essence, this trend, which emerged in the middle of August, combines a cult of Mao's person of an entirely new type with the transformation of the "Thought of Mao Tse-tung" from an ideology into a kind of Marxist Koran endowed with magical virtues. . . .

This development is intimately linked with the growth and transformation of the Mao cult, which has attained in the past few months a level which leaves that of Stalin completely in the shade. This is true, first of all, in simple quantitative terms. Mao's photo and Mao's name are far more ubiquitously and insistently present in the Chinese press than were Stalin's in the Soviet press fifteen years ago. But qualitatively the difference is even more striking.

Until very recently, although Mao and his thought were the object of the highest respect, his physical presence as such did not play any great role in his leadership style. With the exception of the banquet and parade on the occasion of the Chinese national day, he seldom appeared in public. Though he was not obliged, like Stalin, to avoid crowds for the sake of security, he preferred to make known his views either through written statements or through speeches before closed groups for the party or state apparatus, and leave the mass meetings to others. A certain element of mystery and withdrawal was apparently thought desirable to enhance his prestige. . . . But it was the rally of August 18 in T'ien An Men Square, the first of several such gatherings, that marked the veritable starting point for the singular developments we are now witnessing in China.

It was on this occasion that the Red Guards made their first official appearance, though they had been seen on the streets of Peking for several days previously. In the course of the afternoon's proceedings, a girl student placed a Red Guard armband on Mao's arm, thus symbolizing the personal union between the "great teacher, great leader, great supreme commander, and great helmsman" (as Mao is henceforth called) and the young activists who are his instrument in carrying out the "cultural revolution." The Red Guards waved in the air their red-bound volumes of *Quotations from Chairman Mao*, thus producing a characteristic effect which has been repeated and amplified on each subsequent occasion. . . .

It is not easy to pass judgment on a phenomenon of this magnitude. Clearly more is involved than an artificially created mass hysteria. Although there is undoubtedly deep and widespread dissent both within the party and outside it, Mao probably still enjoys a degree of popular adhesion substantially greater than that in the Soviet Union under Stalin, who ruled by sheer police terror. At the same time, there is reason to wonder whether Mao's popularity has not already been gravely undermined by the massive use of violence in recent months. During the wave of terror unleased by the Red Guards in August and September 1966, the number of people savagely beaten was probably several tens of thousands, of whom several thousand were actually beaten to death. And back of the Red Guards stands, as everyone knows, Lin Piao with his army. This situation is hardly calculated to encourage the public expression of dissent, but neither is it likely to strengthen the citizen's feeling of identification with his government. . . .

Understandably the most enthusiastic support comes from youth. The great majority of the Red Guards were born after 1949, and all of them have been taught during the whole of their conscious lives to regard Chairman Mao as the savior of China and a kind and solicitous father figure. Moreover, they have not been steeped like their elders in the culture of the past, and this, joined to youthful exuberance, makes them the natural and enthusiastic instruments of the smashing of statues, burning of books, and defacing of pictures which occurred in Peking and other cities in August and September of 1966. Quantitatively, this vandalism probably has been less than in France at the time of the revolution, or in England at the time of the dissolution of the monasteries by Henry VIII. But given the profound respect for the heritage of the past which undoubtedly still exists among many older Chinese, the psychological shock may be even greater. The numerous suicides among the elite of China's writers and artists may well be the result not merely of the harassment to which they have been subjected by the Red Guards, but of despair at the wanton destruction of elements in China's literary and artistic heritage which only primitive-minded fanatics can regard as reactionary.

A More Distant Perspective

ROSS TERRILL

By 1967 Mao himself was tired of the Cultural Revolution and the increasing arrogance and excesses of the Red Guards. Moreover, it had served his purposes. It had reminded China and the Communist Party of Mao's deepest revolutionary theories—that people are more important than things, that purge and renewal are necessary for a continuing revolution, that revolution is best left to the proletarian/peasant masses, and that China rather than Russia is the inevitable leader of world communism— that "yellow and brown are the colors of the future." Moreover, he had used the Cultural Revolution to overcome those who opposed him in the Chinese Communist Party and Politburo. But most of all, the Cultural Revolution had reasserted Mao's position as the embodiment of the Chinese communist revolution. Mao's "cult of personality" was so firmly in place that he was, in fact, "the people's emperor" right up to the time of his death in 1976.

The true dimensions of the Cultural Revolution and its significance have become considerably clearer since Schram wrote of it in 1966. This is revealed in the excerpt that follows, from Ross Terrill, Mao: A Biography. This book, published in 1980, is the best full-scale contemporary biography of Chairman Mao. Ross Terrill is a distinguished authority and a prolific writer on contemporary China, and positions his account of Mao firmly in the setting of recent Chinese history.

In the 1940s and 1950s it would not have been apt to speak of "Mao-ism" or "Maoists." While collegial authority endured in the CCP, *every* Party member was to a large degree a Maoist. Maoism was pretty much the Chinese Communist Way.

Now things were different. Mao's following had shrunk from al-most the whole, in the 1950s, to merely one part, in the 1960s. In a split Party he was reduced to latching on to one wedge.

But he did have a substantial wedge. Its color was khaki. Mao launched a drive for all of China to "Learn from the PLA [People's Liberation Army]."

What exactly would China learn from the PLA? First signs were odd. "Comrade Jiang Qing talked with me yesterday," Lin Biao told a group in Shanghai. "She is very sharp politically on questions of literature and art."

For years Jiang Qing's health had been spotty and her mood brittle. Mostly she had stayed home and looked after the two daughters. Mao had spent much time away from her. "A man with few words," was how she found him even when they were together.

But her topic—culture—was Mao's chosen weapon for the first round of the fight he was preparing for. "Green Waters"[1] plunged into art and literature circles with a heavy baggage of resentment at her long exclusion from them.

Soon soldiers were doing songs and dances at her behest. Her ter-rible crusade to put China's artistic life into a straitjacket had begun. . . .

Mao left Peking for Shanghai in the autumn of 1965. Jiang Qing was with him. . . .

The spell away from Peking was one more of his retreats, prior to a strong return with batteries recharged. He came to Shanghai to re-cruit some bright young intellectuals as political tools.

One day the Shanghai daily *Literary Currents* carried a heavy piece of drama criticism. That at least is what the strollers on the Shanghai Bund, opening their papers after work on November 10, thought it was.

The article was the first shot in the most amazing gunfire that any Marxist government has ever inflicted upon itself.

The Cultural Revolution had begun. Only in China could an epic of political theater begin with a dry slice of real theater.

The author of the drama column was Yao Wenyuan, a 44-year-old Shanghai essayist with a moon face and sly eyes. As drama criticism his review was stale stuff. For the play that he damned was none other than *Hai Rui Dismissed from Office*, the 1961 work by the vice-mayor of Peking.

---

[1]The English translation of Jiang Qing's name.—ED.

Wu Han's play was a cunning allegory that protested Mao's own dismissal of Peng from the defense ministry. Mao had seen the barb behind it four years before. Now he felt he could hit back. . . .

Only Mao would have made a big issue of Wu Han's play—because Mao was its target. In remarking to some Albanian visitors that the Cultural Revolution began with the *Literary Currents* article, Mao admitted that his own role in Chinese politics was its first bone of contention.

Yet Mao did have some broad and even noble motives for his "Great Proletarian Cultural Revolution." Villagers so wretched that they ate bark, he told Malraux, made better fighters than glib chauffeurs from Shanghai. He was worried about the softness of the 300 million young people born since 1949. They must be put through a struggle of their own.

Mao was also reasserting his belief that people count more than things. "Should we attach more importance to men, to things, or to both?" he asked in a directive on labor reform. It was a question that Chinese tradition had long concerned itself with and Mao gave an answer that was very Confucian. "If we do our work on men well," he concluded, "we shall have things as well." Mao was trying to reestablish, amid the shifting sands of the Chinese Revolution, a priority for social relations over economic output.

The man believed deeply in purge and renewal. "If you have to fart, fart!" he once cried out at a Party meeting. "You will feel much better for it." As in the past, it was nature that lent him the patterns of thought he felt comfortable with.

"Don't peasants weed several times a year? The weeds removed can be used as fertilizer." The sentiment was macabre in its implications. Yet Mao was rousing himself not without hope.

He was in search of immortality for Mao Zedong—but also for the Chinese Revolution.

Mao started with a shot at *Hai Rui Dismissed from Office* for reasons beyond mere wounded vanity. Like any Chinese leader, he had a healthy regard for the role of literature in cementing, or undermining, the legitimacy of a political dynasty.

Being a semi-intellectual himself, he did not quite trust the species, yet he was fascinated by it too. He had come to believe—and told an audience of economic planners so in mid-1964—that in Russia the new privileged elite had sprung first from literary and artistic circles.

"Why are there so many literary and artistic associations in Peking?" he inquired in irritation. "They have nothing to do." At the festivals, "army performances are always the best, local troupes rank second, and those from Peking are the worst."

His obsession with Russia, his chauvinism, his craving for immortality, all tumbled out before the same group of economic planners.

"You have this association, that organization—it's all just a transplant from the Soviet Union . . . all ruled by foreigners and dead men. . . ."

If Mao was furious with Peking cultural officials, he also had bigger fish to fry. Shooting at the vice-mayor, he hoped to splatter some blood of accusation on the mayor.

Peng Zhen was a man of taste and stature. In some eyes he was a possible successor to Mao. His urbane, routinized ways turned Peking into a city that Mao found as soulless and self-important as some Deep Southerners find Washington.

Mao angrily refused to read *People's Daily* during these years. He preferred the army paper *Liberation Army Daily*. . . .

Two outlooks were about to collide.

Using a crablike technique to bring pressure to bear on Peng Zhen and the Peking establishment, Mao appointed a group that included the mayor himself to guide what he had already labeled a Cultural Revolution. Nothing could come of that, except a fight.

The mayor tried to limit the Yao article to the realm of academic debate. Mao was bent on far-reaching political change. The first wave of the Cultural Revolution was against those officials who had come to regard the edifice of PRC rule as an end in itself. A fight was just what Mao had in mind.

He watched it brew during the spring of 1966 from the vantage point of Shanghai. . . .

Mao had made a new analysis of international relations which put Russia and America theoretically on a par as class enemies of China. It was a confused analysis—gaily mixing up national and class factors, arbitrarily reclassifying Russia as capitalist—yet it carried the seed of a coherent new foreign policy line for China.

Mao's problem in calling a plague on both superpowers was that most of the Politburo disagreed with him.

It was clear to everyone in Peking that the U.S. was still a threat to China. Mao did not deny it. The novelty of Mao's position was that he asserted *Russia could be no help* to China in this predicament. Liu and many PLA leaders, on the other hand, still believed in the possibility of "joint action" with Moscow in the face of the American threat. . . .

Mao's strategic view was not changed by the outcome of the Vietnam War. He had already decided by the mid-1960s that Russia was a rising menace and the U.S. a falling one. The U.S. failure in the rice paddies of Indochina merely gave a delayed illustration to his thesis. . . .

While in retreat from Peking, Mao reread *Journey to the West*. The hero of the novel is a monkey with a red ass named Sun. He performs wonderful feats.

Sun steals and eats the peaches of immortality in the gardens of paradise. He storms the gates of hell in order to strike his name off the cosmic blacklist. He covers 180,000 leagues in one bound to reach the pillars that mark the boundary of the world, and once there pisses on a pillar to show his independent spirit.

Daring fate, Sun the monkey king has a trick for coping with adversity. He plucks hair from his body—the term for "hair" happens to be the same Chinese character as Mao's name—bites it into fragments and cries "Change!" Each piece then turns into a small monkey and he has at his side an army of supporters.

"We must overcome the king of hell and liberate the little devils," Mao remarked to a Politburo colleague in March 1966. "We need more Suns from the various local areas to go and disrupt the heavenly palace."

He—and Peking—got them before the year was out. . . .

By mid-1966 Mao was ready to spring back in person to the public arena and he did so clutching a packet of surprises worthy of Sun the monkey king.

He let China know he was alive (but not where he was sojourning) by receiving the premier of faithful Albania at an undisclosed location. Then he offered proof of his physical vigor. He went to Wuhan and swam the Yangze before a battery of TV cameras.

People's Daily reported—perhaps in the spirit of the monkey king legend—that Mao covered fifteen kilometers in sixty-five minutes and showed no sign of fatigue afterward.

Mao returned to Peking to summon some real-life "little devils" to his cause, and to write in his own hand a wall poster that asked the whole nation to revolt.

So the Cultural Revolution really began.

"We need," Mao ruminated of China's future, "determined people who are young, have little education, a firm attitude, and the political experience to take over the work."

His own experience was his guide. "When we started to make revolution we were mere 23-year-old boys," he pointed out, "while the rulers of that time . . . were old and experienced. *They had more learning but we had more truth.*"

The Cultural Revolution put this idea to the test. Young people were supposed to be untainted with old ways. Their education had been purely Chinese and without distortions from the non-Chinese world. As pristine products of new China, would they not prove to have "more truth"?

In that sense the Cultural Revolution was a fresh effort to do what the Hundred Flowers had failed to do: crystallize a moral consensus.

In another sense the Cultural Revolution was a departure from anything Mao had tried before. The "political experience" that Mao wished youth to have was to be gained by a *struggle against the Party!*

This gamble, too, stemmed from the shocks of 1956–1957. At that time Mao lost his faith in the established doctrines of Marxism-Leninism. Truth and the authority of the Party were thereafter quite separable in Mao's mind. So much so that by 1966 he believed that truth could be established *over against* the authority of the Party.

For the Great Leap Forward Mao trusted the Party as vehicle. For the Cultural Revolution he did not. He called in the little devils to assault the Party.

Mao set the Red Guards loose by assuring them that "To rebel is justified" is the gist of Marxism. He invited them to "Knock down the old."

At first their targets were cultural. They smashed temples. They ransacked the homes of intellectuals and better-to-do folk for items that seemed "bourgeois" or "revisionist."

Sunglasses were unacceptable on the first score; chess was too Russian to pass the second test. Almost all books other than those of Marxist doctrine were suspect. Burning them made rousing bonfires which were fun to watch.

If the Red Guards seemed at times like religious zealots, Mao had handed them an apt doctrine. His line of thought was reminiscent of the maxim "Love God and do what you like," which some Christians down the ages have believed in.

If the heart is in the right place, it presumes, then good conduct will flow as naturally as water down a slope.

Mao in 1966 gave Marxism a similar twist. He put "rebellion" in the center, where the Protestant sectarian put "love." If youth has the spirit of rebellion, the Mao of 1966 and 1967 believed, then it will do good deeds for China.

It was a mindless theory and it issued in mindless practice.

The Red Guards had their own reasons to find satisfaction in rebellion. They were a lost generation who suddenly had a sense of being found. They had been to high school, but the expectations aroused there could not be fulfilled. Neither college places nor city jobs existed for them.

A generation that had never had the chance to let its hair down now did so to an extreme. High school kids, who would not have known a capitalist if they saw one, accused veterans who had battled against capitalism for decades of being fingers on capitalism's black hand!

A group of Red Guards broke into Peng Zhen's home in the middle of the night, switched on the light in his bedroom and ordered the mayor to rise and come downtown to be criticized. "Peng Zhen's face turned ashen out of surprise," the young zealots wrote in a breathless report, "and he could not even dress himself properly." . . .

The Red Guards seemed to be devoted to Mao as believers to a prophet. It was in some cases a sincere devotion. But a student of seventeen could not really share Mao's perspective on the Cultural Revolution. For him or her it was exciting to shout insults at "evil ones." It lent self-importance to travel up to Peking by special train to see Chairman Mao and "take part in revolution."

The mechanics probably meant more than the message.

"The Central authorities constantly urged us," one Cantonese youth who eventually swam to Hong Kong recalled, "to take along Mao's *Quotations* and study them whenever there was time. What we did was take along a pack of cards and play whenever there was time."

It seemed that Mao had forgotten the difference between student politics, with all its instability and mixed motives, and the politics of administering a country of 700 million people. . . .

At first the Red Guards wrote posters that merely criticized everything old. But in late 1966, Mao handed graver tasks to the little devils. He asked them to knock power from the hands of half of the Politburo. As if to anoint them for their labors, Mao met eleven million of them at ten sunrise rallies by the Gate of Heavenly Peace.

The young people wore khaki—what did the seasoned veterans of the PLA think of that?—with a red armband and the white words "Red Guard." Each one clutched a copy of *Quotations*. Waved in the air, the red covers made the square resemble a field ablaze with butterflies.

Mao contributed to the rather forced military atmosphere by wearing his PLA fatigues and cap with the red star. The floppy green garments hid a figure that was by now pear-shaped.

At none of the rallies did Mao make any kind of speech (it was frequently Lin Biao who spoke). He merely stood on top of the gate, Jiang Qing beside him (also in PLA uniform), and raised an arm. Yet hundreds of thousands wept from joy, biting their sleeves and jumping up and down in response to his mere presence.

The Cultural Revolution brought all kinds of formalization of self-expression. In a weird way, Mao revived old China's ritual in his waning years.

The philosopher who had written books wrote 200-word posters instead.

The leader who used to lecture for hours to persuade his followers of the merits of a new policy now merely appeared before them with an upraised hand and a glassy smile.

The teacher who always wanted his students to think for themselves seemed content to have them chant a phrase of adoration which they no more understood than does a child understand the catechism it repeats.

Artists signed their paintings, during the mad months of late 1966 and 1967, not with their own name—not with any name—but with the sycophantic phrase: "Ten Thousand Years to Chairman Mao."

How could Mao look at himself in the mirror each morning amid such disgusting nonsense? Had he not asked in his 1949 speech on "Methods of Work" for a "stop to flattery and exaggerated praise"? Had he not forbidden even the naming of a street after a Party leader?

Yet now his own statue stared down over every lobby, his phrases were treated like magic charms, and urban China had come to resemble the interior of a Catholic cathedral with Mao as a red Mary.

Why had Mao changed? Because in his old age he did not any longer believe in the collegial authority of the Communist Party, and his own self-image reverted toward that of a traditional Chinese ruler. . . .

Because Lin Biao was pushing the Mao cult, for his own purposes, and a mixture of lack of energy and lack of will prevented Mao from scotching it.

"You should be concerned about the national crisis," he told a throng outside the Central Committee building one day, "and you should carry out the Great Proletarian Cultural Revolution to the end." He needed more turmoil, for inside the building he was in danger of being outvoted. . . .

The Mao-Liu split began to open up at the time of de-Stalinization. Mao's eventual response to the shock from Moscow—a decision to find a Chinese Way to socialism even if it was not still a Marxist way—left Liu behind in dogged orthodoxy and sheer incomprehension at the pranks of the monkey king. . . .

Liu proved obdurate. The split might have been arrested if Liu had the willow's suppleness, as Zhou had, but he did not. Speaking to an Albanian group in late April 1966, when Mao was starting to crack the whip for his new adventure, Liu did not once mention the words "Cultural Revolution" or even "Mao"!

Liu's most drastic step of resistance was typical of his organization-mindedness: he tried to summon a full Central Committee meeting and have Mao's Cultural Revolution reviewed. But 1966 was not a moment for the triumph of the letter of Party law; a Caesar had much of the nation mesmerized. . . .

Mao's responses grew more and more anti-leftist. The opening stage of the Cultural Revolution, 1965–1966, had been directed against those "veteran cadres encountering new problems" (the code word was "capitalist roaders").

The next stage, from 1967, was directed against young firebrands who proved less good at building than at smashing (the code word was "ultra-leftists").

The wind shifted. *People's Daily* still managed to urge rebellion. Yet between the lines was a very different admonition to law and order.

Well before Liu was formally dismissed from office, in October 1968, Mao's focus of anxiety had switched from Liu's errors to the errors of the "little devils" who had attacked Liu and who wanted "communism now."

The turning point came in Shanghai. Militant leftists "seized power" as Mao had invited them to. They proclaimed a "Shanghai Commune" along the lines of the utopian Paris Commune of 1871. Mao did not approve.

He summoned to his office in February 1967 the two leaders of the Cultural Revolution in Shanghai: Zhang Chunqiao, a former journalist whose career was closely linked with Mao's patronage; and Yao Wenyuan, the moon-faced propagandist who had written the critique of *Hai Rui Dismissed from Office.*

Mao could hardly wait to see them. As their plane flew up from Shanghai he kept asking his secretary if it had arrived at Peking airport yet. The supreme leader ended up waiting in the doorway for the two firebrands to enter his quarters.

He poured cold water on them. Anarchism should be avoided, he said. Organizations must have someone in charge of them.

Shanghai leftists had been quoting a statement of Mao's from the May Fourth period. "The world is ours," ran this cry of youth, "the nation is ours, society is ours." Don't quote it anymore, Mao said, murmuring that he didn't "altogether recall" using those exact words.

As for a Shanghai Commune, Mao backed out of it with a curiously thin objection. If all China's cities set up communes would China's name not have to be changed from PRC to something else? Would foreign countries grant recognition to a "People's Commune of China"?

Zhang and Yao went back to Shanghai and turned down the thermostat of the Cultural Revolution from hot to lukewarm. The Shanghai Commune lasted just nineteen days.

The reason for Mao's change of heart was his dismay at the factionalism of the leftists. They had excelled at knocking down. But when it came to building, there were hundreds of supervisors and no bricklayers.

Mao took trips around China. He did not like what he saw. Not only were Red Guards fighting among themselves, but Red Guards as a whole were coming into bitter conflict with industrial workers. Rumblings of discontent could be heard in the army. . . .

By late 1967 Mao was in favor of law and order. The "little devils" were ordered back to school. They were still to "make revolution," but in practice the reopening of the schools rendered that impracticable.

"If leftists remain uneducated," he murmured in Jiangxi, "they will become ultra-leftists." . . .

Mao scolded the Red Guard leaders for using violence in the factional struggles. . . .

He tried to switch the Cultural Revolution back to its academic beginnings: "We want cultural struggle, not armed struggle."

Mao dealt with the Red Guard leaders bluntly as a veteran politician talking to neophytes. "I am the black hand that suppressed the Red Guards," he said to these young people who had expected that "seizing power" would lead to a new political system. . . .

Was the Cultural Revolution the culmination of Maoism? By no means. It was a charade in a hothouse.

Mao wanted a new society. But in the Cultural Revolution he was driven less by a vision of the future than by a flight from a recent past that he did not like. . . .

Mao also entered on the Cultural Revolution determined to establish more deeply his long-standing socialist values.

- Relations between people are more important than production of things.
- Struggle has a therapeutic benefit that goes beyond attaining the object of the struggle.
- Life is a battleground on which few victories are final and the low and the high change places often.

Here Mao had *some* success. He reminded China of the Maoist faith, even if he did not convert China to it.

The Cultural Revolution did not produce a new type of rule—only some new assistants to the ruler and, for a season, a new social atmosphere. It did, though, put untrammeled power back in Mao's pale and aging hands.

Review and Study Questions

1. In what fundamental ways did Chinese communism under Mao Tse-tung differ from Soviet communism?

2. What prompted Mao to take such radical measures as the Great Proletarian Cultural Revolution? How successful was it?

3. What role did Mao see for China in the so-called Third World?

4. To what extent was the Great Proletarian Cultural Revolution a means to greater power for Mao and the perpetuation of his cult of personality?

5. To what extent was the Great Proletarian Cultural Revolution a genuine effort on the part of Chairman Mao to reenergize and reinvigorate the Chinese Communist revolution?

Suggestions for Further Reading

Mao Tse-tung was a prolific writer, but the entire corpus of his works is not available in English. There are two "official" collections: Mao Tse-tung, *Selected Works*, 5 vols. (New York: International Publishers, 1954) and a British edition of the same collection; and *Selected Works of Mao Tse-tung*, 5 vols. (Oxford and New York: Pergamon Press, 1977), prepared by the Foreign Languages Press in Peking and authorized by the Central Committee of the Chinese Communist Party. Both these editions are devoted to public documents, proclamations, position papers, and the like. Neither contains a shred of biographical material. And further, both editions have been heavily edited and revised by the Communist authorities. To an extent the same is the case with *Selected Military Writings of Mao Tse-tung* (Peking: Foreign Languages Press, 1966). The first of a projected six-volume set of *The Writings of Mao Zedong, 1949–1976*, vol. I, *September 1949–December 1955*, ed. Michael Y. M. Kau and John K. Leung (Armonk, N. Y.: M. E. Sharpe, 1986) has appeared.

There are two English-language versions of Mao's writings in *Mao Tse-tung's Quotations: The Red Guard's Handbook*, ed. Stewart Fraser (Nashville: George Peabody College for Teachers, 1967) and *Quotations from Chairman Mao Tse-tung*, ed. Stuart R. Schram (New York et al.: Praeger, 1967). Somewhat more useful are two carefully edited and selected collections, *The Political Thought of Mao Tse-tung*, ed. Stuart R. Schram (New York et al.: Praeger, 1963) and *Chairman Mao Talks to the People, Talks and Letters: 1956–1971*, ed. and intro. Stuart Schram, tr. John Chinnery and Tieyun (New York: Pantheon, 1974). Of a similar sort are *Mao Tse-tung on Revolution and War*, ed. M. Rejai (Garden City, N. Y.: Doubleday, 1969), and Philippe Devillers, *Mao*, tr. Tony White (New York: Schocken Books, 1969), in the "What They *Really* Said" series. There is no autobiography as such. There is, however, a work that has been used as a substitute for an autobiography for Mao's early career: Edgar Snow, *Red Star over China*, rev. ed. (New York: Garden City Publishing Co., 1939), in which Snow reports a long series of private conversations with Mao about his childhood and early life. There are two books that present selections from Mao's works in a chronological order and hence are biographical or autobiographical in structure: *Mao Papers: Anthology and Bibliography*, ed. Je-

284 *Makers of World History*

rome Ch'en (London: Oxford University Press, 1970), and *Mao,* ed. Jerome Ch'en (Englewood Cliffs, N.J.: Prentice-Hall, 1969). The latter of these, part of the series "Great Lives Observed," is the most useful; it not only presents Mao in his own words but has a section called "Mao Viewed by His Contemporaries" and one called "Mao in History." Another book by Jerome Ch'en, *Mao and the Chinese Revolution,* has an interesting section consisting of "Thirty-seven Poems by Mao Tse-tung," tr. Michael Bullock and Jerome Ch'en (London et al.: Oxford University Press, 1965). Mao was famous as a poet in China.

There is no end of books analyzing Mao's thought. One of the best of them is Arthur A. Cohen, *The Communism of Mao Tse-tung* (Chicago and London: University of Chicago Press, 1964). Cohen's book deflates the exaggerated Chinese representation of Mao as a political philosopher and makes the case for his being simply a skillful revolutionary strategist. There is still no better guide to Mao's thought than this one, in spite of such later books as Alain Bouc, *Mao Tse-tung: A Guide to His Thought,* tr. Paul Auster and Lydia Davis (New York: St. Martin's, 1977) and Frederic Wakeman, Jr., *History and Will: Philosophical Perspectives of Mao Tse-tung's Thought* (Berkeley et al.: University of California Press, 1973).

In general, with the conspicuous exceptions of Stuart Schram's *Mao Tse-tung* (New York: Simon & Schuster, 1966), excerpted for this chapter, and Edgar Snow's *Red Star over China,* the older biographies of Mao can be dismissed in favor of those written in the decade following his death. The best of these is Ross Terrill, *Mao: A Biography* (New York et al.: Harper & Row, 1980), excerpted for this chapter. Two others can also be recommended: Dick Wilson, *The People's Emperor: Mao, A Biography of Mao Tse-tung* (Garden City, N.Y.: Doubleday, 1980), stresses the earthy, peasant quality of Mao and his preoccupation with the traditional Chinese cult of the ruler rather than his Marxism or his higher political skills. It is impressionistic and anecdotal and very readable, as is the work by an able Chinese-American journalist, Eric Chou: *Mao Tse-tung: The Man and the Myth* (New York: Stein and Day, 1982). Two books can be recommended that deal specifically with the Great Cultural Revolution. Roderick Macfarquhar, *The Origins of the Cultural Revolution,* vol. I, *Contradictions among the People 1956–1957;* vol. II, *The Great Leap Forward 1958–1960* (New York: Columbia University Press, 1974, 1983), with a third volume to come, is a definitive, detailed, and altogether convincing analysis of the origins of the Cultural Revolution in the failure of the Great Leap Forward. A less demanding but satisfactory work that also focuses on the Cultural Revolution is Stanley Karnow, *Mao and China: From Revolution to Revolution* (New York: Viking, 1972).

Two books attempt to assess the place of Chairman Mao in modern history: Stuart R. Schram, *Mao Zedong: A Preliminary Reassessment* (New York: St. Martin's, 1983), and *Mao Tse-tung in the Scales of History: A Preliminary Assessment,* organized by the *Chinese Quarterly,* ed. Dick Wilson (Cambridge et al.: Cambridge University Press, 1977).

Of the many books on the history of revolutionary China, there are two that can be especially recommended: Chalmer A. Johnson, *Peasant Nationalism and Communist Power: The Emergence of Revolutionary China* (Stanford: Stanford University Press, 1962), and John King Fairbank, *The Great Chinese Revolution, 1800–1985* (New York: Harper & Row, 1986).

JOMO KENYATTA: "THE BURNING SPEAR"

c. 1894	Born
1914	Joined a Church of Scotland mission and was baptized
1922	Joined the East Africa Association political protest movement
1928	General secretary of the Kikuyu Central Association
1929	Went to London to protest white domination of East Africa
1936–38	Studied anthropology at London School of Economics
1946	Returned to Kenya to become president of the Kenya African Union
1952–53	Arrested and tried as the "manager" of the Mau Mau terrorist organization
1961	Released from prison
1963–64	Became prime minister, then president of Kenya
1978	Died

Jomo Kenyatta of Kenya was the most widely known and charismatic of the leaders of the several African peoples who were clamoring for independence from colonial rule in the 1950s. He was a large, powerfully built man, with a commanding presence, a penetrating, transfixing gaze, and a deep, kettle-drum voice. He was a spell-binding orator, well educated, and an experienced political leader and consensus builder among the many factions of his people. He was clearly a danger to continued white supremacy in Kenya. He knew it and the white settlers knew it.

He was born about 1894, near Mount Kenya, the grandson of a Kikuyu witch doctor. His life coincided with the period of white penetration of East Africa. He later recalled, as a boy, seeing the first white men to reach the interior. He was fascinated by them, by their bustling progress and their literacy. At about the age of twelve he presented himself at a Church of Scotland mission school, clad only in three wire bracelets and a strip of cloth around his neck. He became a student and a Christian. He took the baptismal name Johnstone, from his admiration for the Apostles John and Peter (the "rock" or "stone" of the early church), adding it to his tribal name Kamau.

After five years in the mission school he went to Nairobi, the rapidly growing political and economic hub of East Africa. Here he held a succession of jobs that provided him with a living and the ability to buy fancy clothes, including a decorated belt which in the Kikuyu language is called *kenyatta*. He took this as a new name symbolizing his new life of affluence.

In 1922 Kenyatta joined the fledgling East Africa Association, the first political protest movement in Kenya against white domination. Government pressure forced this organization to disband, but its members shortly reorganized as the Kikuyu Central Association. Kenyatta became its general secretary in 1928. That same year a British colonial commission recommended a union of Kenya with Uganda and Tanganyika, with the prospect of self-government. Such a prospect spelled ruin for native Kikuyu interests, and the following year Kenyatta went to London to work against the scheme.

He made no progress at all with British authorities, but he and his cause were championed by various radical groups and individuals in England, including Fenner Brockway, a socialist member of parliament who was an outspoken critic of imperialism. Under the sponsorship of radical groups, Kenyatta traveled to Moscow and to the International Negro Workers' Conference in Hamburg. He was becoming identified with European radical politics—but he was radical only in the interests of his own people. In 1932 he was finally permitted to testify on behalf of Kikuyu land claims before a British government commission, but his testimony was generally ignored. He continued to travel on the Continent, visiting the Soviet Union again, where he studied at Moscow University for a year. Returning to England, he worked as a phonetic informant at University College, London, and from 1936 to 1938 studied anthropology at the London School of Economics. His thesis, *Facing Mount Kenya*, a study of Kikuyu tribal life, was published in 1938. For that book he took yet another name, Jomo "Burning Spear."

After the start of World War II Kenyatta was unable to return to Kenya. In England he lectured on African affairs for the Workers Educational Association and continued to write pamphlets advocating African rights. With the end of the war he helped organize the Fifth Pan-African Congress, which met, not in Africa, but in Manchester. Resolutions were passed demanding African independence from colonial rule. Shortly thereafter, he was able to return to Kenya, where, in 1947, he was elected president of the newly formed Kenya African Union. Under his leadership the union grew into an enormous, mass nationalist party, with an increasingly insistent agenda for self-government.

Suffering without Bitterness

JOMO KENYATTA

In the face of the intransigence of the white settler government of Kenya, some sort of violent reaction was nearly inevitable. It came in 1952 with the outbreak of the black terrorist movement called Mau Mau. It was a widespread secret society, its members pledged, by the most gruesome oath-taking ceremonies, to violence against both whites and temporizing fellow blacks.

The Mau Mau created a nationwide panic. White settlers barricaded themselves in their farm compounds, fearing even their most faithful native retainers. Black tribal leaders who advocated anything short of violent solutions were in danger of their lives. A climax was reached with the murder of a revered senior chief of the Kikuyu, Chief Waruhiu, in the fall of 1952. On October 20, at the request of the newly appointed governor, Sir Evelyn Baring, the British government issued an Emergency Proclamation. Jomo Kenyatta was widely perceived among the white settlers to be the leader of the Mau Mau. Under the Emergency Proclamation he was arrested, along with nearly two hundred other African leaders. Kenyatta was immediately flown to a remote northern village, Kapenguria, where he was charged with "management" of the Mau Mau and brought to trial.

The book from which the following excerpt is taken, Suffering without Bitterness, *was published under the name of Jomo Kenyatta. While it does contain substantial excerpts from his speeches and writings, it was actually written by two close associates of Kenyatta, his former secretary Duncan Nderitu Ndegwa, and Anthony Cullen, a member of his personal staff. Kenyatta himself read and contributed to the manuscript as it took shape. It is thus an "official biography." It deals with the famous Kapenguria trial, with Kenyatta's subsequent imprisonment, and with his eventual release and triumphant return to Kenyan national leadership.*

The excerpt selected is a refutation of the charge against Kenyatta that he was the leader of the Mau Mau. Quite the reverse: it depicts him as an opponent of the movement and the leading advocate of Kenyan nationalism by peaceful, constitutional means.

The record of evidence at this point illustrates beyond rational doubt that, far from being a catalyst of disaster, Kenyatta was an implacable opponent of lawlessness and violence. By all his words, and by his very presence, he stood unyieldingly for nationalist demands, to be secured by the forces of peace.

He risked his life, before he was arrested, to strengthen his national Party. His principles, rooted in personal philosophy tempered by wide experience, were those of constitutional means. Beyond this, he could envisage how terrorism must provoke such reprisals, and permit such propaganda, as to undo—or set right back—the effect of solid preparation and persuasion over thirty years.

It seems remarkable in retrospect that, in 1952, men of ingrained honesty, and often of undoubted brilliance, should have stifled or have found themselves deserted by such attributes. . . . All were caught up in a monstrous lie.

The national Swahili newspaper *Baraza*—one of the *East African Standard* group of publications—covered a meeting at Muguga, about fifteen miles from Nairobi, in its issue of April 12, 1952. This account was quoted in evidence, incidentally, during the Kapenguria trial.

Baraza was staffed by professional journalists, who reported that: "Mr. Jomo Kenyatta, the President of the KAU, said last Saturday that, because of the rumours that had spread everywhere that KAU is connected with an Association which was proscribed—that is, Mau Mau—there should be no other meetings after the close of KAU meetings". . . .

Also quoted in the Court records was a report in the newspaper *Sauti ya Mwafrika* of June 20, 1952, in reference to a speech by Jomo Kenyatta at Naivasha at that time. In this speech, he emphasized that demands must be pursued peacefully, and warned against racial intolerance. This—be it noted—was not a subtle or strategic address to a select group of intelligentsia, but one of a series of orations to the ordinary people who gathered in thousands to hear him, standing in groups or perched in trees or seated on the ground. . . .

Then came two enormous mass meetings, of the greatest possible significance to any appraisal of Mzee[1] Kenyatta's activities and objectives over this period. The first of these was a KAU meeting at Nyeri on July 26, 1952, with an attendance of at least 50,000 people.

There is an official record of his words at this meeting. As an orator on such occasions, Kenyatta had—and indeed still has—a magic touch and a capability without peer. He could have inflamed this crowd and turned the country onto any chosen path, bending the future to his will. In the event, this was the occasion when he called for national unity rather than subversion, and for the faithful pursuit of democratic principles. He proclaimed that violence and

---

[1]*Mzee* is a Kikuyu term of respect.—ED.

thuggery could only delay Kenya's independence. Denouncing Mau Mau and lawlessness, he urged this vast assembly, and through them the millions to whom his words would gradually seep, to renounce force and rely instead on the supreme power of justice and brains. . . .

The second of these equally large mass meetings was held at Kiambu on August 24, 1952. . . .

Jomo Kenyatta started his speech with these words—"Many people were asked what this meeting is about and who the organizers are. The meeting is of the Kikuyu elders and leaders, who have decided to address a public meeting and see what the disease in Kikuyuland is, and how this disease can be cured. We are being harmed by a thing which some people seem to call Mau Mau."

Kenyatta went on to ask all those who were against Mau Mau to raise their hands. Response was immediate and unanimous. He then went on to talk about the objects of the KAU, and to disclaim any association between the Union and Mau Mau activities. He ended his speech with these words—"Let us agree not to engage in crime. We have pleaded for more land for many years. A Commission will soon be coming out to look into the land question. If you do not stop crime, those people who come out on the Land Commission will be told that we are thieves, that we are this, that we are that, which would do us immeasurable harm. We must now work together". . . .

He went on: "Mau Mau has spoiled the country. Let Mau Mau perish for ever. All people should search for Mau Mau and kill it. . . ."

Only 57 days elapsed after these declarations before Kenyatta was arrested. It is possible to ascribe motivation, not with the assurance of testimony, but at least with the confidence that has to emerge from the absence of alternative assumption. It must have been thought, by those responsible, that here was a man drawing inconveniently near to the attainment of at least some legitimate demands, by lawful means. It must have been thought that here was the one mature and powerful leader, in whose absence ambition—or even rebellion—could speedily be crushed. But whatever the composite of motives and emotions, Kenya was plunged into disaster. And those annals of justice to which the British people cling, with such modest and seemingly-casual devotion, were made to look shoddy, by the work of frightened servants of the Crown. . . .

After Kenyatta's arrest the Mau Mau violence grew worse. But the trial hastened on. In the course of the trial, Kenyatta made the following statement during testimony as a witness, called by his leading defense council, Mr. D. N. Pritt.

'I blame the Government because—knowing that the Africans have grievances—they did not go into these grievances: shortage of houses in places like Nairobi, land shortage, and poverty of the African people both in the towns and in the Reserves. I believe if the Government had looked into the economic and social conditions of the people, they could have done much good.

'And instead of joining with us to fight Mau Mau, the Government arrested all the leading members of the Kenya African Union, accusing them of being Mau Mau. It should have been the Government's duty to co-operate with KAU to stamp out anything that was bad, such as Mau Mau. Instead of doing that, they have arrested thousands and thousands of people who would have been useful in helping to put things right in this country. It is on these points that I blame the Government; they did not tackle the business in the right way.

'They wanted—I think—not to eliminate Mau Mau, but to eliminate the only political organization, the KAU, which fights constitutionally for the rights of the African people, just as the Electors Union fights for the rights of the Europeans and the Indian National Congress for the rights of the Asians. I think and believe that the activity of Government in arresting all the leading members of KAU, who are innocent people engaged in ordinary business, is not the right way of combatting Mau Mau. Most of the people behind bars today are people who would be helping to adjust things and eliminate Mau Mau from the country.

'We know pretty well that the reason for our arrest was not Mau Mau, but because we were going ahead uniting our people to demand our rights. The Government arrested us simply because, when they saw we could have an organization of 30,000 or 40,000 or more Africans demanding their rights here, they said: we have an excuse to stop this—Mau Mau.'

This clearly went to the root of the matter, and the presentation of this truth has been curiously hushed up—or simply unseen by superficial observers of Africa—in almost all subsequent literature and discussion.

But what of the trial itself? How was this conducted, and what was the calculated arrangement of the Prosecution case?

This may be gauged from Mr. Pritt's final address, spread over two days beginning on March 2, 1953. . . .

What follows now is an accurate precis, employing a selection of Mr. Pritt's unaltered words, of the case as he saw it at that stage:

'The prosecution case in this very serious litigation was scarcely properly prepared at any stage, either in the weeks or months preceding the charges, or in the weeks or months when the accused were already in detention, or during the period of the case itself.

'It does not seem that the prosecution has ever made up its mind on what is the essence of its case against the accused.

'I could understand the prosecution attitude if some political or other pressure had brought about the launching of a case that never should have been launched, but in no other way can I understand it.

'Some of the witnesses we wanted to call were in England, and the Government of Kenya refused to give us any safe conduct for them to come here.

'I have constantly wondered why so much of the prosecution evidence, and so much of their examination of the accused and witnesses, has seemed so remote from the allegations contained in the charges, which relate to management and membership of Mau Mau.

'Managing Mau Mau? Well, where? In what fashion, with what assistance, in what office, with what policy, with what documents? There was never anything.

'In order to convict Mr. Kenyatta of managing, the evidence would have to show that he is the manager, that is to say the one person who is at the head of the management, and not just one of a number of persons taking part in management. Therefore I would submit that Mr. Kenyatta not only cannot be convicted of being a manager, as a matter of law, because there is no evidence of his management in that sense of the word, but that he cannot be convicted of assisting in the management, since he is not charged with assisting in the management.

'The prosecution's case is sought to be built up out of all sorts of little bits and pieces, and little items on the periphery, and never any real evidence of anything seriously connected with Mau Mau. . . .

'You have to prove something grave and terrible, that the accused participated in a terrorist organization, whereas there is very substantial evidence that the body in which they are most prominent—the Kenya African Union—is a plain and outspoken enemy of that organization'. . . .

On April 8, 1953, the 58th day of the Kapenguria trial, judgment was delivered by the magistrate, Mr. R. S. Thacker, Q.C. The record shows that Kenyatta was convicted on both counts, sentenced to seven years imprisonment, with a recommendation that he be confined thereafter.

In all the history of legal process, there can hardly have been a more astounding verdict as an outcome of trial proceedings. It caricatured—rather than echoed—those farcical performances of law in Police States which, before and since, have been widely condemned by humanists and liberal-minded men. . . .

Mau Mau from Within

DONALD L. BARNETT AND KARARI NJAMA

In spite of the government's best efforts to keep Kenyatta's trial secret, it quickly became an international event. India's Premier Pandit Nehru sent a team of Indian lawyers to defend him; he had the best available Kenyan lawyers; and his English radical friends secured the services of D. N. Pritt, one of Britain's most famous defense attorneys and a noted advocate of minority and subversive causes.

But the government pressed on with its case. The main charge was that Kenyatta was the active, managing leader of the Mau Mau. Despite the most blatant lapses in judicial process and the witch-hunt atmosphere of the trial, despite the perjured testimony of the leading prosecution witness (to which he later admitted), the presiding judge found Kenyatta guilty as charged. It was a judgment thoroughly approved by the Kenyan white settler community, who were unanimous in their belief that Kenyatta was indeed the leader of the Mau Mau. This was a belief shared by many native blacks, perhaps even a majority.

The following account is excerpted from a sensational book, Mau Mau from Within, *the recollections of a Kikuyu teacher named Karari Njama, who joined the movement and whose book is a defense of it. In the account of his oath-taking it is clear that Kenyatta was regarded as the leader of the movement. It is equally clear that the distinction between Mau Mau terrorism and legitimate protest—which was the heart of Kenyatta's defense—was totally ignored by Njama and the Mau Mau. Njama explicitly identifies Mau Mau with the Kikuyu Central Association (KCA), the radical political movement Kenyatta had once headed.*

Njama had been persuaded by a friend to attend a feast at a neighbor's house. Only after he arrived did he begin to suspect that it was actually to be a Mau Mau initiation. Here is his account of his oath-taking.

Groups of men and women continued to come until there was very little room for anyone to sit. A few persons would be called by names and moved in the next hut. When I was called to go to the next hut, I was very pleased, but arriving outside in a clear moonshine, I could see hundreds of people standing some armed with *pangas, simis* (swords) and clubs. They formed a path on both sides leading to the door of the next hut. I became certain that the day had arrived for me to take the oath, and I had to face it manly, I thought.

As I led my group marching in the cordoned path, they waved their *pangas* and swords over our heads and I heard one of them asking whether there was an informer to be 'eaten.' With a reply that we were all good people from another person, we entered the next hut.

By the light of a hurricane lamp, I could see the furious guards who stood armed with *pangas* and *simis*. Right in front of us stood an arch of banana and maize stalks and sugar cane stems tied by a forest creeping and climbing plant. We were harassed to take out our coats, money, watches, shoes and any other European metal we had in our possession. Then the oath administrator, Githinji Mwarari—who had painted his fat face with white chalk—put a band of raw goat's skin on the right hand wrist of each one of the seven persons who were to be initiated. We were then surrounded [bound together] by goats' small intestines on our shoulders and feet. Another person then sprayed us with some beer from his mouth as a blessing at the same time throwing a mixture of the finger millet with other cereals on us. Then Githinji pricked our right hand middle finger with a needle until it bled. He then brought the chest of a billy goat and its heart still attached to the lungs and smeared them with our blood. He then took a Kikuyu gourd containing blood and with it made a cross on our foreheads and on all important joints saying, 'May this blood mark the faithful and brave members of the Gikuyu and Mumbi Unity; may this same blood warn you that if you betray our secrets or violate the oath, our members will come and cut you into pieces at the joints marked by this blood.'

We were then asked to lick each others blood from our middle fingers and vowed after the administrator: 'If I reveal this secret of Gikuyu and Mumbi to a person not a member, may this blood kill me. If I violate any of the rules of the oath may this blood kill me. If I lie, may this blood kill me.'

We were then ordered to hold each others right hand and in that position, making a line, passed through the arch seven times. Each time the oath administrator cut off a piece of the goat's small intestine, breaking it into pieces, while all the rest in the hut repeated a curse on us: '*T'athu! Ugotuika uguo ungiaria maheni! Muma uroria muria ma!*' ('Slash! may you be cut like this! Let the oath kill he who lies!').

We were then made to stand facing Mt. Kenya, encircled by intestines, and given two dampened soil balls and ordered to hold the left hand soil ball against our navels. We then swore: 'I, (Karari Njama), swear before God and before all the people present here that. . . .

(1) I shall never reveal this secret of the KCA oath—which is of Gikuyu and Mumbi and which demands land and freedom—to any person who is not a member of our society. If I ever reveal it, may this oath kill me! ([Repeated after each vow while] biting the chest meat of a billy goat held together with the heart and lungs.)

(2) I shall always help any member of our society who is in difficulty or need of help.

(3) If I am ever called, during the day or night, to do any work for this society, I shall obey.

(4) I shall on no account ever disobey the leaders of this society.

(5) If I am ever given firearms or ammunition to hide, I shall do so.

(6) I shall always give money or goods to this society whenever called upon to do so.

(7) I shall never sell land to a European or an Asian.

(8) I shall not permit intermarriage between Africans and the white community.

(9) I will never go with a prostitute.

(10) I shall never cause a girl to become pregnant and leave her unmarried.

(11) I will never marry and then seek a divorce.

(12) I shall never allow any daughter to remain uncircumcised.[2]

(13) I shall never drink European manufactured beer or cigarettes.

(14) I shall never spy on or otherwise sell my people to Government.

(15) I shall never help the missionaries in their Christian faith to ruin our traditional and cultural customs.

(16) I will never accept the Beecher Report.[3]

(17) I shall never steal any property belonging to a member of our society.

(18) I shall obey any strike call, whenever notified.

(19) I will never retreat or abandon any of our mentioned demands but will daily increase more and stronger demands until we achieve our goals.

(20) I shall pay 62/50s. and a ram as assessed by this society as soon as I am able.

(21) I shall always follow the leadership of Jomo Kenyatta and Mbiyu Koinange.'

We repeated the oath while pricking the eye of a goat with a kei-apple thorn seven times and then ended the vows by pricking seven

---

[2]Female circumcision had been opposed by white missionaries and, to some extent, whites generally, as a cruel and dangerous practice—but it had become one of the nationalistic issues to the Kikuyu.—ED.

[3]A report on public education in 1949, seen as inimical to black interests.—ED.

times some seven sodom apples. To end the ceremony, blood mixed with some good smelling oil was used to make a cross on our foreheads indicating our reception as members of Gikuyu and Mumbi [while] warning us: 'Forward ever and backward never!' . . .

After we had all been sworn, the house was very crowded that contained about 80 people; nearly all of whom were initiated on that night. About the same number of old members were working outside as guards. A speech was made by the oath administrator, Githinji Mwarari, and his assistant Kariuki King'ori, who told us that they had been sent from the Head Office in Nairobi to give people an oath that could create a real unity among all the Africans which would make it easier for the African to gain his land and freedom. . . .

When he sat down, his assistant administrator, Kariuki King'ori, stood and taught us greetings—the old Kikuyu greetings rarely used due to changes brought about by the European civilization—such as the shaking of hands and the terminology. 'If any person wants to refer to the society he would not say "Mau Mau" as you have already been warned, but he would refer to the society as *Muhimu* (a Swahili word meaning "Most Important"), *Muingi* (meaning "The Community" in Kikuyu) or *Gikuyu na Mumbi*.' . . .

It was about four o'clock in the morning, the cocks were crowing, the moon and the stars were brightly shining. The footpaths were wet and muddy as it had rained sometime before midnight. I quickly and quietly went home and called my wife to open the door for me. Without talking to her I went straight to my bed.

I spent the whole day in bed, partly asleep, as I had not slept the night before, and partly reciting and reasoning my vows. Reflecting on the crowd at the KAU rally held one and a half months ago at Nyeri Showgrounds supporting national demands under the national leader Jomo Kenyatta assisted by Peter Mbiyu Koinange, the cleverest Africans in Kenya—whose leadership was advertised in Mathenge's song book where Jesus Christ's name has been substituted for by Jomo Kenyatta's—and whereas the Government had taken no action against them proved to me that our true and just grievances were led by powerful and honoured men. I believed that it was an all Kenya African national movement and not a tribal one. With the understanding that African labour is the whole backbone of Kenya's economy, I believed that if all Kenya Africans went on a labour strike we would paralyse the country's economy and the white community who holds the most of it would suffer most and recognize our demands. Furthermore, our national leader, Jomo Kenyatta, had lived in England for 17 years and must have during his stay convinced the British Government of our claims.

Rush to Judgment

JEREMY MURRAY-BROWN

Was the Kapenguria trial and conviction of Jomo Kenyatta a disgraceful and cynical rush to judgment? Kenyatta's assertions that he was never associated with the Mau Mau, but that he sought only the rights of his people under a constitutional government, seem to be borne out by the subsequent course of events.

After the trial and a series of fruitless appeals, Kenyatta was imprisoned in 1954, at Lokitaung. But African independence was on the march. There was a continuous clamor for his release. In 1960 he was elected in absentia as president of the Kenya African National Union, the leading native independence party. He was finally released in the summer of 1961, and he immediately began a speaking tour that brought out throngs wherever he went. Within the next two years he was elected president of KANU and a member of the Legislative Assembly. He was clearly the only black leader of Kenya with a substantial following. Under an agreement reached with the British, the last governor of Kenya, Malcolm Macdonald, invited Kenyatta to form a government on June 1, 1963, and he became the first Prime Minister of a self-governing Kenya. In the following year Kenya became a republic with Kenyatta as its president. In his triumph Kenyatta did not seek vengeance. Instead, he became the most pro-British of African leaders, and generally the most pro-Western, pro-white. He even reached an accommodation with the white settlers. This situation lasted until his death in 1978.

Were his moderation and statesmanlike policies as head of state indicative that he had been innocent of the charges brought against him in the trial at Kapenguria? Most of his detractors have said no, and have continued to characterize Kenyatta as, at best, an adroit politician who permitted his name to be used by the Mau Mau, and allowed himself and his party to profit from their terrorism.

In the excerpt that follows from Jeremy Murray-Brown's Kenyatta, *the most authoritative biography of Jomo Kenyatta, the author treats the trial at Kapenguria in great detail and proves conclusively that it was indeed a rush to judgment, a cynical pretext for removing Kenyatta as a dangerous political influence, and that the Mau Mau charge was a total fabrication.*

The account begins with the appointment of the new governor of Kenya, Sir Evelyn Baring, and the proclamation of a state of emergency.

On taking up his appointment as Governor, Baring took the view that it would be a mistake for him to meet Kenyatta formally since if he then had to arrest him he would appear to have double-crossed the Africans. The first assumption of the Emergency operation was that once the nationalist leaders were out of the way, peace would return among the normally law-abiding natives of the colony.

The government was as shaken as everyone else by the Kikuyu reaction to the loss of their leaders, once the initial numbness wore off. It left them with the problem of having to decide what to do with Kenyatta. In London questions were raised in Parliament where Kenyatta had powerful friends in Fenner Brockway and Leslie Hale. Peter Mbiyu Koinange was also at large and able to denounce the Emergency measures. The confusion of thinking that led to Kenyatta's arrest compelled the government to find some pretext for his detention. Perhaps the most obvious solution was to bring him to trial and to try to make him out to be a common criminal. But of what offence should it accuse him? And how could they make the charge stick?

They made vigorous efforts to find something. A ton and a half of documents, books and papers had been removed from Kenyatta's house at Gatundu the night of his arrest, and a senior police officer was immediately detailed to go through these and prepare a case against him. He was given three weeks to complete his enquiries. It is fair to say he found nothing. . . . As Kenyatta's alleged crimes and the place of his arrest both lay in the Kiambu district of Kikuyuland, the natural and proper course would have been to try him in Nairobi. But the government feared the attention and demonstrations which this would attract and wanted to carry the case through as quietly as possible, at some remote spot.

Kapenguria was ideal for this purpose. It lay in a restricted area, to which no one could go without a permit; the scanty local population was backward and uninterested; it had never had a resident magistrate, so that the government could pick someone on whom it could rely. Had the prosecution been decided on from the start, the accused could have been sent straight to one of the prisons at Kapenguria where it would be simple to 'apprehend' them and give some plausibility to the holding of the trial there. But, as it was, the government had to go through a legal farce. On 18 November Kenyatta and his colleagues Kaggia, Kubai, Ngei and Oneko, all of whom were also executive members of KAU, and Kunga Karumba, who was chairman of an important regional branch of the party, were brought down to Kapenguria, technically released from custody and immediately re-arrested, thus creating jurisdiction for trial in Kapenguria. They were now charged with the management of Mau Mau, which was a proscribed society. The offence carried a maximum penalty of seven years' imprisonment. Their trial was set for 24 November.

This was apparently the first Kenyatta heard of the government's intentions towards him. He managed to get a message out requesting that defence lawyers be briefed on his behalf. Within Kenya, feeling among the European community was running so high that no white man in the colony dared join in the defence, which was now being handled from Nairobi by the Indian supporters of the nationalist movement, led by a young barrister, A. R. Kapila. But immediate offers of help came from elsewhere, and soon an impressive international team of counsel was assembled, including Chaman Lall, a member of the Upper House of the Indian Parliament and friend of Nehru, H. O. Davies from Lagos, and Dudley Thompson, a West Indian practising in Tanganyika. Two Kenya residents also took part, a Goan, Fitzwell de Souza and a Sikh, Jaswant Singh.

To lead this team, Koinange, Brockway and Hale invited the services of D. N. Pritt QC, one of the ablest advocates at the English Bar. On 24 November the six accused were again brought down to Kapenguria where a judge recently retired from the Supreme Court of Kenya, R. S. Thacker, had been specially appointed to hear the case. He adjourned proceedings until 3 December to allow the defence team time to come together.

D. N. Pritt QC had as great an experience of political trials as anyone in the British Commonwealth. A Member of Parliament for fifteen years and known for pro-Soviet views, he had long been an opponent of imperialism. In the Parliament of 1945–50 he had sat as an independent Socialist. His acceptance of the Kapenguria brief made it certain that Kenyatta's case would receive wide publicity. If the Kenya Government hoped to get away with a hole-and-corner affair to cover their blunder in arresting Kenyatta, they badly miscalculated. Their attempt to make Kenyatta out to be an ordinary criminal came unstuck the moment Pritt arrived on the scene. As became clear during the trial itself, the prosecution soon shifted the base of its attack from Kenyatta's alleged criminal activities as manager of Mau Mau to the politics of African Nationalism. . . .

On 3 December 1952, all was ready for the trial proper to begin. The government provided window-dressing in the form of armoured cars, barbed wire and helicopters circling overhead. Troops were everywhere in evidence. The six accused men were brought from their prison a mile away by army truck and marched in handcuffs by armed *askaris* to the door of the court. Only then were the handcuffs removed. The 'public' consisted of wives of settlers and of government officers who applauded every point which seemed to go against Kenyatta. But Nairobi journalists and half a dozen of the best foreign

correspondents of the English Press were there, along with government photographers. The government intended, no doubt, to humili-
ate Kenyatta and impress such Africans as were present with the
power of the colonial regime. In the long run the steps taken to
destroy him in the eyes of his people ensured his resurrection as their
suffering servant.

Kenyatta still wore the clothes in which he had been arrested. The
police had removed his stick and ring. He was to spend fifty-eight
days in court before judgement was passed, but everyone who was
present at the trial felt that his was the dominating personality at
Kapenguria.

On 3 December 1952, then, Deputy Public Prosecutor Somer-
hough opened for the Crown:

> 'May it please your Honour. The charge is that of managing an unlawful
> society. . . . The Crown cannot bind themselves to any particular place
> in the Colony where this society was managed. The Society is Mau Mau.
> It is a Society which has no records. It appears to have no official list of
> members. It does not carry banners. Some details of its meetings and
> rites, the instrument of which are got from the local bush, will be heard
> later in the proceedings. Arches of banana leaves, the African fruit
> known as the Apple of Sodom, eyes of sheep, blood and earth—these
> are all gathered together when ceremonies take place. . . .
>
> The Crown case is going to be that Mau Mau is part of KAU—a
> militant part, a sort of Stern gang, if I may borrow a phrase from
> another country. It is possible to be a member of KAU and have noth-
> ing to do with Mau Mau; yet Mau Mau itself is a definite limb or part of
> KAU as it existed in 1952 when all the accused were closely connected
> with KAU as high office bearers.'

The Crown proceeded confidently to its first witness, a certain
Rawson Macharia. Rawson Macharia was a young man still in his thir-
ties and Kenyatta's neighbour at Gatundu. His evidence contained
obvious untruths which the defence exposed, but its main significance
was that it was the strongest of only three statements that implicated
Kenyatta directly with oath-giving ceremonies. Macharia claimed to be
a drinking friend of Kenyatta's, and to have been present when
Kenyatta personally administered a 'Mau Mau' oath to several people
and tried to make Macharia take it also. He gave convincing details—a
goat's head from which the eyes had been removed and placed on
thorns and the tongue cut out, ceremonial arches, a brew of blood and
earth. Kenyatta, he alleged, made the oath-takers repeat the words:

> "When we agree to drive Europeans away you must take an active part
> in driving them away or killing them."

MAGISTRATE: Jomo Kenyatta said this?
MACHARIA: Yes, Mr. Kenyatta said this: "If you see any African killing anyone, you must not disclose it or tell anyone. If you shall see an African stealing, you must help him. You must pay sixty-two shillings and fifty cents to this society." Then he said: "And that is Mau Mau, and you must not ask how this money is used, and if you shall be asked whether you are a member of this society you must say you are a member of KAU."

Macharia said this incident took place on 16 March 1950, which was before Mau Mau was proscribed and so, even if proved, it was not an offence in itself. Pritt argued that the evidence should be disallowed. Thacker, however, accepted it on the grounds that it was a strong indication that Kenyatta must also have engaged in similar oath-giving ceremonies after the banning of Mau Mau. But the prosecution could produce nothing to substantiate this. . . . In the tensions of the Emergency any hint that a man might have links with Mau Mau was enough to condemn him. At Kapenguria Kenyatta was already cast as the villain by the government, and anything he had done or had said, anything which he now said in court, took on sinister meaning in the eyes of the Europeans.

It was for this reason that Rawson Macharia's evidence was so significant. It set the tone for the prosecution case, and put the judge in a receptive frame of mind. Despite the fact that Macharia's story was refuted by no less than nine witnesses whom the defence were able to bring to Kapenguria, as well as being denied by Kenyatta himself, the judge in his summing up said: 'Although my finding of fact means that I disbelieve ten witnesses for the Defence and believe one for the Prosecution, I have no hesitation in doing so. Rawson Macharia gave his evidence well.'

Rawson Macharia had reason to do so, knowledge of which was denied to Pritt at the time, though not to the government. The reader should now be made aware of it, as it is an important illustration of the peculiar circumstances in which Kenyatta's trial was held.

Almost six years later, towards the end of 1958, Macharia signed an affidavit swearing that his evidence against Kenyatta was false. He was then prosecuted himself for perjury—but for what the government said was a perjured affidavit, not for the perjury at Kapenguria to which he confessed. At his trial in 1959 a copy of a letter was produced which purported to emanate from the office of Kenya's Attorney-General and in which were set out the terms of a government offer to Macharia to pay for his air fare to England, for a two years' course at an English University and two years' subsistence for himself and his family, and a government post on his return. The value of the offer amounted to over £2,500. The letter included the sentence: 'In the event of the above named [Rawson Macharia] being murdered for providing evidence, Government will undertake the maintenance of his family and the education of his two sons.' It carried the date 19 November 1952. . . .

It was not until 19 January 1953 that the prosecution completed its evidence. Pritt then argued at length that there was no case to answer: 'I would submit that it is the most childishly weak case made against any man in any important trial in the history of the British Empire.' The Crown disagreed and Thacker adjourned for a weekend to ponder the arguments in Nairobi. He ran into the most dramatic confrontation between the settlers and the colonial government of the whole Emergency.

On the evening of Saturday 24 January occurred the murder of the Ruck family. The Europeans heard the news on the Sunday and at once gave vent to their feelings. On Monday several hundred of them gathered in Nairobi and marched in a body to Government House brandishing their weapons and shouting for the Governor. They demanded a greater say in the running of affairs; the government seemed on the verge of collapse. . . .

Thacker returned from Nairobi to rule that there was a case to answer. The trial resumed under the shadow of increasing settler discontent. A Kenya newspaper warned the judge against acquitting Kenyatta. An article by Elspeth Huxley comparing him with Hitler was reprinted in a settler periodical. Inaccurate information about his life was circulated by men like W. O. Tait who had known him in the past. Kenyatta was the universal scapegoat.

After lunch that Monday, 26 January 1953, Kenyatta at last entered the witness-box himself. . . .

There follows a grueling cross-examination of Kenyatta.

In the interval the situation with Mau Mau underwent a dramatic deterioration. Two incidents, both on the night of 26 March, shocked all races in the colony.

The first was a daring raid on Naivasha police station, in the Rift Valley. With only five guns between them, the attackers rushed the post in the dark and got away with weapons and ammunition which they loaded on to government trucks and drove off to the forests. It showed the Mau Mau bands were capable of military planning and discipline, and it gave them essential supplies for guerrilla warfare. . . .

The second incident had greater repercussions. For reasons which in part stretched back into the troubled history of the Tigoni removal, all the villagers of a location called Lari who were loyal to their government-appointed chiefs were marked for destruction by rivals. On the night of 26 March some 3,000 embittered men, most of whom had taken the stiffest Mau Mau oaths, swept through the location burning huts and hacking wildly at humans and animals. At least ninety-seven men, women and children in the village died.

Lari and the beginnings of this spiralling descent into nightmare coincided with the closing stages of Kenyatta's trial. They placed him in an impossible situation. The leader of a nationalist movement must always expect to find himself in the dock sooner or later. What he then says will decide his future standing with his people. For Kenyatta to deny the springs of nationalism would have been to deny his whole political life. The judge at Kapenguria could only sentence him to a term of imprisonment; but if he said anything against his own people, who could say what might happen to him. Some of the other accused who played such a subordinate role at Kapenguria were not above murder for their cause.

On 8 April 1953, the court reassembled at Kapenguria for the last time. In the situation just described, an acquittal was politically unthinkable. The judge duly found them all guilty. He dwelt upon Kenyatta's evasive attitude, implying that Kenyatta had virtually condemned himself. Kenyatta then addressed the court. For all he knew it was to be his political testament. In the circumstances it was a remarkable statement.

'May it please Your Honour. On behalf of my colleagues I wish to say that we are not guilty and we do not accept your findings and that during the hearing of this trial which has been so arranged as to place us in difficulties and inconvenience in preparing our cases, we do not feel that we have received the justice or hearing which we would have liked.

'I would like also to tell Your Honour that we feel that this case, from our point of view, has been so arranged as to make scapegoats of us in order to strangle the Kenya African Union, the only African political organisation which fights for the rights of the African people. We wish to say that what we have done in our activities has been to try our level best to find ways and means by which the community in this country can live in harmony. But what we have objected to—and we shall continue to object—are the discriminations in the government of this country. We shall not accept that, whether we are in gaol or out of it, sir, because we find that this world has been made for human beings to live in happily, to enjoy the good things and the produce of the country equally, and to enjoy the opportunities that this country has to offer. Therefore, Your Honour, I will not say that you have been misled or influenced, but the point that you have made is that we have been against the Europeans, and sir, you being a European, it is only natural that perhaps you should feel more that way. I am not accusing you of being prejudiced, but I feel that you should not stress so much the fact that we have been entirely motivated by hatred of Europeans. We ask you to remove that from your mind and to take this line: that our activities have been against the injustices that have been suffered by the African people and if in trying to establish the rights of the African people we have turned out to be what you say, Mau Mau, we are very sorry that you have been misled in that direction. What we have done, and what we shall continue to do, is to demand the rights of the African people as human beings that they may enjoy the facilities and privileges in the same way as other people.

'We look forward to the day when peace shall come to this land and that the truth shall be known that we, as African leaders, have stood for peace. None of us would be happy or would condone the mutilation of human beings. We are humans and we have families and none of us will ever condone such activities as arson that we have been guilty of. . . .

'I do not want to take up more of your time, Your Honour. All that I wish to tell you is that we feel strongly that at this time the Government of this country should try to strangle the only organization, that is the Kenya African Union, of which we are the leaders, who have been working for the betterment of the African people and who are seeking harmonious relations between the races. To these few remarks, Your Honour, I may say that we do not accept your finding of guilty. It will be our duty to instruct our lawyer to take this matter up and we intend to appeal to a higher Court. We believe that the Supreme Court of Kenya will give us justice because we stand for peace; we stand for the rights of the African people, that Africans may find a place among the nations.

'That, in short, is all that I shall say on behalf of my colleagues; that we hope that you and the rest of those who are in authority will seek ways and means by which we can bring harmony and peace to this country, because we do believe that peace by force from any section is impossible, and that violence of any kind, either from Europeans or from Africans, cannot bring any peace at all.'

Thacker turned to sentence him.

'You, Jomo Kenyatta, stand convicted of managing Mau Mau and being a member of that society. You have protested that your object has always been to pursue constitutional methods on the way to self government for the African people, and for the return of land which you say belongs to the African people. I do not believe you. It is my belief that soon after your long stay in Europe and when you came back to this Colony you commenced to organise this Mau Mau society, the object of which was to drive out from Kenya all Europeans, and in doing so to kill them if necessary. I am satisfied that the master mind behind this plan was yours. . . .

You have much to answer for and for that you will be punished. The maximum sentences which this Court is empowered to pass are the sentences which I do pass, and I can only comment that in my opinion they are inadequate for what you have done. Under Section 70 and on the first charge the sentence of the Court is that you be imprisoned for seven years with hard labour, and under Section 71 and on the third charge for three years with hard labour, both sentences to run concurrently, and I shall also recommend that you be restricted.'

Thacker was immediately flown out of Kenya. The settlers were satisfied. Kenyatta was out of the way.

Review and Study Questions

1. In your view, is Jomo Kenyatta's account of his own trial a valid historical document?
2. What were the government's motives in pressing the trial of Kenyatta?
3. Was Mau Mau ever a really serious nationwide problem in Kenya?
4. In your view, was Kenyatta the manager of Mau Mau?
5. To what extent was Kenyatta's trial and imprisonment the springboard to his political success and Kenyan independence?

Suggestions for Further Reading

Jomo Kenyatta himself wrote extensively. We have excerpted, for this chapter, his authorized "official biography," *Suffering without Bitterness: The Founding of the Kenya Nation* (Nairobi: East African Publishing House, 1968). His anthropology thesis is a substantial and respected work: *Facing Mount Kenya: The Tribal Life of the Gikuyu* (London: Secker and Warburg, 1939). Some of his speeches have been collected in *Harembee!: The Prime Minister of Kenya's Speeches, 1963–1964* (New York: Oxford University Press, 1965).

There are several books by contemporaries dealing with Kenya during the early years of Kenyatta's life: for example, Elspeth Huxley, *The Flame Trees of Thika: Memories of an African Childhood* (New York: William Morrow, 1959), and Karen Blixen, *Out of Africa* (New York: Random House, 1970). There are several more dealing with the years of the Mau Mau crisis in the early 1950s. One is excerpted for this chapter: Donald L. Barnett and Karari Njama, *Mau Mau from Within: Autobiography and Analysis of Kenya's Peasant Revolt* (New York and London: Modern Reader Paperbacks, 1966). Barnett is an American anthropologist who annotates and interprets the account of Njama. A similar account is Josiah Mwangi Kariuki, *"Mau Mau" Detainee: The Account by a Kenyan African of His Experiences in Detention Camps, 1953–1960* (London and Nairobi: Oxford University Press, 1963). Another book of the same type is J. Wamweya, *Freedom Fighter* (Nairobi: East African Publishing House, 1971). The story is told from a white perspective in *So Rough a Wind: The Kenya Memoirs of Sir Michael Blundell* (London: Weidenfeld and Nicholson, 1964). There are two other worthwhile books representing the colonialist viewpoint—one by a former civil servant, N. S. Carey Jones, *The Anatomy of Uhuru: Dynamics and Problems of African Independence in an Age of Conflict* (New York and Washington: Praeger, 1966), the other by a journalist whom President Kenyatta personally had escorted out of the country, Richard Cox, *Kenyatta's Country* (New York and Washington: Praeger, 1965).

There are several biographies of Kenyatta. By far the best is Jeremy Murray-Brown, *Kenyatta*, 2nd ed. (London: George Allen and Unwin, 1979), excerpted for this chapter. George Delf, *Jomo Kenyatta: Towards Truth about "The Light of Kenya"* (Garden City, N.Y.: Doubleday, 1961), is limited since it was written in 1960 while Kenyatta was still in prison, his future uncertain. There are two somewhat laudatory and superficial illustrated biographies: Anthony Howarth, *Kenyatta: A Photographic Biography* (Nairobi: East African Publishing House, 1967) and Mohamed Amin and Peter Moll, *Mzee Jomo Kenyatta: A Photobiography* (Nairobi: Trans Africa Publishers, 1973). A good political biography is Guy Arnold, *Kenyatta and the Politics of Kenya* (London: J. M. Dent, 1974). An excellent straightforward account of Kenyatta's trial is Montague Slater, *The Trial of Jomo Kenyatta* (London: Secker and Warburg, 1955).

There is a useful assessment of the Mau Mau movement in Carl G. Rosberg, Jr. and John Nottingham, *The Myth of "Mau Mau": Nationalism in Kenya*, Hoover Institution Publications (New York and Washington: Praeger, 1966). There are two useful works on the Kenyan economy under Kenyatta: Arthur Hazlewood, *The Economy of Kenya: The Kenyatta Era* (New York: Oxford University Press, 1979) and Norman

N. Miller, *Kenya: The Quest for Prosperity* (Boulder, Colo. and London: Westview Press, 1984).

There is a specialized historical study of Kenya's fight for independence following World War II in David F. Gordon, *Decolonization and the State in Kenya* (Boulder, Colo. and London: Westview Press, 1986). A good, even-handed one-volume history of Kenya is A. Marshall Macphee, *Kenya* (New York and Washington: Praeger, 1968). Also useful is *The Oxford History of East Africa,* especially vol. 3, ed. D. A. Low and Alison Smith (Oxford: Clarendon, 1976).

Courtesy of the British Information Service

MARGARET THATCHER: "THE IRON LADY"

1925	Born
1947	Graduated Oxford
1954	Called to the bar
1959	Elected to Parliament
1970	Secretary of state for education and science, privy councillor
1975	Conservative Party leader
1979	Prime minister
1982	The Falklands War
1982–1990	Continued service as prime minister

Margaret Thatcher, the first woman to serve as Great Britain's prime minister, was also the longest continuously serving prime minister in modern British history. She was one of the architects of the resurgence of British conservatism and, as prime minister, was the manager of that resurgence. Thatcher, the relentless enemy of Labourite socialism, the welfare state, and easy money, was a tough-minded and realistic politician, a skillful parliamentary tactician, and an unforgiving opponent. Shortly after coming into office, she was nicknamed the "Iron Lady," a label she wore with some rueful pride.

Thatcher was born Margaret Hilda Roberts in Grantham, Lincolnshire, in 1925, the daughter of a grocer who was also the town mayor. After attending Grantham Girls' School, she entered Oxford University, where she studied chemistry and served as president of the Oxford Conservative Association. After graduating with an M.A., she worked as a research chemist from 1947 to 1951, when she married Denis Thatcher; they have twin children, a son, Mark, and a daughter, Carol.

By 1951, Margaret Thatcher already had made two unsuccessful bids for a seat in Parliament. She had also begun to study law, and she was admitted to the bar in 1954. She tried again for a parliamentary seat and was elected in 1959 as Conservative member for

Finchley, a constituency in North London. She began immediately to rise through the ranks of the Conservative Party. From 1961 to 1964 she was a parliamentary secretary to the Ministry of Pensions and National Insurance. From 1964 to 1970 she was the opposition spokesperson for economic affairs and education. In 1970, under the Conservative government of Edward Heath, she was appointed secretary of state for education and science. In this cabinet post she served with some distinction and considerable criticism—for example, when she eliminated free milk for over three million schoolchildren, an outraged Labourite member called her "Mrs. Scrooge with a painted face."

Under the Labour government of 1974 she became opposition spokesperson for the environment, treasury, and economic affairs, and in that capacity she advocated a balanced budget and tight monetary policies. By this time she was able to contend with Edward Heath for the post of Conservative Party leader and in 1975 was elected by her Tory colleagues in a stunning upset. For the next four years she tirelessly championed a long list of conservative causes—reduced taxes, law and order and crime prevention, opposition to the power of the trade unions, and less government interference. In March 1979 the Labour prime minister James Callaghan narrowly lost a vote of confidence in the House of Commons. In the ensuing election of May 3 Margaret Thatcher became prime minister.

In Thatcher's view the preceding Labour government had failed utterly to deal either with the unreasonable demands of the trade unions or with inflation. She resolved to deal with both problems and put in place a right-wing ideological program. She continued to belabor the remnants of the British welfare state; she privatized several government industries; she took drastic measures to control inflation. Indeed, Thatcher made headway against inflation but at the cost of sharply rising unemployment—over three million were left jobless. As a result, she was the most unpopular prime minister in more than twenty years.

Thatcher very likely would have been forced out of office had it not been for the disarray of the Labour Party. The more radical Labourites formed a new party, the Social Democrats, dedicated to unilateral nuclear disarmament and pulling Britain out of the European Common Market. The Social Democrats allied with the Liberals, and the alliance came close to commanding a majority in the Commons against the Conservatives. Margaret Thatcher's government was not faring well through 1981 and into 1982: it was criticized on every hand and on nearly every issue. Then, on April 2, 1982, Argentina invaded the Falkland Islands. This event was to transform the fortunes of Thatcher's government.

The Falklands Crisis

MARGARET THATCHER

The Falklands, a British crown colony, are a cluster of flyspeck islands located in the South Atlantic, off the southern end of Argentina, 8,000 miles from Britain. Almost no one knew where they were or cared much about them until the Argentine invasion. Two centuries before, Samuel Johnson had called the Falklands "a bleak and gloomy solitude . . . thrown aside from human use."[1] *This had continued almost literally to be the case. The islands had a population of fewer than 2,000 people, most of them tending more than half a million sheep.*

The invasion itself was a surprise, although Britain had had a long-simmering dispute with Argentina over the ownership of the islands, which the Argentines called the Malvinas. The dictatorial Argentine regime of General Leopoldo Galitieri apparently decided to launch the invasion as an effort to distract his people from domestic problems. The British themselves had unwittingly contributed to the decision. The previous year the aging ice-patrol ship HMS Endurance *was scrapped in the annual Defence Review. It had been stationed in the Falklands, the sole token of British naval presence in the South Atlantic. The Argentine government regarded this action as a symbolic withdrawal of Britain from the Falklands.*

The invasion produced a universal reaction of shock and anger in Britain, both in the nation and in Parliament. It was demanded that immediate military action be taken to regain the Falklands. While "the fate of the country was not at stake in the Falklands," "the fate of the government was."[2] *Mrs. Thatcher needed no prompting. Here was a popular cause that she and the Conservatives could seize on to revive their flagging popularity; moreover, it was a cause that was totally consistent with Thatcherite conservatism. All efforts at conciliation or diplomatic solution were swept away— including the shuttle-diplomacy of the American secretary of state Alexander Haig. This was a matter to be resolved by arms.*

Within days elements of a massive naval task force had been assembled and dispatched. The force would eventually include the aircraft carriers Hermes *and* Invincible *and more than fifty other warships, as well as*

---

[1]"Thoughts on the Late Transactions respecting Falkland Island" [1771], *Works of Samuel Johnson* (London: J. Buckland, 1787), X, 56.

[2]Lawrence Freedman, *Britain and the Falklands War* (Oxford: Blackwell, 1988), p. ix.

some fifty civilian ships mobilized as troop transports, including the luxury liners Canberra *and* Queen Elizabeth 2. *The military force consisted mainly of special troops—Royal Marine Commandos, Parachute battalions, and the Special Air Service, as well as some troops from the Guards Division and even Nepalese Gurkhas—a total of some 28,000 including naval personnel, and a substantial number of aircraft.*

Britain imposed a 200-mile blockade around the islands, and by May 1 air raids and naval bombardment against Argentine positions had begun. On that same day the task force attacked and sank the Argentine cruiser General Belgrano, *with the loss of over three hundred lives. Three days later the British destroyer HMS* Sheffield *was disabled by an air-launched French Exocet missile: twenty sailors were killed and the vessel was sunk. The war was becoming serious and, with the approach of winter in the South Atlantic, a British landing was imperative. On May 21 it began, directed at the capital of Port Stanley. Within three weeks the war was over. On June 14 the Argentine commander of the garrison at Port Stanley surrendered on behalf of all his forces in the Falkland Islands. From beginning to end the war effort had been directed by Prime Minister Thatcher and her "war cabinet." The prime minister had held at bay demands for a diplomatic solution from factions in Parliament, from allies such as the United States, and from the United Nations.*

Even before the Argentine surrender, Thatcher gave an assessment of her war. The occasion was a speech to the 52nd Annual Conservative Women's Conference in London.

Your conference takes place at a time when great and grave issues face our country. Our hearts and minds are focused on the South Atlantic. You have been debating defence policy at a time when our fighting men are engaged in one of the most remarkable military operations in modern times.

We have sent an immensely powerful task-force, more than a hundred ships and 27,000 sailors, marines and soldiers, 8000 miles away in the South Atlantic. In a series of measured and progressive steps, over the past weeks, our forces have tightened their grip on the Falkland Islands. They have retaken South Georgia. Gradually they have denied fresh supplies to the Argentine garrison. Finally, by the successful amphibious landing at San Carlos Bay in the early hours of Friday morning, they have placed themselves in a position to retake the islands and reverse the illegal Argentine invasion.

By the skill of our pilots, our sailors and those manning the Rapier missile batteries on shore they have inflicted heavy losses on the Argentine Air Force—over fifty fixed-wing aircraft have been destroyed.

There have, of course, been tragic losses. You will have heard of the further attacks on our task-force. HMS *Coventry* came under repeated air attack yesterday evening and later sank. One of our Merchant Marine ships, the *Atlantic Conveyor*, supporting the task-force, was also damaged and had to be abandoned. We do not yet know the number of casualties but our hearts go out to all those who had men in these ships.

Despite these grievous losses, our resolve is not weakened. We know the reality of war. We know its hazards and its dangers. We know the formidable task that faces our fighting men. They are now established on the Falkland Islands with all the necessary supplies. Although they still face formidable problems in difficult terrain with a hostile climate, their spirits are high.

We must expect fresh attacks upon them, and there can be no question of pressing the Force Commander to move forward prematurely—the judgement about the next tactical moves must be his and his alone.

It was eight weeks ago today that information reached us that the Argentine Fleet was sailing towards the Falklands. Eight thousand miles away . . . At that stage there were only two ways of trying to stop it—through President Reagan, whose appeal to Argentina was rebuffed, and the United Nations, whose plea was also rejected.

There were those who said we should have accepted the Argentine invasion as a *fait accompli*. But whenever the rule of force as distinct from the rule of law is seen to succeed, the world moves a step closer to anarchy.

The older generation in this country, and generations before them, have made sacrifices so that we could be a free society and belong to a community of nations which seeks to resolve disputes by civilized means. Today it falls to us to bear the same responsibility.

What has happened since that day, eights weeks ago, is a matter of history—the history of a nation which rose instinctively to the needs of the occasion.

For decades, the peoples of those islands had enjoyed peace—with freedom, with justice, with democracy. That peace was shattered by a wanton act of armed aggression by Argentina in blatant violation of international law. And everything that has happened since has stemmed from that invasion by the military dictatorship of Argentina.

We want that peace restored. But we want it with the same freedom, justice and democracy that the islanders previously enjoyed.

For seven weeks we sought a peaceful solution by diplomatic means: through the good offices of our close friend and ally, the United States; through the unremitting efforts of the Secretary-General of the United Nations.

We studied seven sets of proposals and finally drew up our own. Without compromising fundamental principles, we made a variety of reasonable and practical suggestions in a supreme effort to avoid conflict and loss of life. We worked tirelessly for a peaceful solution. But when there is no response of substance from the other side, there comes a point when it is no longer possible to trust the good faith of those with whom one is negotiating.

Playing for time is not working for a peaceful solution. Wasting time is not willing a peaceful solution. It is simply leaving the aggressor with the fruits of his aggression.

It would be a betrayal of our fighting men and of the islanders if we continued merely to talk, when talk alone was getting nowhere.

And so, seven weeks to the day after the invasion, we moved to recover by force what was taken from us by force. It cannot be said too often: we are the victims; they are the aggressors. As always, we came to military action reluctantly. But when territory which has been British for almost a hundred and fifty years is seized and occupied; when not only British land, but British citizens are in the power of an aggressor, then we have to restore our rights and the rights of the Falkland Islanders.

There have been a handful of questioning voices raised here at home. I would like to answer them. It has been suggested that the size of the Falkland Islands and the comparatively small number of its inhabitants—some 1800 men, women and children—should somehow affect our reaction to what has happened to them.

To those—not many—who speak lightly of a few islanders beyond the seas and who ask the question, 'Are they worth fighting for?' let me say this: right and wrong are not measured by a head-count of those to whom that wrong has been done. That would not be principle but expediency. And the Falklanders, remember, are not strangers. They are our own people. As the Prime Minister of New Zealand, Bob Muldoon, put it in his usual straightforward way, 'With the Falkland Islanders, it is family.'

When their land was invaded and their homes were overrun, they naturally turned to us for help, and we, their fellow citizens, 8000 miles away in our much larger island, could not and did not beg to be excused. We sent our men and our ships with all speed, hoping against hope that we would not have to use them in battle but prepared to do so if all attempts at a peaceful solution failed. When those attempts failed, we could not sail by on the other side.

And let me add this. If we, the British, were to shrug our shoulders at what has happened in the South Atlantic and acquiesce in the illegal seizure of those far-away islands, it would be a clear signal to those with similar designs on the territory of others to follow in the footsteps of aggression.

Surely we, of all people, have learnt the lesson of history: that to appease an aggression is to invite aggression elsewhere, and on an ever-increasing scale.

Other voices—only a few—have accused us of clinging to colonialism or even imperialism. Let me remind those who advance that argument that the British have a record second to none of leading colony after colony to freedom and independence. We cling not to colonialism but self-determination.

Still others—again only a few—say we must not put at risk our investments and interests in Latin America; that trade and commerce are too important to us to put in jeopardy some of the valuable markets of the world.

But what would the Falklanders, under the heel of the invader, say to that? What kind of people would we be if, enjoying the birthright of freedom ourselves, we abandoned British citizens for the sake of commercial gain?

Now we are present in strength on the Falkland Islands. Our purpose is to repossess them. We shall carry on until that purpose is accomplished.

When the invader has left, there will be much to do—rebuilding, restoring homes and farms, and above all renewing the confidence of the people in their future. Their wishes will need time to crystallize, and of course will depend in some measure on what we and others are prepared to do to develop the untapped resources and safeguard the Islands' future.

Madam Chairman, our cause is just. It is the cause of freedom and the rule of law. It is the cause of support for the weak against aggression by the strong.

Let us then draw together in the name, not of jingoism but of justice. And let our nation, as it has so often in the past, remind itself, and the world:

> Nought shall make us rue,
> If England to herself do rest but true.

The Falklands Factor

ROBERT GRAY

Amid the victorious trumpeting of the British popular press and the congratula-
tions of politicians at home and abroad, Prime Minister Thatcher resolved to ex-
ploit the Falklands victory and transform it into a victory on a broader front.
This became clear in an impassioned speech she made to some 5,000 Conserva-
tive partisans at Cheltenham Racecourse on July 3, 1982. In that speech, for
the first time, she talked about the "Falklands Factor" and how it had irrevoca-
bly changed British attitudes to produce a "new mood of the nation." The
immediate subject of her speech was an impending rail strike, which she
contrasted with the patriotic achievements of the Falklands Task Force. She
went on from the recalcitrant rail workers to those "waverers and fainthearts"
who had doubted Britain's ability at the outset of the Falklands campaign to "do
the great things which we once did." "Well," she said, "they were wrong. The
Falklands Factor is a new major force in British politics. Things are not going
to be the same again." She continued: "All over Britain, men and women are
asking—why can't we achieve in peace what we can do so well in war? And
they have good reason to ask. Now is the time for management to demonstrate
professionalism and effectiveness. Now is the time for the trade unions 'to match
the spirit of the times.' The government will no longer print money: the nation
won't have it. That too is part of the Falklands Factor."[3]

Thatcher plainly intended to identify the Falklands Factor with her own
conservative program in every area of public policy. Neither the prime min-
ister's tactic nor its likelihood of success were lost on her Labourite oppo-
nents in Parliament or on their advocates in the left-wing journalistic and
intellectual community. A spate of publications poured out analyzing
Thatcher's intentions and challenging them. The following excerpt is typi-
cal. From "The Falklands Factor," an essay by Robert Gray, a left-leaning
labor historian, it deals generally with the new Thatcherite political initia-
tive and specifically with its implications for foreign policy.

The Argentine occupation of the Falklands/Malvinas represents one
of those historic moments when the capacity to respond to unexpected events can decisively strengthen or weaken political forces. In

---

[3]The speech was reported in the *London Sunday Times,* July 4, 1982, and the forego-
ing quotations are from that account.—ED.

this case the effect was to strengthen the right, and specifically the Thatcherite right. Not only did this greatly improve Thatcher's chances of electoral success and a renewed mandate, it also threatened, and still threatens, to roll back the advances made by widespread popular demands for peace and disarmament, by exposing historic weaknesses and dilemmas in the left, and in the peace movement. Thatcher may thus have won some ground from what has perhaps been the most deeply and broadly based area of dissent from her government's policies.

This essay attempts to explore the wider implications of the Falklands adventure for British politics. I shall argue that these events represent a new application of Thatcher's distinct kind of politics, now in the arena of foreign affairs; the appeals of this initiative expose certain weaknesses of other forces—from Tory "Wets" to the left and the peace movement—which might have resisted it. An effective fight-back requires the left to confront historically awkward issues, so as to redefine the national identities and loyalties which Thatcher has so powerfully mobilized. This is a challenging and daunting task, and one which the left has been reluctant to undertake, but until it is tackled the right will draw a strategic political advantage from its hegemonic definitions of "national interest" and "national unity."

The aggressive military response to the Argentine occupation bears the marks of Thatcherism, extended to foreign affairs. . . .

Two features of this policy stand out. First, not only did the Government opt for a military response, but it also chose one of the more extreme possibilities. The task force was dispatched, not with diplomatic pretexts about safeguarding lives and properties (the classic formula of gunboat diplomacy), but with declarations of intent to dislodge the Argentinians (even if only temporarily) by any means necessary: "Failure is a word we do not use." Most wars since 1945 have begun in a shamefaced way, with growing military entanglements kept secret from both world and domestic opinion; this war began with flags flying, drums beating and cameras rolling, and with the revival of a rhetoric which many people, especially on the left, too easily assumed to be dead. The course pursued may not be that different in content from what other political leaders might have done; but, as so often with Margaret Thatcher, the style and rhetoric were crucial to the political effect.

Second, the sheer audacity of this response, the speed with which events moved, and their relaying to the British public through carefully orchestrated media have muted opposition. Those elements of center opinion, in all the parliamentary parties, which might have preferred a "softly softly," if still basically military approach were consistently outmaneuvered. . . .

Once the force was on its way, with support from the majority of the media and a bi-partisan parliamentary consensus, the whole grotesque enterprise took on a life of its own. The formation of a "war cabinet" reinforced Thatcher's authority. Popular opinion was frightened, but also excited by the creation of a war atmosphere, and the tendency for the control of events to pass a purely military logic (for example, the way that the safety of the troops became a strong reason for getting them ashore as soon as possible, regardless of the progress or otherwise of diplomatic efforts). With the commitment of forces to combat, identification with the men became a compelling motive, even for people who had reservations about the initial dispatch of the task force. The *Guardian* and the *Mirror* which, to their credit, had maintained a relatively balanced and critical attitude nevertheless carried reports from the battle-zone written in a stereotyped rhetoric familiar from every war this century (the assault troops waiting patiently, sipping cups of tea, etc.). Perhaps most compelling of all were the photos of "British" children welcoming liberating British soldiers. This atmosphere of national emergency and danger inevitably strengthened the authority of Government; opposition leaders have indicated that their criticisms of Government responsibility for the origins of the situation were merely postponed till after the crisis—by when criticism could well be too late and politically marginalized.

"Victory" and the long drawn out return of ships and men provided the occasion for a seemingly endless prolongation of media exposure. This was in many ways the ideal war—short, sharp, "successful," directly involving small professional armed forces and their families, but consumed vicariously through press and TV—for cementing a reactionary chauvinist consensus. The bellicose atmosphere was quite quickly and directly projected against such domestic enemies as ASLEF.[4] The euphoria will of course one day die down and the nagging question of "what next?" will surface, given the apparent difficulty of a continued British presence in the face of an embittered Argentina, or of the cession by negotiation of what has been won with lives.

However it would be a mistake to underestimate the extent to which Thatcher (helped by the passivity of the official oppositions) gained the initiative on this issue, or to assume that the emergence of these problems will automatically discredit her. Even if Thatcher suffers subsequent defeats over the future of the Falklands, the whole

---

[4]The rail union.—ED.

issue may by then be quietly marginalized. Its political effect anyhow rests on the gratifying Palmerstonian spectacle of the British lion punishing a Latin despot, rather than on Thatcher's wilder visions of maritime imperial rebirth centered on the South Atlantic.

To say that Thatcher has won an important initiative is not therefore to say that the eventual outcome will be what she would favor. Nor does it imply that she has gained the near-unanimous support portrayed in the more sycophantic elements of the media—there has certainly been more dissent, some of it in unexpected quarters, than the media and parliamentary balance would suggest. But that dissent has been largely isolated and leaderless, in terms of mainstream electoral politics. Tail-ending behind Thatcher's war, the official opposition parties added to her glory, rather than gained any for themselves. Winning the political initiative is reflected in the demoralization and division of opposing forces—something less tangible than numerical support, but nonetheless real.

Thatcher's seizure of command in any case has consequences that extend beyond the conjunctural strengthening or weakening of her position, or that of her party. We may be faced with a relatively permanent and organic shift in the political landscape. As is argued elsewhere in this volume, "Thatcherism" constitutes a shift of this kind, to which the personal fate of Thatcher herself is relatively marginal; whatever happens to her, or the government she leads, she has already done her political work. That work may be characterized as the mobilization of hitherto subterranean and politically incoherent currents of right-wing populism, in a way that is something of a new departure within the conservative political tradition, to build support for reactionary "solutions" to Britain's chronic economic and social crisis, This has succeeded by drawing on popular experience and a pervasive sense of crisis and decline, and articulating them in reactionary decisions. The expression of this in foreign affairs had previously been confined to enthusiastic support for the new cold war and the new arms race, Britain's role as Reagan's best friend, and thumping the table at EEC negotiations. Now, the articulation of a distinctly British nationalism has been added to this.

Like the domestic formula of the "free market and the strong state," this assertion has drawn on a sense of crisis related to Britain's long decline and articulated it in a reactionary, and very dangerous direction. One striking, and alarming feature of this has been the backward-looking, atavistic rhetoric, the motif of imperial nostalgia. At the crudest level, this appeals as a sign that Britain is still Great, that, despite change and decay we can still, when pushed, get it together. "Thank God the most professional armed forces in the world are BRITISH," one poster seen in Portsmouth proclaimed (together with "Britain does not appease dictators" and "Congratulations to the Royal Navy"). Debate at the parliamentary level at times presented the grotesque spectacle of different protagonists all reenacting some moment in the national past from which they draw comfort and hope, in a magic ritual to exorcise the facts of twentieth-century life, an attempt to "conjure up the spirits of the past to help them" (Marx, *Eighteenth Brumaire*). Thatcher dons the mask of Churchill or Lord Palmerston, while Foot[5] appears to believe that the Falklands are part of the Sudetenland and that he is about to "speak for England."

It is easy enough to laugh at all this, to see it as a wave of hysteria aided by media manipulation. But it has powerful appeals, expressed in varied languages, not all of them as crude as the version propagated by the *Sun*; the resonances are not simply of Victorian "gunboat diplomacy," but also of the popular experience and memory of the Second World War. Thatcherism benefited from the organization of all these currents into more or less enthusiastic support for a war that Thatcher made her own.

Atavistic rhetoric makes sense of an experience of crisis, uneasy decline and lack of forward-looking political leadership. The national past, or a selectively mythologized version of it, is a source of identity and hope. Like all such rhetorics this is in reality the creation of something new, since the old cannot in its entirety be restored. The new factor is the clear assertion of distinctly "British" interests and power in a post-imperial world dominated by the stalemate of the cold war and the "nuclear balance." A language of chauvinism that had seemed out of place in this world is thus given renewed credence.

One aspect of this is the re-definition of Britain's relations with the U.S. Conservative policies since the 1950s have sought to come to terms with the diminished position of British imperialism by asserting Britain's special role as the senior European ally in the Atlantic alliance, but at the same time as a world power with interests transcending the purely regional ones of the NATO pact. These pretensions have at times seemed hollow: at Suez, for instance, the refusal of American support made the British posture untenable. There has always been a residual anti-Americanism on the Tory right, relating to this and other grievances. Now the Suez debacle has been neatly reversed; it is the Americans who have been forced, after a singularly unconvincing attempt at "mediation," to support British claims, at least for the crucial period of armed confrontation. This had demonstrated the value of the Atlantic alliance (and thus of British hospital-

---

[5]Michael Foot, the Labour Party leader.—ED.

ity to existing and proposed U.S. nuclear weapons), while at the same time asserting British independence and appealing to residual anti-Americanism of the right. In the same way, EEC sanctions have shown the value of an association that had been questioned, not just by the left but by a nationalist right. Britain, in short, is not just one more European country, but can call the tune for its allies on an issue of extra-regional interest. Apart from its short-term effect in helping Thatcher to seize the initiative, this may have a longer-term effect on national consciousness and the production of a new nationalism.

This poses dangers and challenges for the left. It can be a potent force in winning renewed support for the cold war and the arms race, as well as the reassertion of a British imperial role. The Falklands war is likely to reinforce the ideology of war preparation and "negotiation from strength." While the failure of a nuclear strategy to protect the Falklands may demonstrate the incoherence of British military doctrines, this can be masked by less discriminating perceptions of the need for military strength. The spectacle of an actual war, and the atmosphere surrounding it, threatens to erode the widespread popular support for peace and disarmament, which has limited enthusiasm for the new cold war and the new arms race.

A New View of the Falklands War

PETER JENKINS

No one can deny the remarkable political success of Margaret Thatcher and her equally remarkable impact upon modern Britain. One of her former ministers, Francis Pym, has observed that "she has shifted the political ground away from the leftward drift of Socialism. There is little doubt that she would view this as her main achievement: it is the thing she was most determined to do." [6] *Sarah Benton, in* New Statesman and Society, *in the spring of 1989, wrote of Mrs. Thatcher:*

> *She has, with considerable difficulty, transformed her ideology from one of gaining power to one of holding it. Her supporters are no longer victims and martyrs, longing only for a safer Britain. They are innovators and leaders. It is "we Conservatives who set the pace, generate the ideas and have the vision," she*

---

[6]Francis Pym, *The Politics of Consent* (London: Hamish Hamilton, 1984), p. 11.

tells the 1988 conference. "Inventiveness" has replaced thrift as their number one virtue. The old enemies are vanquished. "Whatever happened to Socialism?" she jeers. "Communism is in retreat," she reassures them.[7]

This piece of doggerel appeared in the same journal:

> *When weary Britain languished*
> *For lack of faith and drive,*
> *And commentators anguished*
> *That we could not survive,*
> *You broke our chains and freed us,*
> *O Mighty Margareen!*
> *Ten years and you still lead us,*
> *Our rare and rightful Queen!*[8]

But to what extent was the Falklands War the turning point in the political triumph of Margaret Thatcher? In the immediate aftermath of the war, as we have seen, she clearly thought it was the turning point, as did her critics. A somewhat more measured answer is provided by the British journalist Peter Jenkins in Mrs. Thatcher's Revolution: The Ending of the Socialist Era, *one of the best and most perceptive of a glut of recent books on Thatcher and Thatcherism. In his analysis of the "Falklands Factor" Jenkins argues that, while the war itself was a trivial affair, it provided an opportunity for the prime minister to demonstrate the strong leadership Britain yearned for and thus contributed to the eventual success of Thatcher's revolution.*

His analysis follows.

What of the Falklands Factor? One may doubt its salience in any literal sense by the time voters came to enter the polling booths, one year after Port Stanley was retaken from the Argentinians. At least that is what they would have had the pollsters believe. The Falkland Islands were of no concern to the electorate before the war and it would not be surprising if they became of little concern once more soon after it was over. Indeed, an important cause of the war was that a small but single-minded pro-Falklands lobby had been able to take advantage of governmental timidity and huge public indifference to prevent some negotiated arrangement with Argentina which would guarantee the status of the islanders while ending a territorial dispute

---

[7]*New Statesman and Society,* 28 April 1989, vol. 117, No. 3030, p. 11.

[8]*New Statesman and Society,* p. 31.

which had been going on for longer than anyone could remember. It had been the policy goal of successive governments to liquidate a post-imperial commitment which Britain, at a distance of 8,000 miles, no longer had the means of honouring except by expensive distortion of her other defence requirements.

For some months before the Falkland Islands were thrust upon the national consciousness the government had been regaining popularity, chiefly at the expense of the SDP [Social Democratic Party]–Liberal Alliance, whose bubble had reached bursting point at the time of the Crosby by-election in December 1981. In that month the standing of the parties (according to Gallup) was: Conservatives 23; Labour 23; Alliance 50. By March the parties were running virtually neck and neck. The figures were 31: 33: 33. Nevertheless, the war did transform the political scene. In July, with the war won, the government had a 19 point lead: Cons. 46: Lab. 27: All. 24. On the eve of the 1983 General Election the figures were 49: 31: 16. The actual result was 43·5: 28·3: 26. The mould was thus set by the Falklands War but that does not mean that it might not have been set in the same way for other reasons. That we can never know.

The Argentinian invasion of those remote and unimportant islands threw the nation into a patriotic fit. Parliament set the lead. When news of the invasion was first rumored this commentator failed totally to grasp the significance of the matter. The Falkland Islands were a post-imperial leftover of no strategic or economic value and far removed from the real problems facing the country, at home and abroad. I left London that Friday for the country and the next day, annoyed at the disturbance of my Saturday, listened to the emergency debate in the Commons on the radio. Had I been in my place in the Press Gallery perhaps I, too, might have been carried away by the excitement of the moment but as it was, listening at my kitchen table, I could scarcely believe my ears. That the Commons was sitting for the first time on a Saturday since the Suez crisis of 1956 was an invitation to exaggerate the importance of the occasion. One speaker went further and solemnly compared the invasion of the Falklands with the fiasco of the Norwegian campaign in 1940, one of the darkest moments of the war which led to the fall of the Chamberlain government. The most jingoistic speech of the morning came from Michael Foot, who having proclaimed Britain's role as 'defender of people's freedom throughout the world' and asserted the 'absolute right' of the Falklanders to British protection, called upon the government to 'prove by deeds—they will never be able to do it by words—that they are not responsible for the betrayal and cannot be faced with that charge.'

It seemed to me then, and it seems to me now, extraordinary that it should be supposed that Britain could be responsible for 1,800 people and their 600,000 sheep in the remoteness of the South Atlantic. That we should hold ourselves responsible was honourable, noble in the extreme, but foolhardy. It had been irresponsible to continue with such a commitment without the capability of discharging it. The defence of the Falklands had for some time rested on bluff. Now that the bluff had been called the proper course was to seek to discharge our responsibility to the islanders as best we could through negotiations to guarantee their status as British citizens or to repatriate and compensate them as need be. It was preposterous, it seemed to me, to assert their absolute right to self-determination. Rights could not exist without the means of upholding them and it was quite unrealistic to expect Britannia to rule the South Atlantic in the year 1982.

Karl Marx had said that history repeated itself as farce but then had gone on to say that when it repeated itself for a second time it did so as tragedy. In 1956 the folk-guilt of the ruling class had led an out-of-touch generation to mistake the nationalisation of the Suez Canal by Gamal Abdul Nasser for another Munich. Suez had been a post-imperial farce, a tilting at windmills; but now, it seemed, young lives were to be sacrificed tragically in the Quixotic cause of making a world safe for South Atlantic sheep-shearers. For it was questionable to claim—as Mrs Thatcher did throughout the affair—that liberty was indivisible to the extent that if aggression were allowed to succeed in this case licence would be given to aggressors everywhere, in Afghanistan and Cambodia or wherever. We were deluding ourselves if we supposed that the rest of the world, even our American allies and Common Market partners, would regard a dispute over an insignificant outpost of a lost Empire as an event on the same footing as the Nazi invasion of Poland. Thus:

> At the State Department, in the early hours of the crisis, most of the staff shared the amusement of the press and public over what was perceived as a Gilbert and Sullivan battle over a sheep pasture between a choleric old John Bull and a comic dictator in a gaudy uniform.

In his memoirs General Haig, then the Secretary of State, disassociated himself from this mockingly contemptuous view of the matter but when shown maps he was alleged to have said at the time: 'Gee, it's only a pimple on their arse.'

Indeed, there seemed to me, and here I consulted theologians, something disproportionate about the British response to the Argentinian invasion, reprehensible though it was. St Thomas Aquinas had laid down three conditions for a 'just war'—it must be authorised by the sovereign, the cause must be just, and the belligerents of valid moral intention. Recent Catholic moralists have stressed a fourth condition, most relevant to modern times: a war, to be just, must be

waged by proper means (*debito modo*). Could this be said of the des-
patch of a large naval Task Force (which on its way would sink a
cruiser and drown 308 young men) to avenge an act which, if the
truth were admitted, was more costly of national pride than of true
national interest? The Falklands, as we know, were recaptured in
glorious fashion and the Union Flag flies once more over Government House, Port Stanley. The death toll all round was about a thousand, plus some 1,700 wounded—for 1,800 islanders and 600,000
sheep. *Debito modo?*

There were two flaws to this analysis, more apparent in hindsight
than at the time perhaps. The first was that it pointed to no clear
alternative course of action. It would have been disproportionate
equally to have done nothing. The Junta in Buenos Aires were a nasty
lot ('a gang of thugs' Haig told the Cabinet) and their aggression
could in no way be condoned; even the Security Council of the United
Nations had condemned it. Resolution 502 required Argentina to
withdraw but, if she did not, Britain had the right under Article 51 of
the Charter to repossess her territory by the use of reasonable force.
Diplomacy backed up by the threat of force, it seemed to me, was the
appropriate and proportionate strategy.

The Prime Minister's intention from the beginning was to get the
islands back and undo the humiliation which had been done. The
Foreign Office was in such disrepute as a result of the invasion that it
was, literally, *hors de combat;* a peace strategy never really received a
hearing. Nevertheless, the Cabinet was from the outset united on the
total war objective. The services had many options but no clear plan.
The Americans stepped into the diplomatic action. The 'war cabinet'
in London in fact went a long way in co-operating with the Haig
mission but it was his reports on the character of the Junta in Buenos
Aires, anecdotes of drunkenness and imbecility, which convinced the
doubting members of the inner group that the 'Argies' would be
neither willing to make peace nor capable of it. And, as it turned out,
it was the Junta which rejected, first, terms to which Mrs Thatcher
had reluctantly agreed, and subsequently—to her huge relief—terms
which she would herself have declined to put to Parliament had
Galtieri had the wit to accept them. Meanwhile, as the Task Force
approached its destination, the options narrowed until the only
choice was between all or nothing. Her military strategy achieved its
goal; looking back, it is hard to see how a diplomatic approach could
have succeeded.

Be that as it may, we are concerned here with the politics of the
matter, with the contribution of the 'Falklands Factor' to the realign-
ment in British politics brought about by, or under, Mrs Thatcher.
The second flaw in the position of those of us who at the time were

critics of the war is that we underestimated, perhaps, the psychological needs of the nation. I do not mean by that a need for crude chauvinistic distraction, for one thing which was striking about those ten weeks was how rare it was to hear of the spirit of high patriotism degenerating into hatred or crude 'Argie' bashing. It might have been otherwise if the horrendous sinking of HMS *Sheffield* had preceded the tragic sinking of the *Belgrano*. Nor do I mean simply that the country was willing to have its attention diverted by an external adventure, the oldest trick in the book, from three million unemployed at home, although diverted it was for a while as the places of public entertainment emptied and all eyes became riveted to the nightly television news bulletins. No, the psychological need was for a success, a success of some kind, an end to failure and humiliation, to do something well, to win. Nostalgic knee-jerk reaction it may have been, vainglorious posturing in a post-imperial world of Super Powers, but it made people feel better not worse.

Moreover, it aroused genuine admiration around the world and, where not that, reluctant respect. There is a slight note of astonishment in Haig's account of how:

> In a reawakening of the spirit of the Blitz that exhilarated Britain, warships were withdrawn from NATO, civilian ships, including the liner *Queen Elizabeth II*, were requisitioned and refitted, troops were embarked, and in an astonishingly short time a task force of over 100 ships and 28,000 men was steaming under the British ensign toward the Falklands.

Perhaps no people were more surprised than the British, accustomed to being told they did not know how to run a motor car factory. By jingo they knew how to launch a Task Force. The point was not lost upon the Prime Minister in her heady hour of victory. On 3 July a great throng assembled on the race course at Cheltenham—where better?—and she said:

> It took the battle in the South Atlantic for the shipyards to adapt ships way ahead of time; for dockyards to refit merchantmen and cruise liners, to fix helicopter platforms, to convert hospital ships—all faster than was thought possible; it took the demands of war for every stop to be pulled out and every man and woman to do their best.

On she went, dishing out the medals to British industry, the British people—the British worker! Of course, Churchill had to be quoted at such a moment—he had said something somewhere about the need to work together in peacetime as in war, a banal enough sentiment, and now—thirty-six years on—the truth of it at last was dawning on the British people, or so she said.

We saw the signs when, this week, the NUR came to understand that its strike on the railways and on the Underground just didn't fit [we can hear the voice]—didn't match the spirit of these times.

And on she went. Printing money was no more.

Rightly this Government has abjured it. Increasingly this nation won't have it. . . . That too is part of the Falklands Factor.

Not only was the Falklands Factor making the trains run on time, it was—it seems—rallying the nation behind the Medium Term Financial Strategy. And as the climax is approached, the sentences grow shorter:

What has indeed happened is that now once again Britain is not prepared to be pushed around.

We have ceased to be a nation in retreat.

We have instead a new-found confidence—born in the economic battles at home and tested and found true 8,000 miles away.

That confidence comes from the rediscovery of ourselves, and grows with the recovery of our self-respect.

Britain found herself again in the South Atlantic and will not look back from the victory she has won.

Such oratory is not to be taken too literally; it is indicative of a state of mind, not of the state of the nation. War is a celebrated midwife but it is improbable that the loss and recapture of the Falkland Islands in 1982 will prove to have been the rebirth of Britain, or the apotheosis of Thatcherism. What it may have done, however, is to help link in people's minds their images of her with this powerful image of success. She was a winner. Luck was on her side. What she said she would do she would do. She was a sticker whose determination paid off. What had worked so brilliantly abroad, would work at home. And she was quick to reinforce these thoughts in people's minds: 'I think people like decisiveness, I think they like strong leadership,' she told an interviewer. In this way the Falklands Factor became the Thatcher Factor.

Review and Study Questions

1. In what ways did the Falklands crisis transform the fortunes of Mrs. Thatcher's conservative government?

2. Did the prime minister make any good-faith effort to avoid war over the Falklands? If not, why not?

3. Can the British government's behavior in the Falklands War be persuasively compared to the United States government's behavior in the Persian Gulf War?

4. In the new international climate produced by the end of the cold war and the nuclear arms race, what are the implications for such old-fashioned nationalist policies as those of the Thatcher government?

Suggestions for Further Reading

The only collection of Margaret Thatcher's own writings, to date, is Margaret Thatcher, *In Defence of Freedom: Speeches on Britain's Relations with the World, 1976–1986,* intro. Ronald Butt, foreword by President Ronald Reagan (Buffalo, N.Y.: Prometheus Books, 1987), excerpted for this chapter. Her speeches, parliamentary positions, and news releases, however, are fully covered in both the British and American press and exhaustively analyzed in such British opinion journals as *New Statesman and Society* and *The Economist.*

There are many books on Mrs. Thatcher, including one comprehensive biography, Russell Lewis, *Margaret Thatcher: A Personal and Political Biography,* rev. ed. (London et al.: Routledge and Kegan Paul, 1983). A briefer and more strictly political biography is Patrick Cosgrave, *Margaret Thatcher: A Tory and Her Party* (London: Hutchinson, 1978). Another book by Patrick Cosgrave, *Thatcher: The First Term* (London: The Bodley Head, 1979), concentrates even more on questions of national policy and politics in her first term as does Jock Bruce-Gardyne, *Mrs. Thatcher's First Administration: The Prophets Confounded* (New York: St. Martin's Press, 1984).

There are a large number of books that attempt to analyze the Thatcher government, Thatcher conservatism, or simply Thatcherism. The best of these is Peter Jenkins, *Mrs. Thatcher's Revolution: The Ending of the Socialist Era* (Cambridge, Mass.: Harvard University Press, 1988), excerpted for this chapter. Another excellent, and politically neutral book, is Dennis Kavanagh, *Thatcherism and British Politics: The End of Consensus?* (Oxford et al.: Oxford University Press, 1987). Two books that reflect the Tory viewpoint are Francis Pym, *The Politics of Consent* (London: Hamish Hamilton, 1984), by a Tory politician and former member of Thatcher's government; and Peter Riddell, *The Thatcher Government* (Oxford: Robertson, 1983), also one of the most intelligent assessments of its subject.

Because of the success of Thatcher's brand of conservatism she has attracted the criticism of the left like a lightning rod. The essay by Robert Gray, excerpted for this chapter, is an example, as are most of the other essays in the volume in which it appeared, *The Politics of Thatcherism*, ed. Stuart Hall and Martin Jaques (London: Lawrence and Wishart, 1983). Joel Krieger, *Reagan, Thatcher, and the Politics of Decline* (New York: Oxford University Press, 1986), is highly critical of the New Right conservatism exemplified by Reagan and Thatcher. The Falklands War in particular exercised the critics of the left. One of the most comprehensive and strident attacks was by Anthony Barnett, "Iron Britannia: War over the Falklands," *New Left Review*, No. 134 (July–August 1982). Another is Norman Gelb, "Thatcher's Victory: The Falklands Factor," *The New Leader*, vol. 65, No. 14 (July 12–26, 1982), 5–6. Yet another is an editorial in *New Statesman*, "A Victory Beyond Our Means," vol. 103, No. 2673 (18 June 1982). There is an interesting survey and analysis of this left-wing criticism in an article by Clive Christie, "The British Left and the Falklands War," *The Political Quarterly*, vol. 55, No. 3 (July–September 1984), 288–307.

There are a large number of books on the Falklands War itself. The most lively and complete are Max Hastings and Simon Jenkins, *The Battle for the Falklands* (New York and London: Norton, 1983) and a book by Martin Middlebrook that takes its title from the British codename for the war, *Operation Corporate: The Falklands War, 1982* (London: Viking, 1985). A briefer general work in the "Making Contemporary Britain" series is Lawrence Freedman, *Britain and the Falklands War* (Oxford: Blackwell, 1988). Devoted more to analysis than narrative are Peter Calvert, *The Falklands Crisis: The Rights and the Wrongs* (New York: St. Martin's Press, 1982), *The Falklands War: Lessons for Strategy, Diplomacy, and International Law*, ed. Alberto R. Coll and Anthony C. Arend (Boston: Allen and Unwin, 1985), and Virginia Gamba, *The Falklands/Malvinas War: A Model for North-South Crisis Prevention* (Boston: Allen and Unwin, 1987). A good section on the contribution of the *Queen Elizabeth 2* to the Falklands War is included in Captain Ronald Warwick and William H. Flayhart III, *QE2* (New York: Norton, 1985). Warwick was chief officer of the *QE2* during the experience, and Flayhart is an American maritime historian.

Acknowledgments (continued from p. iv)

From *Relation of Some Years Travel, Begun 1626 into Africa and the Greater Asia, Especially the Territories of the Persian Monarchy,* by Sir Thomas Herbert, 1634, pp. 96–99, 101–102, English Experience Series, Vol. 349. Reprinted with permission of Walter J. Johnson.

From *Medieval Persia 1040–1797* by David Morgan. Reprinted by permission of Longman Group UK Ltd.

Peter the Great: "Panegyric to the Sovereign Emperor Peter the Great" by Mikhail Vasilevich Lomonosov, translated by Ronald Hingley from *Russian Intellectual History* edited by Mark Raeff. Reprinted by permission of Humanities Press International, Inc., Atlantic Highlands, N.J., and The Harvester Press Ltd.

From *On the Corruption of Morals in Russia* by Prince M. M. Shcherbatov, edited by A. Lentin, 1969. Reprinted with the permission of Cambridge University Press.

From *A History of Russia,* Second Edition by Nicholas V. Riasonovsky, 1969. Reprinted by permission of Oxford University Press.

Napoleon: From *Napoleon: From 18 Brumaire to Tilsit* by Georges Lefebvre, translated by Henry F. Stockhold. Copyright © 1969 Columbia University Press, New York. Used by permission.

Shaka Zulu: From *Shaka Zulu* by E. A. Ritter. Penguin Books, 1978. Copyright © E. A. Ritter, 1955. Pages 12–18, 21–26, 30–32, 34–35, 44–47, 55, 57–61, 71. Reproduced by permission of Penguin Books, Ltd.

From *The Diary of Henry Francis Fynn,* ed. by James Stuart, and D. Malcolm, 1950, pp. 28–30, 71–79, 84–86, 132–136, 156–157, reprinted by the kind permission of Longman Group, Ltd.

From *The Zulu Kings* by Brian Roberts. Copyright © 1974 by Brian Roberts. Reprinted by permission of Brandt and Brandt Literary Agents.

Cecil Rhodes: Stuart Cloete, *Against These Three: A Biography of Paul Krugar, Cecil Rhodes, and Logenbula the Last King of the Matabele,* pp. 180–186, 382–384. Reprinted by permission of the JCA Literary Agency, 242 West 27th Street, New York, NY 10001.

From Robert E. Rotberg, "The Enigma of Rhodes" from *The Founder, Cecil Rhodes and the Pursuit of Power,* 1988, pp. 674, 681–682, 685, 687, 690–692. Oxford University Press, New York.

V. I. Lenin: From *The Young Lenin* by Leon Trotsky, translation by Max Eastman, translation copyright © 1972 by Doubleday, a division of Bantam, Doubleday, Dell Publishing Group, Inc. Used by permission of the publisher.

From *Encounters with Lenin* by Nikolay Valentinov, translated by Paul Rosta and Brian Pierce, 1968. Reprinted by permission of Oxford University Press.

Reprinted with permission of Charles Scribner's Sons, an imprint of Macmillan Publishing Company, from *Red October* by Robert V. Daniels. Copyright © 1967 Robert V. Daniels.

Adolf Hitler: From *Mein Kampf* by Adolf Hitler, translated by Ralph Manheim. Copyright © 1943 and copyright © renewed 1971 by Houghton Mifflin and Company. Reprinted by permission of Henry Holt and Company, Inc.

From *The Three Faces of Facism* by Ernest Nolte. Copyright © 1963 by R. Piper and Co. Verlag. Translation © 1965 by R. Piper and Co. Verlag. Reprinted by permission of HarperCollins Publishers.

From *Hitler: A Study in Tyranny* by Alan Bullock. Copyright © 1962 by Alan Bullock. Reprinted by permission of HarperCollins Publishers.

Albert Einstein: "Atomic War on Peace" by Albert Einstein as told to Raymond Swing, *Atlantic Monthly,* 176, No. 5, (November 1945). Reprinted from *Einstein on Peace* edited by Otto Nathan and Heinz Norden, published by Schocken books. Copyright © 1960 by the estate of Albert Einstein. This and excerpts from pp. 290–302 of *Einstein on Peace* reprinted by permission of the Hebrew University in Jerusalem, Israel.

333

From G. Solton and Y. Elkano, editors, *Albert Einstein Historical and Cultural Perspectives: The Centennial Symposium in Jerusalem.* Copyright © 1982 by Princeton University Press. Excerpt pp. 371–387, reprinted by permission of Princeton University Press.

Mahatma Gandhi: From *Gandhi and Civil Disobedience: The Mahatma in Indian Politics* by Judith M. Brown, 1977. Reprinted with permission of Cambridge University Press.

From Jawaharlal Nehru, *Mahatma Gandhi.* Asia Publishing Co. A-32 College Street, Market, Calcutta 700007.

Mao Tse-tung: From *Post Revolutionary Writings* by Mao Tse-tung and Lin Pias, translation by K. H. Fan, translation copyright © 1972 by K. H. Fan. Used by permission of Doubleday, a division of Bantam, Doubleday, Dell Publishing Group.

From *Mao Tse-tung,* 1966, pp. 298, 312–315, 317–320. Stuart Shram, 4 Regel Lane, London, NW1, 7th.

Jomo Kenyatta: Jomo Kenyatta, *Suffering without Bitterness: The Founding of the Kenya Nation,* 1968, pp. 46–63. East African Publishing House, P.O. Box 30571, Lusaka Close, Nairobi, Kenya.

From *Mau Mau from Within, Autobiography and Analysis of Kenya's Peasant Revolt* by Donald L. Barnett and Karari Njama. Copyright © 1966 by Donald L. Barnett and Karari Njama. Reprinted by permission of Monthly Review Foundation.

From *Kenyatta,* Second Edition, by Jeremy Murray Brown, 1979. Reprinted by permission of Unwin Hyman Ltd., part of HarperCollins Publishers.

Margaret Thatcher: Reprinted from *In Defense of Freedom: Speeches on Britain's Relations with the World 1976–1986* by Margaret Thatcher, with permission of Prometheus Books, Buffalo, NY.

Reprinted by permission of Lawrence and Wishart Ltd. from *The Politics of Thatcherism* by Robert Gray, edited by Stuart Hall and Martin Jaques, 1983.

Reprinted by permission of the publishers from *Mrs. Thatcher's Revolution: The Ending of the Socialist Era* by Peter Jenkins, Harvard University, Cambridge, Mass., Harvard University Press, copyright © 1987, 1988, Peter Jenkins.